REVIEW 2

REVIEW

Volume 2 1980

Edited by

James O. Hoge and
James L. W. West III

University Press of Virginia
Charlottesville

THE UNIVERSITY PRESS OF VIRGINIA
Copyright © 1980 by the Rector and Visitors
of the University of Virginia

First published 1980

ISSN 0190-3233
ISBN 0-8139-0865-5

Printed in the United States of America

Contents

Preface   xi

From Burnt Norton to Little Gidding: The Making of T. S. Eliot's *Four Quartets*   1
  by A. Walton Litz
    Review of Helen Gardner, *The Composition of Four Quartets*

"The Whole Book": Medieval Manuscripts in Facsimile   19
  by A. S. G. Edwards
    Review of *The Auchinleck Manuscript*, intro. by Derek Pearsall and I. C. Cunningham; *The Thornton Manuscript*, intros. by D. S. Brewer and A. E. B. Owen; *The Findern Manuscript*, intro. by Richard Beadle and A. E. B. Owen

The Editing of Harold Frederic's Correspondence   31
  by Stephen E. Meats
    Review of *The Correspondence of Harold Frederic*, ed. George E. Fortenberry, Stanton Garner, and Robert H. Woodward; text establ. by Charlyne Dodge. The Harold Frederic Edition, Vol. I

Swift's Poetry and the Critics   41
  by Louise K. Barnett
    Review of Nora Crow Jaffe, *The Poet Swift;* John Irwin Fischer, *On Swift's Poetry*

Romantic Unity, High Seriousness, and Chaucerian Fiction   49
  by Robert M. Jordan
    Review of Robert B. Burlin, *Chaucerian Fiction*

Editing Geniuses: Max and Saxe   71
  by Thomas L. McHaney
    Review of A. Scott Berg, *Max Perkins: Editor of Genius;* Dorothy Commins, *What Is an Editor? Saxe Commins at Work*

The Whole Duty of Composition 91
  by Donald J. Gray
    Review of E. D. Hirsch, Jr., *The Philosophy of Composition;* Mina Shaughnessy, *Errors and Expectations: A Guide for the Teacher of Basic Writing*

Understanding Middle English Romance 105
  by Derek Pearsall
    Review of Susan Wittig, *Stylistic and Narrative Structures in the Middle English Romances;* Velma Bourgeois Richmond, *The Popularity of Middle English Romance; Le Bone Florence of Rome,* ed. Carol Falvo Heffernan

Stillinger's Keats 127
  by Ronald Sharp
    Review of *The Poems of John Keats,* ed. Jack Stillinger

Reconstructing Hawthorne 137
  by Kent Bales
    Review of Nina Baym, *The Shape of Hawthorne's Career;* Richard H. Brodhead, *Hawthorne, Melville, and the Novel;* Kenneth Dauber, *Rediscovering Hawthorne;* Edgar A. Dryden, *Nathaniel Hawthorne: The Poetics of Enchantment*

"Learning to be Joyce's Contemporaries": *Ulysses* 165
in the Mid-1970s
  by Michael Groden
    Review of C. H. Peake, *James Joyce: The Citizen and the Artist;* Marilyn French, *The Book as World: James Joyce's* Ulysses; Suzette A. Henke, *Joyce's Moraculous Sindbook: A Study of* Ulysses; James H. Maddox, Jr., *Joyce's* Ulysses *and the Assault upon Character;* John Henry Raleigh, *The Chronicle of Leopold and Molly Bloom:* Ulysses *as Narrative;* Hugh Kenner, *Joyce's Voices;* Robert Martin Adams, *Afterjoyce: Studies in Fiction after* Ulysses; Robert H. Deming, comp., *A Bibliography of James Joyce Studies*

Contents

To Teach and to Please: The Literary Achievement　　189
of Nicholas Rowe
   by Richard H. Dammers
     Review of Annibel Jenkins, *Nicholas Rowe;* J.
     Douglas Canfield, *Nicholas Rowe and Christian
     Tragedy*

Mirror Tricks: An Interdisciplinary Exercise　　197
   by Carl Ficken
     Review of William Mallard, *The Reflection of
     Theology in Literature: A Case Study in Theology
     and Culture*

Editorial "Jamming": Two New Editions of　　211
Piers Plowman
   by David C. Fowler
     Review of The Vision of Piers Plowman: *A
     Complete Edition of the B-Text*, ed. A. V. C.
     Schmidt; Piers Plowman: *An Edition of the
     C-Text*, ed. Derek Pearsall

Letters, Parables, and Guides: Some Recent Work　　271
on Flannery O'Connor
   by Diane Tolomeo
     Review of *The Habit of Being*, ed. Sally
     Fitzgerald; John R. May, *The Pruning Word: The
     Parables of Flannery O'Connor;* Robert E. Golden
     and Mary C. Sullivan, *Flannery O'Connor and
     Caroline Gordon: A Reference Guide*

Dickens and the Business of Authorship　　287
   by Peter L. Shillingsburg
     Review of Robert L. Patten, *Charles Dickens and
     His Publishers*

Elizabeth Bowen: A Portrait　　297
   by E. C. Bufkin
     Review of Victoria Glendinning, *Elizabeth Bowen*

Medieval Texts and the Editor　　307
   by Richard A. Dwyer
     Review of *Editing Medieval Texts, English, French,
     and Latin Written in England*, ed. A. G. Rigg

Posterity's Stepchildren: Two Bibliographies 317
of Living Authors
  by John Bush Jones
    Review of James L. W. West III, *William Styron: A Descriptive Bibliography;* Joe Maynard and Barry Miles, *William S. Burroughs: A Bibliography, 1953–73*

Women's Biographies of Women: A New Genre 337
  by Carolyn G. Heilbrun
    Review of Gloria G. Fromm, *Dorothy Richardson;* Cynthia Griffin Wolff, *A Feast of Words: The Triumph of Edith Wharton;* Janet Hobhouse, *Everybody Who Was Anybody: A Biography of Gertrude Stein;* Phyllis Rose, *Woman of Letters: A Life of Virginia Woolf;* Renee Winegarten, *The Double Life of George Sand: Woman and Writer;* Paula Blanchard, *Margaret Fuller: From Transcendentalism to Revolution;* Nancy Cardozo, *Lucky Eyes and a High Heart: The Life of Maud Gonne*

Old English Sermons 347
  by W. F. Bolton
    Review of Milton McC. Gatch, *Preaching and Theology in Anglo-Saxon England: Ælfric and Wulfstan*

Hemingway: The Writer as Researcher 351
  by Charles J. Nolan, Jr.
    Review of Michael S. Reynolds, *Hemingway's First War: The Making of* A Farewell to Arms

Dante, Shakespeare, and the Common Heritage 361
  by Calvin S. Brown
    Review of Francis Fergusson, *Trope and Allegory: Themes Common to Dante and Shakespeare*

A New Edition of the Poems of the *Gawain*-Poet 367
  by Alexandra F. Johnston
    Review of *The Works of the* Gawain-*Poet,* ed. Charles Moorman

Contents

Basic Books 373
   by T. H. Howard-Hill
      Review of Robert C. Schweik and Dieter Riesner,
      *Reference Sources in English and American
      Literature, an Annotated Bibliography*

Experiencing the Nineteenth Century: 385
Two New Collections
   by Stephen W. Canham
      Review of *Nature and the Victorian Imagination,*
      ed. U. C. Knoepflmacher and G. B. Tennyson;
      The Victorian Experience: The Novelists, ed.
      Richard E. Levine

Professor Davis's Colonial South 399
   by Bruce Granger
      Review of Richard Beale Davis, *Intellectual Life in
      the Colonial South, 1585–1763*

"Shadows and the shows of men": The London 407
Exhibition World
   by G. Blakemore Evans
      Review of Richard D. Altick, *The Shows of
      London*

Contributors 418

Editorial Board

Felicia Bonaparte
City College, CUNY

Jerome H. Buckley
Harvard University

Paul Connolly
Yeshiva University

A. S. G. Edwards
University of Victoria

Robert L. Kellogg
University of Virginia

James R. Kincaid
University of Colorado

Cecil Y. Lang
University of Virginia

James B. Meriwether
University of South Carolina

Hershel Parker
University of Delaware

Martin Roth
University of Minnesota

George Stade
Columbia University

John L. Sharpe III
Duke University

G. Thomas Tanselle
John Simon Guggenheim Memorial Foundation

Stanley Weintraub
Pennsylvania State University

Preface

The first volume of *Review* has met with wide approval; perhaps it is not too much to say that thus far our enterprise is flourishing. The state of academic book reviewing, in literary studies at any rate, has for some time been unhappy, and *Review* was conceived in large part to help remedy this situation. The journal has provided a new forum for lengthy and rigorous examinations of significant new books and, by so doing, has challenged the intellectual community to recognize the high value of tough-minded reviewing. Every review submitted to this journal is appraised by the editors and by outside referees. Reviews are *accepted* for publication; they do not just automatically appear. It is our keenness to dignify reviewing as a separate genre of scholarship, together with our exclusive publication of reviews and our dismissal of restrictions on length, that sets *Review* apart.

Our conviction that *Review* fills an important need has been supported by the strongly favorable response to our maiden volume and by our continued success in commissioning reviews. Initially we feared that herculean efforts might be required to persuade first-rate people, foremost in their various fields, to write for a brand-new journal. Such has not been the case. Even when assigning reviews for the first volume, we found that most of the scholars we approached were eager to write for *Review,* and in the months since publication of volume I we have been even more fortunate in this regard. Occassionally an individual has been too busy or has had to decline for some other reason, but almost without exception the first choice who declined has been able to suggest an excellent alternate. Naturally the best possible reviewer for a particular assignment need not always be an established author, and we have received excellent work from less well known scholars.

In part because of expressions of approval for volume I, and in part because of our desire to spread the word about *Review*, we published in the October 1979 issue of *Scholarly Publishing* an essay entitled "Academic Book Reviewing: Some Problems and Suggestions." In this article we describe in detail our hopes and aims for *Review* and recount some of the problems we dealt with in founding the journal and getting the first volume into print. Like the preface to volume I, this article is also a kind of manifesto, offering our thoughts about scholarly reviewing—its nature, importance, and proper practice.

Included in volume I of *Review* is an essay that considers a book written by a member of our editorial board. And volume II contains a review of a coeditor's book, West's *William Styron: A Descriptive Bibliography*. Though some readers may disagree, we believe it best to exclude no book from review. We intend to subject our own works, and works by members of our editorial board, to the same rigorous examination applied in these pages to the works of other persons. Likewise, we will not shy away from treating books issued by the University Press of Virginia, our publisher. While guarding against sycophancy on the one hand and ill temper on the other, we will publish any commissioned review, favorable or unfavorable, so long as it meets our standards. The careful selection of books of real consequence and of reviewers with strong credentials, coupled with a painstaking editorial scrutiny, should enable *Review* to avoid publishing any essay that smacks of either the sales pitch or the gratuitous hatchet job. The editors of *Review* support conscientious scholarship and reviewing and will continue to oppose all inferior writing—the biased, the bland, the imprecise, and the irresponsible—in our campaign to improve the quality of academic book reviewing.

JAMES O. HOGE

JAMES L. W. WEST III

From Burnt Norton to Little Gidding: The Making of T.S. Eliot's *Four Quartets*

A. Walton Litz

Helen Gardner. *The Composition of* Four Quartets. New York: Oxford University Press, 1978. xiv, 239 pp.

It seems inevitable and wholly appropriate that Helen Gardner should have been chosen to edit the drafts of *Four Quartets* and the correspondence relating to the growth of the poems. Her pioneering essay on the first three quartets ("The Recent Poetry of T. S. Eliot," *New Writing and Daylight*, Summer 1942), which was subsequently revised to include *Little Gidding*, is the best by far of the early commentaries on *Four Quartets* and later became the basis for *The Art of T. S. Eliot* (1949). Helen Gardner was almost uniquely qualified to appreciate the scope and power of Eliot's last major work when it first appeared. She had come to Eliot's poetry through the study of medieval religious literature and seventeenth-century devotional verse; therefore, many of the crucial sources were already familiar to her; and she read the last three quartets against the dark background of the wartime London that produced them. In a lecture delivered at the Morgan Library on 22 March 1978, Helen Gardner spoke movingly of the comforts that *East Coker* offered when it was published in early 1940, "at the dreariest moment of the war." With its long view of history and deeply felt sense of place, the poem gave assurance that certain values, both poetic and beyond poetry, would survive the disasters of the present. This recollection of how *Four Quartets* "spoke so powerfully to our condition in the dark years when they first appeared" informs much of Helen Gardner's commentary, giving a special emotional force to her scrupulous scholarship, just as Eliot's personal recollections were intended to give his poems "power from well below the surface" (Eliot to John Hayward, 5 August 1941, p. 24).

Helen Gardner opens her study with a description of "The Documents in the Case," most importantly the drafts Eliot gave to his friend John Hayward and the correspondence of 1940-42 between Hayward and Eliot. By the end of the 1930s Hayward had appointed himself the "Keeper of the Eliot Archive," and sometime before the war Eliot presented him with the corrected typescript of *Burnt Norton* used by the printer (Helen Gardner's sketch of Hayward's career and of Eliot's growing friendship with him is fascinating). In June 1940 Eliot gave Hayward five typed drafts of *East Coker* and the proof for magazine publication; later Hayward received a draft of *The Dry Salvages* and five drafts of *Little Gidding*. He carefully bound up all these drafts of *Four Quartets*, along with the relevant letters from Eliot, and bequeathed them to his Cambridge college, King's. As Helen Gardner points out, wartime conditions often forced Eliot to resort to letters rather than conversation with his friends, and we therefore have an unusually full record of the criticisms of *Four Quartets* made by Hayward, Geoffrey Faber, and others, as well as Eliot's responses to them.

Other important materials are in the Library of Magdalene College, Cambridge. After Rudyard Kipling's death in 1936, I. A. Richards persuaded his colleagues at Magdalene to offer Eliot the Honorary Fellowship that Kipling (and before him Thomas Hardy) had held, and in 1941 Eliot gave to the Magdalene Library four drafts of *The Dry Salvages* (one heavily annotated by Geoffrey Faber). The next year he presented the college with thirteen *Little Gidding* typescripts and the remaining pages of two or three "scribbling pads" that contain manuscript notes and rough drafts for parts of *The Dry Salvages* and *Little Gidding*. Speaking of his "pleasure" in this gift, Eliot added his usual qualifications about genetic evidence, reminiscent of his ambiguous comments on the "lost" *Waste Land* manuscript.

When I say that this would be a pleasure, I do not wish this quite truthful assertion to be construed as expressing general approval of the preservation of my own or indeed of most manuscripts. As a general rule, to which I cannot perceive my own work to provide any exception, it seems to me that posterity should be left with the product, and not be encumbered with a record of the process, of such compositions as these. Their presentation, however, affords an author one of the few means at his disposal for showing his gratitude and appreciation, such as I owe towards Magdalene: and it is in this spirit that I have proposed subtracting these papers from the national supply of pulp. [p. v.]

These complex materials from the Magdalene and King's College libraries, augmented by a few documents from other collections (such as the manuscript of *East Coker* IV that Eliot gave to Hugh Walpole to sell for the Red Cross), have been carefully ordered and transcribed. Faced with the bulk and repetitive nature of the many drafts, Helen Gardner decided (I think rightly) not to reproduce all the documents in full, but to cut up the texts and the letters so as to provide a running account of the growth of the poems. The second part of her book, which comes after introductory chapters on "The Documents in the Case," "The Growth of *Four Quartets*," and "The Sources of *Four Quartets*," presents the final 1944 text of the *Quartets* divided into logical verse-movements, each section of final text followed by a record of changes on manuscript and typescript and by commentary on individual passages that includes excerpts from the letters of Eliot's friends and relevant passages from Eliot's own prose or the scholarly literature. In both the running commentary and the introductory chapters, Helen Gardner has not hesitated to quote at length from essays by Eliot and others that are not easily available (such as Adm. Samuel Eliot Morison's "The Dry Salvages and the Thacher Shipwreck," which appeared in *The American Neptune* in 1965). The result of these editorial decisions is a book that provides both a record of the evolving text and a rich commentary on individual lines or verse paragraphs. Usually this commentary is occasioned by textual revisions, but the book is also a repository of useful background information and Helen Gardner's incisive critical opinions.

These editorial decisions inevitably led to some problems in presentation. Critical and textual discussion is carefully segregated from the textual record, but that record is not always easy to read. One must constantly keep in mind the sigla for various drafts and manuscripts, which change from poem to poem, and must reconstruct earlier versions from a dense apparatus of notes and symbols. The difficulty is rather like that faced by a reader of the *Variorum Yeats*. When the textual history becomes overwhelmingly complicated, as in Parts II–IV of *Little Gidding*, Helen Gardner wisely gives a narrative account of the many drafts and revisions, interspersed with quotations from the correspondence that accompanied each stage of revision. One wishes she had made a wider use of this method and included more complete transcriptions of individual stages in composition. Appendix A, a transcription of the entire first draft of *Little Gidding* with John Hayward's marks and suggestions printed in red, makes one long for more such transcriptions, especially since it is accompanied by the full text of Hayward's letter to Eliot. Clearly the large amount of material and the frequent similarities between texts preclude the method adopted by Valerie Eliot in the *Waste Land* facsimile, where every manuscript or typescript is reproduced first photographically and then in type, with Ezra Pound's annotations printed in red. But in a book this expensive ($32.50) one could legitimately expect more facsimiles, particularly of the early manuscripts, and full additional transcriptions of key drafts. A generous format would also have helped, allowing the textual notes to be spread out or even offered on a facing page.

A neat example of the difficulties for the reader which stem inevitably from Helen Gardner's editorial methods can be found in the fascinating quotation from Eliot's letter to Hayward of 5 August 1941 that stands as an epigraph to Chapter 3. Hayward has queried a line near the end of the first draft of *Little Gidding* II, "He turned away, and in the autumn weather," commenting: " 'Autumn weather': I do not

The Making of Eliot's *Four Quartets*

get the significance of *autumn*? It struck me as having a greater significance than you may have intended it to have." Eliot replied: " 'Autumn weather' only because it *was* autumn weather—it is supposed to be an *early* air raid—and to throw back to Figlia che piange (but not having my Poems by me I may be misquoting) but with less point than the children in the appletree meaning to tie up New Hampshire and Burnt Norton (with a touch, as I discovered in the train, of 'They' which I don't think I had read for 30 years, but the quotation from E. B. Browning has always stuck in my head, and that may be due to 'They' rather than to the Bardess herself)." This may be the most revealing passage in all of Eliot's correspondence about *Four Quartets*: it compounds his immediate sense of time and place (the autumn of 1940 and the London blitz) with the landscapes of time lost in "New Hampshire" and *Burnt Norton*, and then links these emotional landscapes with that most poignant of the early poems, "La Figlia che Piange," where the poet-spectator stands at a Jamesian remove from experience. But to appreciate the quotation fully one must turn to Helen Gardner's discussion of "They" and the Browning poem later in the chapter, and then ferret out the relevant passages from *Burnt Norton* and *Little Gidding* presented in the second half of the book. *The Composition of Four Quartets* is not an easy work to use, demanding that we hold the introductory discussions in mind while shuttling nervously from top to bottom of each page of text.

Helen Gardner's introductory chapters are rich in new information and fresh interpretations. After surveying the basic documents in Chapter 1, she provides in Chapter 2 a narrative account of "The Growth of *Four Quartets*." Like so many of Eliot's poems, *Burnt Norton* grew out of an earlier work, in this instance a passage of thirteen lines written for the Second Priest in Act I of *Murder in the Cathedral* but never used (the producer had thought Act I was "too static," and Eliot had obliged with additional speeches). These lines with a few alterations became the opening paragraph of *Burnt Norton,* where they are fused with the memories and intense personal regrets prompted by Eliot's visit to Burnt Norton in 1934 or

1935. *Burnt Norton* grew naturally out of *Murder in the Cathedral* and the "Landscape" poems, where we can feel the quickening of imagination (as well as the keen sense of time lost) that resulted from Eliot's return to the United States in 1932-1933. In contrast, the occasions for the last three quartets were as much public as personal. In his 1963 *Paris Review* interview with Donald Hall, Eliot said that "in 1939 if there hadn't been a war I would probably have tried to write another play" (p. 15). The dislocations of the war precluded the regular habits needed for playwriting, and Eliot turned to verse as the threats to his two native lands sharpened his interest in the themes of history and time redeemed.

The impulses behind the last three quartets are revealed in Eliot's critical writings of 1941-1942: the introduction to *A Choice of Kipling's Verse*, the Glasgow lecture on "The Music of Poetry," the address to the Classical Association on "The Classics and the Man of Letters," and the BBC talk on Tennyson as "The Voice of His Time." Here we find Eliot confronting the paradox of the expatriate writer who like Kipling—or James—is "everywhere a foreigner" and yet can see more clearly precisely because of his "otherness." We also find Eliot assuming, however reluctantly, the role of unofficial poet laureate for two nations linked more closely than ever before by a common ancestry and a common enemy. Most of all, we find him wrestling with the problems of musical organization and the "long poem" that had been thrust upon him by the writing of the *Quartets*. Helen Gardner's commentary makes it clear that *Burnt Norton* was conceived as a single poem, modeled after the five-part structure of *The Waste Land,* and that Eliot did not visualize a cycle of four poems until he was well into the writing of *East Coker*. (Whatever their wider implications may be, the epigraphs from Heraclitus belong to *Burnt Norton* alone.) In February 1940 John Hayward wrote to Frank Morley that Eliot was at work on a successor to *Burnt Norton* "provisionally entitled 'East Coker'," the "second of three quatuors" (p. 16). By the time *East Coker* was finished, Eliot must have already formulated his four-part plan based on the symbolism of the four elements and the cycle of the four

The Making of Eliot's *Four Quartets*

seasons. When he came to write *Little Gidding*, he confessed to Hayward (July 1941) that "as it is written to complete a series, and not solely for itself, it may be too much from the head and may show signs of flagging" (p. 22). The next month he repeated his uneasiness, saying that "the defect of the whole poem, I feel, is the lack of some acute personal reminiscence (never to be explicated, of course, but to give power from well below the surface) and I can *perhaps* supply this in Part II" (p. 24). This attempt to make *Little Gidding* a fitting summary in structure and theme, while at the same time recapturing the personal intensity of *Burnt Norton*, gives a special interest to Eliot's tortured rewritings of the last quartet.

In the long third chapter, "The Sources of *Four Quartets*," Helen Gardner provides much new and exciting information, as well as evidence from obscure or uncollected essays. Among the most interesting passages are those on Gide's *Le Prométhée mal enchaîné* as a source for *East Coker* IV and on the historical backgrounds of the four "places" that give their names to the *Quartets*. There are, however, some problems in Chapter 3. One stems from a reluctance to discuss the deeply personal backgrounds of the *Quartets*, especially *Burnt Norton*. Given Eliot's insistence on the role of "acute personal reminiscence," it is surprising that the author does not explore further Eliot's relationship with his youthful sweetheart, Emily Hale, and their visit to Burnt Norton. She buries in a footnote the speculation that the moving line in "New Hampshire," "Twenty years and the spring is over," resulted from a visit to New Hampshire with Emily Hale before Eliot's return to England in 1933. Without violating her admirable tact, Helen Gardner could have given us more on the American background and perhaps less on Eliot's involvement with his Kensington literary circle.

Another problem derives from Eliot's habit of thinking and feeling through literature. How are we to distinguish the mere source, interesting but not crucial to the final text, from the allusion which demands that we align Eliot's world with that of some past or present master? And what of the indeterminate ground between source and allusion, what we might call the "umbra" of the poem, inhabited by ghosts that are intensely felt by the reader but scarcely visible in the text (I am thinking especially of the way in which Poem VII of *In Memoriam*, describing Tennyson's Hamlet-like encounter with the ghost of Hallam during a dawn patrol, casts its shadow over Part II of *Little Gidding*). One wishes that such an accomplished reader as Helen Gardner, with her instinctive understanding of the workings of Eliot's imagination, had made a more rigorous attempt to discriminate between peripheral sources and the more profound literary presences in *Four Quartets*.

The surviving typescript of *Burnt Norton* contains relatively few significant revisions, and there is no available correspondence about the writing of the poem. Perhaps the most interesting question in the making of *Four Quartets*—how Eliot arrived at the five-part scheme that would govern the shape of the later poems—must remain largely unanswered. We do know that *Burnt Norton*, like most of Eliot's poetry, was written rather quickly in late 1935. When Eliot returned to poetry in 1939–1940, after finishing *The Family Reunion*, he was faced with a problem that would vex him throughout the writing of the last three quartets: how to repeat the form and styles of *Burnt Norton* without becoming "an imitation of myself."

By the time John Hayward received a complete draft of *East Coker* in February 1940, most of the large structural problems comparable to those Eliot and Pound struggled with in the revisions of *The Waste Land* had been solved. The five-part form of each poem had been determined, and the principle of stylistic and thematic parallels between the separate poems had been fixed. This makes the process of composition of *Four Quartets*, insofar as we have a record, radically different from that which produced *The Waste Land*, and the role of Eliot's wartime "critics" quite different from that played by Ezra Pound. Pound was confronted by the fragmented record of a spiritual and physical breakdown, out of which he and Eliot pieced together a condensed symbolist epic. In the course of Pound's maieutic efforts the balance of *The Waste Land* was tipped from drama and narrative to symbol and myth, enhancing the "cinematographic" effect and bringing the entire poem closer to the form of Pound's early Cantos. In a review of Cocteau's poetry published in January 1921, Pound had called for a new poetry "where the reader must not only read every word, but must read his English as carefully as if it were a Greek that he could not rapidly be sure of comprehending." "The life of a village is narrative. . . . In a city the visual impressions succeed each other, overlap, overcross, they are 'cinematographic,' but they are not a simple linear sequence. They are often a flood of nouns without verbal connections." This is the model for a long modernist poem realized later that year in the revisions of *The Waste Land*. But large structural decisions, such as the paring down of Part IV of *The Waste Land* (followed by Pound's insistence that the Phlebas lyric "must stay in"), were denied to Eliot's friends—and to Eliot himself—by the time *East Coker* had been drafted. The poem that Pound and Eliot faced in late 1921 was still problematic in form, with closure not yet in sight. The poems that Eliot shared with his friends in 1940-1942 were already partially closed in form. The prose outlines that Eliot drafted for parts of *The Dry Salvages* and *Little Gidding* (rather like Yeats's prose schemes for some of his poems) testify to this sense of a closed form. *The Waste Land*, on the other hand, had been one of those poems "neither didactic nor narrative" that Eliot describes in "The Three Voices of Poetry":

[The poet] does not know what he has to say until he has said it, and in the effort to say it he is not concerned with making other people understand anything. He is not concerned, at this stage, with other people at all: only with finding the right words or, anyhow, the least wrong words. He is not concerned whether anybody else will ever listen to them or not, or whether anybody else will ever understand them if he does. He is oppressed by a burden which he must bring to birth in order to obtain relief. Or, to change the figure of speech, he is haunted by a demon, a demon against which he feels powerless, because in its first manifestation it has no face, no name, nothing; and the words, the poem he makes, are a kind of form of exorcism of this demon. In other words again, he is going to all that trouble, not in order to communicate with anyone, but to gain relief from acute discomfort; and when the words are finally arranged in the right way—or in what he comes to accept as the best arrangement he can find—he may experience a moment of exhaustion, of appeasement, of absolution, and of something very near annihilation, which is in itself indescribable.

The Waste Land had a necessary obscurity that Eliot, fresh from the writing of plays and committed to a new relationship with his audience, could never have recaptured in 1940-1942, even if he had wished to do so. He said as much years later in his *Paris Review* conversation with Donald Hall: "That type of obscurity comes when a poet is still at the stage of learning how to use language. You have to say the thing the difficult way. The only alternative is not saying it at all, at that stage. By the time of the *Four Quartets*, I couldn't have written in the style of *The Waste Land*. In *The Waste Land,* I wasn't even bothering whether I understood what I was saying" (p. 4). These large differences between the recasting of *The Waste Land* and the composition of *Four Quartets* are reflected in the local matters of style and substance where Eliot often took the advice of John Hayward, Geoffrey Faber, and others. Many of the suggestions made by Eliot's friends strike me as judicious, and perhaps he should have acted on more of them. But they are not marked by the sense of a high shared purpose—the justification of "modernism"—that makes Pound's detailed comments on *The Waste Land* so exciting. In Pound's minor changes the eye and ear of a master translator are always evident; his marginalia culminate a long struggle to purify the dialect of the tribe. The slogans of Imagism and the new poetry are validated by the *Waste Land* manuscript.

The comments that John Hayward made on the drafts of the last three quartets are minute and highly intelligent, the work of a cultured reader devoted to Eliot's poetry and the traditions it builds upon. His long letter of 1 August 1941 concerning the first draft of *Little Gidding* (reprinted in full in Appendix A) is filled with sound advice, like his suggestion that Eliot insert a comma to avoid "a possible Empsonism."

But other remarks seem prissy or pedantic, and Hayward's inability to fit Part IV of *Little Gidding* "into the scheme of the poem as a whole" stands in revealing contrast to Pound's immediate understanding of the importance of the Phlebas lyric to *The Waste Land*. The bookishness and often tedious humor of Eliot's Kensington circle pervade the exchanges between Hayward and Eliot. For this reason alone we may be glad that the original title, *Kensington Quartets*, was abandoned. Eliot obviously intended an allusion to those prewar years when, after the separation from his first wife, he tried to reconstruct himself with the help of attentive friends. But Hayward wisely recognized that " 'Kensington' is too likely to suggest to the uninformed majority of readers a private joke of some kind or an allusive jibe at all that 'Kensington' is commonly thought to stand for—the decaying rentier, frayed respectability and the keeping up of outmoded conventions" (pp. 26-27).

Perhaps the best way to illustrate the special nature (and special interest) of the *Four Quartets* drafts is to focus on one much-revised passage, the imitation of a canto from the *Purgatorio* that closes Part II of *Little Gidding*. (In addition to Helen Gardner's detailed treatment, there is an excellent discussion of the revisions in J. A. W. Bennett's essay " 'Little Gidding': A Poem of Pentecost," *Ampleforth Journal*, 79 [Spring 1974], 60-73). As Helen Gardner remarks, this passage "gave Eliot more trouble than any other section of the poem"; its growth was so complex that she was forced to adopt a narrative method in presenting the successive drafts. From the beginning Eliot felt under intense pressure to make *Little Gidding* a true summation ("In my end is my beginning"), and after completing the first draft he felt that Part II was "the centre of weakness." It took many recensions to make this Dantesque encounter with a ghostly alter ego one of the strongest and most moving passages in *Four Quartets*.

One of Eliot's initial problems was purely technical. Whereas the second movement of Part II in each of the three preceding quartets had been loose and discursive, in Part II (b) of *Little Gidding* he set himself the difficult task of imitating in English Dante's terza rima. The metrical solution, a triple pattern of light and heavy endings suggesting Dante's rhymes, strikes me as brilliant, but the form did not come easily to Eliot and throughout the passage we can see him struggling with this newly imposed restriction. We can also see him striving for that narrative clarity and precision of detail he associated with the *Divine Comedy*. In his 1929 Dante essay Eliot had joined with Matthew Arnold in singling out a simile from Canto XV of the *Inferno* for particular praise:

[Dante] is speaking of the crowd in Hell who peered at him and his guide under a dim light:
> *e si ver noi aguzzevan le ciglia,*
> *come vecchio sartor fa nella cruna.*
> and sharpened their vision (knitted their brows) at us,
> like an old tailor peering at the eye of his needle.

The purpose of this type of simile is solely to make us see *more definitely* the scene which Dante has put before us in the preceding lines.

The precision of Dante's comparison was Eliot's aim in his "imitation," but when he first tried to render these lines he missed the mark:

> And as I scrutinised the downturned face
> With the pointed narrowness of observation
> By which we greet the first-met stranger at dawn.

After some revision these lines became:

> And as I scrutinised the down-turned face
> With that pointed narrowness of observation
> We bear upon the first-met stranger at dawn.

Hayward queried several turns of phrase, and Eliot responded with a new version:

> And as I bent upon the down-turned face
> That pointed scrutiny with which we challenge
> The first-met stranger in the first faint light.

Hayward then questioned "bent" and "first faint light," suggesting "daybreak" for the latter (in spite of the injury to the meter). Eliot agreed with Hayward's doubts about "first faint light," altered it to "The first-met stranger after lantern-end," then rejected this phrase as too imprecise and strained. After accepting nearly all of Hayward's suggestions about surrounding lines, he was still "wrestling with the demon of that precise degree of light at that precise time of day." He wanted "something as universal as Dante's old tailor threading his needle." He even toyed with the Miltonic "The stranger at the antelucan hour," then finally accepted one of Hayward's many suggestions, "waning dusk."

> And as I fixed upon the down-turned face
> That pointed scrutiny with which we challenge
> The first-met stranger in the waning dusk.

When this, the fifth draft of the passage, was sent to Hayward, Eliot thanked him for "invaluable assistance." "You will observe that I have accepted 'waning dusk', and my observation conducted during the last few days leads me to believe that it will wear."

The full record of Eliot's "wrestling" with this tercet occupies three pages in Helen Gardner's study and reminds us forcefully of his comment on *Little Gidding* II (b) in his 1950 lecture "What Dante Means to Me": "This section of a poem — not the length of one canto of the Divine Comedy — cost me far more time and trouble and vexation than any passage of the same length that I have ever written." The vexation came partly from the difficulties Eliot encountered in imitating Dante's austere, disciplined style and partly from the restrictions of the mock terza rima. Sustained imitation of Dante's style and atmosphere proved far more difficult than the method of allusion, or "luminous detail," employed in the early poetry, as Eliot acknowledged in "What Dante Means to Me."

Readers of my *Waste Land* will perhaps remember that the vision of my city clerks trooping over London Bridge from the railway station to their offices evoked the reflection "I had not thought death had undone so many"; and that in another place I deliberately modified a line of Dante by altering it — "sighs, short and infrequent, were exhaled." And I gave the references in my notes, in order to make the reader who recognized the allusion, know that I meant him to recognize it, and know that he would have missed the point if he did not recognize it. Twenty years after writing *The Waste Land*, I wrote, in *Little Gidding*, a passage which is intended to be the nearest equivalent to a canto of the Inferno or the Purgatorio, in style as well as content, that I could achieve. The intention, of course, was the same as with my allusions to Dante in *The Waste Land*: to present to the mind of the reader a parallel, by means of contrast, between the Inferno and the Purgatorio, which Dante visited and a hallucinated scene after an air-raid. But the method is different: here I was debarred from quoting or adapting at length — I borrowed and adapted freely only a few phrases — because I was *imitating*.

In *Little Gidding* II (b) we find the technical rewards of a lifetime devoted to study of the *Divine Comedy*. The imitation is so successful because Eliot had been obsessed throughout his career with a few touchstone cantos from the *Inferno* and *Purgatorio*, making them part of his inner life.

When we trace the recensions of *Little Gidding* II (b), the general movement is from an encounter with "the dead masters" of the poetic tradition, modeled after Dante's emotional meeting with Brunetto Latini in *Inferno* XV, to a more mysterious encounter with "a familiar compound ghost" who is both the masters of the past and Eliot's complex other self. It is as if the dramatic encounters of the *Inferno* and *Purgatorio* had been merged with the psychological encounters of Henry James's "The Jolly Corner." In the first draft the poet's strange meeting at dawn is specifically Dante's with Brunetto in *Inferno* XV, and Dante's appalled cry (*Siete voi qui, ser Brunetto?*) is directly repeated:

> And I, becoming other and many, cried
> And heard my voice: "Are you here, Ser Brunetto?"

But Brunetto was soon replaced by a more ambiguous figure:

> So I assumed another part, and cried
> Hearing another's voice cry: "What? are *you* here?"

When Hayward questioned the disappearance of Ser Brunetto, Eliot replied that he "wished the effect of the whole to be Purgatorial" rather than Infernal. But he had another reason for enlarging the alter ego: the insistent presence of the ghost of William Butler Yeats. Eliot told Hayward that "the visionary figure has now become somewhat more definite and will no doubt be identified by some readers with Yeats though I do not mean anything so precise as that. . . . I do not wish to take the responsibility of putting Yeats or anybody else into Hell and I do not want to impugn to him the particular vice which took Brunetto there" (p. 176).

Memories of Yeats were intimately bound up with the making of the last three quartets. Two early versions of *Little Gidding* IV were drafted on the versos of pages which contain notes for the memorial lecture on Yeats that Eliot delivered in Dublin in June 1940, and the attitude toward the "dead master" expressed in that lecture is reflected in the moving first lines of *East Coker* V. Eliot had come late to an appreciation of Yeats's achievement, but by the time *Four Quartets* was underway he had recognized Yeats as "the greatest poet of our time." In an unpublished lecture delivered in Dublin to the English Literary Society on 29 January 1936, Eliot spoke of his fate (and perhaps his good fortune) to have come to poetic maturity at the time when Yeats was least powerful, and therefore least threatening as an influence. The argument of the entire lecture (now at Harvard) reminds one of the later arguments of Walter Jackson Bate and Harold Bloom; Eliot even speaks of the special impact of poetry that is *misunderstood.* But Eliot's conclusion, of course, is just the opposite of Bloom's, and in *East Coker* V he speaks of the need for humility and submission in the presence of the dead masters, not struggle and denial.

This theme of accommodation with the past is developed in the 1940 Yeats lecture, where Eliot remembers that Yeats's early poetry had little to give him in his youth when he was "looking for masters." It was only after 1919 that the older Yeats gradually emerged for Eliot as an exemplary figure, "one of those few whose history is the history of their own time, who are a part of the consciousness of an age which cannot be understood without them." Eliot speaks of the process by which Yeats made himself "universal," returning once more to his old theme of "impersonality" in a way that clarifies many of the earlier comments.

I have, in early essays, extolled what I called impersonality in art, and it may seem that, in giving as a reason for the superiority of Yeats's later work the greater expression of personality in it, I am contradicting myself. It may be that I expressed myself badly, or that I had only an adolescent grasp of that idea — as I can never bear to re-read my own prose writings, I am willing to leave the point unsettled — but I think now, at least, that the truth of the matter is this. There are two forms of impersonality: that which is natural to the mere skilful craftsman, and that which is more and more achieved by the maturing artist. The first is that of what I have called the "anthology piece," of a lyric by Lovelace or Suckling, or of Campion, a finer poet than either. The second impersonality is that of the poet who, out of intense and personal experience, is able to express a general truth; retaining all the particularity of his experience, to make of it a general symbol.

It is exactly this process of turning "intense and personal experience" into "a general symbol" that Eliot followed in the making of *Little Gidding* II (b).

At the same time as Eliot was transforming the dead masters, Brunetto and Yeats, into a "familiar compound ghost," he was looking for "some sharpening of personal poignancy" to animate the canto. Such personal urgency was already there in the last twenty-four lines of the first draft, which were later replaced by the movement beginning "But, as the passage now presents no hindrance."

> ["]Remember rather the essential moments
>   That were the times of birth and death and change
>   The agony and the solitary vigil.
> Remember also fear, loathing and hate,
>   The wild strawberries eaten in the garden,
>   The walls of Poitiers, and the Anjou wine,
> The fresh new season's rope, the smell of varnish
>   On the clean oar, the drying of the sails,
> Such things as seem of least and most importance.
> So, as you circumscribe this dreary round,

The Making of Eliot's *Four Quartets*

> Shall your life pass from you, with all you hated
> And all you loved, the future and the past.
> United to another past, another future,
> (After many seas and after many lands)
> The dead and the unborn, who shall be nearer
> Than the voices and the faces that were most near.
> This is the final gift of earth accorded—
> One soil, one past, one future, in one place.
> Nor shall the eternal thereby be remoter
> But nearer: seek or seek not, it is here.
> Now, the last love on earth. The rest is grace."
> He turned away, and in the autumn weather
> I heard a distant dull deferred report
> At which I started: and the sun had risen.

Here there is "acute personal reminiscence" in abundance, memories of Cape Ann, of London in the autumn of 1940, and perhaps of the visit to the south of France made with the Pounds in the summer of 1919. Hayward objected to the Whitmanesque catalogue, while Helen Gardner feels that the passage "is slackly written and the 'essential moments' lose their individual poignancy and are trivialized by being set in a catalogue" (p. 185). I do not agree. I find the passage extremely moving, but it does not match the austere Dantesque style Eliot was aiming at, and I suspect the "essential moments" were too openly biographical for his taste. In any event, he began to rework the passage by writing a prose draft in which the details of Yeats's exemplary life replaced moments from his own, yet he ended the draft with a reference to Canto XXVI of the *Purgatorio*, always a touchstone to his deepest feelings.

> Those who have known purgatory
> here know it hereafter—so shall you
> learn when enveloped by the coils
> of the fiery wind, in which you
> must learn to swim.

A later prose version, which ends with a Yeatsian echo —"there is only the one remedy, pain for pain, in that purgative fire which you must will, wherein you must learn to swim and better nature" — was then versified:

> From ill to worse the exasperated spirit
>   Proceeds, unless restored by that refining fire
>   Where you must learn to swim, and better nature.

Hayward queried "swim," Eliot's literal rendering of Guido's disappearance in Canto XXVI, "like a fish going through the water" (*come per l'acqua pesce andando al fondo*). Eliot changed "swim" to "move," then brilliantly recast the line to combine Yeats's image of the dancer with the experience of joyful pain presented by Dante in *Purgatorio* XXVI-XXVII. Eliot surely did not know that one of the influences behind Yeats's Byzantium poems was Blake's illustration to *Purgatorio* XXVII, where the figures entering purgatorial fire are portrayed as dancers. The image of the dance was Blake's invention, not present in Dante, but it seems entirely fitting that Eliot should have inherited this Romantic image from Yeats and used it to recreate that moment in the *Divine Comedy* which had obsessed him throughout his poetic life: Arnaut Daniel's willing acceptance of the purifying flames.

> From wrong to wrong the exasperated spirit
>   Proceeds, unless restored by that refining fire
>   Where you must move in measure, like a dancer.

"The Whole Book": Medieval Manuscripts in Facsimile

A. S. G. Edwards

The Auchinleck Manuscript: National Library of Scotland Advocates' MS. 19.2.1. With an Introduction by Derek Pearsall and I. C. Cunningham. London: The Scolar Press, in association with the National Library of Scotland, 1977. xxiv, 334 leaves.

The Thornton Manuscript (Lincoln Cathedral MS. 91). Introductions by D. S. Brewer and A. E. B. Owen. London: The Scolar Press, 1975; revised reprint, 1977. xxii, 321 leaves.

The Findern Manuscript: Cambridge University Library MS. Ff. I. 6. Introduction by Richard Beadle and A. E. B. Owen. London: The Scolar Press, 1977. xxxiv, 185 leaves.

The codicological method—the analysis of a manuscript as a total construct rather than of particular texts within that construct—is not one that has been extensively practiced in Middle English studies. There have, of course, been admirable examinations of particular codices. One thinks, for example, of the Early English Text Society facsimiles of Bodley 34, Harley 2253, and the former Winchester manuscript of Malory, all with introductions by Neil Ker,[1] or of admirable analyses of particular manuscripts by such scholars as A. I. Doyle[2] and A. G. Rigg.[3] But codicological work has been hampered by the inability of scholars to present the work itself in its entirety, to make the total evidence for conclusions available for scrutiny. There is as yet for the Middle English period no counterpart to the excellent Early English Manuscripts in Facsimile series, which has made available a number of important codices from earlier centuries.

The three facsimiles under review here are, therefore, to be particularly welcomed. They make available for the first time, in facsimile, three of the most important English manuscripts of the fourteenth and fifteenth centuries. The Scolar Press is to be congratulated for its vision and enterprise. The quality of the facsimiles is remarkably high; moreover, each volume is accompanied by a detailed physical description (including — most usefully — a quire-by-quire analysis) and a succinct introduction assessing the significant features of the manuscript.

The obvious virtue of all these volumes is the opportunity they afford for uninterrupted scrutiny of the complete manuscript. The introductions to each volume reflect, to a greater or lesser degree, the results of such a scrutiny by experienced scholars. It seems important here to summarize their conclusions and to record my own reservations as well. For in each case an examination of "the whole book" suggests modifications or qualifications to the arguments advanced by these scholars.

The earliest manuscript of the three is the Auchinleck, now Adv. MS 19.2.1 in the National Library of Scotland (together with fragments in the Edinburgh, St. Andrews, and London University libraries). It is notable for many reasons: its early date — c. 1330-1340; its remarkable size — more than 386 leaves in its original state; the diversity of its contents, ranging from romances to devotional works to satires — all (with one exception) in verse; and the high number of unique or early texts it preserves.[4]

Derek Pearsall, in his introduction, can therefore write: "The manuscript is thus the first, and much the earliest, of those 'libraries' of miscellaneous reading matter, indiscriminately religious and secular, but dominated by the metrical romances, which bulk large in the popular book-production of the late Middle Ages in England" (p. vii). This is a judicious appraisal. Other aspects of Pearsall's assessment, however, are more controversial, for they break new ground in our understanding of the production and dissemination of vernacular manuscripts in the fourteenth century.

Pearsall argues, for example, that the Auchinleck manuscript is fascicular: "The bookshop produced a series of booklets or fascicles, consisting of groups of gatherings with some integrity of content . . . which were then bound up to the taste of a particular customer, at which point catchwords were supplied" (p. ix). This assumption seems plausible for a number of reasons. Pearsall points to the clear evidence of scribal collaboration, involving at least six scribes, and to the way in which some attempt was clearly made to place related items within a particular gathering or group of gatherings. These loosely related groupings could then be shuffled into an order that would juxtapose certain kinds of material (or focus on a particular kind) according to the inclinations of a prospective purchaser.[5] This argument has some important implications for our understanding of the manuscript and indeed for other Middle English manuscripts. It has been argued recently that there may be significance in the conjunction of the romance *Sir Orfeo* with texts of a religious and devotional nature in Auchinleck and in other codices.[6] Pearsall's arguments provide a caution to all who would look for such evidence of design, moral or aesthetic, in the overall structure of a particular manuscript. It may well be that, as here, such "design" is wholly arbitrary, reflecting merely a sequence of texts congenial to the taste of a particular purchaser or compiled from whatever materials were at hand in the shop. It is clear that a full understanding of methods of manuscript production must precede conclusions about the finished manuscript.

Pearsall's second important point about Auchinleck may win less ready acceptance. Following and developing the work of L. H. Loomis,[7] he sees the shop producing Auchinleck as not merely a scriptorium but also a center where "translation and versifying were as much the activities of the place as scribing, illuminating, binding and selling" (p. ix). The evidence for such a view seems rather tenuous. Pearsall demonstrates that there is a "large amount of material borrowing and verbal reminiscence between items in the manuscript" (p. x). A number of texts can in fact be linked by distinctive verbal borrowings. These include the *Arthur*, *Kyng Alisaunder*, and *Richard* group, *St. Katherine* and *St. Margaret*, and *Sir Orfeo* and *Lay le Freine*. But whether this amounts to a likelihood of common authority is a moot point. We probably are not yet in a position to make confident pronouncements about notions of "originality" in the transmission of early popular texts.[8] For instance, if *Sir Thopas* were the only work of Chaucer's to survive, would the stanzaic and couplet versions of *Guy of Warwick* then be claimed for the Chaucer canon on the evidence that there are striking verbal parallels between Chaucer's work and the romances? The arguments advanced here might allow us to do so. And even if a case could be made for common authorship, this does not provide an evidential basis for connecting the author directly with the Auchinleck scriptorium. It seems likely that a manuscript the size of Auchinleck would have been produced from a variety of exemplars—probably, given the fascicular nature of the manuscript, exemplars that were themselves generically linked (such as collections of romances or saints' lives). But it scarcely follows from this likelihood that such exemplars would be created directly under the auspices of the bookshop or scriptorium producing Auchinleck. Such an assumption lacks logical necessity, and in this case it seems unsupported by much evidential force.

There may be a related lack of logical necessity in the final aspect of Pearsall's discussion: the relationship of the Auchinleck manuscript to Chaucer. Ever since the researches of L. H. Loomis, there has been a recurrent assumption in Chaucer studies that he may have owned or used the Auchinleck manuscript. Pearsall terms such an assumption "natural, *probable* and pleasing" (p. xi, my italics). Yet there are problems with this view. As I have already noted, there are distinctive verbal parallels between Chaucer's *Sir Thopas* and certain texts unique to Auchinleck: the stanzaic and couplet versions of *Guy of Warwick* and *Horn Child*. (One might wonder, in passing, why Chaucer should have been drawn so distinctively to those if he had the plethora of romances in Auchinleck available to him.) But more to the point, Pearsall's demonstration of the high degree of professionalism of the Auchinleck shop makes it reasonable to assume that it must have produced a number of copies of its available exemplars. These copies would doubtless be constructed in a similar fascicular manner, and would hence not reflect the exact contents of Auchinleck itself. Chaucer may indeed have had direct access to Auchinleck, but it is just as likely that he had access to another manuscript, now lost, deriving from its shop but perhaps smaller in size and composed more exclusively of vernacular romances. Such an assumption is more plausible than a direct link between Chaucer-Auchinleck.

One of the many virtues of Pearsall's introduction is that it stimulates further discussion about the creation and influence of this most important fourteenth-century manuscript. If one wishes to supplement or adjust aspects of the picture Pearsall provides, such qualifications should be seen in the overall context of the freshness and authority of his arguments. Pearsall's introduction, together with the admirable physical description by I. C. Cunningham, will be a fundamental document in any future discussion of Middle English codicology.

The Thornton Manuscript (Lincoln Cathedral MS 91), introduced and described here by D. S. Brewer and A. E. B. Owen, is a different kind of collection altogether. It contains far fewer unique texts of importance: the prose *Alexander*, the verse romance *Perceval of Galles*, and, most notably, the alliterative *Morte Arthur*. It was written by a single named scribe, Robert Thornton. And it was written in Yorkshire in the mid-fifteenth century, far removed in both time and place from the Auchinleck. The Thornton Manuscript is important as "a document of literary, cultural and intellectual history."[9] Brewer suggests that it is "very representative of what must have been a number of manuscripts of a somewhat similar kind"(p. xi). This may be pitching things a little high—for reasons I will return to—but certainly Thornton does exhibit a considerable diversity of material, from romances to scientific works to prayers and devotional treatises.

Such diversity within a single manuscript inevitably raises questions about the intentions, and by extension the identity, of the compiler and scribe (assuming them both to be the same person). The Robert Thornton who signed his name in the manuscript has been identified with a Robert Thornton of East Newton, Yorkshire, a relatively prosperous gentleman in the North Riding. Although identification is complicated by a multiplicity of Robert Thorntons in that region at the relevant period, the identification is plausible.

However, it does pose certain problems, which are perhaps not faced within this facsimile. The chief of these is Thornton's purpose in compiling this manuscript. Is he, as Brewer suggests, a "gentleman amateur" motivated by scholarly enthusiasm? Or does his work suggest the activity of a professional scrivener copying out his works for commercial motives? These questions are of considerable importance in evaluating the Thornton manuscript. They determine whether one sees this as a compilation of private taste—possibly "representative," possibly not—or as an attempt to satisfy a perceived market for such a compilation.

Past scholarly opinion has tended to support Brewer's view of the "gentleman amateur," but this view is not altogether easy to accept. In the first place, Thornton, as has long been known, also transcribed another manuscript, B.L. Add. 31042, which has a similar diversity of content.[10] In total Thornton must therefore have transcribed well over five hundred large leaves, or somewhere between a quarter and a half million words. He did so, moreover, in a manner that shows considerable attention to detail: the hand is relatively regular throughout; the leaves are ruled; there are attempts at decoration of initials and the ascenders of top lines; there is frequent rubrication. Indeed, in the British Library manuscript some of this decoration has been taken to "imply a degree of professionalism and confidence" on Thornton's part.[11] The same can certainly be said of the Thornton manuscript.[12]

Moreover, the actual design of the manuscript seems to have been the outcome of some quite careful organization of the contents into coherent interrelationships. Thus, the first broad division of the manuscript (up to f. 178^v—the end of a gathering) is romance materials, chiefly in verse. From f. 179 there is a shift to predominantly prose materials, and the contents are of a devotional nature. From f. 280 to the end (again from the beginning of a new gathering) the manuscript contains only a scientific treatise, the *Liber de Diversis Medicinis*. Such careful differentiation over such a long manuscript

Medieval Manuscripts in Facsimile

(more than 340 leaves originally) bespeaks organization before the transcription of the manuscript. One must assume that Thornton first assembled a considerable number of exemplars in the form of works owned or borrowed. Then he must have prepared a number of transcripts and methodically planned the shape of his manuscript.[13] Finally he executed this design, with considerable attention to detail.

At what point does such laborious care become the work of a professional scribe rather than a "gentleman amateur"? Would Thornton have been likely to prepare such manuscripts for his own private use with such attention to matters of layout, decoration, script, and design? If not, for what audience did he prepare his manuscripts? I cannot answer these questions, but they seem worth raising. This facsimile points clearly toward the need for further research. There should be a sustained drive to gather all evidence about all Robert Thorntons in the first half of the fifteenth century; and there might profitably be a search of local records of the North Riding for the same period to see whether Thornton's hand appears in other documents, such as local records, in such a way as to shed light on the precise nature of his intentions in preparing his manuscripts — to suggest whether he was, in fact, a professional scrivener.[14] One is grateful to Messrs. Brewer and Owen for providing the material enabling us to raise these crucial questions.

The third facsimile raises different questions for students of Middle English codicology. Cambridge University Library MS Ff. I.6, introduced here by Richard Beadle and A. E. B. Owen, is more generally known as the "Findern Manuscript." The contents and the underlying concerns of Findern differ markedly from those of the two earlier manuscripts discussed here. It contains, for example, only one romance — *Sir Degrevant*. On the other hand, it contains a number of extracts from Gower's *Confessio Amantis*, pieces by Chaucer (but nothing from the *Canterbury Tales*), Clanvowe's *Book of Cupid*, and works by such fifteenth-century versifiers as Hoccleve, Lydgate, Roos, and Burgh. But the major textual importance of the manuscript lies in the number of unique short texts it contains. Of its sixty-two items no fewer than thirty-three appear in it alone, the great majority of these being lyrics. These lyrics in conjunction with the other contents of the manuscripts seem to suggest an audience interested in "courtly" verse. Such an audience was, however, clearly removed from any courtly milieu. As Beadle demonstrates, the provenance of Findern places it in the North Midlands in the late fifteenth to early sixteenth centuries.

Findern is, then, a compilation of "provincial character" (p. xii) perhaps undertaken in a spirit of emulation of the assumed literary attitudes and values of metropolitan culture. If so, it affords a remarkable insight into the nature of late medieval literary taste among the gentry, who were apparently seeking to ape their courtly peers in the production of (rather tepid) love lyrics and who were buttressing their effusions with copies of the work of established figures.

But who compiled it? Beadle offers the view that "the construction of the manuscript involved a surprising number of amateur scribes at work in the same place" (p. xii). There are, it is true, a variety of hands at work in Findern. Here the number is put at "some thirty," of which six are adjudged responsible in varying degrees for relatively extensive portions of the manuscript. This fact together with the irregular collation suggests the very strong probability that this is a "home-made" anthology, perhaps the product of some of those who actually composed certain of the lyrics it contains.

The case for such a view is strong. Many of the hands in Findern do exhibit a singular degree of inexpertness; but the view, first advanced by Rossell Hope Robbins, that professional scriveners may have had a hand in parts of the manuscript merits more examination than the footnote it receives (n. 19).[15] For example, ff. 100-108 of *Sir Degrevant* seem to be the work of someone capable of writing an undistinguished but serviceable text hand. And ff. 22-28 (Clanvowe's *Book of Cupid*) appear to be the work of a competent scribe. Both these hands begin new gatherings. It may be that the compilers did have some access to professional scribes for portions of their work—which may have been initially undertaken in an order quite different from that in which the manuscript is now bound. And there may conceivably have been a scribe working at some point with amateur copyists. Thus, ff. 155-161 are written generally in a hand of superior competence, sufficiently versatile to distinguish some titles and headings in *textura*. But interspersed into the middle of one poem on these leaves (no. 56, f. 158) are stanzas written in a highly inexpert cursive. These features seem to imply, at some stage in the manuscript's preparation, a close collaboration between scribes of professional competence and rank amateurs. One would have welcomed a detailed analysis of the hands in the manuscript to determine their frequency and interrelationships.[16] Together with a study of watermarks, such analysis might have told us more about the composition of the Findern manuscript.[17]

It would also have been useful to know more about the milieu in which Findern was created. Presumably a number of exemplars lie behind it. Most scholars would probably like to know more about the circulation and ownership of books in this part of the Midlands in the later medieval period. What collectors were in the area? What did they own? We need to see Findern in a larger picture to appreciate its significance properly.

Indeed, it is a virtue of all three facsimiles that they suggest directions for future research. One cannot exaggerate the benefits offered by these volumes to teachers and scholars alike. One can only hope that Scolar's enterprise will prompt other presses to follow its example and produce facsimiles of other important medieval manuscripts.

Notes

1. *Facsimile of Bodley 34* (London: Oxford Univ. Press, 1960); *Facsimile of British Museum MS. Harley 2253* (London: Oxford Univ. Press, 1965); *The Winchester Manuscript* (London: Oxford Univ. Press, 1976).

2. See, e.g., Doyle, "The Shaping of the Vernon and Simeon Manuscripts," in *Chaucer and Middle English Studies*, ed. B. Rowland (London: Allen & Unwin, 1974), pp. 328-41.

3. Rig, *A Glastonbury Miscellany of the Fifteenth Century* (London: Oxford Univ. Press, 1968).

4. There seems to be some confusion about the exact number of such texts. It is stated (p. viii) that "fifteen" of the twenty-six nonromance items are unique to Auchinleck. My own count reveals only thirteen (3, 4, 5, 9, 12, 14, 15, 16, 20, 27, 36, 39, 42), with the status of another item (6) not altogether clear. There are seven wholly unique romance texts (23, 24, 30, 31, 32, 37, 41) and one (26) that is unique beyond its first quarter.

5. One small piece of supporting evidence not noted here is the occasional variation between catchwords at the end of a gathering and the opening words at the beginning of the next gathering. At times (e.g., at the ends of gatherings 17, 20, 21, and 23) there is substantive variation between the wording of the catchword and the following text. This suggests that the catchwords were intended to be no more than an approximate indication of the sequence of gatherings rather than a precise instruction to the scribe about where he should take up the transcription of his exemplar.

6. See P. B. R. Doob, *Nebuchadnezzar's Children* (New Haven: Yale Univ. Press, 1974), pp. 170-71.

7. Loomis, "The Auchinleck Manuscript and a Possible London Bookshop of 1330-1340," *PMLA*, 57 (1942), 595-627.

8. See, for example, A. J. Bliss's review of Mills's edition of *Libeaus Desconus* (London: Oxford Univ. Press, 1969) in *Studia Neophilologica*, 42 (1970), 491-92.

9. I quote from G. R. Keiser, "Lincoln Cathedral Library MS. 91: Life and Milieu of the Scribe," *Studies in Bibliography*, 32 (1979), 158-79. I am grateful to Professor Keiser for providing me with a copy of his paper in advance of publication.

10. For an excellent recent description and discussion of this manuscript, see Karen Stern, "The London 'Thornton' Miscellany: A New Description of British Museum Additional Manuscript 31042," *Scriptorium*, 30 (1976), 26-37, 201-18.

11. Stern, p. 210, apropos the "London" Thornton manuscript.

12. Cf. the rather elaborate initials on ff. $19^{r\text{-}v}$, 27^r, 109^r and 154; Owen suggests that "there is no reason to believe these are by a different hand [than Thornton's]." If he is correct, Thornton's competence stands in

Medieval Manuscripts in Facsimile

very favorable comparison with journeyman professional work of the period. If he is incorrect (and he does not develop his assertion), then we must wonder how likely it is that an amateur would have sought the assistance of a professional illuminator.

13. Keiser usefully assembles much evidence about the kinds of texts to which Thornton might have had access in preparing his manuscript.

14. See the work of Carter Revard (to be published shortly) on the implications of local records for identifying the scribe of Harley 2253; see the very summary account in *Manuscripta*, 22 (1978), 18-19. I am indebted to Professor Revard for discussing his work with me.

15. Robbins, "The Findern Anthology," *PMLA*, 69 (1954), 610-42. Robbins's argument about scribes appears on p. 630 and is discussed by Beadle and Owen in a footnote (p. xvi, n. 19).

16. We are told on p. xi that there are "some thirty," but no effort is made to discuss more than three of them, even though we are told that some appear in more than one "section [gathering?]."

17. See the important study by Stephen Spector, "Symmetry in Watermark Sequences," *Studies in Bibliography*, 31 (1978), 162-78.

The Editing of Harold Frederic's Correspondence

Stephen E. Meats

The Correspondence of Harold Frederic. Edited by George E. Fortenberry, Stanton Garner, and Robert H. Woodward. Text established by Charlyne Dodge. The Harold Frederic Edition, Volume I. Fort Worth: Texas Christian University Press, 1977. xxvi, 615 pp. An approved text of the Center for Editions of American Authors.

The information this volume contains about Harold Frederic the man and the writer and about his business relationships with publishers will interest all persons studying American literature of the late nineteenth century. The letters are rich in what they reveal of Frederic's mind and character, his style of living (especially in London), the stages of his literary career, and the nature and progress of various friendships. This edition allows readers, for the first time, to put together their own assessment of Frederic based on the unvarnished portrait he paints of himself and the varied reports of him by his friends and associates. The biographical notes interspersed throughout the text conveniently summarize the significant biographical data in the letters and can be seen as brief supplements to and corrections of omissions and errors in the earlier biographical study of Paul Haines and that of Thomas F. O'Donnell and Hoyt C. Franchere.[1]

The extensive correspondence between Frederic and his several publishers—Scribners, Heinemann, Stone and Kimball, the *New York Times,* and others—is particularly valuable for what it reveals of Frederic's writing career and of author-publisher relationships and publishing practices of the period. For example, O'Donnell and Franchere note that royalty information could not be obtained from Scribners at the time of their 1961 study. Such information abounds in these letters, however, not only for Scribners but for Frederic's other publishers as well. We are shown a reasonably complete record of what Frederic was paid for short stories, for serial publication of novels, and for his various book publications in both England and America. Also available in varying amounts is information on publishers' advertising practices, author-publisher contracts, arrangements for subsidiary rights, transfer of publishing rights from one company to another, the role of the literary agent, and more.

Frederic's correspondence with Scribners gives us a good inside look at what must have been the typical relations they maintained with their authors. They consistently treated Frederic with kindness, understanding, fairness, and patience—even during the unpleasant circumstances of the publication of *The Damnation of Theron Ware*. Scribners handled this clearly capricious and questionably legal action with tact and good grace, and even after Frederic's betrayal of them, they continued to show concern for him personally and to express a desire to publish his future books. Some of the most interesting letters in the collection are those of Edward L. Burlingame, senior editor at Scribners. Besides being models of diplomacy and firm principle, they also give us an early glimpse of the role of literary editor as it would develop later in such persons as Maxwell Perkins.

As the Frederic editors point out, these letters contain little about Frederic's artistic and aesthetic theories, though an occasional paragraph or entire letter may be illuminating, such as the one in which he discusses the relationship between history and fiction (pp. 393–95). Similarly, the letters are quite reticent about his family life. But of Frederic the man and author, and of publishing practices of the period, the edition is a particularly rich and valuable source and therefore a welcome addition to American literary scholarship.

I wish I could be as enthusiastic about the editing of *The Correspondence of Harold Frederic* as I am about the information it contains. In saying this, my intention is not to downgrade the edition's many good features of format and editorial method: the inclusion of letters to Frederic, the calendar of inferred and unlocated correspondence, the reluctance of the editors to regularize usage among letters, the concise biographies of close Frederic associates — to name only a few. Nor do I wish to imply that the editorial decisions that shaped the volume were made hastily or without careful examination of numerous alternatives. Both the introduction and the editorial appendix set forth at some length the processes and justifications of these decisions. Yet these decisions and the edition's features and methods should still be brought under the microscope, not so much to indict the volume as to benefit future editors who find themselves confronted with similar problems. We shall start with the annotation, proceed through various aspects of format, and end with the text.

For the most part, the annotation of the letters is thorough, appropriate, and informative. In fact, if an error is committed, it is on the side of too much rather than too little. Of course, the question of how much to include in annotation is always a matter of judgment, and what one editor might exclude, another would think essential. Still, there are a number of clear-cut areas in which annotations could have been reduced in size without sacrificing quality. First, a good general rule to follow is, "Do not annotate the annotations." It is a common temptation for editors to annotate names or references which turn up in the notes (in quotations, etc.) but which have little bearing on the letters themselves. In several instances in this volume, a name mentioned in one of the notes, but not in the letter, is given a separate biographical annotation of its own. (Representative examples appear in the notes on pp. 311-12, 440, and 463-64.) Until I caught on to this quirk, biographical notes of this sort sent me back to the text of the letter to find a name I thought I had overlooked. And, since the editors do not use a number or symbol reference system for notes, such a search was awkward and time-consuming, especially for long letters. Annotating the annotations not only draws attention away from the letters, but it can also lead to an unnecessary, inefficient, and almost indefinite expansion of annotative materials.

Another sound rule: "Make all annotations as brief as possible." In the Frederic letters, violations of this rule occur most often when letters or other documents are extensively—and unnecessarily—quoted in the notes. Some letters, especially those of Frederic's publishers, are quite rightly quoted in their entirety in the notes, but others would have been better dealt with in summary. (For examples, see p. 40, graphologist's comments; pp. 49–50, Wilkinson's description of a dinner; pp. 113–14, Copleston's letters; and p. 440, Walker-Miner material.) The same is true for the many quotations from personal memoirs, newspaper articles, and so on. Even quotations from Frederic's *New York Times* dispatches must be included in the same category. For purposes of annotation, all should have been summarized, quoted far less extensively, or cut entirely. (Representative examples appear on pp. 35, 83–84, 138, and 264–65, but the supreme instance is the entire dinner menu printed in a note on pp. 447–48.) In recommending that such materials be summarized or cut altogether, I am not claiming that they are uninteresting. I am simply saying that they are unessential and therefore unnecessary to our understanding of the letters. Since needless annotations can swell the cost of a volume considerably, they are also economically inefficient. The Frederic correspondence shares with most other editions of letters the flaw of not documenting sources of information for the notes. Space would have been much better committed to documentation than to dinner menus and expansive textual appendixes.

The second major feature of the volume's format I wish to discuss is its index. Although the editors are scrupulous in explaining and justifying their procedures and methods for most other aspects of the volume's apparatus, they say not a word about their rationale for the index. The index is not comprehensive. It consists mostly of names of persons and titles of books, journals, stories, and articles (though article titles are indexed inconsistently). Names of cities, as well as sections of cities and streets, seem to be regularly excluded, as are the names of countries. Occasionally, though, a placename does appear in the index. It is apparent, then, that some conscious limits must have been set upon the index, but even those categories selected for indexing are marred by numerous omissions. Listing even a representative number of the specific problems I found in spot-checking the index would be far too cumbersome, but a clear measure of its inadequacy is its lack of an entry for Harold Frederic. As a result, much of the biographical information cited as the volume's chief value is inaccessible except by complete reading. For example, if one wanted to study Frederic's royalties, he would search the index in vain for entries identifying such references in the letters or notes. The index of *The Correspondence of Harold Frederic*, because of its intentionally narrow limits and its unintentional lapses, is by far the volume's weakest feature. Considering what this does to the edition's potential usefulness to scholars, it is indeed a crippling weakness. If half the effort expended on the textual apparatus had been put into the index, it could have been made into a superbly useful reference tool. It might be noted here that the CEAA editorial manual sets forth no standards for indexing the volumes it sponsors.

The numbering of the letters presents another problem. The system of numbering adopted by the editors (e.g., "89.5.12," using the year, month, and day) does indeed eliminate the difficulty caused by later discovery of letters that interrupt the conventional "1-2-3" numbering sequence. This new system, however, does not eliminate the need for "a," "b," and "c" suffixes since multiple letters written on the same day still necessitate their use. Also, this new method makes it necessary to use different systems for dated and for undated letters. The conventional method at least makes it possible to include all letters under the same system. More serious is the potential confusion resulting from the use of dates as part of the numbering system. In many cases the dates of the letters are conjectural, yet the letter numbers derived from those conjectural dates are not printed in brackets as are other editorial conjectures throughout the volume. This, it seems to me, creates a dangerous type of confusion since letter numbers and dates, even when conjectural, are made indistinguishable. The conventional numbering system at least has the advantage of being neutral in this respect.

Finally, I want to take up the textual apparatus and the editing of the text itself. It seems to me that in modern textual scholarship we have now reached a point at which the lengthy detailing of editorial procedures, a standard feature of CEAA sponsored volumes, has become not only prohibitively expensive with today's printing costs but redundant. CEAA procedures are well enough known for the appearance of the seal on a volume to guarantee sufficiently the care taken in editing the text. Why, then, is it necessary to add forty or more pages to every volume published under CEAA sponsorship merely to prove that the seal is justified? Why cannot editors simply record the data and make them available to interested scholars upon request, perhaps through the central agency supervising such editions: CEAA, CSE (Center for Scholarly Editions), or whatever organization will now evolve to replace them? Or perhaps the textual material could be published in a bibliographical journal for which printing costs are not so high. In editions of correspondence such as the Frederic, essential substantive variants and emendations could even be recorded in the notes to individual letters, thus eliminating the need for textual tables altogether. The CEAA editing manual, by the way, suggests this method as a feasible alternative to textual tables for certain types of editions.

A similar problem. In the Frederic volume the textual tables are broken down into so many different parts that it is necessary to repeat over and over, substantially unchanged, the introductory notes to the several subsections. Such a waste of space (and therefore money) is impossible to justify. One might even suspect that such wastefulness is at least partially responsible for a great deal of the current official disenchantment with practices of modern textual scholarship.

In reading many textual introductions and appendixes over the past several years, I have also been struck by a vaguely disagreeable, though certainly unintentional, tone of editorial self-adulation. While reading the textual appendix of the Frederic volume, I was reminded of the Dr. Seuss book in which the "cat in the hat" attempts to entertain two children by balancing simultaneously a dozen impossible things and then saying to them, in effect, "Look, look at the marvelous and difficult feat I am performing." Now, lest I be misunderstood, let me make it clear that I in no way oppose setting high, strict, conservative standards for editorial methods and having the application of those methods to individual volumes inspected and approved by an agency established for that purpose. But I do oppose the costly, redundant, and somewhat self-adulatory parading of editorial procedures in long textual introductions and appendixes. This may have been necessary at one time, but I am convinced that that time is now past.

Concerning the editing of the texts of the letters, except for a few apparent typographical errors (p. 99, "achievment"; p. 142, "accomodation"; p. 360, "respectfly"), I have total faith in the accuracy of the texts, within the limits of the governing editorial policy. But certain aspects of the governing policy itself can be called into question. It has always seemed to me that CEAA editorial methods, although well suited to literary texts, are not particularly appropriate for the editing of correspondence and other types of personal documents. Take, for example, the practice of silent emendation. Within very narrow limits, as for such typographical anomalies as inverted or broken characters, silent emendation can perhaps be justified in editing letters. But when the policy is extended, as it is in this volume, to include silent emendation of the author's supposed writing errors and errors in dating, clearly the editors have been led into second-guessing the author as well as into possible errors and blunders of their own. Two small examples. On page 55 "pleased you people" is silently emended to "pleased your people." Surely, "you people," like "you folks," is an acceptable informal construction in American English. The change to "your people" alters what was very likely Frederic's intentional phrasing while also changing both tone and meaning.

A second instance is far more serious. On page 127 the editors have changed the date of a letter from October to August, citing internal evidence to justify the change, without giving any indication in the text that the change of date was made.[2] The date written on a letter by the author should always be allowed to stand unless the editor can prove that it is wrong. The internal evidence cited in this case is far from conclusive since any letter written after the events referred to, whether dated August or October, could contain the same information. The earlier date may indeed be probable, but silent emendation should be based on certainty, not probability.

If one glances through the tables of emendations for this volume, one will find, fortunately, that the editors have not made many substantive alterations. But minor alterations abound. In fact, most are so minor that one asks what is gained by emending them at all, especially since they pose no threat to the reader's understanding, and correcting them removes an element of the eccentricity characteristic of all personal correspondence. As a general rule, the less editing (that is, the less editorial emending and altering) done to the text of letters, the better the job of editing. A letter is, after all, a primary historical document; one might even call it a "fact." As such, it should be kept as close to its original state by the editors as the transition from copy text to print will allow. If a letter in its original state presents problems for the reader's understanding, the editor can speculate on the intended meaning in the notes. If an alteration of any sort is deemed necessary, it should be indicated in brackets. In any case, silent emendation in the editing of letters should be severely restricted. It might be appropriate at this point to suggest, if the CEAA editing manual or some similar document is to continue as the guide for scholarly editions, that a special section be included which defines more fully the differences between personal documents and works of literature and establishes appropriate editorial guidelines and standards.

There are other questions I could explore about the editing of the Frederic letters. For example, why were addresses and postmarks not considered parts of the essential texts? Why were Frederic's printed letterheads not indicated for each letter in the main text of the book at least by some symbol or number? Further, why was Frederic's unusual indentation in some of his later letters (indenting all lines of a paragraph except the first) regularized to conform to all other letters, when the editors were otherwise so careful to avoid the temptation to normalize usage from letter to letter? For all those personal touches that could not be reproduced in print, why did the editors not include representative illustrations as they did with the letterheads?

This list of unexplored questions could be even longer. But let me conclude by reemphasizing, perhaps at the risk of repeating myself unnecessarily, that the apparently disproportionate amount of space in this review allocated to "blame" rather than to "praise," so to speak, should not leave one with the impression that I am condemning *The Correspondence of Harold Frederic* as a bad job. On the contrary, as I tried to establish at the outset, this edition has many good things to recommend it. I would, in fact, rank it quite high, both informationally and editorially, among editions of correspondence in general. But the questions I raise in this review should indicate that the editorial decisions and methods adopted by the Frederic editors are not conclusive and definitive. There is a great deal more room for thought, as well as for trial-and-error exploration, by future scholars trying to find their way a little more successfully through the complex and difficult labyrinth of editing correspondence.

Notes

1. Paul Haines, "Harold Frederic," Diss., New York University, 1945; Thomas F. O'Donnell and Hoyt C. Franchere, *Harold Frederic* (New York: Twayne, 1961).

Many of the views on editing correspondence expressed in this review are similar to those in my earlier review-essay, "The Responsibilities of an Editor of Correspondence," *Costerus*, NS 3 (1975), 149-69.

2. This emendation is mentioned in the notes to the letter. By silent emendation, I mean editorial alteration without any indication *in the text* that a change has been made.

Swift's Poetry and the Critics
Louise K. Barnett

Nora Crow Jaffe. *The Poet Swift*. Hanover: University Press of New England, 1977. x, 190 pp.

John Irwin Fischer. *On Swift's Poetry*. Gainesville: University Presses of Florida, 1978. 207 pp.

These two volumes are the first book-length studies of Swift's poetry since Maurice Johnson's *The Sin of Wit* appeared in 1950, and they illustrate both the rewards and the frustrations of taking on a hard but needed job of criticism. I can think of no comparable body of English poetry that has been similarly slighted—certainly many lesser figures have yielded up their mysteries to critical scrutiny while Swift's poetry has remained virtually untouched. A few celebrated poems have always been preserved by anthologies, but the almost total absence of critical comment on all but these few suggests that Swift's poetry as a body has been unpopular within the scholarly world. When Johnson did his doctoral dissertation and subsequent book in the 1940s, Swift's poetry was a novel choice that others did not hasten to follow. In his 1968 survey, "Recent Swift Scholarship," George P. Mayhew does not mention the poetry except to take notice of the 1958 Harold Williams edition of it.[1] And as late as 1971 the distinguished Swift scholar Irvin Ehrenpreis could write: "Swift survives as the author of half a dozen prose satires and a few humorous or complimentary poems. Who reads more?"[2]

There may be no one explanation for this anomaly; however, a common theme of the arguments made against Swift's poetry is its failure to meet some kind of generic expectation. Herbert Davis has called Swift "the most extreme example that we have ever had in England of reaction against the historic or romantic view of the poet's function and art."[3] The poetry itself—its mockeries and burlesques of traditional genres and conventions, its refusal to idealize, and its open contempt for certain kinds of poetic diction—has supported this characterization of Swift as a subversive figure within the poetic universe, a writer of "anti-poetry."[4] The occasional nature of much of Swift's poetry and his own offhand remarks about it have contributed to another pejorative view, that Swift is a mere "verse man" (W. R. Irwin's term),[5] a writer whose successful poetry is light verse and whose serious talents found their best expression in prose satire. A dichotomized perspective of this sort, whose standard of measurement is *A Tale of a Tub* and *Gulliver's Travels* (a likely second to *Ulysses* in the amount of criticism it has generated), inevitably and unnecessarily reduces the poetry. If Swift was not seriously interested in poetry, it follows that his poetry is not worth taking seriously; hence the judgment of Dr. Johnson, among others, that "in Swift's poetry there is not much upon which the critic can exercise his powers."[6]

Still another objection, the prevalent nineteenth-century attitude that the poetry is morally or philosophically repugnant, was given new currency in the twentieth century by such well-known writers as D. H. Lawrence, Aldous Huxley, and F. R. Leavis.[7] Here, too, a significant difference in attitude toward the poetry and the prose obtained. What was disturbing in the prose could be distanced from Swift the man and discussed critically. The poetry, in contrast, tended to be interpreted more as direct personal statement, evidence of Swift's own deficiencies. For Lawrence, the excremental vision of "Cassinus and Peter," rather than of *Gulliver's Travels,* demonstrates that Swift is a "mental lunatic."[8] Because the poetry often uses a character or speaker named Swift, or an unidentified speaker not readily separable from the writer, it has been easier to confuse Swift with his poetic speakers than with his prose personae.

Even those commentators sympathetic to the poetry have remarked on its resistance to standard modes of literary analysis. As Charles Peake wrote in 1962: "For exact discussion of those very aspects of poetry in which Swift excels we still lack adequate tools."[9] In other words, the singularity of Swift's poetry rather than any sort of deficiency makes it difficult to categorize and discuss. Just as "pastoral" connotes what is least interesting in "A Description of a City Shower," so the most obvious handles to many of the poems are equally unrewarding or misleading. Given the violation of rhetorical expectations and resistance to conventional rubrics which characterize Swift's poems, it is understandable that they were traditionally read and dismissed as tokens of madness, misanthropy, coprophilia, or "insane egotism" (Leavis's phrase).

Since the late sixties, however, a steadily developing interest in Swift's poetry has accomplished some of the work of interpretation that David M. Vieth found "scarcely begun" in 1966.[10] The Delany poems, the poems associated with Market Hill, and the early Pindaric odes have joined "Verses on the Death of Dr. Swift," the scatological poems, and the two city descriptions as objects of critical attention. *The Poet Swift* and *On Swift's Poetry* thus appear against a now substantial background of recent journal criticism.

Like *The Sin of Wit*, Jaffe's book is a general introduction to Swift's poetry: it suggests certain approaches to the poetry as a whole and reads a large number of poems organized into seven groups, but it does not provide the intensive analysis and interpretation that need to be done. Although Jaffe is promulgating the values of Swift's poetry, she is not totally free of those timeworn ideas that can only hamper an aesthetic appraisal. In defining that accessibility which has made Swift's poetry seem unworthy of critical attention, she writes: "The scholarly intelligence that battens on Pope will starve on Swift, whose prosody rarely calls for analysis, whose argument seldom moves between and within half-lines, whose allusions seldom bring a whole literary world into being" (pp. 2–3). In her eagerness to stress rhetorical strategies and the projection of Swift's own personality as the most important keys to the poetry, Jaffe too sweepingly denies everything else; imagery, "matters of form," and "technical interest" (pp. 6, 7) join prosody and allusion as unworthy of consideration. More disturbing is an occasional tendency to read the poems biographically in an irresponsible way. In a detailed and otherwise illuminating discussion of "The Legion Club," for example, Jaffe gratuitously remarks that Swift "knew that the madness was in himself and he strove to deny it" (p. 152).[11] Invoking the discredited myth of Swift's "madness" can only undercut her efforts to analyze the conscious artistry of the poem.

While Jaffe seems to be familiar with much of the criticism published since Johnson's study, she surprisingly does not utilize it. C. J. Rawson, surely the most exciting and original mind to work on Swift's poetry during this period, is mentioned but not cited; yet Jaffe's idea of Swift's cruelty indicates that she would find Rawson's approach congenial.[12] Other commentators — Denis Donoghue and A. B. England especially come to mind — are also notably absent. The first book on Swift's poetry in twenty-six years would undoubtedly have been more valuable if it had taken account of significant recent criticism.

What Jaffe does well is to read a number of poems with unfailing intelligence and write about them in a clear and direct way. Her discussion of the scatological poems (which have inspired numerous critical excesses) is particularly balanced and thoughtful, the best treatment of these difficult poems that I know. Jaffe analyzes persuasively the puzzling disruption of the satire in "Strephon and Chloe" and demonstrates the wrongheadedness of applying current attitudes of tolerance and sympathy to the Swiftian world of vice. In countering John M. Aden's interpretation of "A Beautiful Young Nymph Going to Bed" she writes:

[The] argument ignores the obvious contempt implied by such lines as "Who sees, will spew; who smells, be poison'd." It rests on the very dubious assumption that Swift could not realize so vividly the sordid details of Corinna's life without commiserating with her. And last, the argument neglects the capacity for harshness in the service of morality revealed in a work like "To Stella, Who Collected and Transcribed his Poems." . . . Aden's remarks on "A Beautiful Young Nymph" are symptomatic of the modern inclination to fend off the emotional effects of Swift's satire. The need to fend them off

Swift's Poetry and the Critics

is unfortunate for criticism, but it proves indirectly the power of Swift's poetry. [pp. 106-7]

Jaffe insightfully observes that the preoccupation with excretion in several of the poems (and elsewhere in Swift's writings) shows that "for Swift, excrement becomes the symbol for life's disappointments and defeats" (p. 113).

Unlike Jaffe, Fischer has not written an introductory work; rather, *On Swift's Poetry* is a specialized study that not only treats far fewer poems than either Johnson or Jaffe but also omits the Delany and scatological poems entirely and gives only passing mention to one of Swift's greatest poems, "The Legion Club." Fischer's thorough scholarship and critical sensitivity make it unfortunate that his book is not more comprehensive.

The difference between the approaches of Jaffe and Fischer is well defined by their treatment of the early odes. Jaffe discusses the poems in a general way in fourteen pages. She mentions Swift's "staggering" debts to Pindar, Cowley, Homer, Virgil, Milton, Dryden, Shakespeare, Donne, and Spenser; instead of exploring these debts in detail, her main interest in the odes is to reveal Swift's satiric genius struggling to express itself within an alien form. Jaffe is consistently readable and suggestive, but, here as elsewhere, too brief. Fischer, in contrast, devotes forty-eight pages to the odes. His discussion is primarily an investigation of allusions, and it enriches poems that have been universally conceded to be of little merit and interest. Fischer's attention cannot transform bad poems into good, but it does transform our experience of reading them.

What Fischer does with an allusion to Cato in the "Ode to Sancroft" is typical of his method. He first identifies it as an echo of Lucan's famous *Victrix causa deis placuit, sed victa Catoni;* then he explains its significance in Swift's context:

Given Swift's proudly desperate predilection for seeking the significance of human life in models of monumental strength, he must have once greatly admired the way this ringing line celebrates Cato's worth by opposing him — as an equal — to the gods themselves. But by the end of the *Ode to Sancroft* Swift knows that Lucan's line

—powerful as it is—is wrong and must be changed. For finally, by portraying Cato as a just man who pits his will against the unjust gods, is defeated, and commits suicide, Lucan leads us only to a vision in which the very greatness he extols is lost in a wild and pointless universe. [p. 37]

Clearly, the reader should begin with Jaffe for a cogent placing of the odes as a group and move on to Fischer for detailed readings.

The strength of Fischer's approach is the solid formation of scholarship which he builds upon carefully and imaginatively. Time and again his attention to detail pays off in new insights: he follows up Swift's direction that "Lady B—— B——" is "To the Tune of the Cutpurse" and discovers that Jonson's *Bartholomew Fayre* is central to the poem's meaning. He similarly finds that Plutarch's *On Moral Virtue* clarifies Swift's advice in "To Stella, Visiting Me in My Sickness." In neither case is the source mechanically imposed; Fischer is characteristically aware of the complex interplay between Swift and the earlier writer.

Fischer locates the dramatic character of Swift's poetry in his efforts "to attain a poised tension between self and larger-than-self" (p. 3). "Self" is Swift's own powerful personality, but it is also an archetypal satiric spirit, doubting and judging in opposition to "larger-than-self," the orthodox Christian perspective of faith and acceptance. This thesis is convincing. From the tortured vocational struggle recorded in the early odes to the violence of the epitaph he composed for himself, Swift reveals a constant disposition to take the issues of existence seriously. His orthodox Anglicanism was a refuge from the chaos and irrationality he observed and hated; this tension between system and anarchy which Swift felt so personally informs all of his greatest poetry. Even at its most amusing and playful, Swift's poetry usually has a serious import because he was himself always serious about and emotionally engaged by the human condition, moved "to perfect rage and resentment," as he wrote to Pope, by "the mortifying sight of slavery, folly, and baseness."[13] In Fischer's words, "Swift's trust was powerful, but it was so . . . because it was much exercised by his doubts" (p. 138). *On Swift's Poetry* is predicated upon this dynamic, whether it takes the form of flesh versus spirit in the Stella poems, love versus reason in "Cadenus and Vanessa," or the ideal of Christian charity versus the flawed reality of egotism in "Verses on the Death of Dr. Swift."

We can hope that after the promising start made by these two books, future critics of Swift's poetry will take up some of the possibilities Jaffe and Fischer have not addressed: an overall conception that would treat the poetry as a coherent whole; departures from the predictable organization of the poems to consider other, potentially enlightening, groupings; a rigorous aesthetic examination of more poems; and a more systematic consideration of satiric strategies. Although different in method and scope, Jaffe and Fischer have both illuminated aspects of Swift's poetic praxis and read individual poems with sensitivity. Their work firmly establishes the value of Swift's poetry as a worthy object of continued critical and scholarly research.

Notes

1. Mayhew, in *Jonathan Swift 1667-1967: A Dublin Tercentenary Tribute*, ed. Roger McHugh and Philip Edwards (Dublin: Dufour Editions, 1968), pp. 187-97.

2. Ehrenpreis, "Swift's Letters," in *Focus*, ed. C. J. Rawson (London: Sphere Books, 1971), p. 197.

3. Davis, "Swift's View of Poetry," in *Fair Liberty Was All His Cry: A Tercentenary Tribute to Jonathan Swift, 1667-1745*, ed. A. Norman Jeffares (London: Macmillan, 1967), p. 62.

4. Bonamy Dobrée, *English Literature in the Early Eighteenth Century, 1700-1740* (Oxford: Clarendon Press, 1959), p. 466, applies the term "anti-poetic" to Swift's two descriptions. For a similar characterization of Swift's poetry see Oswald Johnson, "Swift and the Common Reader," in *In Defense of Reading*, ed. Reuben A. Brower and Richard Poirier (New York: Dutton, 1962), p. 189.

5. Irwin, "Swift the Verse Man," *Philological Quarterly*, 54 (1975), 222-38.

6. Samuel Johnson, "Swift," *Lives of the Poets*, ed. George Birkbeck Hill, 3 vols. (Oxford: Clarendon Press, 1905), III, 65.

7. Lawrence, Introduction to *Pansies*, rpt. in *Phoenix: The Post-*

humous Papers of D. H. Lawrence, ed. Edward D. McDonald (London: Heinemann, 1936), pp. 281-82; Huxley, "Swift," in *Do What You Will* (London: Chatto & Windus, 1929), pp. 93-106; Leavis, "The Irony of Swift," in *Determinations* (London: Chatto & Windus, 1934), pp. 79-108.

8. Lawrence, p. 282.

9. Peake, "Swift's 'Satirical Elegy on a Late Famous General,'" *Review of English Literature,* 3 (1962), 88.

10. Vieth, "Introductory Note," *Papers on Language and Literature,* 2 (1966), 291.

11. Fischer states in a similar vein: "In 'The Legion Club' he bravely exploits for our edification his own incipient degeneration" (p. 5).

12. Some of Rawson's articles on Swift and other literary figures have been collected in *Gulliver and the Gentle Reader* (London: Routledge & Kegan Paul, 1973).

13. Letter of 1 June 1728, *The Correspondence of Jonathan Swift,* ed. Harold Williams, 5 vols. (Oxford: Clarendon Press, 1963), III, 289.

Romantic Unity, High Seriousness, and Chaucerian Fiction
Robert M. Jordan

> Robert B. Burlin, *Chaucerian Fiction.* Princeton: Princeton University Press, 1977. x, 292 pp.

Robert Burlin's *Chaucerian Fiction* exemplifies the proposition that criticism grows by fits and starts of accretion rather than by neat stages of displacement, generation by generation. This is a book that moves two steps forward and one step back as it wars with itself over two opposing approaches to its subject. The subject is Chaucer's attitude toward fiction, his own and his literary sources', as that attitude is revealed through his art. A poet as self-conscious and as eclectic as Chaucer provides fertile ground for this very modern interest in the relationship between self and form, between maker and made, poet and narrating persona. But despite his interest in the structuring of fictions, Burlin is not to be mistaken for a confrere of Barthes and Foucault. To the contrary, his heart is with Arnold and Coleridge, with high seriousness and the Romantic Imagination. These are his standards of value, and despite a considerable amount of critical detachment, in accordance with his seemingly formalist approach, they inevitably absorb him in the works and characters that he most admires and provide him with a rationale of value that often appears more an invention of Coleridge, Arnold, and Burlin than an intrinsic possession of the Chaucerian texts. But if *Chaucerian Fiction* is not an entirely consistent book, it is by no means a trivial one. It is a book with presence, a book that demands attention and repays it. Unlike many books on Chaucer, it consistently pursues a theme, one that is not banal but central to the pressing need for a theoretical groundwork for Chaucer studies.

In undertaking to "scrutinize imaginatively what the poet's

own work implies about his understanding of the uses of fiction," Burlin distinguishes three kinds of fiction—poetic fictions, philosophic fictions, and psychological fictions. This synchronic differentiation yields some interesting formal perceptions, but for Burlin these are less important than the artistic progression which these three kinds of fictions represent. Through them he undertakes to trace the growth of the poet's mind, the development of his "shaping imagination." Thus he proposes a development from youthful technical experimentation with poetic forms (mainly the dream visions) through an adaptation of poetry to serious philosophical content (mainly *Troilus and Criseyde*) to full maturity in the merger of content and form in poetry powerfully dramatic and psychological (the tales of Canterbury, some more than others). If the evolutionary paradigm is familiar, Burlin nevertheless develops it in an arresting and provocative manner.

Burlin traces the poet's development through a study of the changing relationships between narrator and narrative. These changes, often very subtle, denote a development in the poet's orientation toward poetry and its nature and uses, beginning with an externalized narrator closely associated with the poet himself (*Prologue to the Legend of Good Women* most notably, but also the *House of Fame* and the *Book of the Duchess*) and culminating in dramatized narrators with "unspoken motives," namely, the Canterbury pilgrims. Complicating and enriching this argument, Burlin embeds it in an ongoing discussion of the well-known antinomy of "auctoritee" and "experience." He finds in Chaucer's poetic imagination more than an ambivalence over these two opposing claims upon the poet. He also discerns, paradoxically, an interpenetration and finally a union as fiction becomes the instrument of authority—but an authority inevitably fallible and hence "fictive" because it is human. Moving at times rather laboriously through these paradoxes, Burlin emerges with some rather inconclusive speculations in his concluding discussion of cosmic analogies and the limitations of language. He finds that Chaucer's continuing struggle with the paradox of experience and authority renders him a skeptic but that his understanding of the uses of fiction is "profoundly Christian," though his description of Chaucer's Christianity conveys distinctly Romantic overtones: "The Creation of a fictive universe assumes an analogy of human invention to the transcendent power of Nature, whose divine authorization transmutes the disparities of human experience into an accordant whole" (p. 242).

Following these comments, Burlin alludes briefly to "another, less promising analogy," one that lies close to the surface throughout the book. The literary process itself is based upon the essential ambiguity of language, the problems of which further complicate the authority of fiction. Burlin observes finally that Chaucerian irony, especially as evident in the deeply ambiguous implications of the Canterbury narrator's Platonic rationale "The wordes moote be cosyn to the dede," is what allows the poet "to entertain the viciousness of fictions in the very process of creating them" (p. 244).

Within this theoretical framework Burlin conducts detailed discussions of four dream visions, *Troilus and Criseyde,* and ten of the Canterbury tales. As I have suggested, the thoughtful theoretical orientation strengthens the book, but it also produces some difficulties. These become increasingly troublesome in the second half of the book, which deals with "psychological" fictions. These Burlin regards as "the logical final step in a life-long exploration of the nature and uses of fiction" (p. 151). Here Burlin's predilections appear to interfere with the detached pursuit of his theoretical concerns. Burlin's own prose increases in fervor and virtuosity as he proceeds into the psychological fictions, and for this reason I infer that he would not share my view that the opening chapters, dealing with dream visions as "poetic fictions," are the most interesting and valuable parts of the book.

Burlin recognizes the limitations of his taxonomy and acknowledges some interpenetration among the three types of Chaucerian fictions. Of the three the category of "poetic fictions" is the most autonomous and self-defining, requiring less labor of the critic. Exemplifying that category are the *Prologue to the Legend of Good Women,* the *House of Fame,* and the *Book of the Duchess,* which Burlin discusses in that order.

Whereas all of Chaucer's poems, Burlin maintains, display an awareness of the fiction-making process, these three possess the highest degree of self-consciousness. In them the famous Chaucerian persona appears in its early and protean form, a device Chaucer adopted from the French practice but made very much his own. Central to Burlin's approach to these forms is his perception of the crucial importance of the Chaucerian "I," not merely to the general notion of irony, but more profoundly to the epistemological orientation Chaucer's poetry retains throughout the poet's career.[1] He begins with the *Prologue to the Legend of Good Women*, chronology being less important than his theoretical point—namely, the palpable relationship in that work between the narrating persona and the poet himself, a relationship Chaucer experiments with in his other works, reaching varying degrees of ironic detachment, and, finally, in the "psychological" fictions, deploying the relationship itself among dramatized fictional narrators.

Burlin finds the dream vision to be a peculiarly appropriate form for Chaucer's early explorations into the nature of fiction: "The disengaged attitude of the dreamer throughout his narrative carries an intriguing resemblance to that of the poet when he steps back from his manuscript and suddenly sees his poem, not as a vital experience in which he has been deeply immersed, but as ink on parchment to be copied by a scribe" (p. 28). Chaucer's consciousness of fiction-making and his sensitivity to its significance are represented within the dream by the interplay of old books and immediate experience. Thus the Ceyx and Alcyone story, the Dido and Aeneas story, and the occasion of the legends of good women all represent, to varying extents and in conjunction with differing contexts, the "authority" of old writings which the protagonist must evaluate in relation to the dream "experience" he is reporting. Such is the paradox that animates Chaucer's life-long self-consciousness about the office of the poet, that the "authority" of fiction is a transmutation in a shifted temporal perspective of the recorded "experience" of the writer. In the act of composing, the poet is both an innocent and an authority.

The aesthetic implications of this paradox are subtle but

crucial to a proper understanding of Chaucer's art. Burlin's discussion of the *House of Fame* is a compelling explication not merely of this puzzling poem but of its direct relevance to these theoretical concerns as well. In his treatment of the poem Burlin reveals certain of his own biases, especially an impatience with such rhetorical devices as the enumeration of the petitioners to Fame — a typically Romantic impatience one would have thought Chaucerians had outgrown with the help of rhetorical studies published within the past fifty years, since Manly's innovative but badly biased contribution. Nevertheless, within the thirteen pages devoted to the *House of Fame* Burlin produces a superlative illumination of Chaucer's creative processes and infers a deep epistemological ambivalence in a poet troubled by the contention between versions of truth, "authoritative" and "experiential."

Although much of the originality of Burlin's analysis has been anticipated by Sheila Delany, to whose book on the *House of Fame* he pays tribute,[2] Burlin nevertheless adds further to our understanding of a poem whose form is diffuse, whose tone is unsteady, and whose theme cannot be substantially formulated because it is the self-reflexive issue of poetic construction. If there is a "meaning" in the poem, Burlin would identify it, as Delany does, in the poem's ironic or skeptical valuation of meaning. The poem subjects everything to irony or parody and arrives finally at the position that "neither written authority nor observed experience has any claim to truth, but combined in the efforts of the poet they provide the best available access to earthly fame" (p. 58). Nothing is what it seems: the "authoritees" the dreamer reveres, his book as well as his pedantic guide, produce in him an emotional "experience" that he authoritatively recounts; the Eagle, espousing empirical experience, professes to demonstrate the reasonableness of Ovid's poetic fiction, the House of Fame. Burlin relates these insights to the theoretical concern that runs through his book: "This undermining of traditional categories is itself provocative, neither the first nor the last time Chaucer will intimate that the opposition of experience and authority is an illusion . . . that they are perhaps merely aspects of a single process, different facets of a unified way of knowing through the imagination" (p. 56).

Burlin's discussions of the *Prologue to the Legend of Good Women* and the *Book of the Duchess* are less successful in demonstrating the importance of his thesis, and for differing reasons. Nevertheless, they offer keen interpretations of those works. Burlin admires the *Prologue* for its intricately unified and controlled network of symbolic associations, which so thoroughly differentiates it from the *House of Fame*. He sees the dreamer's reverence for the sacred (St. Bernard), the secular (the classics), and the natural (the daisy/lady) as the agent for fusing the oppositions of authority and experience into a "supernal" authority. In achieving this unified vision, the poem borrows the language and the processes of religious experience and parodies them in a secular vein. While such observations are discerning, Burlin's claims for their significance seem extravagant, as represented by his comment on the line "Bernard the monk ne saugh not all, pardee!": "With such incidental strokes as these, Chaucer prepares the way not merely for the language of devotion but for a thoroughgoing transformation of the conventional dream-vision into a secular parody of the greatest reward a contemplative may receive, the gracious animation of the object of his veneration into the divine reality itself—the mystical vision" (p. 39). I find that excessive emphasis on such incidental strokes, and the rush to interpret them anagogically, leaves too much of the poem, in all its rhetorical complexity, too far behind. In the concluding sentence of this chapter Burlin returns to the text and attempts to retrieve the threads of his thesis, but the assertion seems forced: "Deeply embedded in the artifices of court charade and the multilevelled audacities of comic ingenuity, lies an intuitive sense of the constructive powers inherent in the poetic imagination" (p. 49). Thus we move from the heights of mystical vision to the depths of intuition, above the text and below it. The stress on intuition and the powers of the imagination points to Burlin's Romantic orientation and reveals once again his impatience with the rhetorical aspects of Chaucer's art, which of course are especially prominent in the poems

Burlin treats as "poetic fictions." The third and last of these, the *Book of the Duchess,* receives a reading that is distinctly "Romantic" and traditional in that it concentrates on the thematic concerns of grief, consolation, and love and dwells on the psychological processes of the characters, all of which it treats with sensitivity and attention to detail and nuance. But the discussion does not produce a striking advance in our understanding of the poem, nor does it advance our understanding of Burlin's theme. Once again at the chapter's conclusion Burlin strikes a gratuitous blow for the creative imagination: "The young poet smuggles into his remarkable elegy a subversive claim for the creative imagination and the constructive use of fiction." (p. 74). This declaration is not sufficient to redeem for theoretical considerations a running commentary that is more fully absorbed in the fiction than the detached student of the art of fiction can afford to be.

The line between "poetic" and "philosophic" fictions is somewhat blurred, as Burlin admits, and neither chronology nor genre is a definitive factor, since the *Prologue to the Legend of Good Women* is a "poetic" fiction and the *Parliament of Fowls* is a "philosophic" one, neither being an early work but the "philosophic" *Parliament* being earlier than the "poetic" *Prologue.* But by and large chronology and genre do define Burlin's categories, since the "poetic" fictions are all dream visions and at least predate the Canterbury period. Burlin's distinction between poetic and philosophic fictions enforces the evolutionary model against which he undertakes to measure the growth of Chaucer's creative imagination, and it raises important theoretical issues.

By "philosophic fiction" Burlin means "a work in which the narrative has been pressed into the service of a philosophic idea or speculation" (p. 79). This is the second stage of Chaucer's inevitable progress toward high seriousness, from the merely aesthetic to the philosophical: "The self-consciousness and underlying seriousness of the 'poetic fictions' lead predictably to the awareness of a potential purpose for fiction other than the principal incarnation of a particular occasion or the meditation upon the process by which such metamorphoses are affected" (p. 79). The emphasis upon content, aside from implying that philosophy enjoys a higher status than literature in the scale of cultural values, exerts a strain upon Burlin's professed concern, "not so much [for] the fiction itself, but the shaping of it" (p. 81). His discussions of the "philosophical fictions," which stress Chaucer's Boethian affinities, are distinctly oriented toward theme and "meaning" and deal accordingly with the subjects of love, nature, and fortune. For generations these subjects have preoccupied students of the *Parliament of Fowls,* the *Knight's Tale, Troilus and Criseyde,* and the *Clerk's Tale,* and Burlin's contribution, though always astute and eloquently expressed, is in the end more interesting for its failures than for its successes. These are failures of theory, and they are interesting and valuable because they provoke thought about important issues that Chaucer studies have largely neglected.

The discussion of the *Parliament of Fowls* illustrates the clash between Burlin's predispositions and his adopted method. Consistent with the methodological detachment and the formal orientation implied in his preface, Burlin asserts that "the *Parliament* is an epistemological process" (p. 92). To demonstrate such a proposition would require the kind of sustained analysis Burlin performs on the *House of Fame,* a finely tuned perception of what the poem *does,* of how, through the ambivalent role of its narrator, it mediates in subtly varying ways between the poem's fiction and the poet's and reader's reality, or, in the terms Burlin uses so provocatively, between the authority of fiction and the experience of reality. Although Burlin exerts a strong effort at this kind of sophisticated analysis, the bulk of his discussion leads him into the old, all too familiar questions. We are told that the poem is about love, "the principle of love binding the discordant into harmony, the contentious into unity" (p. 91). To the considerable extent that he is preoccupied with the poem's content, Burlin is studying not the "process" which he claims the poem to be but a stasis, a fixed and presumably recoverable "meaning."

Burlin's rediscovery of the meaning of the *Parliament* illustrates his affinity with the orthodox view on the more fundamental issue of "unity," what it is and where it resides. Finding that the poem is about love as the unifying force in the cosmos, Burlin moves on to assert, as many have before him, that the poem is not only about unity but is itself unified: "The principle of a divine force that binds discordant and contentious elements informs every aspect of the poem and regulates its structure" (p. 89). This view, widely held though it is, presents difficulties both practical and theoretical.

While the *Parliament* can be *about* the classical concept of cosmos, of a balanced and unified order of creation, it nevertheless exists as a medieval mixture of diverse poetic elements: classical lore (Scipio's dream), ornate description (the garden), courtly debate (the suit for the formel), and obstreperous, "realistic" dialogue (the avian conclave). The Romantic critic, whose eye is focused on the abstract idea of the unifying imagination, fails to see clearly these stubborn insoluble realities of the poem's verbal structure. Without questioning the Romantic assumption that form and content interpenetrate inseparably (particularly in an admired work), the critic moves easily from the deep meaning of love as unifier of Creation to the transcendent vision of the poem as itself a unified structure. In the process of this movement from theme to structure the verbal substance of the poem receives short shrift. Thus, subordinating the concrete and unique elements of the poetic work to more exalted abstractions, presumed to be both higher and deeper than the individual text, seems to me an unjustifiable form of reductionism that is of more service to the critic than to the poem.

The kind of unity Burlin perceives resides in the mind of the beholder and perhaps in the theme of the poem, but not demonstrably in its formal order. With our eye persistently on the text I think the most we can say is that Chaucer achieves a form of accommodation to hold together a multiplicity (not a "unity") of poetic elements and verbal styles. Such a view is supported by a number of recent studies that propose non-Coleridgean models of unity. Brief allusion to some alternate approaches to this important theoretical question will perhaps help to place Burlin's presuppositions in perspective.

Arthur Moore has decried the excesses of "unity studies," especially as applied to medieval narrative poems, which are characteristically diffuse, digressive, and "amplified" rather than dense and tightly ordered. He also points out the tendency of much modern criticism of medieval literature to use the term *unity* in an evaluative rather than a descriptive sense—the result being reduction or distortion of medieval poems in order to attribute to them admired qualities they do not intrinsically possess.[3]

In a wide-ranging (though non-Chaucerian) study of medieval narrative William Ryding devotes a chapter to "The Question of Unity" and observes that "we seldom stop to consider whether there might not be some advantage in relinquishing the idea of unity altogether and admitting at least hypothetically the validity of artistic duality, trinity, or some other form of multiplicity."[4] Eugène Vinaver has commented similarly on the limitations of "organic unity," which "turns out to be a metaphor whose validity is strictly limited in time, and it is our failure to grasp this simple fact that has caused us to overlook the very things that give life and meaning to medieval literary art." Vinaver goes on to observe that, contrary to the requirements of Romantic unity, the most prominent feature of Romanesque art and also of medieval romance is *acentricity*.[5] Pamela Gradon's broad-ranging study of medieval narrative reaches the similar conclusion that "medieval narrative appears to spring from a principle of multiplicity rather than unity."[6]

Burlin reveals no acquaintance with any of these important studies of medieval narrative. Therefore, his lapse into traditional Romantic preoccupation with theme and character is less surprising than it might have been, though no less disappointing. Yet another version of aesthetic wholeness is the structuralist alternative, which posits a network of books and other language within which an individual text assumes infinitely varying conditions and relationships. "The book is not simply the object that one holds in one's hands," states Michel Foucault, "and it cannot remain within the little parallelepiped that contains it: its unity is variable and relative. As

Chaucerian Fiction

soon as one questions that unity, it loses its self-evidence; it indicates itself, constructs itself, only on the basis of a complex field of discourse."[7] While the applicability of structuralist theory to medieval texts is problematic, it is perhaps no less promising than continued adherence to Romantic theory, which, in relation to medieval literature, is not significantly less anachronistic. Perhaps the least we can do, in the face of increasing dissatisfaction with the unity criterion, is to entertain the idea that theories of multiplicity and of variable unity are potentially valid models against which to examine medieval poetry.

At any rate, the unity problem remains unresolved in *Chaucerian Fiction*. As Burlin leaves the dream visions and proceeds to consider other "philosophical fictions," he becomes increasingly involved in content and, therefore, increasingly susceptible to the interpretative problems adumbrated in his discussion of the *Parliament of Fowls*. His philosophical readings of the *Knight's Tale* and *Troilus and Criseyde* are penetrating and sensible but fully predictable in their emphasis on theme and "meaning." Thus, for example, Boethius receives his due, as does Boccaccio. Theseus' "profoundly resonant" final speech expresses symmetry, love, and justice in the cosmic, pre-Christian setting of the poem. The treatment of *Troilus and Criseyde* is largely a running commentary paraphrasing the action and touching on most of the familiar issues: the depth of characterization ("something almost Jamesian about many of its scenes" [p. 114]); the contrast between the idealistic, ennobled, but intelligent Troilus and the practical Pandarus; Criseyde's philosophical intelligence; Troilus' pagan limitations of perspective; the paradox of the poem's ending, whose "double vision" Burlin finds to be the ambivalence of a poet rather than the dogma of a theologian. Surprisingly, in view of the pervasively problematic role of the narrator in relation to Burlin's interest in the processes of fiction-making, that figure receives very little attention. He is more important to Burlin as a fictional character than as an instrument in the structuring of the fiction. The narrator is found to be ambivalent, to be sure—he is both a servant of the servants of love and a mere historian—but he is distinguished by personal qualities of compassion and "doting sentimentality." "He is fully immersed in the life of the lovers when he likes what is happening, as in Book *III*" (p. 131), but when things are not going well he becomes detached and bookish. Burlin's study of *Troilus* slights the theoretical questions and concentrates on the subjects of philosophy, love, and "the experience of life" as depicted in a great poem. Within these limitations, however, Burlin offers as sane and sensitive an appraisal as we have of *Troilus and Criseyde*.

The treatment of the *Clerk's Tale*, the last of Burlin's "philosophic" fictions, is brief, but it is useful, apparently, as a transition to the "psychological fictions." The link is the dramatic characterization of the Clerk, whose "imaginative sympathy may aspire to the ideality of a Griselda, but [who] also concedes the reality of a Wife of Bath" (p. 146). Burlin proposes a concise, cogent rationale for the narrative's well-known difficulties and contradictions by containing them within the "implied wit and perspicacity" of the Clerk, upon whom Chaucer confers "complete mastery over the materials of his fiction" (p. 144). The Clerk's "performance" is distinguished by his capacity to hold in suspension three distinct points of view: that of the Griselda story, with bias toward the heroine and against her "villainous" husband; that of the "allegorization" of the story, with its view of Walter as an analogue of divinity and "God's right to test his creatures, as He chooses"; and finally that of the Envoy, in which the Clerk balances the ideality of Griselda and the reality of the Wife of Bath within his "fine humanity." The concept of the creative imagination as the resolver of discords has been transferred from the poet to his fictional surrogate. This is a crucial turn in the progress of Burlin's argument, for it commits him to the dramatic fallacy and thereby begs or at least obscures the issue he set out to examine. "Drama" is too facile an explanation for attributing to fictional creations the same degree of autonomy, the same "fine humanity," that their human creator possesses. The implications for a sound theory of Chaucerian fiction are not promising.

"Psychological Fictions," the section that comprises almost half the book and presents the culmination of Chaucer's artistic achievement as Burlin views it, opens and closes with brief but provocative discussions of the large theoretical questions. Unfortunately, the intervening discussions of several tales do not fulfill the promise or develop effectively the implications of these theoretical passages. We are told in particular that "Chaucer's method consistently depends upon a recognizable distinction of the narrative from the narrator" (p. 150), and yet the thrust of the ensuing readings is to claim an organic connection between tale and teller, the tales being seen as extensions of the personality and character of their tellers. So powerful is Burlin's drive to humanize the narrators that he might well have entitled this section "Fictional Psychology."

Allowing for the unevenness of the *Tales* and their spread over some twenty years of Chaucer's career, Burlin maintains nonetheless that "there is little reason to doubt that Chaucer's insight into the nature of fiction led him toward the increasing involvement of an identifiable teller in the act of fiction-making" (p. 152). In developing this theme, Burlin resurrects the roadside drama theory and in so doing consistently violates his own theoretical insights. How can the critic maintain a cool eye on the processes of fiction-making when he persists in regarding fictional characters as real people, sketchily rendered figures as psychologically complex beings? Burlin is a skillful rhetorician—he will detest the term—and duly acknowledges certain limitations to his claims, such as the lesser degree of "involvement" of the Knight and Miller in their tales than that of the Reeve in his. Nevertheless, once embarked upon demonstrating the psychological wholeness and complexity of the Reeve, the Pardoner, the Canon's Yeoman, the Monk, the Prioress, the Franklin, the Merchant, the Wife of Bath, and finally and oddly the Nun's Priest, Burlin marshals his considerable resources of resonant and persuasive language and intricate and subtle argumentation to demonstrate how much the tales tell about their tellers. Contradictions, digressions, or inconsistencies in the narrative are dismissed with reiterated emphasis upon character, particularly the character of the (fictional) teller. The forms of the assertion are infinitely varied, and Burlin employs luxuriant, often extravagant prose to enforce his psychological interpretations. For example, such meager evidence as the *Monk's Tale* affords is surveyed in a page or two and leads to this typical claim: "In spite of the overextended tediousness of his tragedies, the Monk's performance is admirably conceived to explore the personality of a man whose lust for power and material pleasure has found comfortable expression in a vocation regrettably intended to serve other purposes" (p. 185). It is difficult to see that any of the Monk's simply told tales demonstrate their teller's "lust for power and material pleasure," and Burlin's assertions to the contrary do not convince. These narratives display stylistic features that are found everywhere in Chaucer and can hardly be taken as definitive characterization of a unique narrator:

> A lemman hadde this noble champioun,
> That highte Dianira, fressh as May;
> And as thise clerkes maken mancioun,
> She hath hym sent a sherte, fressh and gay.
> Allas! this sherte, allas and weylaway![8]

These lines from the story of Hercules would be easily attributable, with as much and as little suitability as they bear for the Monk, to the Clerk, the Merchant, the Man of Law, the narrator of *Troilus,* and many other Chaucerian narrators.

Similarly, we find in the *Franklin's Tale* that Dorigen's complaint, disproportionately long and bristling with exempla not always relevant, demonstrates the Franklin's comic inadequacy as a storyteller: "Where the Franklin had intended to give us the elevated style of a noble lady faced with a tragic dilemma, a peek over Chaucer's shoulder confirms that he has produced a much more human and engaging, if somewhat hysterical and even silly woman" (p. 200). As an autonomous personality, with inferrable if not stated intentions, the Franklin "lurks" behind the assemblage of "elegant but artificial puppets" he has gathered "from bits of faded romance, clichés of character, and conventions of courtly manners. . . . It is the reality, the everpresent personality of the Franklin, that gives the lie to the posturing and self-conscious nobility of the characters" (p. 202). What Burlin sees as flaws or ineffectual elements in the narrative are thus interpreted, by a process of imaginative transference, as facets of the personality of the narrator.

This mode of reasoning reaches an apotheosis, as one would expect, in the interpretation of the notoriously difficult *Merchant's Tale*. By a deft sleight of mind the focus is shifted from the palpabilities of a verbal text to the inferred abstraction of a human character; a confusing text is explained as a complex personality, unified and understandable, because, a priori, the human personality, though perhaps infinitely quirky, is yet one. If the narrative lacks a consistent point of view toward the characters, in fact frequently contradicts itself, it is because the Merchant neglects his duties as a narrator. Further, the "stylistic and even generic confusion . . . tells us something about the general meaning the Merchant intends his tale to imply" (p. 214). And finally we have unity: "The imaginative coherence of the *Tale* bespeaks a dramatic creation of psychological intensity" (p. 215). The critic infers a complex personality from a complex text and then "explains" the complexities of the text as manifestations of the "dramatic creation" of the character's personality. Rather than indulge in such circular procedures, we would be well advised, as I suggested earlier, to question the presupposition that motivates such zealous and ingenious quests for "unity." In resurrecting the drama theory, Burlin succumbs to the assumption that the stubborn realities of medieval narratives—their diversities, prolixities, incongruities, and imbalances—can be rendered consistent and "unified" through the alchemy of the critic's creative imagination.

As we have long known, the Wife of Bath provides more grist than any of the other pilgrims for the "dramatic" critic's mill, and Burlin makes the most of it in a virtuoso critical performance. He also comes closer here than anywhere else to reconciling his preoccupation with character and personality with his interest in Chaucer's attitudes toward fiction-making.

The critic's theme of psychological unity is sounded early as he states that the Wife's story, which "would seem a conundrum of ungainly digressions and misshapen materials . . . can only be understood in terms of its teller" (p. 217) and that "in spite of its apparent contradictions and multiple poses, the Wife of Bath's performance exhibits underlying consistency" (p. 218). This underlying consistency is found to exist in the "imaginative reach" of the Wife's performance, which "penetrates those depths of the human personality where contrarieties coexist in oxymoronic tolerance" (pp. 223-24). By such Coleridgean means Burlin is able to explain such contradictions as the unexpected *gentillesse* of the old hag's sermon, which is a part of the Wife's fiction-making and self fantasy and hence a facet of her capacious and complex personality. But from what evidence do we perceive such a personality? From the diversities and contradictions of the text. The hermeneutic circle is complete.

Readers accept or reject Burlin's interpenetration not because of his argument but because of his premise, namely, that the conceptual whole, the Wife's "personality," precedes the parts, which consist of literary material from a variety of sources in a variety of styles and genres on a variety of subjects representing a variety of viewpoints. Burlin appreciates the literary diversity of the text, but he finally transcends it and discovers unity in his own construct, the psychological reality of the Wife. For unity he requires an organic model. The result — or is it the preconceived cause? — is as fully realized a character as, say, Isabel Archer. To derive such a character from a Chaucerian text is finally to devalue the text, to override its most palpable characteristics and press it to subserve a preconceived psychological paradigm.

The deficiencies of the drama theory have become apparent in recent decades, as the theory's affinities with turn-of-the-century psychological realism and the doctrine of character-as-destiny have assumed their place in the perspective of modern history. In an effort to do fuller justice to Chaucerian texts, some critics have sought other models to help account more accurately for the looseness, the inconsistencies, the imbalances, the peculiar rhythms, and unpredictable cadences of Chaucerian narrative. The mosaic, the interlace, the labyrinth, even the Gothic cathedral—all such models seem to illuminate in some way the special structural properties of Chaucer's fictions. In particular, they provide analogies to the poet's uses of language, his disposition of the verbal materials of his craft.

It is this view of the poem as a crafted work that Burlin cannot regard as sufficient, despite his putative emphasis on "making" fictions. "Craft" is insufficient for him, for example, to raise the Prioress's "performance" to the level of great art. He follows his sensitive and admiring interpretation of the *Prioress' Tale*—which he compares to a medieval artisan's application of his skill to a "program" supplied by those with greater learning—with an explicit disclaimer: "That is not to say that the work of the Prioress satisfies the demands of great art" (p. 192). What the Prioress lacks is original genius: "Lacking the overpowering force of original genius or intellect, she does her best, with the appropriately submissive technique of the 'illuminator' " (p. 194). The key, once again, is personality, which Burlin characteristically values above art. The "submissive" technique of the Prioress differentiates her pejoratively from the Wife of Bath. It is the latter who proves the genius, the high seriousness, of Chaucer. Burlin exalts the Wife in passages of extravagant prose and sometimes obscure meaning, as exemplified by this concluding tribute: "The interpenetration of fiction and reality, so astonishingly embodied by the Wife of Bath, serves as a timeless insight into the nature of literary creativity and, like Dame Alys herself, transcends the limits of Chaucer's self-effacing art" (p. 227). In this manner Burlin consistently employs the idea of transcendence in which oppositions are unified to express evaluative judgements. In the process poetry is inevitably reduced to the status of an instrumentality, serving character and finally something higher. Thus the Wife of Bath "is a reflex of [Chaucer's] sure dramatic instinct, his intuitive knowledge of the workings of the human mind and psyche, which could create in a fictional being, compounded of fictions, a character that transcends the limits of its own fictive universe" (p. 225).

In his analysis of the *Nun's Priest's Tale* Burlin's critical faculties almost subdue his Romantic predispostions. He accords to that tale the honor of final place, following the Wife of Bath and concluding his discussion of the *Canterbury Tales*. Judging by the reduced fervor of the treatment, however, I think the honor was reluctantly bestowed. Certainly Burlin finds in the *Nun's Priest's Tale* none of the high seriousness of dramatic characterization (the teller being virtually anonymous), though he does lay great stress on the personality of Chauntecleer and the human vanities it represents. The final assessment of the tale is derived from its rhetorical character, an aspect of Chaucer's fiction-making which Burlin is loath to acknowledge throughout the book but to which he pays due if brief acknowledgment in some perceptive paragraphs on the *Nun's Priest's Tale*.[9]

Compared to Alys of Bath, the Nun's Priest offers little for the critic's heart, but his head recognizes how apposite the *Nun's Priest's Tale* is to the theme of fiction-making. After citing E. Talbot Donaldson's defense of rhetoric as a "powerful weapon of survival," Burlin summarizes the well-known uses and satiric abuses of rhetoric in the tale, but he still cannot escape entirely the imperatives of his preconceptions. Apparently sensing that rhetorical poetry poses a threat to the doctrines of Romantic unity, Burlin makes a brief, convoluted effort to redeem Chaucer, as a genius standing apart from his age, from the sterility of rhetoric: "The *Nun's Priest's Tale* testifies to a creative instinct on Chaucer's part, however obliquely revealed, that stands outside the critical strictures of his age and rejects the deathly separation of form and meaning, the body and soul of literature. Yet, paradoxically, in so doing he offers the Parson a 'meaning' very much to his taste" (p. 232). The "paradoxically" allows us, characteristically, to have it both ways, to "unify" the oppositions of rhetorical poetry and "real" poetry. Burlin finds the operative "moralitee" of the tale to be the fox's admonition against imprudent "jangling." "The tale is about that point at which the abuse of language touches upon the abuse of reason, when language separates itself from thought and takes on a meaning of its own" (p. 232). Finally, the *Nun's Priest's Tale* enforces a strong philosophical connection with Burlin's ostensible theme: "On the one hand, the fable may seem to imply that the act of fiction-making is nothing but 'worldly vanitee,' a hubristic imitation of his Creator by fallen man, doomed from the start to authenticate little more than the authority of authorial pride. On the other hand, even such a self-deflating moral as this can only be properly expressed by the *experience* of fiction" (p. 234). The central role of fiction in this paradoxical merger of the oppositions of experience and authority is the subject of a brief concluding chapter in which Burlin offers a shrewd but not entirely lucid recapitulation of the difficult theoretical issues he posed at the beginning. He speaks of the "binary structure of Chaucer's imagining" but also insists, still compelled toward unity, that Chaucerian fiction is a "unitary structure [which contains] bipartite elements that seem to be in opposition but interpenetrate imaginatively" (p. 239). I interpret this to mean that Burlin regards Chaucer's imagination to be unitary and his fictions to be binary, hence the unifying function of the imagination. However, he would shun such a simplification because he sees *all* of these elements as interpenetrating, the binary elements of the fiction merging with one another, and the fiction being an expression of the poet's imagination. This kind of argument, positing both unity and its opposite, demands faith as well as evidence and leaves us somewhat uneasily suspended between the maker and the made, the poet's elusive imagination and his difficult but palpable fictions.

Chaucerian Fiction is a book to be conjured with. Of its kind it is an outstanding example, comparable to the work of Kittredge and Lumiansky; and there would be no point in regretting that it is not of another kind were it not for its own explicit and provocative gropings toward a more critical, less subjective analysis of Chaucer's art. To recall Moore's distinction, I think it is time to acknowledge the limits of interpretive criticism of medieval poetry and to encourage a descriptive criticism more rigorously oriented toward the properties of the text. Burlin will provoke discussion of the essential question of critical orientation toward Chaucerian fiction, and if his own answer is in large part retrogressive, it nevertheless points us toward promising alternatives.

Notes

1. Studies of the Chaucerian narrator have proliferated in the past two decades. Some of these are germane to Burlin's sense of Chaucer's self-consciousness about his art (rather than about himself). See especially Robert O. Payne, *The Key of Remembrance: A Study of Chaucer's Poetics* (New Haven: Yale Univ. Press, 1963), which Burlin briefly acknowledges. See also Payne's "Making His Own Myth: The Prologue to Chaucer's *Legend of Good Women, Chaucer Review*, 9 (1975), 197-211. See also Laurence K. Shook, "The *House of Fame*," in *Companion to Chaucer Studies*, ed. Beryl Rowland (New York: Oxford Univ. Press, 1968), pp. 341-54; Gabriel Josipovici, *The World and the Book* (London: Macmillan, 1971), pp. 52-99; Alice S. Miskimin, *The Renaissance Chaucer* (New Haven: Yale Univ. Press, 1975), pp. 116-45; Alfred David, *The Strumpet Muse: Art and Morals in Chaucer's Poetry* (Bloomington: Indiana Univ. Press, 1976), pp. 9-26, 215-31.

2. Delany, *Chaucer's House of Fame: The Poetics of Skeptical Fideism* (Chicago: Univ. of Chicago Press, 1972).

3. Arthur K. Moore, "Medieval English Literature and the Question of Unity," *Modern Philology*, 65 (1968), 285-300. This study includes brief discussions of the *Parliament of Fowls, Beowulf, Piers Plowman,* and the *Morte d'Arthur*. For a detailed study from this point of view, see Robert M. Jordan, "The Question of Unity and the *Parlement of Foules*," *English Studies in Canada*, 3 (1977), 373-85.

4. William W. Ryding, *Structure in Medieval Narrative* (The Hague: Mouton, 1971), p. 115.

5. Vinaver, *The Rise of Romance* (Oxford: Clarendon Press, 1971), p. 77.

6. Gradon, *Form and Style in Early English Literature* (London: Methuen, 1971), p. 150.

7. Michel Foucault, *The Archeology of Knowledge*, trans. A. M. Sheridan Smith (New York: Pantheon/Random House, 1972), p. 23.

8. The *Monk's Tale*, ll. 2119-23, *The Works of Geoffrey Chaucer*, ed. F. N. Robinson, 2nd ed. (Boston: Houghton Mifflin, 1957).

9. Alfred David's recent book (see note 1) also accords pride of place to the *Nun's Priest's Tale*, which David calls "an omnium gatherum of lore and learning that holds up to scrutiny the various means by which man seeks to understand his world." David is less ambivalent than Burlin about the "manipulative" artistry that distinguishes this tale: "In this block of tales . . . the poet begins to reassert his 'authority,' not in his own person, but by manipulating his fiction" (pp. 223-24).

Editing Geniuses: Max and Saxe
Thomas L. McHaney

A. Scott Berg. *Max Perkins, Editor of Genius*. New York: E. P. Dutton, 1978. ix, 499 pp.

Dorothy Commins. *What Is an Editor? Saxe Commins at Work*. Chicago: University of Chicago Press, 1978. xv, 243 pp.

As the book business in America has evolved over the last half century, the editor has become more than a functionary who corrects and styles manuscripts. Though there were and are editor-publishers, the independent editor is replacing the publisher now as the seeker, nurturer, inspirer, shaper, purveyor, and advocate of literary talent. Publishers are seldom elegant or flamboyant or even slightly shady connoisseurs of books, authors, and chorus girls; more often they are corporate structures with full staffs of managers, marketing specialists, and cost accountants, as easy to get close to, for the serious writer, as the computer that charges him for airline tickets he never bought.

A. Scott Berg's *Max Perkins, Editor of Genius* is the chronicle of a man who, in a sense, is the prototype of this trend in publishing, and the book is itself a sign of the times, a "Thomas Congdon Book," where Berg's editor can fly his own flag alongside the corporate logo at the bottom of the title page. One wonders whether such books will come to have individualistic traits like symphony performances or play productions or films done by specific conductors and directors. One wishes that this question had been put to the work of Max Perkins, whose life Berg tells, and to the career of Saxe Commins, whose widow has prepared a brief memoir based on his diaries and letters. Are there such things as "Max Perkins Books" and "Saxe Commins Books"? What would it matter to literary history and criticism if this were demonstrably so?

The question is raised, obviously, because it probably would matter a good deal. These two roughly contemporaneous editors handled—and possibly sometimes mishandled—the greatest display of literary talent that America at any one time has produced. They were neither born to it nor trained for it. Can one imagine a couple of Renaissance worthies stumbling into the management of Shakespeare, Spenser, Marlowe, Wyatt, Surrey, Sidney, Donne, and Thomas Nash, or two Victorian gentlemen of no great means, educated for business and medicine, becoming editors for Dickens, Thackeray, Browning, George Eliot, Trollope, Tennyson, Swinburne, and Wilde? A capricious daydream, to be sure, but perhaps also an instructive one if we are to appreciate what it means for Maxwell Perkins, a serious New England Harvard man who left newspaper reporting to work in Scribner's business department, and Saxe Commins, who studied dentistry at the University of Pennsylvania and began a practice in Rochester, N.Y., to have played major roles in the literary careeers of Scott Fitzgerald, Ernest Hemingway, Thomas Wolfe, Erskine Caldwell *and* Taylor Caldwell, Ring Lardner, Marjorie Kinnan Rawlings, James Jones (a partial Perkins list) and Eugene O'Neill, Theodore Dreiser, Sinclair Lewis, William Faulkner, W. H. Auden, Gertrude Stein, Walter Van Tilburg Clark, Robinson Jeffers, Isak Dinesen, and Irwin Shaw (a partial Commins list). What wouldn't we give to know a great deal about the work of these men and how it formed, helped, or harmed the writing they brought into print? We know where twentieth-century literature would be without these writers; but do we know where it would be without—or even with—these editors?

Perkins's story has been told many times, at least piecemeal, in biographies of Hemingway, Wolfe, Fitzgerald, and Lardner; in collections of his letters like *Editor to Author, Dear Scott/Dear Max,* and *Ring around Max;* in early portraits by Van Wyck Brooks and Malcolm Cowley; and in Perkins's own accounts of his relations with Wolfe and others, his rare speeches, and his essays. Berg goes beyond this material by working his way through the original documents in the Scrib-

Editing Geniuses: Max and Saxe

ner archive at Princeton, the Wolfe papers at Harvard, Van Wyck Brooks's letters and notebooks, Fitzgerald's papers, Scribners' current files, Malcolm Cowley's interview notes, and letters and documents held by Perkins's family and friends. Berg has interviewed scores of people. He has pried loose a cache of letters, only a few of which have been printed before, that reveal something of Perkins's private thinking and a special but supposedly Platonic friendship with a well-to-do young Virginia woman, Elizabeth Lemmon. He has added Perkins's work with other authors to a new synthesis of the editor's ongoing relations with his most famous clients. The result is a substantial "life" though, as we shall see, it is not everything one might have wanted.

Saxe Commins is not the legend that Perkins was, nor was he apparently quite the "editor of genius" that Perkins's peers and his authors seem to agree upon, but first at Liveright and then at Random House Commins too worked with writers of great stature, including O'Neill and Faulkner, both of whom liked him as a man, relied upon him as a friend, and benefited from his sympathy. The brief memoir *What Is an Editor?* by his wife Dorothy is constructed from Commins's correspondence and diaries, now on file at Princeton, and from Mrs. Commins's recollections. She does not appear to have used Random House files, from which *Selected Letters of William Faulkner* drew for correspondence with Commins, but she quotes and uses as illustrations several letters not in the Faulkner volume; it may be assumed, then, that the Commins archive contains a number of literary documents which remained the editor's personal property. Mrs. Commins calls this archive a "partial" record of her husband's work with authors, because so many of his literary discussions were carried on at his office or at his home. Beginning with these limitations, she has inevitably constructed only a partial portrait, and as a result the question in her title is answered only in a limited, general way.

What is an editor? When one dips into the small body of literature devoted to modern editors and editing, he finds that there is agreement upon the answer and evidence to illustrate.

Numerous men and women have reputations as solid as Maxwell Perkins's; others, like Commins not so well known, have nevertheless played important parts in the literary lives of both serious and popular authors, who are grateful and bestow credit and praise for encouragement and help received. Authors are a lonely lot; they can be as out of touch with their own talents and literary affinities, at times, as they are with current commercial trends, and an editor with a good second sense and a firm but tactful hand can put them on either of the two tracks to success—make them grow into artists or turn them into best-sellers. A writer as tough as Faulkner could confess to Commins, as he neared the end of his long struggle with *A Fable*, "My judgement is still good; what I have done is all right, but very slow, difficult. I must have peace again; I have almost got to teach myself again to believe in it. I seem to have reached a point I never believed I ever would: where I need to have someone read it and tell me, Yes, it's all right. You must go ahead with it"(p. 208). By this time, 1953, Max Perkins had been dead for six years, so "might-have-beens" are more than usually futile speculation, but comparing Perkins's work with what we learn of Commins's, it is still intriguing to think what a writer with Faulkner's energy and self-discipline might have accomplished at a house like Scribners, under Perkins's eye.

Both biographies claim special status for their subjects, of course, Berg confirming in his title the widely held view that Perkins was "editor of genius"—in both senses—and Mrs. Commins suggesting in her title that Saxe Commins was prototypical. Perkins's case is illustrated by the work he did, the letters he wrote, and by the success of authors whom he literally made. Commins's case is established chiefly by testimonials and anecdotes. The claims of both biographies can be judged, along with the quality of their documentation, organization, and presentation of the available facts, but before these matters are considered it will be useful to consider some previous estimates of editorial excellence and some accounts of what an editor is supposed to do.

Charles A. Madison's *Irving to Irving: Author–Publisher*

Relations, 1800-1974 is a lively synthesis of existing anecdote and scholarship about how publishers and authors treat one another. Joseph Conrad, for example, once wrote the young Alfred Knopf, then working for Doubleday, about his wish for a lasting "connection" with a house that would take him up as an investment to be trusted and nurtured. Conrad, Madison writes,

> here touched on an aspect of publishing that came close to the heart of the industry. Ideally publishers are expected to nurse new authors and do their utmost to build up their readership, so that in time their books become profitable to both author and publisher. In reality most publishers are neither astute nor idealistic—and are particularly shortsighted currently, when editors must show an immediate profit to satisfy their corporate employers. More in the past, and less so recently, a publisher will take a book by a new author on the chance that it will prove profitable. . . . When it doesn't sell well enough at last to repay the investment, the tendency of most publishers is to drop the author and seek others—a gamble that usually benefits neither party. It is only the exceptional publisher who has the wisdom and the critical insight to pick authors of promise and promote their work for the long-term rewards that often come with persistent effort.[1]

Madison might have gone on to say that editors, more often than not, are now the ones who make these commitments and gambles, though with a corporation's sharply watched money. They pick, groom, and promote; they lose positions over authors who have not succeeded financially; and they leave for jobs with greater freedom, when they can find them, taking with them the authors whom they have found or helped. As Gerald Gross wrote in *Editors on Editing* seventeen years ago, "The editor has only just about come into his own as a power in the publishing world. As the old-fashioned publisher—the man who selected, backed and 'personalized' his books—grows fewer in number, the editor supersedes him in power and influence."[2] Today, as noted, we have the personalized book, its editor's name given equal billing with that of the "house" which is no longer a home.

A modern editor must first of all be an author's advocate,

and he must understand and appreciate what an author can do and wants to do so he can transmit enthusiasm for a book into editorial counsels and sales meetings. He must bring an objective view to the author's manuscript and try to help the author achieve his own potential. Once a book is published, he must be sensitive to reviews and sales figures, partly to help his author and partly to protect himself, learning not to repeat unnecessary mistakes.[3] John Farrar, a publisher and editor himself, says that great editors, in his experience, have been "strongly individualistic in their characters and methods . . . had a deep appreciation of the finest things in literature . . . were not literary snobs; all of them liked authors as friends and all liked to read and enjoyed a good story; they worked night and day and loved publishing even as it became more and more a business and less a profession. Naturally preferring to work with books they admired, they were willing to undertake more routine jobs . . . men of affection, industry, and enthusiasm."[4] He points out that only a few books on any publisher's list are "by any test works of literature," and that editors must spend large portions of their time working with poorly executed manuscripts not produced by seasoned writers and with ghost-written hackwork.[5]

Editors create books; they may even create authors. A subject that an editor believes to be "commercial" is assigned to a writer considered capable of making a successful book. A writer with ability cannot find a subject; the editor suggests one, elaborates it, even purchases and sends reference works to get the author going. If in either case the germ grows, an author is suddenly born, and the writer who has a single triumph and is willing to repeat it, exercising a certain amount of quality control, may do very well indeed. William Charvat pointed out many years ago that Longfellow made America safe for poetry and became the first of a long succession of brand-name authors, turning out a product that was consistent in tone, theme, and size, year after year, uniform as our famous brands of soup, or candy bars, or ketchup. That is the way to hold an audience, and publishing is full of standard-brand authors, many of whom have been conceived and maintained by self-effacing editors.

An editor of genius, then, is not a man who spends all his time contemplating the ideal and chatting with the next classic author. He has a number of jobs to do, and he must walk a very narrow path, must be sensitive to the aroma of genius, the smell of success, and the odor of turkey. He must be literarily and psychologically and commercially astute; he cannot be a snob or a boob. Often he must cajole, encourage, admonish, and finance people who betray and abuse him. Being a good editor is not easy, and being a great editor, one comes to believe, is a bit like raising a well-behaved and happy family of intelligent youngsters while running an efficient and successful no-holds-barred whorehouse.

The "ordinary editorial services" are "correcting, adding, deleting, substituting, transposing."[6] But these can be done by a copy editor, and in the mind of John Farrar "the gift of meticulous care in the correction of punctuation, spelling, and so on does not usually combine with the abilities of an editor who concerns himself with the earlier problems of an author's creative period."[7] An editor of genius like Perkins is better employed detecting the author's intentions, discerning underlying patterns, and suggesting ways for development that have not been fully pursued. As much as possible, at least when the editor of genius is really editing genius — and he must be able to judge that — he should stay in the background and not meddle with structure or style.

The foregoing are the ideals, derived from the practice of the best in recent times. Since Perkins is, by all accounts, one of the models, we have only to examine Berg's *Max Perkins* to determine how satisfactorily and completely the story is told and Mrs. Commins's *What Is an Editor?* to judge how well, considering both subject and treatment, it matches up.

Berg's biography has been expanded from a 1971 undergraduate thesis at Princeton. It was conceived, or perhaps reconceived, at an editor's suggestion, as a commercial book. This is not an inherent fault, necessarily, as W. A. Swanberg's scholarly but entertaining lives of Hearst or Dreiser demonstrate. Berg's model appears to be the work of his teacher, Carlos Baker, who directed the Princeton thesis and to whom the book is partially dedicated. Berg uses the same style of documentation that Baker employed in *Ernest Hemingway: A Life Story,* avoiding footnotes and organizing his references by subject subheadings in the back of the book; unlike Baker, he does not boldface his key phrases, and the references are difficult, though not impossible, to track from text to notes. Since he relies primarily upon manuscript materials rather than published accounts, the accuracy of most of his quotations and dates can only be checked fully by a visit to the collections he used. A comparison of published versions of the same letters did turn up several nonsubstantive differences, and a spot check of quotations from published works revealed a number of similar discrepancies, some of which seem to be the result of editorial styling. Page references to published texts seem complete and accurate; the index is also apparently accurate.

As to the story Berg tells, it is familiar because of the attention already devoted by scholars and biographers to Perkins and his most famous authors. There are few if any surprises to change our view of the editor, and all the famous letters are there, ones we have read before in *Editor to Author* or *Dear Scott/Dear Max* or the biographies. Berg's accomplishment is putting more of Perkins's work together: what he did for the famous and the not-so-famous and even the obscure. The focus, naturally, is on Perkins, not his authors. But even here we most likely do not have a full portrait of the average Perkins day; we seem to see him in leaps of weeks and months, and because his major authors were so interesting they raise the scale of everything. Perhaps they made his days and weeks worth the tedium he must have felt during some of the jobs he had to do. We do see the energy, intelligence, and warmth he applied to his craft. .

As Berg portrays him, Maxwell Perkins is a bit like a figment of a late nineteenth-century imagination—the Last Puritan of the Genteel Tradition entering the Modern Age, except, miraculously, he not only accepts the twentieth century, he becomes the advocate and promoter of the age's spokesmen. But if Perkins felt comfortable in the modern period, he did so without ever taking off his coat and hat, a polite, fascinated, and indispensable visitor. He created a revolution at Scribners without being a revolutionary. He did it by accepting the work of as yet undeveloped authors in whose writing he discerned special promise. Then he either let them grow or he worked with them, encouraged them, drew from them what his judgment told him was there. "Before Perkins nobody at Scribners had edited so boldly or closely as he did Fitzgerald, and some of the older editors considered the practice questionable. They liked Max and sensed his ability, but they did not always understand him. . . . It took some time for the older editors to appreciate what Max was accomplishing . . . or indeed to value the new writers Perkins had brought into their house" (p. 70).

Perkins apparently never concerned himself with manufacturing best-sellers as such, though he turned out more than his share of successes. When the Great Depression came and the book business looked bleak, Perkins's books, including S. S. Van Dine's *The Bishop Murder Case* and Hemingway's *A Farewell to Arms*, helped Scribners enjoy "the palmiest year they had ever had" (p. 158). By 1930, when Charles Scribner died at seventy-six, Perkins was an officer of the firm, on his way to becoming editorial director, and he did not have to defend his judgments. He suffered failures, like any editor, gambling on writers whose books never materialized or shaped up, publishing work that did not succeed, and, according to Berg, he literally suffered when these things occurred. He had a preference, Berg writes, for "reminiscences and autobiographical fiction by people he felt had lived interesting lives filled with colorful characters and dramatic events. But often, he eventually realized, these were the very people who lacked the perseverance or talent to write" (pp. 371-72).

How he worked with Fitzgerald and Wolfe is well known, but what some of that work meant can be better appreciated now that we see it occurring within the context of busy days and the need to keep up with many other authors. Perkins's self-image was complex but self-effacing. In 1943 he told Malcolm Cowley, who was engaged upon research for his *New Yorker* profile, "that the man he would most like to resemble was Major General John Aaron Rawlins . . . 'the most nearly indispensable' officer of General Grant's staff. It was his job to keep Grant sober; edit his important papers and put them in final form; apply tact and persistence in order to make critical points; and often restore the general's self-confidence" (p. 421). Berg makes no connection between this image and Fitzgerald's application of the life of Grant to Dick Diver in *Tender Is the Night*, though the opportunity for discussion seems obvious, especially coupled with another incident Berg reports. Fitzgerald reacted sharply when Perkins sent him a cartoon that seemed to reflect upon the author's drinking, but later he apologized and "reminded Perkins of the time he accused Max of sending him Grant's memoirs to show him the life of another failure" (p. 384).

Perkins's most famous authors, we know, sometimes had troubled relationships not only with him but with one another, and yet most of the time he managed to serve them all, convince them of his loyalty and keep theirs, listen to their complaints or take their abuse, and maintain for himself an undeceived perception of their weaknesses as well as their strengths. In 1931, apparently, he gave some thought to annexing William Faulkner to the Scribners list, but he did not follow through. Perhaps, as John Hall Wheelock told Berg, it was "because he was afraid of arousing Hemingway's jealousy" (p. 181).

What Perkins did for writers whose books did not make literary history and whose lives did not make headlines is less well known than his work with Fitzgerald, Hemingway, Lardner, or Wolfe, but his reputation as an editor rests as surely on that work as it does upon the other. He helped Arthur Train, a criminal lawyer who wrote true crime stories, to create the popular Mr. Tutt, an eccentric Yankee lawyer-detective who bears some resemblance to Perkins's own forebears. His suggestions apparently freed Train's imagination and started him on a long successful writing career, Perkins often contributing plot and characterization for the Tutt series and for other work by Train as well. He accepted the writing of Janet Reback, worked with her to cut and shape it; and her first book for Scribners, under her new pseudonym, Taylor Caldwell, became the first of a number of best-sellers. Berg observes that "Taylor Caldwell was worth the extra hours that Perkins had devoted to her book, time that probably would not have been available if Thomas Wolfe still had been on the Scribners list" (p. 346), a statement that puts a professional context around the labor Perkins often did for his authors and especially around the emotional parting of Scribners and Thomas Wolfe. Wolfe's books exacted a high price in time and energy, but Perkins never complained.

For Caldwell, as for Marcia Davenport, Nancy Hale, and Marjorie Kinnan Rawlings, Perkins contributed ideas, reference works, suggestions for structural and stylistic revision, pushing them toward action and drama and extracting from them, somehow, the kind of writing he had perceived each could do best. Caldwell wrote him that it was like a course in fiction-writing to work with him. Perkins wrote his Virginia lady-friend that he had believed Hale could write "before she had written," as "Virginians think a colt could run when he could barely stand" (p. 206). He had to wait through several novels before Hale achieved the success he predicted, but he stuck by her and encouraged her. He stuck with an enormous and chaotic manuscript by Marcia Davenport because "it would not do to allow Marcia to fail on this big undertaking. It might ruin her career to get beaten that way" (p. 403). He urged Marjorie Kinnan Rawlings to write the book that became *The Yearling*, urging her on for years while supporting her in other writing tasks. Her remark to him one time was, "Do you realize how calmly you sit in your office and tell me to write a *classic?*" (p. 213). When she finally began the "boy's book," she asked Perkins if he liked *The Fawn* as a title, and he replied encouragingly: "I think *The Fawn* is a good title, but I am not sure that it would be a wise one for it might seem too poetic, or even a little sentimental" (p. 297).

Perkins's judgments so often proved uncannily correct that it is remarkable to see him continue as a self-effacing editor constantly reminding his authors to resist him, to write their books according to their own conceptions, to ignore the "conditions of the trade" (p. 299). In an odd way this advice was a reflection of his own approach to life; he was true to his heritage, but eccentric, determinedly "responsible," and sufficiently sure of his judgments to believe they were not entirely subjective, at least not willful, and he was able to accept resistance or counterargument without personal involvement or rancor. He knew his business, though he was without any specific training for it; in fact, he practically invented or reinvented it for himself.

As for Perkins's troubles with authors, except for the famous case of Wolfe, they were comparatively few (at least few are chronicled in Berg) and, in general, such things are par for the profession, as a glance at Madison's *Irving to Irving* proves—for instance, his chapter on Henry Holt and William James. The Wolfe episode is dramatic, but this is partly so because it has been dramatized so many times by so many people, including Wolfe himself. Berg follows modern scholarship in demythologizing the editing of *Look Homeward, Angel*, which was paramountly a matter of cutting the book by almost a third to keep focus upon the hero and his reactions to his family. No one believed in and supported Wolfe more than Perkins, and the editor himself apparently anguished, even in later years, over some of the fine pieces he had insisted upon removing. Harry Maule, himself an editor with Doubleday and Random House, observed in *Editors on Editing* that "to invest so much time in one book implies supreme confidence in the ultimate result. (I dread to think of the extra hours Max Perkins had to put in to catch up on the affairs of other authors he was handling at the time—Hemingway, for example.)"[8]

Berg's life of Perkins is well written, except for artificial transitions that close the opening chapters, and it is well paced. Berg drops back from an opening in medias res to proceed chronologically through Perkins's life. Dates are given often enough to keep the reader aware of when events occurred. Berg avoids the temptation to provide an artificial plot or to milk our emotions too heavily as, inevitably, the circle narrows and some of Perkins's friends and authors begin to die. The letters to the Virginia lady, Elizabeth Lemmon, provide a love interest of sorts, but it is low key; the ones which have not seen print before (letters from Perkins to her have been used in previous biographies of Fitzgerald and Wolfe, but not the more intimate letters) do not force any reevaluation of Perkins's character or his work. They confirm what his friends and colleagues, like Van Wyck Brooks or John Hall Wheelock, knew about Perkins long ago. Berg's interpretation of Perkins does not appreciably differ from Andrew Turnbull's; it is only more detailed. Since Perkins did confide to Elizabeth Lemmon things he apparently did not record in letters to others, the letters to her provide an occasional insight into other literary lives.

John Hall Wheelock said in 1950 that it was too soon to measure Perkins's achievement as an editor. Berg quotes this remark at the beginning of his acknowledgments section as if to announce that he has accepted the challenge. Certainly he seems to have worked through the available resources diligently, and he has shown us Perkins's achievement, but that he has measured, analyzed, or explained it is to be doubted. From a scholarly point of view, at least, some things are lacking. There is, for example, more room for consideration of Perkins's effects upon the work of his authors, consideration that must be based on comparative study of manuscripts he edited and possibly comparison of what he did for admittedly popular writing with what he did for the work of genius. To what extent did he leave his stamp upon the books he edited? To what extent did his reputation, his known prejudices and preferences, intimidate his authors while they wrote? How do "Maxwell Perkins books" differ from those of some noted contemporaneous editors? A summary of the personal and corporate financial considerations under which he worked would be useful and informative. What kind of money did he have to work with; what kind of money did he make for the house? A year-by-year analysis, set beside the books he accepted and produced in each year, would be useful.

Perkins did tell his authors to resist him, but he was often irresistible. What was the effect of his position on profanity in the novel? In *A Farewell to Arms* Hemingway was determined not to make the concessions he had made regarding obscene language in *The Sun Also Rises*, but Perkins won him over in the end, only later to write Hemingway that he had finally seen "that any circumlocutions, etc. would be inconsistent with the way you write. I tried to explain this [to Owen Wister], but I really never fully grasped how you do write, so I couldn't very well" (p. 143). A summary chapter on the general nature of Perkins's editorial impact, though it is not the kind of thing a popular audience is interested in, might have been included as an appendix without costing Berg too much extra effort, and it might have been illustrated with examples of typical work on manuscripts, if that had been possible. A rough idea of what such a synthesis would contain may be had by skimming Berg's index of entries under Perkins's name.

Dorothy Commins makes claims for her late husband that are almost as extravagant as the praise Perkins has received. Praise, with testimonials from authors with whom Saxe Commins worked, seems to be the reason for her book, but the fact is that Commins did have supporters and friends among the authors he handled, and he did for them the kinds of things Perkins did for the Scribners stable. Since Mrs. Commins's book appeared, Irwin Shaw has added more evidence: "Editors can be very useful. I had a great editor, Saxe Commins at Random House, who helped me cut more than 100,000 words out of *The Young Lions*. If I had kept it in it might have been a terrible flop."[9] That is more than Perkins urged Wolfe to remove from *Look Homeward, Angel*, but, for whatever reasons, it has not become a legend or a cause célèbre in the world of letters. On the other hand, just as Perkins did not understand the deliberate purposes of Hemingway's artful prose sufficiently well to appreciate the sparing use of obscenity, Commins seems never to have perceived what Faulkner was doing or the purposes of his fictional methods. The result is not discussed in Dorothy Commins's book, but anyone who has studied Faulkner's manuscripts is aware that beginning with *Absalom, Absalom!*—the first novel with Random House and the first one that Commins worked on—the editing is inconsistent and often destructive of Faulkner's intentions.

The story of Commins's editorial work at Random House is really not told in *What Is an Editor?* It is a small book, chiefly anecdotal, interlaced with letters and excerpts from Commins's diaries and a few letters from his authors, most of them not concerned with editorial matters. If Perkins seems a bit like a character invented by George Santayana, Commins sounds as if he were a product of the imagination of Sherwood Anderson. "My colleagues would set up a derisive snicker at the notion that I am a businessman," he once wrote an admirer. "I am merely a working editor who has accumulated a set of naive concepts about publishing" (p. xiii). In a lecture prepared for delivery at Columbia, his style even seems unconsciously to mimic Anderson:

Now what is an editor? To know what an editor "is," it becomes necessary to inquire into what he has been and what he became. He is first of all a worker, proud of his craft, sensitive to ideas of all kinds and responsive to them; he is discriminating against ineptitude, inaccuracy, misinformation, nonsense, and humbug; he fights for talent, for the free interchange of opinion and the widest possible dissemination of information. . . . He is nimble in his thinking and his guessing and prophesying. He prays that he will be lucky . . . an editor is any semiliterate who reads with a pencil in his hand. [p. xiii]

Commins trained as a dentist and began a practice; metaphorically, that does not seem to be a terribly unlikely preparation for editorial work: filling, extracting, polishing. He always had literary ambitions, and he cultivated literary friends, including Eugene O'Neill. On the eve of the Great Depression he married Dorothy, abandoned his dental practice, and set out for Europe to be a writer; but he soon returned to America and settled into editing, first with Covici-Friede and then, after a year, with the firm to which O'Neill had given him an introduction, Boni and Liveright. When

O'Neill moved from Liveright's sinking ship to Random House, part of the deal was that Saxe would come along, and he worked there until his death in 1958, at which time he was senior editor.

Dorothy Commins has constructed her book out of Saxe's personal papers, which are by no means a complete record of his editorial work or his life. The longest section of the book is devoted to his friendship with O'Neill, but he came into O'Neill's literary life quite late, when the great playwright had an enormous reputation, a large body of completed work, and a great confidence in his own abilities. Commins's editorial work with O'Neill was essentially copy editing, but there is less information about that in Dorothy Commins's book than in the undocumented biography of O'Neill by Arthur and Barbara Gelb, which Mrs. Commins has not used. Similar problems exist in her account of Commins's dealings with other authors. The story of Commins and Faulkner does not begin until the post-Nobel Prize period, though Faulkner went to Random House in 1936 with *Absalom, Absalom!* Commins apparently worked on that complex book, which is poorly edited, but in *What Is an Editor?* we do not learn anything about Saxe's editorial work until *A Fable*. Just how bewildered Commins must have been by *Absalom, Absalom!* is perhaps revealed in one of his notebook entries about the galley proofs of *A Fable*: "On second and third and fourth reading, one gains a deeper impression of order rather than involution for its own sake or because it is so much what Bill himself is—involuted. Who isn't? Still a little bewildered by some of the rhetorical extravagances and the involuted progressions and regressions in the unfolding of a tale that is overwhelming and so simple, full of questionable coincidences and yet with a narrative substructure that holds the whole edifice from collapse" (p. 202). He also confesses to his notebook, "I acquire a nervous psychological block which makes it almost impossible to open its covers and see what we have wrought. There will be much to answer for—and I, not Bill, will be called on to answer questions" (p. 202). Commins continued to worry over what Random House and the world would say about his work on *A*

Editing Geniuses: Max and Saxe 87

Fable — and it is not clear from Dorothy Commins's book why — until a friend, the Harvard scholar Perry Miller, felt the need to console him: "above all things, you must not — repeat NOT — let any implication, spoken or implied, that Faulkner's editor is at fault, you must NOT give it house room" (p. 211). Exactly what Commins believed he would have to answer for is never spelled out; Dorothy Commins reveals that Saxe wrote a long letter to Faulkner and a report to Random House about *A Fable*, but both, she says, have been lost. Commins's reaction seems both despairing or obtuse and paranoid, a strange reaction for a man who had worked with Faulkner on *Absalom, Absalom!, The Unvanquished, The Wild Palms, The Hamlet, Go Down, Moses, Intruder in the Dust, Knight's Gambit*, and *Requiem for a Nun*, except the sad fact is that Commins appears not to have understood some of those earlier books either, to judge by his editorial work on them.[10]

Dorothy Commins does not have the documentation for her husband's editorial work; she reports very little of it, does not analyze what she reports, and occasionally does not comprehend what she describes. As she tells it, Budd Schulberg came to Saxe with the idea for a novel and, working weekends, they "made" *On the Waterfront*. But the circumstances suggest that they were doing a novelization of a screenplay that Schulberg already had written and sold. The film appeared before Random House could produce the book.

Commins did do ghostwriting, though his activities in that area are not covered thoroughly either. The most detailed account of Commins's editing comes from a journal he kept while putting together a biography of Lillian Russell for a man named Parker Morrell, who was to write it, at Bennett Cerf's suggestion, to capitalize upon a movie about her. Commins did all the work; Morrell got all the credit.

What Is an Editor? is intended as monument of praise to Saxe Commins; the biographical anecdotes about him or about his authors and the letters sent to his widow after his death serve that function. Commins became senior editor at Random House, but he does not seem to have received much credit; whether his role was really small there, despite his position, or his role has been diminished by recent biographical works like Blotner's *Faulkner* and the posthumous Cerf memoirs, *At Random*, is hard to say without a full study of the publisher's records, which Mrs. Commins has not used. Commins did a lot of editorial work that is recorded, apparently, in the letters of Robert Haas, a Random House partner who brought Faulkner and authors like Isak Dinesen with him when his firm, Smith and Haas, merged with Random House in 1936. Haas continued to handle the authors, though Commins seems to have handled their books; hence the letters between Faulkner and Haas in Blotner's recent *Selected Letters of William Faulkner* may be a part of the iceberg whose tip, according to Mrs. Commins, is the archive of her husband's personal papers with which she is working.

Her defenses of Saxe Commins do not always come out the way she intends. She quotes a weak and apologetic letter from Robert Haas to Isak Dinesen. Dinesen had found errors and objectionable styling features in her *Last Tales*; she did not like the jacket copy. Haas is unable to defend the book's editor, Commins, except to claim that Saxe had devoted "loving care" to the book; he consoles the author with the suggestion that the errors won't be noticed as much as she supposes. Cerf's memory of Commins in *At Random* is mixed: "One of the conditions made by Eugene O'Neill was that I give a job to his old friend Saxe Commins, who had come to Liveright just about the time I was leaving. We gave Saxe a job, and he turned out to be one of the great men of Random House, a wonderful man, and was our senior editor for many years, until he died."[11] But, Cerf also records, Saxe was

a frustrated writer. When he himself wrote, it was purple prose, the kind of thing he would have laughed at if somebody brought it in to him. He infuriated John O'Hara with editorial suggestions to the point that O'Hara finally refused to work with him any longer. On the other hand, with James Michener, who came to Random House because of Saxe, the trouble was of a different kind. Jim brought in a manuscript that he regarded as an unfinished first draft and that he wanted to discuss with his editor before giving it the final polishing. When he learned that Saxe had copyedited the

Editing Geniuses: Max and Saxe

manuscript and sent it to the printer, he asked for a different editor.[12]

Dorothy Commins mentions the break with O'Hara, giving some examples of the author's rebukes and outbursts to Commins, but she does not explain the whole story. She does not mention the break with Michener, though she quotes a letter in which the author gives Commins a short lecture on the style and content of an introduction the editor had written for the *Selected Writings of Robert Louis Stevenson* (pp. 102-3).

What Is an Editor? is not in the same class as *Max Perkins*, nor was it intended to be, but it does not fulfill its own modest aims. At best, it is an announcement of a small archive that is important to literary history and to the writing of several literary lives. It is not documented, and the materials have been assembled into a narrative without scrupulous attention to chronology or context. There is no need to belabor the small book's limitations, but it might have included a handlist of the Commins papers, which Princeton, where they are now located, could have provided without too much trouble; then the editors at Chicago might have devised a system of references from the text to the handlist to provide some modest documentation. There is an index that seems to be adequate and accurate.

These two accounts, so differently scaled whatever their individual merits and demerits, demonstrate the importance of studying the lives of men like Perkins and Commins. It is true that the amount of published material about Perkins is a reflection of the interest in his authors as much as it is a reflection of his own abilities. But the incomplete account of Commins and the other writing devoted to editors like him illustrate the need for more research upon the editorial relation. The mediocre editor may have more effect on great writing than the great one. By studying what the great editor does for the mediocre writer we may learn more of his tastes, abilities, prejudices, and interests than by studying his work with geniuses whom he lets go their own way or who resist him successfully. We also stand to learn a great deal about conditions of publishing, the taste of the times, and general literary relations, while we gather materials for a full history of various publishing houses. As any enterprising editor could see, there are books out there waiting to be written.

Notes

1. Madison, *Irving to Irving: Author-Publisher Relations 1800-1974* (New York: Bowker, 1974), p. 119.

2. Gross, Introduction, *Editors on Editing* (New York: Grosset & Dunlap, 1962), pp. xiii-xiv.

3. Harry Maule, in *Editors on Editing*, pp. 122-23.

4. Farrar, in *Editors on Editing*, p. 35.

5. *Ibid.*

6. John Kuehl and Jackson R. Bryer, Introduction, *Dear Scott/Dear Max: The Fitzgerald-Perkins Correspondence* (New York: Scribners, 1971), p. 13.

7. Farrar, in *Editors on Editing*, p. 34.

8. Maule, in *Editors on Editing*, p. 123.

9. Irwin Shaw, "The Art of Fiction IV," *Paris Review*, 21 (Spring 1979), 256.

10. There is sufficient basis for this observation in my own study of the Faulkner papers at the University of Virginia, but very little published information exists yet on Commins's editing of Faulkner. Some of the problems with *Absalom, Absalom!* are discussed in Noel Polk, "The Manuscript of *Absalom, Absalom!*" *Mississippi Quarterly*, 25 (Summer 1972), 359-67. The editing of *The Wild Palms* is treated in the textual appendix to Thomas L. McHaney, "William Faulkner's *The Wild Palms*: A Textual And Critical Study," Diss. University of South Carolina 1968.

11. *At Random: The Reminiscences of Bennett Cerf* (New York: Random House, 1977), p. 85.

12. *Ibid.*, p. 220.

The Whole Duty of Composition
Donald J. Gray

E. D. Hirsch, Jr. *The Philosophy of Composition.* Chicago: University of Chicago Press, 1977. xiii, 200 pp.

Mina Shaughnessy. *Errors and Expectations: A Guide for the Teacher of Basic Writing.* New York: Oxford University Press, 1977. viii, 311 pp.

Both these books begin with a brief account of what E. D. Hirsch calls a "conversion experience." While he was chairing the department of English at the University of Virginia, Hirsch "began to wonder how long our university would continue its big expenditures on literary teaching and scholarship without insisting that we devote comparable energies to the teaching that was paying for so many of our literary courses—namely the teaching of composition" (p. xii). After the doubt, the conversion: "I felt ashamed of my neglect of composition during my chairmanship" (p. xii), and Hirsch undertook the direction of his department's composition program and the course of reading and thinking that resulted in his book. Mina Shaughnessy, characteristically more particular than Hirsch, opens her book with a memory of "sitting alone in the worn urban classroom" in which a group of students who were poorly prepared for college had just written their first compositions at the City College of New York. Their writing was "so stunningly unskilled" that "I could only sit there, reading and re-reading the alien papers, wondering what had gone wrong and trying to understand what I at this eleventh hour of my students' academic lives could do about it" (p. vii). Like Hirsch, she assumed that she was being paid to do something about it. Her book began when she started to analyze student writing—four thousand student essays by the time she was through—to find the logic of their misuse or neglect of the conventions of standard written English. She then began to speculate on the reasons for these errors and to try out some ways to teach students to unlearn them.

I suspect that such conversions, in kind if not in quality, are becoming common in the profession of teaching college English. After years in the deer parks of graduate and undergraduate courses in literature, a lot of us, in mid-career or fresh from graduate school, are moving or being moved to where the students and the jobs are, in courses and programs designed to teach people to write. For Hirsch and Shaughnessy, conversion was a thorough and extensive commitment of mind, heart, and conscience. For others of us it may be a mechanical making over and making do—not Saul changed to Paul; more like a gas station being converted into a doughnut shop. The principal benefit of Hirsch's book and Shaughnessy's is that in each of them an intelligent writer and teacher shows that it can be an attractively diverse and complicated matter to think long and hard about composition. The religious connotations of the metaphor of conversion are apt. These books do bear a kind of witness to what can happen when one turns one's whole mind to the teaching of composition; they are calls to our duty as teachers of literacy. However grudging our own conversions, it cannot but do us good to learn how these smart and confident colleagues found their ways to a complex engagement in a responsibility many of us can no longer slip past.

Most of Hirsch's book is in fact a speculative essay on some ideas about the history of language and the psychology of reading that he thinks will furnish an "authentic ideology of literacy" (p. xiii). In his first chapter he argues that the difference between oral and written speech required the development of conventions to help readers understand a discourse that must do without the clues and constraints of a "definite situational context" (p. 21) and a physically present speaker. These conventions, Hirsch argues, established themselves as the grapholect of a language, its normative, "transdialectal" code (p. 44). Hirsch draws on Jespersen and others to claim that the history of prose shows that the grapholect develops toward increased "communicative efficiency" (p. 53) in its standard orthography, regularity of syntax, and use of such conventions as proleptic devices. This tendency toward efficiency, which Hirsch sees as probably an historical inevitability, provides him with a term and measure that teachers of writing can put to practical use. The term is *relative readability*, and the test, in Hirsch's italicized words, is: *"Assuming that two texts convey the same meaning, the more readable text will take less time and effort to understand"* (p. 85). He then brings in his studies in psycholinguistics and the psychology of reading to argue that this test furnishes an "intrinsic and truly universal norm of writing" (p. 89). For he thinks that the reason one text is more readable than another lies not in culturally learned habits and expectations but in capacities and limits of human intelligence that are universal. For example, experiments show that we cannot hold more than about seven items in our short-term memories. It follows that we will all find readable that prose which keeps us moving ahead by frequent syntactic and semantic closures that resolve the relationships between words and phrases and let us store their meaning somewhere out of our immediate attention. The experiments in long-term memory, reports of which Hirch has read, suggest that we store the meaning but not the words of paragraphs and passages. We therefore find it relatively easy to read prose in which frequent "thematic tags" and "prospective-retrospective links" help us to recall the meaning of earlier parts of the discourse (p. 129). Hirsch closes his book with some familiar maxims about writing he thinks have been freshly accredited by this research: keep related words together, use positive statements and concrete words, use integrative devices between clauses and sentences. He adds some practical advice about teaching composition (ask for lots of revision), and he concludes with some suggestions of topics for further research. He thinks, for example, that we might find a "best" way to organize a course of instruction in writing, or at least "a small number of ways that are better than any others" (p. 164). And he claims that he and his colleagues at Virginia are close to proving a system of evaluation in which the efficiency (and thus the quality) of student writing can be consistently judged.

When I first read Hirsch's book in manuscript, at the request of one of the editors at the University of Chicago Press, I was excited by the chapters on psycholinguistics and the psychology of reading but a little let down by the homely familiarity of the maxims and advice with which he closes the book. In my several rereadings since its publication I have come to wonder if even in the earlier chapters Hirsch makes the lessons of linguistics and psychology, and the progress of what might be called the cultural history of literacy, a little too simple. But my rereadings have also ratified my first conviction that the book is important. He does give intellectual size and dignity to the study, "more complex and challenging than any which I had undertaken in literary history or literary theory" (p. xii), of how people make sense out of writing. But, for Hirsch, composition and its teaching are practical arts. His intention in writing a book about its philosophy is not to prosecute an argument in epistemology, cognitive psychology, or the nature, history, and sociology of language. Nor is it his intention to describe and sponsor new forms of practice. He wants rather to urge the way of his study on us so that we will begin to rescue the teaching of writing from hunch and whim and settle it on theoretical ground. If the practice he finally recommends is familiar, and if its foundation is still imperfectly charted, Hirsch nonetheless shows us where to go and what to study to work out the philosophy of composition his book points toward rather than completes. There is, he demonstrates, something solid and satisfying to be learned about reading and writing. English teachers can learn and even help to make this knowledge. This knowledge will in turn make us consistently effective teachers of composition. That does indeed look to be a good life after the conversion, one in which we can feel as smart and purposive as ever we did in our teaching of literature.

Mina Shaughnessy is as optimistic as Hirsch. But the pleasures of her book and the successes it promises are less speculative than those to be found in Hirsch's way. She simply adopts two premises which Hirsch demonstrates in a chapter each: that writing is different from speech (and therefore students competent in speech must learn an additional set of conventions in order to write), and that the conventions of standard written English are normative in the United States. Sometimes she considers how competence in speech or in another language might interfere and cause errors in the student's use of written English. Sometimes, and always acutely, she remarks how the history of an unskilled writer's failures in academic English make him or her hesitant to begin a sentence or a paragraph, often hypercorrect in punctuation and falsely grand in diction, and sometimes childish in the psychomotor skills of handwriting. Like Hirsch, she sees the teaching of composition as an intrinsically interesting professional enterprise that ought to attract talented people who will learn in it not only something about psycholinguistics and discourse theory, but also something about the structure, responsibilities, and social meaning of their own profession.

But for the most part Shaughnessy attends closely to the data, rather than to their origins and implications, of the four-thousand compositions written by the unskilled writers she calls "basic writing students." She assumes that many of their deviations from standard written English are not random but may be sorted into categories and then corrected by special instruction that addresses entire classes of error. A kind of Linneaus of the tangled flora of basic writers' prose, she classifies in separate chapters the kinds of errors these students make in punctuation, syntax, the number and tense of verbs and their agreement with nouns, spelling, and vocabulary. In another chapter she considers how and why the compositions of unskilled writers are so skimpily and disjunctively developed. In her final chapter she moves from errors to expectations and argues from her own experience that students do learn when they and their teachers figure out patterns of error and sequences of their correction. She offers advice about the means of such correction all through the book. In the chapter on common errors in number, tense, and agreement, for example, she quotes a passage of student writing in which thirteen of eighty-nine words are wrong. Yet she shows that there are only three patterns of error in the passage, "all common to large numbers of students who err not for want of intelligence or care but because of opposing language habits and analogical thinking" (p. 118). Then, as usual, she describes some exercises to change the patterns.

None of Shaughnessy's advice comes from or adds up to a consistent idea about the nature of written English and how students learn to be proficient in its use. Such an idea may be out there, waiting to be mined from the learning theory or psycholinguistics to which Shaughnessy recommends teachers at the end of her book. But she can't wait; she constantly invokes the urgency of Monday morning, when the teachers to whom she is writing must show up in class whether the theory is ready or not. To get them through she puts together "rough and ready" classifications of spelling errors (p. 163), advises teachers to rig up "Rube Goldberg" grammars (p. 156), and tells them about other tactics whose authority is only that they have worked for her. Her book is narrow in its pragmatism as well as in its exclusive attention to the difficulties of basic writing students. But the professional reality she writes about is common enough. She imagines her readers as "teachers trained to analyze the belletristic achievements of the centuries" (p. 3) who are sitting, as she once sat, baffled and dispirited before student writing so apparently random in its unconventionality that they don't know where to begin. She tells them, Begin: "a teacher must be prepared to move, with the student, straight into the tangle, systematically scrutinizing and classifying . . . until patterns of difficulty begin to emerge" (p. 186). That looks to be a hard life, after the conversion. Its successes will mostly be local, improvised, and expended in the occasion; all must be won again in the next tangle, on the next Monday morning. Yet for all of that, such successes are no more evanescent than those we used to win with our neat classroom explications of one of the belletristic achievements of the centuries. None of us needs Shaughnessy's book to remind us that our good days as teachers leave few monuments behind them. The gift of her book, and of the intelligent, generous, optimistic sensibility that shines through it, is that she persuades me that there can be good days in teaching composition too.

Hirsch and Shaughnessy of course write from very different experiences as teachers of writing. The difference shows in the character of the objections to their arguments they anticipate in their books. I think that they meet these objections well, but I will consider them briefly because they and the responses to them help to describe the character and uses of each book. Then I will bring an objection of my own to their conception of the process of writing, for I think their idea encourages other ideas about the means and purposes of teaching composition that are narrow and limiting.

Hirsch expects that the "gravest misunderstanding" of his readers will concern his advocacy of communicative efficiency as the test of good writing (p. 74). He moves to correct this misunderstanding by emphasizing that in the notion of relative readability he considers the semantic intention of the text. Efficient writing is not necessarily easy to read. Difficult prose, prose which uses words surprisingly and holds its syntactic relationships in suspension for a long time, may be efficient if its semantic intentions require such practices. The test is not whether we have trouble reading the prose but whether the same intentions can be realized in words, sentences, and paragraphs that are easier to read. This test summons up the question of synonymy, a familiar question for Hirsch—his idea that the same meaning can be expressed in different words. He does not stay to engage this question in *The Philosophy of Composition,* referring his readers to its discussion in *The Aims of Interpretation* (1976). I think that Hirsch is on solid ground in both these matters. He is, after all, writing a book about teaching students to write. If we did not think that students could say the same thing better and more plainly we would not spend so much time reading their revisions and rearranging the phrases and clauses of their prose. That Hirsch should anticipate these objections, however, interests me because in them I see the reality that he (and I) work in—the reality of colleagues who are solicitous of the unique integrity of the literary text and worried about the heresy of paraphrase, and of students whose problem is not so much getting down a first draft but remaking their prose so that its intention and meaning become clear and emphatic.

The students about whom Shaughnessy writes, on the other hand, have a lot of trouble getting out a first draft, at least in the beginning. And she seems to anticipate that her colleagues are likely to accuse her of betraying the integrity not of the text but of the working-class and minority students who enroll in basic writing programs in urban universities and colleges. Is it, in Shaughnessy's phrase, "academic colonizing" (p. 239) to move students who are fluent in a register of the spoken language, say, into a competence in the standard written English of the academy? Hirsch also engages that question, and answers it by saying that "merely to be a teacher of literacy is already to be committed to linguistic social engineering" (p. 45). He justifies this office by arguing that even though any set of linguistic conventions may be "correct" in its community, all sets are not equal, for one—especially the "transcendent norm" of the grapholect—may be more widely understood than another, carry more status, and allow the statement of more complicated relationships. Shaughnessy's answer is similar and equally sure. But she is readier than Hirsch to consider the conditions from which the question arises. She writes: "When we remember the ways in which the majority society has impinged upon the lives of most [basic writing] students . . . it is difficult to see how the desire to identify with the majority culture, and therefore its public language, could possibly have survived into young adulthood" (p. 125). She also writes of the cost of forgetting where these students come from when we "take from them their distinctive ways of interpreting the world. . . [and] assimilate them into the culture of academic writing without acknowledging their experience as outsiders" (p. 292). But she knows too that the desire to identify, to move up, to be assimilated has survived, and she knows why. The noblest note of Shaughnessy's book is her consistent understanding not just of how errors in student writing might be found in a logic learned from competence in another reg-

The Whole Duty of Composition

ister of language but also of how the solecisms and hypercorrectness of this writing reveal a yearning for a formal register that will help students explain their experience. She writes of a student who wants to learn "to talk analytically, with strangers, about the oppression of his parents and his own resolve to work against that oppression" (p. 197). She imagines college as "a place where people come together for a short time to be immersed in words" (p. 224), and she conceives of a composition course as a place in which students begin to learn to think of themselves as writers, people whose mastery of words and rhetorical forms enables them to talk of their ideas and feelings to strangers in a code no longer strange.

Much as I admire the clarity and sympathy with which Shaughnessy confronts the question of educating students in the code of the academy, I see at its bottom an idea about the process of writing that troubles me. She shares the idea with Hirsch. Both think of writing as a process in which students translate their ideas into the code of the grapholect or, in Shaughnessy's words, "the common language not only of the university but of the public and professional world outside" (p. 187). In a sense, in the act of writing both the meaning and the proper language of its expression are already there. Writing, and its teaching, become centrally a matter of fitting meaning and code together so that others will understand. Hirsch and Shaughnessy acknowledge that the purpose of writing can be defined as only self-satisfying and self-expressive. Both also think that meaning is discovered as well as communicated in the act of writing. As Shaughnessy puts it, "The idea that a writer begins with is seldom fully formed. Submerged in his mind, it must be drawn to the surface by words. But once the words are there, the writer begins testing them against the thought that evoked them, discovering his meaning as he chooses and rejects" (p. 204). But when Hirsch and Shaughnessy buckle down to think about the real business of writing, they imagine a writer with an idea looking for words that will communicate it most efficiently to a reader who expects to be addressed in the "dominant code of literacy" (Shaughnessy, p. 13). Deviations from the code will be counted against the writer, and so will inefficiencies in its use that tire, confuse, or annoy the reader. The pressure always comes from outside the writer—from the ordained usages of the code, the established expectations of the audience. Shaughnessy's exercises, Hirsch's maxims, the notions of error (the others do it right) and relative readability (the others set the measure of efficiency), the entire weight of the history and universal psychology Hirsch uses to elevate the grapholect to a transcendent norm, and the equivalent weight of the sociology of ambition Shaughnessy sees working in her students: all tell student writers to fit themselves and their ideas to words, forms, and expectations that are not, at the beginning, theirs. The job of writing, the role of the writer, and the role of the teacher threaten to flatten into the spiritless business of putting ideas into words that carry as little as possible of the perplexities, qualifications, and particular voice of someone actually thinking something out.

The kind of prose predicted in that last sentence is in fact described by Shaughnessy and Hirsch. Shaughnessy tells a basic writing teacher what to expect after a semester of instruction: a composition in total agreement or disagreement with one idea, supported by one example (p. 283). The system of evaluation that Hirsch finds promising will ask listeners to judge writing read to them by "the standard of least effort"; compositions written to this standard will almost certainly be mechanical and predictable in their use of the concrete words, frequent closures, integrative devices, and other features legislated in Hirsch's maxims. This is the kind of writing variously described as "black rot" (Jacques Barzun), "Engfish" (Ken Macrorie), and the "official style" (Richard Lanham). It is, undoubtedly, better than the writing that dismayed Shaughnessy when she first read the compositions of basic writing students, better than the string of loosely related sentences that constitute the single piece of student writing quoted by Hirsch in his book (p. 158). But, to return to the metaphor in which I began, there ought to be more to be won by our conversions, more to the whole duty of composition to which Shaughnessy and Hirsch call us.

The Whole Duty of Composition

What I miss is of course the note of the personal in which Hirsch and Shaughnessy begin their own books, and what I wish were given more attention are some notions of writing often associated with the personal: writing as self-expression, as an instrument of discovery, as a liberal study whose worth is the knowledge and discipline it confers on the writer. Were I writing this review five or six years ago I would just summon up such powerful phrases, evoke the names of Peter Elbow, Ken Macrorie, and some others, and leave it at that. The teaching of composition then, at least according to the most interesting people writing about it, still had to do mostly with helping students get ideas and an authentic voice in which to tell them, with journals and "free-writes," prewriting and group editing, autobiographical episodes and arguments which retain the uncertainties and urgent confusions of writers finding their own relationships to matters they care about. But the circumstances which require our conversions are also pressing strongly against the idea of writing as a self-expressive or liberal enterprise. The practical worries that have taken students out of literature courses have also created some quite practical composition courses. In my two years as editor of *College English* (the occasion of my own conversion) I have read about one thousand essays on composition and its teaching. Most of them tell me that courses in technical and professional writing are popular. So are "adjunct" courses in which composition teachers are detailed to teach in other departments and help students learn to read and write in the matter of these disciplines. The research paper seems to be coming back as the standard culmination of first-year composition programs. I would guess that in most programs the writing of journals and autobiographical essays is assigned as a prelude to or respite from the earnest work of writing in the standard forms of argument, explanation, definition, analysis. Even the recent and extremely promising emphasis on audience (how do I arrange it for them?) can become a deflection from a regard for the turns and possibilities of one's own engagement in the writing (where am I, literally, in this discourse?). We are, in short, being asked to teach students to write for others, on topics, for purposes, and in forms and perhaps in a register of language strange to students, and sometimes even to us.

That is all quite proper. But it is no more complete than the idea of composition as a mode of discovery and self-expression. I am not discouraged by the persistence of these competing ideas of writing and its function. I know of no reason that teachers in a composition course or program cannot put equal emphasis on the self-expressive and communicative functions of writing, on process and product, invention and audience, prewriting and revision, practice in writing in an individual voice and in satisfying the requirements of common forms and the expectation of readers. I am sure that many teachers, eclectic and nonideological as always, are improvising such mediations, in the style that Shaughnessy displays as she helps teachers make do until the theory arrives. What is discouraging is to remember how those who write about the teaching of composition have swung from one pole to the other, at least in the twenty-five years I have been teaching in college. And even more discouraging is the prospect that Hirsch's book and Shaughnessy's may be used to encourage our present swing toward the objective, public, and utilitarian, as opposed to the personal and liberal uses of writing and its teaching.

This is not the right use of these books. Their right use is not to tell us what to do but rather to show us how to think about what we are doing. Shaughnessy's book asks us to think about how and why student writers make mistakes. Hirsch's book asks us to think about how and why the conventions from which student writers deviate have become normative. One can make a whole composition teacher out of Hirsch's bent for theory and Shaughnessy's intelligent practice, out of his attention to how readers make sense of writing and her attention to what really happens when unskilled writers try to make meaning in written words. But it is more important to learn from them both how little most composition teachers have known about how people write and read. Our ignorance has not inhibited us from framing pieties about our duty as we bounded from purpose to purpose, program to program, tactic to tactic

The Whole Duty of Composition

to try to keep our pious hopes together. Hirsch and Shaughnessy do know something. Their books are important as ethical and political statements, calls to a way of being and doing as members of a profession. They are also important as reports on their close study of the acts of literacy. I don't much like the narrow and joyless competence that might be the issue of the instruction they describe and the idea of writing on which it is founded. But in the presence of these books, it is fatuous just to say the magic words of a decade ago and imagine that the polarities have been reconciled or that the utilitarian gnome has been struck dead. I must begin to think as hard and as consecutively as they have if I am to correct or complement their premises and programs. These thoughtful books, in short, require us to take thought. That effect can prevent us from again settling too simply on one or another of the several reasons for writing, and the more than several motives and means of its teaching.

Understanding Middle English Romance
Derek Pearsall

Susan Wittig. *Stylistic and Narrative Structures in the Middle English Romances*. Austin: University of Texas Press, 1978. x, 223 pp.

Velma Bourgeois Richmond. *The Popularity of Middle English Romance*. Bowling Green, Ohio: Bowling Green University Popular Press, 1975. xii, 237 pp.

Carol Falvo Heffernan, ed. *Le Bone Florence of Rome*. Manchester: Manchester University Press; New York: Barnes and Noble, 1976. Old and Middle English Texts Series. x, 205 pp.

Anyone who has spent time reading and studying those literary works known as the Middle English romances will have become aware that there are a number of things that need explaining. From the point of view of literary history and the study of genre, it is difficult to understand how a form so apparently amorphous and so resistant to definition can create so powerful an impression of homogeneity. From the point of view of literary and critical understanding, it is even more difficult to understand why poems that are so bad according to almost every criterion of literary value should have held such a central position in the literary culture of their period. Attempts to define the nature of Middle English romance on the basis of content or of form have usually ended up with formulations so vague as to be useless, while explanations of the absence of the literary qualities one would normally look for, or, more desperately, claims that they are really there, have only served to make more unbridgeable the apparent gulf between medieval and modern literary expectation. Nevertheless, one has remained convinced that there is a lost "grammar" or "morphology" to this body of writing, a set of methods that it used to satisfy certain needs, of which we retain some glimpses in our own culture but to which we now need more clues.

Susan Wittig has written a bold, intelligent, and interesting book that attempts to tackle these problems. Her goal is clearly stated: "What we need now is a generic description based on linguistic and structural analysis which will not only clarify the formal and stylistic affiliations of this group of narratives, but will also attend to the problems of why this form came into being and what cultural needs it satisfied" (p. 6). She simplifies the problem at the outset by choosing to concentrate on twenty-seven noncyclic romances. As she explains, the cyclic romances "are built on a different structural framework" (p. ix), and one would readily accept this explanation both for its inherent likelihood — since story-patterns in the cyclic romances are complicated by their relation to a larger narrative framework and corrupted by their more or less tenuous connection with real or supposed historical fact — and for the immediate clarity it brings to the subject. The romances to be dealt with are those, essentially, that have in the past been loosely categorized as "exile-and-return" stories, and they are the ones where the impression of homogeneity has been strongest.

The method of analysis chosen for the study is one based on the models provided by structural linguistics, principally the tagmemic linguistics of Kenneth Pike and Lévi-Strauss's analysis of the deep structural patterns of myth. The reader may at this point have a sinking feeling as he sees the batteries of technical terms — syntagmeme, motifeme, allomotif, emic and etic units, etc. — being wheeled into place, and may have the familiar sense that the subject is about to disappear under the weight of formalist jargon. But Susan Wittig is well aware of the prejudices she has to overcome, and she both recognizes the elements in structuralist criticism that have nourished those prejudices (pp. 5-6) and also herself gives a very lucid account of the strength of the basic structuralist position:

Literary structuralists and tagmemicists alike view works of verbal art as componential systems of opposing elements which depend for their meaning and effect upon the interrelated functions of other elements in the same system. These elements are subject to certain fundamental structural laws in terms of which the whole system is defined. The system is not static but dynamic—that is, a shift in the formal relationships of components constitutes a change in the entire system. No part of it can be isolated and viewed without consideration of its relationship to other parts, because a single element has meaning only on its relationship to other elements, only as part of a whole. [p. 7]

The further refinements introduced into this system by "the tagmemic assumption" (that language is generated by means of the substitution of variables within a stable framework) are explained somewhat later: "Tagmemics assumes that language is built by a series of grammatical hierarchies of *emic* units, units which have particular and distinctive significance within a given system. . . . On any given structural level the distribution of *emic* units takes place in a pattern of *slots*. . . . The *slot* is one functional position in a syntagmatically ordered sequence of such positions, while the individual set members are paradigmatically related by virtue of the fact that any one of the members could be substituted for any other without altering the functional nature of the slot itself" (pp. 37-38). The claim made for this method of analysis is that it can be transferred from the analysis of sentence structure to the analysis of larger and larger structures, and ultimately to the analysis of those deep patterns of psychic need that are the generative power of recurrent narrative forms. The book is structured according to this claim, moving chapter by chapter from the analysis of formulaic phrases (syntagmemes), through stanzas, narrative incidents (motifemes), scenes and episodes to the larger narrative patterns in which a whole romance can be subsumed.

The language of analysis employed is a mixture of the traditional and the structuralist, which means that Wittig will probably annoy everyone, but one has to recognize the difficulties of applying a new methodology to an old subject. One of the characteristic consequences is the way every part of the discourse seems obliged to begin by clearing away a mass of terminological debris, and depositing more of its own, before it can move on, rather in the manner of a modern building program, and with some of the same aesthetic results: "When the motifeme has been established as the viable structural unit on this level, the term *allomotif* can be adopted for those variant manifestations of the motifeme which occur in any given poem; the common term *motif* (understood as an *etic* unit) is useful here as well" (p. 60). There is a constant barrage of categorization, and a proliferation of italicized forms which are there presumably to demonstrate the inadequacy of "normal" language. The effect, in terms of communication, is sometimes counterproductive; and what we have, it seems, is an obsession with tidying-up definitions and categories for their own sake, rather as if the analysis were being prepared for submission to a computer. "As we have seen, in many narratives the challenge may become a major element, perhaps even more important than the battle which follows it. When this occurs, we are probably justified in treating the *challenge* as a separate motifeme in its own right, manifested by a number of allomotifs, rather than as one of the components in the *single-combat* motifeme of the single-combat scene" (p. 95). One would be wrong to be too much put off by these habits, since precision is on the whole preferable to imprecision, but Wittig is occasionally guilty of straying into quite gratuitous terminological asides: "The treatment of time is usually very simple in these narratives. The tale is almost always executed in a straightforward chronological fashion, and not even the simple device of the flashback is available to the poets. To put it in structuralist terms, the *histoire* and the *discours* are almost identical as far as the manipulation of chronology is concerned" (p. 203, n. 1). If the characteristic recognized in the structuralist distinction is not present in the romances, then it seems hardly worth talking about it in structuralist or any other terms.

These are minor irritations. What is interesting about this

book, in its demonstration of a structuralist methodology at work, is its uneasy marriage of the two models it proposes, those of Pike and Lévi-Strauss. The one moves constantly toward formal abstraction, the other toward significant content; and the embarrassments created by this conflict are fascinating to observe as they are revealed in successive chapters.

Wittig begins her opening chapter, on "Problems of Stylistic Analysis," by stating her belief that the formulaic element so noticeable in the style of the romances is intrinsically functional and is not owing to mere incompetence or to the pragmatic requirements of oral delivery. The analysis that follows, however, does little to demonstrate the truth of this belief: it is not persistent or systematic enough in its own terms to compel acceptance of a structuralist explanation of the function of formulaic language; and that explanation, even if it were made fully convincing, is still only obscurely related to the further claims for the significant function of formulaic language made at the end of the chapter. Wittig goes into some detail in her analysis of the formulaic phrases of the romances, but the various charts and lists that she gives are based on a hand-count of subjectively identified formulas (p. 17), and they show very little, except that the romances contain a lot of formulas, some more than others—which we knew already. It is not the only time in this book when one feels that the quality of mind addressed to the problems is not matched by a comparable rigor in the collection of evidence. Wittig criticizes Waldron's "syntactical mould" approach (p. 36) as involving an artificial separation of form and content, but this is a facile criticism, for the separation is necessary at this stage of analysis. Another point about Waldron's approach is that he was clear about the problems he was trying to deal with through his method of analysis, and he tackled them systematically. Wittig, who is not interested in theories of oral-formulaic composition, offers the tagmemic approach (p. 38) as an alternative method of solving "the problems of formulaic analysis," but it is not clear what problems she has in mind or what solution to them might be offered by this kind of analysis:

The first of the two-line patterns, for example, demonstrates a fixed, homologous pattern in the relative clause (*that was* ADJECTIVE *and* ADJECTIVE) within the larger two-line pattern of NOUN + RELATIVE CLAUSE:

> Many a doghty knyght there was levyd
> That was wylde and wode (107-108)

> For to make the lady glade
> That was bothe gentyll and small (768-769)

In the following two-line slot patterns from *Toulous* a different kind of homologous, embedded pattern is evident (*that* VERB + ADVERBIAL/PREPOSITIONAL PHRASE):

> And asked gode for god allmyght
> That dyed on the tree (383-384)

> And sithen he thanked god of hys grace
> That syttyth in trynyte (119-120) [p. 40]

The problems she has in mind, one might guess, are like the problems of leveling texts to a standard form so that they can be read by a computer. But such problems are not worth solving for their own sake; they should be addressed only if some use is to be made of the solution. Wittig's problem here, I think, is a half-hearted adherence to the principles of structural analysis which leads her to make sporadic gestures in the direction of analysis which in the end demonstrate only familiar truths. She begins to reveal the nature of her real interest in "the slot-pattern notion of formula" in a following paragraph:

It is obvious at the outset that these syntagmemes are not surface structures but rather generate surface structures by certain elementary processes of transformation. Nor are they deep structures (in the sense of the deep structures of transformational grammar), because their constituents can be further reduced; they are, rather, intermediate between deep and surface structures. It is beyond the scope of this study to undertake an examination of the deep structures which through a series of transformations generate surface-structure syntagmemes. All of the results to this point, however, justify the hypothesis that these deep structures are relatively few in number compared to the more various deep structures of literary language, and that they produce a limited number of syntagmeme types which in turn produce a limited number of highly homologous surface structures. [p. 41]

In other words (though in truth there are no other words for statements like this), the language of romance is more than usually formulaic, which suggests that the range of things it has to express is more than usually limited. We always thought this, and it seems a fair enough assumption, but it has not been shown to be any more true by the analysis that precedes or by that roundabout way of putting it. I would not wish to be rude about that paragraph, but I think that, as an emic unit, it could be syntagmemically analyzed so as to demonstrate that its surface structure is generated by a choice of variables drawn from a matrix chiefly distinguished by the redundance of its components.

What follows, though, is more to the point, since Wittig ends the chapter by describing some of the relations she sees between a highly stereotyped poetic language and the needs of the society which takes pleasure in it. She speaks of it as a kind of ritual in which certain preconditioned responses are encoded. This kind of ritualistic language has, she says, "a very real beauty" (p. 43). It has "a kind of psychological comfort, an assurance that the social institutions in which the audience has invested itself are stable and secure, that the traditions have been preserved, that the future is safe" (p. 44). It "supports, reinforces, and perpetuates the social beliefs and customs held by the culture, perhaps long past their normal time of decline" (p. 45). It is "a kind of third-order linguistic phenomenon, a closed referential system twice removed from reality and confined to the social conventions and codes of etiquette of a highly ritualized society" (p. 46). This is an interesting and illuminating approach, and it demonstrates, I think, that Wittig's real interests are in the sociology of romance, in the significant statements that can be made about the relation of the romances to the society for which they catered. The attempt at a structuralist analysis of formulaic language seems to move only a small part of the way to making such statements more credible, and the confusion over the function of such analysis is compounded by the introduction of the word *beauty*. One could speak, I suppose, of the beauty of a revealed structure or structural principle, and on the whole structuralists should expect to be satisfied with this. Wittig is not, however, and she compromises the purity of the structuralist approach by claiming that it has led her to a position where she can make large evaluative statements like these.

The second chapter moves on to stanzas, motifemes, and scene-patterns as structural units, again analyzed tagmemically. The discussion of the formulaic nature of stanzas is very peremptory and is unfortunately based on a specialized group of stanzas in which the narrative content is already distributed into units of meaning which lend themselves to structural analysis (stages in growing older; the different recipients of shared gifts). It is just too easy to do it in this way, and again the analysis has been disablingly compromised by its failure to recognize the distorting effect of similarities and differences of content, or at least to disregard these in a systematically random manner. The model for the larger structural unit, the motifeme, is again specialized: inexplicably, it is the opening address to the audience that has been chosen. Everyone knows that these openings are stereotyped in romances, and they have been subjected to some quite careful analysis in the past. Wittig's point is that motifemes are tagmemically structured —that is, they fill a slot in the pattern of slots—but what can be the point of saying this about units that are bound to come first anyway? It seems a lazy way of establishing a new method of analysis. With the other motifemes that are selected for analysis—the *Now-we-leave-and-turn-to* unit, the *procession*, the *bidding-to-battle*, the *battlefield description*, and the *confession of love*—it is emphasized again that they are emic units (rather than etic units) since their function is essentially structural; they cannot be considered in the same way as motifs, the older term favored by folktale analysts. Wittig is very good on the limitations of the older type of motif analysis, less convincing when she comes to establish her own, for the motifemes that she selects provide little insight into the function-

Understanding Middle English Romance 113

ing of tagmemic structures. The fact that they have to be where they are and nowhere else is not due to any structural considerations but because of what they mean, their content. A bidding-to-battle cannot come anywhere but before a battle. Again, the desire not to be confined within the clinical vestments of the structuralist, and the reluctance to purge analysis of reference to content, means that the analysis is compromised. It is also made more lengthy, because the statement of some general category to which an incident belongs in several romances has to be followed by a listing of the differences in content between them (this is called the demonstration of the allomotifs of the motifeme). At the end one wonders sometimes whether it was worth establishing the category in the first place. The exceptions and qualifications prompted by the interest in the content of the romances, an interest which Wittig is understandably reluctant to abandon, clutter the analysis and prevent it reaching the simple conclusions it is capable of.

The scene-pattern is the next unit chosen for analysis. "The scene-pattern has essentially the same formulaic nature as the two smaller systems (the syntagmeme and the motifeme) which it subsumes. Typical scenes consist of ordered and/or unordered sequences of a limited number of motifemic slot patterns (usually only four or five) which are filled by variants of syntagmemic patterns, often in repeated sequences of twos and threes" (p. 81). The treatment is devoted to scenes of single combat, which seems a good choice for structural analysis. Even here, though, there are the embarrassments which a recognition of content, in this case reference to reality, is bound to incur and which Wittig is too honest (or too halfhearted) a structuralist to ignore. In reference to certain repetitions within the descriptions of single combats, she says: "These redundant patterns are not contingent upon any other element in the narrative, it seems, but are stylized representations of real medieval tournaments, which, like any other games, were played by a recognized set of rules. In this case, however, it is very difficult to say where realism ends and ritual representation begins" (p. 91). When she attempts to make a distinction between realism of content and tagmemic structure, the effect, by this stage, is comic: "The effect of such a rapid-paced narrative account is one of speed and confusion, with horses and men tumbling about the field in a flurry of limbs and broken armor, but hidden within the confusion is a careful patterning which lends structure to the whole" (p. 93). To be sure, we hardly need to be told about this "careful patterning"; we really did not expect a confused flurry of syntagmemes and broken allophones to accompany the combat, any more than one would expect to feel pain when saying "I was hit." The only thing that we are being reminded of here is that old favorite, "the miracle of language," and the unique and extraordinary nature of the relation between verbal sound or sign and reference in reality. It all makes one a little dubious about the validity of the original transfer of methodology from linguistic to narrative structures.

Chapter 3 deals with the type-scene, a term chosen to avoid the nonemic associations of the old-fashioned word "theme." The *death of the hero's father* is the model of the type-scene, which may be substituted by *irregular birth*; either may be followed by the *expulsion of the hero*. Wittig makes a very cogent defense of emic as against etic units here, and of structuralist analysis as against the type of analysis that allows an element of causality in the ordering of events. There is, to be frank, some discrepancy throughout the book between the significance of the analysis actually provided and the quality of the abstract discussion occasionally entered into concerning the necessity for such analysis. The account of the reasons for the apparently meaningless repetition of events in type-scenes, on pages 125–26, for instance, could hardly be bettered. But it may be contrasted with a comment made in the course of the analysis of the *death of the hero's father*: "The head of the victim sent as proof of the slaying is a motifeme manifested in various ways depending upon its narrative context: in *Octavian*, the head of the giant, the princess's would-be paramour, is sent to her as proof that he is dead; Torrent, Eglamour, and Bevis return the heads of their victims as witness to accomplished tasks. *Bevis* is the only narrative, however, in which a husband's head is sent to his widow" (p. 200, n. 19). Here we seem to be coming, by a very circuitous route, to the description and listing of "motifs" of the old-fashioned kind — and, furthermore, insufficiently frequent to be significantly compared, insufficiently formulaic to be significantly structural, and in the end little different from the naive recital of the events of the story which occupies much elementary writing on literature. Wittig's strictures on Propp, and his use of *lack* and *lack liquidated* as slot-names, seem to be all the more out of place: "In my view, the Proppian terminology is much too broad and admits far too many possible fillers into its function-slots. Almost all stories, in one way or another, can be seen to begin with a *lack*. It would seem important to be able to describe much more specifically and completely what kind of scenes manifest the pattern in any group of narratives" (p. 199, n. 13). It would seem, on the contrary, that structuralist analysis must travel, if it is not to be constantly compromised and embarrassed by matters beyond its competence, in the direction of a higher and purer abstraction.

Chapter 4, on the type-episode, begins with some characteristic agonies of definition: "How do we know whether to call the narrative unit under examination a *scene* or an *episode*? Where do these units begin and end? What are the criteria for segmentation?" (p. 136). Wittig deals here with larger episodes, in sequences such as *threatened marriage-rescue-marriage*, educing in the end two major patterns, *love-marriage* and *separation-adoption* (i.e., loss and regaining of identity and patrimony), which seem persistent throughout the romances. The persistence of such patterns suggests that they "may in some way represent a basic situation which generates the narrative energy that brings the tale into being" (p. 160). This idea is developed later, in Wittig's final chapter, and it is an idea worth developing. In fact, the book develops real strength in these later chapters, as the author moves away from more narrow structuralist positions and adopts a broader approach to the significant ordering of contents in the romances. Tagmemics is not irrelevant here, since it helps to demonstrate the significant nature of the ordering, but it is tagmemics in the service of a larger and on the whole more traditional approach to literature. The analysis of episode sequences referred to above, for instance, with its clear acknowledgment of the importance of social concepts and of shared assumptions about those concepts, would hardly be tolerable to a structuralist. A further embarrassment follows from this, however, for Wittig's acceptance of history, and of the existence of these romances in a social and historical context as a significant aspect of their being, means that she can no longer claim the privilege of the structuralist to ignore variant texts, manuscripts, sources, analogues, date, author, audience, historical allusions, and all the other paraphernalia of the literary scholar, and to work with the naked text. In admitting the sociological significance of the romances and in asserting the bearing upon that sociological significance of her own analysis of them, Wittig lays herself open to the charge that she has neglected important kinds of evidence which would certainly affect her thesis. The relation of variant versions of romances (e.g., of *Launfal* or *The Squire of Low Degree*), or of romances to their originals, is rarely so much as mentioned, even though changes in the pattern of social expectation are clearly involved. Audiences have to be talked about, and poets too, and all sorts of responsibilities are incurred which are not laid upon the structuralist. It may be that the neglect of traditional literary history and scholarship is a mere defect of omission, which does not invalidate the general argument; but when the propriety of talking about a poet's purposes or an audience's expectations is even admitted, as it is admitted here, then the author has got to make sure that she does not make any mistakes. Speaking of the two romances of *Guy of Warwick* and *Reinbroun* (as they appear in the Auchinleck manuscript—which Wittig nowhere mentions), Wittig says: "In the composite tale of *Guy* and *Reinbroun* (treated here as a single tale made up of two separable parts), the Reinbroun story is composed exclusively of the *separation-restoration* sequence, while the Guy-Felice portion of the story is composed entirely of the *love-marriage* se-

Understanding Middle English Romance 117

quence. It is likely that the poet felt some structural requirement for bringing the two stories together" (pp. 176-77). The trouble with this supposition about the poet's feelings is that we know that in this case the poet's contribution was the disentangling of the two stories from the original Anglo-Norman romance, and not the bringing of them together. The happy isolationism of the structuralist, whose only "mistakes" can be mistakes of reasoning, evidently has much to commend it.

Wittig ends by developing certain ideas that have provided much of the sense of purpose through the book. The romances, she observes, are constructed according to a systematic narrative "grammar," in which the choices allowed to the individual writer are limited. This grammar in its turn encodes certain social and political beliefs held by the community and serves to reinforce and perpetuate them. The basic structure of the Middle English romance is in a twofold sequence, the *separation-restoration* sequence and the *love-marriage* sequence, combined in such a way that "one of the sequences provides the necessary means for resolving difficulties and restoring imbalances found in the other" (p. 182). Mythic and other early origins can be identified in the sequences, but the stories have been converted to deal with problems of human relationships in the more contemporary social and political world. The extraordinarily systematic nature of the pattern educed, one in which marriage restores the imbalance created by the hero's loss of filial rights, leads Wittig to some further speculations:

The singular pervasiveness of this male-Cinderella pattern suggests, perhaps, an important fact about the romance: that it serves as a means by which the culture can resolve certain conflicts it feels about the restrictiveness of its class system. In one sense, the romance serves as an apparent vehicle for upward mobility; it offers the hope to the lower class that even a princess can be won by a worthy man, whatever his economic and social status. But at the same time, it endorses the upper-class belief that worth and birth are synonymous, that only a nobleman can be a noble man, fit by nature to gain the princess and the kingdom and to rule over both. Perhaps this ability to bridge two distinctly different classes within the culture, implicit in the two linking structures of the narrative, is one of the most important aspects of the Middle English romance and accounts in large measure for its importance as a community ritual and for the culture's determination to preserve it. This double structure can be viewed as a problem-solving structure, enabling the culture (the producers and audiences of the tales) to mediate certain important contradictions within its social, economic, and mythic structures and to provide a set of categories in terms of which a coherent reality could be constituted. [p. 189]

These final remarks, though they remain speculative, are extremely suggestive and full of insight. They ring true, and seem to open a way to a deeper understanding of the Middle English romances and two of the basic questions one wants to ask about them: why are they so alike (and so alike in being so bad) and why were they so popular? Wittig clearly has some important things to say about the Middle English romances, and if paying observance to certain current fashions concerning the objective analysis of narrative structures was the only way in which she could get round to saying them, then maybe that has something to do with certain historical necessities in the condition of criticism. As I have perhaps made clear, I am not convinced that the elaborate program of structuralist analysis undertaken in this book was necessary to prove that the narrative procedures of the Middle English romances are very stereotyped; indeed, it seemed often that the essential function and purpose of structuralist analysis was obscured by the manner in which it was being used. But the book is never less than highly intelligent, and in demonstrating the limitations of its own methodology it nevertheless does not fail of its purpose.

Passing from Susan Wittig's book to that of Velma Bourgeois Richmond is like going from a strenuous and rather self-conscious postgraduate seminar into a Sunday school. Richmond faces one of the problems that confronted Wittig in attempting to understand the Middle English romances—the need to explain "their undenied early and sustained popularity but subsequent lack of reputation" (p. 1)—and she makes some similar comparisons with modern best-sellers and the

Understanding Middle English Romance

challenge they present to literary criticism. The difference, though, is that Richmond accepts quite wholeheartedly for herself and for us a simple version of the explanation that Wittig proposed for the medieval audience, namely, that the romances reinforce conventional values. Richmond says that romance has more than the surface appeal and fascination of surprise, suspense, and the extraordinary: "It offers exposition of a system of value" (p. 18). This view is supported by parallels drawn with modern thrillers and science fiction and by a children's history of the Middle Ages, which generally comes to the conclusion that life was so grim that people looked for moral uplift as well as escapism in their popular entertainment. The popularity of Middle English romance results from its firm sense of moral purpose.

The book demonstrates the truth of this assertion by examining a number of different kinds of romance. "Fortune's Heroes" (Chapter 2) deals with Troy, Alexander, and Arthur, where the romances aim to place wordly ambition in the context of Christian values. In the *Destruction of Troy*, for instance, "we have an explicit exposition of traditional religious values which gives the whole of the Greek expedition a quality of falsity" (p. 33). The stories associated with Troy "repeatedly illustrate the inadequacy of the non-Christian view" (p. 34). *Kyng Alisaunder* likewise is "notable for its moral tone," and is full of "evidence of the poet's basic Christian viewpoint" (p. 35)."God is frequently mentioned," we are told (p. 47), in the *Morte Arthure*. In the next chapter, "Fiendish Origins Transformed," which is about *Emare, Gowther, Robert the Devil*, and the Melusine romances, we are relieved to find that "the undeniable fascination of evil . . . is allowable because of a belief in a God-controlled universe where evil will not finally prevail" (p. 58). The popular audience can therefore enjoy its *frissons* whilst knowing that all will be well in the end. In *Emare* it is this assurance that provides "the inspiration and optimism that are the mainstays of popular fiction" (p. 65). "Friendship and Brotherhood" is the title of Chapter 4, and we are assured that these are good things, though not as good as "the more comprehensive charity of Christianity" (p. 89).

Richmond thinks well of the Christian religion and is continually stressing its good points. To those who complain that Amiloun, in *Amis and Amiloun*, gets a good deal out of behaving very badly and that the moral scheme of the romance is rather obscure, she answers that God offers his grace where it is unearned and unmerited. "Thus it is the most hopeful of religions" (p. 94). She says nothing of God's not offering his grace where it *is* earned and merited, a situation which has caused thinking men a headache now and again. But the great thing about the romances, repeats Richmond, is that "there is never any doubt that good will triumph, and it is that kind of reassurance which attracts many readers" (p. 108).

In the chapter on "The Delights of Love," English romances are much approved for their lack of enthusiasm for adultery and for their high moral tone. Of the hero and heroine of *Paris and Vienne* it is said: "Their steadfast dedication and loyalty, always preserving honesty in expectation of worthy marriage, offer the moral example and inspiration that are crucial for success in popular fiction" (p. 121). The stanzaic *Le Morte Arthur* is praised for its "diversified exposition of popular Christian values" (p. 129), and the anxiety of critics who find its world of values inconsistent is primly (but forgivingly) reproved as reflecting "readings that either expect sinners to be differently viewed or delight in human loyalties and tragic powerlessness rather than the resolution of Christian forgiveness" (p. 133). At the end, *Guy of Warwick*, as the longest and most enduringly popular of all the Middle English romances, is given a whole chapter to itself. It has "a high sense of moral purpose," we are told, and the critical method is to tell the story at length, with pauses from time to time to applaud Guy's exemplary behavior.

The guileless naiveté of the whole book is such as to disarm criticism almost completely, and no one can say that it is not original, when the things that it finds inspiring are the very things that everyone else has found boring. Indeed, criticism may feel embarrassed as well as disarmed, for there is no doubt that all that Richmond says is on one level perfectly true. She has captured simple meanings that these stories must have had for many of their earlier audiences or readers, and which they may still have, for all one knows, for modern readers in search of moral uplift. If the emphasis upon what ingredients make for popular success in fiction were presented as a matter of objective analysis, one could not in justice complain except at the insistent statement of the obvious. It is the hearty approval given to these simpleminded recommendations to good behavior that sometimes leaves one bemused. At the end of the book, Richmond offers a firm reproof to A. B. Taylor, who thought that the romances "appealed to the child-like mind of our ancestors." Such "modern sophistication," she says, "is both inadequate and inappropriate." The reason that modern commentators find the romances naive and trifling is that they have "less confidence and a lack of firm belief" (p. 196). What is being recommended, it appears, is not the appreciation or understanding of the beliefs that are said to sustain popular romance, but the adoption of them. Richmond's enthusiasm for the Middle Ages, clearly, knows no bounds.

The book is written with a childlike facility, occasionally straying into ineptitude ("Lancelot conceals his identity, thus showing a desire to function as himself," [p. 135]). Richmond carries around with her a capacious bag of comparisons, which she is ready to unload at the lightest provocation. Orson's vision of Judgment, for instance, inspires recall of the tympana at Conques and Bourges, a painting by Roger van der Weyden, the Hereford Mappa Mundi, and the last scene of the Corpus Christi plays (pp. 116-17). The notes are full of "authorities," rather indiscriminately hauled together, but a useful hoard for the beginner to rifle. In fact, it is the beginner, if anyone, who will profit from this book. He will recognize its naiveté, but he may appreciate its enthusiasm and its positive response to the romances.

Neither Wittig nor Richmond, who are perhaps preoccupied with the business of writing books about romances, pays much attention to the texts of the poems with which they work. Nevertheless, those texts are the basis of all that is said and thought about the romances, and they need to be as good as scholarship can make them, and to be kept up to date. The new edition of *Le Bone Florence of Rome*, in the admirable Manchester University Press series of Old and Middle English Texts, is therefore very welcome. The poem has suffered some neglect, having been available only in Ritson and in a German edition of 1893, and it is good to have it presented now with proper modern apparatus and in such an attractive and compact format. Carol Falvo Heffernan has done her editorial work assiduously, and the criticisms that one has to make should be seen in the context of a generally competent and satisfactory piece of work.

The introduction gives a good account of the origins of the story, and the development of the story-type to which it belongs, the *Crescentia-Constance* story. Heffernan uses the emphasis on justice as a means of linking different versions of the story, which may make a structuralist look askance, but of course she is tracing the physical derivation of the story and not its structural characteristics. The account of "Literary Aspects" (a rather unfortunate subtitle) is mostly about the poet's reinforcement of the exemplary function of the story. The discussion of style, especially alliteration, is not very well-informed, and the suggestion that the large amount of alliteration in *Florence* argues for an alliterative English original is quite unnecessary, given the similarly alliterative character of much Middle English metrical romance. Heffernan has some further comments on the relations of *Florence* with *The King of Tars* and the *Man of Law's Tale,* and she ends the introduction with obligatory remarks about what the tale reveals of medieval attitudes towards women: these attitudes, we are unsurprised to hear, were ambivalent, "perhaps stemming from a boy's initial erotic attachment to his mother and his subsequent fear of female dominance" (p. 38). Things would on the whole have been better without this last section. The bibliography is full and useful but is marred by that bad dissertation habit of picking up for inclusion all sorts of oddities that have been mentioned in passing here and there. The text itself is attractively presented, with rather too much punctuation. Emendation is kept to the minimum, and Heffernan does not emend purely for the sake of rhyme. There are arguments on both sides: on the one hand, it is clear that some manuscript readings are not what the author intended; on the other hand, nothing is lost by preserving the manuscript reading, since the emendation is usually obvious, and something may be gained where there is doubt about an author's practice and skill in rhyming—and there nearly always is doubt. Heffernan's refusal to emend, therefore, in line 1140, and in other lines like it, is readily defended. In one instance, the *fame/sawe* reading in 252, she explains how difficult it is to distinguish *fame* from *sawe* in the scribe's hand, and here it does seem a little perverse to have chosen the reading that does not rhyme and makes very poor sense. Otherwise, there is very little to complain about: the emendations in lines 303 (*to* to *do*) and 1947 (*be* to *ben*) are quite unnecessary smoothings of syntax; in line 665, *aveaunt* should be emended to *avenaunt*, though the reading *aveaunt*, "avaunt," is possible in line 128, which may have prompted the later error; in line 1569, *any many* is not "an unusual expression" but a mistake, and should be emended to *any man*.

Heffernan offers very full annotation and an ambitious glossary, but she does not have quite the depth of knowledge or experience of Middle English to inspire the reader with complete confidence. There is also too much fussing in the notes about minor linguistic points and about errors in Ritson's transcriptions (which can surely be buried with him now), and in the glossary there is too much unnecessary subdivision of significations (e.g., entries for *he, hyt, of*). The editor has done a great deal of work with *OED* and *MED*, and mostly done it well, but she has not always had the best of luck. Thus, *rechyd* (line 132) is not an (inexplicably) early example of the nineteenth-century nautical sense (*OED, reach*, 15c), but the perfectly normal ME sense of *OED*, 15a. Likewise, *rekenyth* (line 188) is not an (inexplicably) early example of the nineteenth-century intransitive use, "number, amount to" (*OED, reckon*, 15), but, in the context ("There were kyngys in that halle,/Erlys and dewkys who rekenyth all,/Full a hundurd that tyde"), an element in the conventional parenthetic clause, "Whoever counts (them) all." The note to line 212 seems to have trouble with *hope*, though it is perfectly clearly and sensibly explained in the glossary as "trust, confidence." This is not the only instance of a discrepancy between notes and glossary. Thus, in lines 655-57, ("At þe furste wynnyng of þer schone,/So tyte of lyvys were they done,/That all deryd not a pere"), the last two lines are translated in the notes, "they killed so many straightway that they lost nothing." The last clause, derived through "risked not a thing" (*deryd* taken as "dared"), is intolerably strained. The correct translation is suggested by the meaning given for this occurrence of *deryd* in the glossary, "afflicted, hurt": "So quickly were they done out of their lives that the lot of them caused no one a scratch." This is the only possible sense, too, in the narrative context.

Heffernan seems to have recurrent trouble with conventional phrases, perhaps through unfamiliarity. There is a rather naive explanation of the presence of the phrase *wythowte lesynge* in line 1567; it is the right explanation, but it was hardly necessary. In line 1617, "The sothe ys not to layne," *layne* is translated "forgive," as if a form of *loan*, giving the sense "The truth is unpardonable"; but the formula, with *layne*, "hide," is perfectly conventional. The phrase *godys forbode* in line 955 is quite mistaken in the glossary, where *forbode* is glossed as 3 pt. pl. rather than as a noun. In line 404, to conclude these cavillations, *ware* is "wear," in the sense "wear out, use up," rather than "were," while *tyde* in line 1050 cannot possibly be "tide."

The volume could evidently have been looked over, with advantage, by someone with more experience of Middle English, but I would not wish to give the impression that it is riddled with errors. On the whole, as I have said, it is fairly sound and should be received with gratitude. It should be said, in fairness, though it is not often recognized, that it is more difficult to edit a text properly than to write a respectable critical book. The editor is constantly in a position where his ignorance may be exposed, and he cannot shuffle off his responsibilities; the critic can choose the ground where he knows (or thinks) his footing is firm, and allow the reader to assume that that is not the extent of his knowledge. And if finally it were thought appropriate to apply some general criterion of relative usefulness to the three books we have been looking at, it could be said, I think, that the reader who wants to gain some "kynde knowyng" of Middle English romance would do best to read his way carefully through *Le Bone Florence*, with Heffernan stumbling by his side. There is the thing in itself, as it really is, in all its tawdry glory.

Stillinger's Keats

Ronald Sharp

Jack Stillinger, ed. *The Poems of John Keats.* Cambridge: The Belknap Press of Harvard University Press, 1978. xv, 769 pp.

In the introduction to his new edition of Keats's poems, Jack Stillinger wonders how Keats would have reacted to the publication of this book. Would he have approved of its detailed textual apparatus and elaborate editorial paraphernalia? What about its chronological arrangement and its inclusion of every poem Keats ever wrote, whether he labored at it for months or only for minutes? When he was twenty-two years old, Keats predicted that he would "be among the English Poets after [his] death,"[1] and Stillinger concludes that "the present edition is one more manifestation of his fulfillment of that intention" (p. 4). By itself, of course, the publication of a rigorous scholarly edition of a poet's works is scarcely proof of his greatness; if it were, the hundreds of such editions that line the shelves of any university library would crowd the attribution of greatness into a corner of triviality. But, as Stillinger says, his edition is only "one more" indication of Keats's success. The other indications require no explanation: Keats's reputation could scarcely be higher.

That Stillinger should feel the need for an apologia that would satisfy Keats strikes me as admirable and reassuring. It reveals a perspective on his own enterprise and a self-consciousness about his own procedures that extends even to his sense of audience. Not only does he offer useful examples of thorny textual problems, but he also mercifully accepts the fact that many of his readers will not know what a "copy-text" is, let alone an "accidental." These and a few other such terms Stillinger clearly yet tactfully defines—a practice that many other editors would think superfluous if not vulgar. But Stillinger apparently considers his definitions useful. "The apparatus," he says, "is intended for practical use by the general reader and beginning student of Keats as well as by the textual scholar" (p. vii). Though I find it hard to imagine that very many general readers would even know about this book, let alone read it, I am certain it will be read and studied by many English professors whose familiarity with textual terminology scarcely extends beyond that of the general reader. One consequence of the fundamental revision of graduate curricula in literary studies over the last two decades has been that many students go on to successful scholarly careers with only the sparest training in textual studies and bibliography. Right or wrong, that seems to be our situation, and Stillinger's concern for clarity even in this small detail can only be salutary.

The whole book, in fact, demonstrates an extraordinary clarity about what is known along with a "negative capability" about what is not known. Stillinger refuses to gloss over uncertainty, and he painstakingly attempts to isolate those problems that remain unsolved. Establishing standard texts for Keats is no easy task, since there are numerous variant readings to consider and since Keats's spelling, punctuation, and capitalization are notoriously erratic. Confronted with an average of three or four manuscripts — both holographs and transcripts — for each poem, and considerable uncertainty about which of these represent versions that Keats approved, the editor faces a dizzying number of possible permutations. In his earlier book Stillinger set out to "determine the relationships among the extant MSS . . . the sources of the earliest published versions . . . and the relative authoritativeness of the various texts that might have claims to be the standard."[2] He also listed and described the surviving manuscripts and early printed versions and provided a history of transmission of each poem. "The principal novelty of the present edition," he says, "is that it is the first in the history of Keats scholarship to be based on a systematic investigation of the transmission of the texts" (p. v).

The previous standard edition was H. W. Garrod's *Poetical Works,* published in 1939 in the Oxford English Texts series and revised in a second edition in 1958. But some sixty manuscripts have come to light since Garrod's work, along with some first and early printings that Garrod "either overlooked or chose to ignore" (p. v). Stillinger claims that his new edition differs "in canon, in arrangement, in substantive readings in eighty-five of the 150 texts, and in several thousand particular details of information in the apparatus" (p. v). Garrod's errors cover a wide range, as a few examples from *Endymion* will illustrate. At I.511 Garrod has "Thy deathful bow against some dear-head bent," whereas Stillinger changes "head" to "herd." That may not be as momentous—or pregnant—an error as the infamous "Soldier" for what should have been "Solider" in Yeats's "Among School Children," but it is an error of some substance. At the opposite pole of significance, Garrod prints "Ah! thou has been unhappy at the change" (I.520) for what in Stillinger's view should have been "hast" rather than "has." No reputations should tumble on that change. And then there are lines like III.652, which in Garrod is "Dark clouds, and mutterings of winds morose" and in Stillinger is "muttering" instead of "mutterings." One less *s* might take a bit of wind from the sails of a critic intent on demonstrating a particular kind of sound effect in that line, but there are still three sibilants left, and in any case such a change is not very likely to alter our sense of the line, let alone the poem.

But Stillinger's major point of contention with both Garrod and Miriam Allott, editor of the only other important recent edition,[3] is that they too often combine substantive readings from different sources so that the final text is one that never existed in exactly that form. Instead of navigating by textual eclecticism, Stillinger prefers "to reproduce a single state of text for each poem" (p. 15).[4] Still, the special problems of any given poem usually present enough complications to convince Stillinger of the need for a full accounting. Consequently, he records in his apparatus "all known substantive variants that have any claim to be considered authoritative" (p. v). This information appears at the foot of each page and always begins with a list of all the manuscripts and printed versions that have been collated. At the back of the book Stillinger provides elaborate textual notes "that give dates of composition, describe the relationships among the extant MSS and early printings, explain the choices of copy-text, and discuss matters of special interest or difficulty" (p. v).

In addition to the text, the apparatus, and the textual notes, there is a short, good-humored preface; an introduction that explains and justifies editorial procedures; an index of first lines and (blissfully unlike Garrod, who omits them) titles; and six appendixes covering such topics as "Editorial Emendations of the Copy-Texts," "The Original Preface to *Endymion*," and "Questionable Attributions."[5] Like the rest of this handsome book, these sections are clearly arranged in type that is easy to read and in units that are easy to work with.

One of the most useful features of the apparatus is the careful collation of manuscript variants and alterations, which do indeed, as Stillinger suggests, "frequently illuminate Keats's meaning in a line or passage or even an entire work. . . . 'Was it a vision real' in the draft of *Ode to a Nightingale* 79," says Stillinger, "helps clarify the difference between 'vision' and 'waking dream' in the revised text" (p. 3). But here we must be cautious, for in most cases we do not know why the poet made the change, and the range of possible reasons is so great as to beg the original question. In this particular instance, for example, Keats might have felt that the word *real* made for too sharp a contrast between the two sets of terms; or was not sharp enough; or that, having posed the contrast in this way, he now meant quite the opposite of *real*, or that, though he did mean *real*, it would be too heavy-handed to state the contrast in that way; or that it would be metrically inappropriate for any number of reasons. By itself a manuscript variation or alteration can never be conclusive evidence unless we know why the change was made, and even then we can be certain about its meaning only if we accept a version of intentionalism that most intentionalists would themselves consider crude. A few more examples should help bring these issues into focus.

In "Character of C. B." it is uncertain whether a phrase in line 22 should read "cherry brandy" or "cheery brandy." Stillinger, recognizing that the manuscript authority is ambig uous, opts for the former. Both versions make perfect sense — the former a bit more obvious sense, the latter a bit more subtle. But how can we know whether Keats is being subtle here? On what grounds, in situations like this, can an editor make a choice? The only ground, it seems to me, is a messy but inevitable one: the editor's larger sense of Keats's work — the substantive concerns, the patterns of emphasis and structure, the habits of mind and technique. When the purely textual evidence is inconclusive, the editor must rely on precisely that area of knowledge which is the familiar territory of criticism and interpretation and which is constantly being discussed, debated, and redefined by critics. When Stillinger decides to use the earlier holograph version of "Not Aladdin magian," for example, he does so because the later version seems "more casually written, and the substantive changes in [it], including the omission of several lines . . . may be owing more to carelessness than to conscious artistry" (p. 14). Every editor must occasionally make such judgments: what I want to emphasize is that his decisions about what is casual, careless, or conscious — indeed, about what is substantive — are based on a sense of the poet that is exactly the kind of sense that critics establish, agree to, fight over, and revise.

Let me develop this point with an example that comes out of my own work. In my recent study of Keats. I argue that religious concerns are absolutely central to Keats and that understanding his secular religious humanism alters one's interpretation of the whole body of his work.[6] The usual view is quite the contrary. Walter Jackson Bate, perhaps the most prominent of all Keats scholars, claims that "the poetry is . . . largely untouched by any direct interest in religion," and Robert Ryan, in his book about Keats and religion, says that with one or two exceptions the major poems do "not concern [themselves] in any obvious or direct way with modern religious themes."[7] An editor working with the usual view would presumably have a different sense of what was careless or casual, conscious or substantive, than an editor who was persuaded by my argument. Stillinger, for example, follows Garrod and Allott in considering "On Death" a questionable attribution on the grounds that "we have no evidence to indicate that Keats was the author" (p. 753). John Barnard, on the other hand, in his recent edition of the poems, does include the poem and suggests that "the verses may represent Keats's attempt to reconcile himself to the death of his grandmother. . . . The weakness of the lines is not conclusive evidence against Keats's authorship: he was still ill-formed as a poet at this stage."[8] In my view, however, both editors miss the point, for the substance of the poem makes it clear beyond a doubt that Keats did not write it. If there were a question as to whether Keats wrote a poem condoning mass murder, no editor would cite textual, biographical, or stylistic evidence against Keats's authorship; he could assume that Keats would never have written such a poem. The example seems melodramatic only because there is such wide agreement about certain of Keats's fundamental values. But the importance of radically new interpretations of a poet's work is that, if they are accepted, they redefine exactly those areas of agreement — or at the least they bring into the foreground what before was either obscure or invisible. It is these areas that constitute an editor's working "knowledge" of his poet.

Returning to the matter of Keats's manuscript alterations, we discover the same problems and principles. Lines 223-24 of "The Eve of St. Agnes" originally described Madeline this way: "She seem'd a splendid angel, newly drest, / In wings, for heaven: — Porphyro grew faint." But Keats changed the "In" at the beginning of line 224 to "Save." In "Ode to Psyche," Keats changed line 43 from "I see, and sing, by my *clear* eyes inspired" to "I see, and sing, by my *own* eyes inspired" (emphases mine). Both changes seem significant to me. The first implies that Madeline cannot ascend and thus — consistent, in my view, with the rest of the poem — suggests that whatever heaven she inhabits must be earthly rather than transcendent. The second reverses the tradition of supernatural inspiration by suggesting that the source of Keats's inspiration is himself rather than something beyond, a view consistent with the poem's larger attempt to create a deity rather than worship one that already exists.

But one can imagine a dozen other reasons why Keats might have made these changes, and many of them would have nothing whatever to do with religious matters. The data themselves are mute; they speak only when we regard them in configurations of significance, and that is where the interpreter makes his entrance. Neither the most heroic efforts at self-effacement nor the most disciplined attempts at "objectivity" can eliminate the editor's occasional need to be an interpreter and thus to make critical judgments and decisions that significantly influence the final text. His points of emphasis, his attitude towards his materials, his sense of the urgency or triviality of this or that detail, his knowledge of the myriad contexts in which a given poem is embedded—ranging from the political, economic, and topical, to the metrical, allusive, or purely textual—all affect those judgments, even as they influence our sense of the editor's authority. We may regard these as obstacles to be overcome rather than direct determinants, but even so there will often be cases in which one can overcome the obstacle in many ways, each of which creates new and different obstacles, and each of which involves matters of interpretation that are no less controversial than those that occupy critics after the "actual" text is established. Stillinger claims that his editorial ideal is to establish "final authorial intentions" (p. 1). No one even vaguely familiar with recent developments in critical theory can fail to see how problematic—or at least controversial—such an ideal is in critical interpretation. My point is that the editor confronts similar problems, for he too is engaged in interpretation. Even at this level, the question, What is the text?, is not an easy one to answer.

Stillinger, I imagine, is not unaware of these considerations, but he does not belabor them. Indeed, one wonders whether anyone who did dwell on the hermeneutical dimensions of textual scholarship could muster the iron will and massive patience that textual editing requires. The volume of data that Stillinger confronts as raw material is absolutely staggering. The lists that he must have made, the charts, diagrams, and mountains of notes—just imagining all of this is enough to induce nausea in the average critic. The sheer weight of detail is bewildering enough; but what about the discipline that must have been required to make his way through the layers uncovered by textual excavation and the labyrinths of textual transmission? We come with awe to this archaeological site, and as tourists we have the luxury of remarking its complex beauty and importance, and even of speculating about its ontological status. But we should not forget the dizzying labors that brought it to its present state.

The dust jacket of Stillinger's edition quotes the London *Times* review of his companion book, *The Texts of Keats's Poems*: "Thanks to Mr. Stillinger a revolution in Keats studies is at hand." "Here," says the jacket copy, referring to the new edition, "is the crucial step in that revolution." It would be an act of crass ingratitude for critics to respond to this claim merely with a raising of the eyebrow. Stillinger's edition of Keats, Donald Reiman's Norton selection of Shelley, Leslie Marchand's volumes of Byron's letters and journals, Kathleen Coburn's Coleridge project, the Cornell Wordsworth, David Erdman's Blake—these and other recent editions constitute an advance in Romantic studies that one might well call a revolution. The importance of Stillinger's edition should not be underestimated. It is unquestionably, now, the definitive edition of Keats's poems. Students of Keats will, henceforth, take its texts, canon, and chronology as standard, and textual scholars will certainly find the majority of what remains of their agenda in this book and *The Texts of Keats's Poems*. Editors of other writers will find Stillinger's edition a model of clarity and rigor, and critics of Keats will have an invaluable source book for further studies of Keats's methods of composition and revision.

But this book does not mark a revolution in Keats studies any more than it marks a revolution in Keats's poetry. A great edition—and this certainly is one—stands between a writer and his readers. It may enable a revolution to occur, and in rare cases it may even inspire one; but a revolution in our understanding of a writer can come from an edition only if it provides us with material that is so new, or so different from what we had earlier taken to be the text, that it fundamentally alters our sense of the writer's work. Stillinger's edition provides much that is new and much that is different, but not enough to alter our understanding of Keats. That is not Stillinger's fault, and nothing can be gained from asking of this book more than it could possibly offer. With Keats a revolution will come only when his interpreters take seriously the words of John Middleton Murry: "An attitude of condescension or patronage towards [Keats] is utterly impossible," said Murry over half a century ago. "The thing that Keats actually was is infinitely more perfect than any perfection we can invent for him. The proper attitude of criticism towards Keats is one of complete humility."[9]

Nor should critics adopt an attitude of condescension to Stillinger's edition. Presented with such a magnificent gift, we should not trifle over its inherent limitations. The truest gifts circulate, and in their movement they generate and accumulate value. Keats had the greatest gift, and he gave it to us. Stillinger has kept it moving, and thus renewed it.

Notes

1. *The Letters of John Keats: 1814–1821*, ed. Hyder Edward Rollins, 2 vols. (Cambridge: Harvard Univ. Press, 1958), I, 394.

2. Stillinger, *The Texts of Keats's Poems* (Cambridge: Harvard Univ. Press, 1974), p. vi.

3. *The Poems of John Keats*, ed. Miriam Allott (London: Longman, 1970).

4. Stillinger's desire to "avoid combining readings of discrete states of text" (p. 15) even makes him reject his own earlier proposal (in various articles and in *The Texts of Keats's Poems*) to incorporate in a standard text of "The Eve of St. Agnes" readings which Keats's publishers altered and omitted against his wishes. Stillinger still believes that the 1820 text is faulty, but decides that the methodological imperative "outweighs" that consideration (p. 15).

5. The appendix "Editorial Emendations of the Copy-Texts" is especially useful for a quick overview of the changes, but one wishes Stillinger had divided the entries into substantives and accidentals.

6. Ronald Sharp, *Keats, Skepticism, and the Religion of Beauty* (Athens: Univ. of Georgia Press, 1979).

7. Walter Jackson Bate, *John Keats* (1963; rpt. New York: Oxford Univ. Press, 1966), p. 133n; Robert M. Ryan, *Keats: The Religious Sense* (Princeton: Princeton Univ. Press, 1976), p. 5.

8. *John Keats: The Complete Poems*, 2d ed., ed. John Barnard (Harmondsworth, England: Penguin, 1976), p. 535.

9. John Middleton Murry, *Keats and Shakespeare: A Study of Keats' Poetic Life from 1816 to 1820* (London: Oxford Univ. Press, 1925), p. 5.

Reconstructing Hawthorne

Kent Bales

Nina Baym. *The Shape of Hawthorne's Career.* Ithaca: Cornell University Press, 1976. 283 pp.

Richard H. Brodhead. *Hawthorne, Melville, and the Novel.* Chicago: University of Chicago Press, 1976. vii, 216 pp.

Kenneth Dauber. *Rediscovering Hawthorne.* Princeton: Princeton University Press, 1977. xii, 235 pp.

Edgar A. Dryden. *Nathaniel Hawthorne: The Poetics of Enchantment.* Ithaca: Cornell University Press, 1977. 182 pp.

The study of language has once again become central to the humane disciplines, although in a new sense and with different results. Language is no longer deemed central because to master ancient tongues unlocks sacred and otherwise valuable texts, nor because the history of its development traces the history of culture and its progress; language is instead thought to be central because the study of its structures provides the model for other structural investigations, including the study of supralinguistic forms in literature. To trace the history of these developments would be out of place here, but it is appropriate to remark that one result has been the diminution of historical studies and of the prestige of history itself. Also, although the change has exerted less adverse influence on the study of psychology, there too the idea that our language may think our thoughts and speak through us, rather than the other way 'round, has undercut the imputed power both of consciousness and of a preverbal unconscious mind. In short, two of the greatest fascinations of the past two centuries, history and psychology, have been displaced from the prominence they had so long enjoyed.

Nathaniel Hawthorne shared in that fascination with history and psychology. Indeed, few writers have brooded more than he over the nature of these two mysteries, and fewer have penetrated them as far. But Hawthorne would also have sympathized with the recent fascination exercised by the structures which thought and feeling may be given and which social organizations take, for these are in one sense the very stuff of history, the *differentia* distinguishing one time and people from another. He would have objected, however, to the largely ahistorical way in which these structures are now usually studied. For in order to describe how a language, for example, works, linguists have usually ignored explaining how it came to function in that way or how it will change into a structure that in radical or subtle but important ways will operate in a new way to generate different meanings. To be sure, by limiting their subject in this way, linguists describing a language code or social scientists describing the function of an institution or the configuration of social values can make their analyses quite detailed. They can also describe the internal dynamics of the system, the processes by which the code or institution adjusts itself to the newly felt needs that can define themselves within the institution or coded system. But that is all: the matter of how revolutionary changes occur in the coded meaning, or how new institutions arise, or how radical change occurs in existing institutions, remains a mystery. In some of their forms, history and psychology attempt to resolve that mystery. They offer explanations of changes as well as descriptions of systems in equilibrium, although they often settle for explaining and neglect to describe very fully. Hawthorne's tales and romances frequently try to do both, to describe (or portray) a society in a moment of crisis and to explain what happened to it. In this way Hawthorne also sought to explain how the *we* reading his works came to be and how their institutions and language are uniquely theirs. Such has often been the work of historians, but not all have tried to recreate for us the past as distinctly as did Hawthorne. In the fullest meaning of the term, he had a historical imagination.

His works thus call for an equally historical imagination from their readers.

The new *we* whose habits of thought have been formed on the lasts of synchronic linguistics and structurally related disciplines rarely have such a historical imagination. The study of history seems to them instead either a mystification or an impossibility. It mystifies because it looks for meaning in the past rather than in how our lives are ordered today; it is impossible because new generations have altered (and been altered by) their institutions and codes of communication and hence live in a sense new lives cut off from those lived in earlier and different times—times irrevocably lost. For we lack the data and the leisure to call back to life their codes of communication, to reconstruct in imagination their other institutions. Or, if we attempt such reconstructions, we know that we do so in order to create for ourselves a usable past rather than what really was. This latter enterprise acknowledges the reality of history and the importance of historical study, and it certainly exercises the imagination, but in its relativism it in effect joins in declaring that "we" have moved "beyond history."

The consequences of Babel thus seem even more numerous and various as our awareness of codes, linguistic and otherwise, increases. Not only are we separated from the French and the Ojibwa, we are cut off from our ancestors and even our parents and children by subtle but important changes. Like Hawthorne in "The Custom-House," when we try to communicate with our ancestors we are aware of doing so "across the gulf of time." Not only are they dead and gone, swallowed up by that gulf, but their structures of thought and signs are dead with them. That is one meaning of *The Scarlet Letter*, for it is "about" the transformation of a sign that in turn signals a transformation in the code. Yet that is not the whole story: "the past was not dead," Hawthorne also tells us, slyly insinuating into this remark about his past as a writer the supposedly dead past of his Salem ancestors, both awakened simultaneously when he discovers the cloth sign in the attic, the elaborate symbol of Hester Prynne's being that has survived until it can be placed by Hawthorne into a sign system more sympathetic to its seventeenth-century creator than were his ancestors and the sign system they had tried to define her within.

In this and in other stories Hawthorne brings together two senses of history, what Harry B. Henderson, III, has called "holist" and "progressive" histories.[1] The former describes (like a linguist synchronically studying a language) a people and its culture at a certain time, while the latter proposes a principle of change that is meant to explain how a nation or people or civilization develops (as a language studied diachronically will be shown to change in sound and syntax according to certain laws). The holist describes a gestalt unique to his subject; the progressive explains where we (or they) came from and are going. As holist (and for Henderson, Hawthorne is the definitive holist), Hawthorne looks back and describes how the Puritans, the Quakers, the Indian-fighting frontiersmen, the revolutionaries were; as progressive, he knows that "strong traits" of his Puritan ancestors' "nature have intertwined themselves" with his own and that present and future America has been "caused," variously, by the Puritan ethos (e.g., "The Gray Champion"), or by rejection of it (e.g., "My Kinsman, Major Molineux"), or by a modification of it (e.g., *The Scarlet Letter*). Sometimes the progressive explanation seems instead a degenerative explanation, a disclosure of how low we have fallen. But when this possibility is raised in *The Scarlet Letter*, it is quickly qualified by a holist way of thinking: those, after all, were other times; they, only naturally, had other ways. The judgmental motives behind progressive versions of history yield to an understanding that all judgment is relative, that societies and cultures are intricate systems with their own peculiar strengths and weaknesses. For the holist, to understand all is truly to forgive, or not even to blame in the first place, and very often to admire how cunningly made the other culture was. The richness of Hawthorne's sense of history derives from the mixture of these two historical imaginations, on the one hand a profound sympathy for the past in its very difference from the present, and on the other a conviction that historical change can be explained and is the only promise of a better future. He may thus be inconsistent, but as a holist he is faithful to our certain knowledge that all structures of codes and conventions, and the feelings felt through them, are intricately complex; as a progressive historian he also fulfills the need to explain change, to account for how we came to be by exposing the root of our present and giving us the wisdom to shape the future—or the hope of escaping the nightmare.

Hawthorne's psychology likewise consists of a wise catholicism, nicely brought into accord with the historical imaginations that he exercises. For example, varieties of behaviorism seem best suited to a holist history, for both the history and the psychology are unevaluative, descriptive, functional. Indeed, the concepts of psychological conditioning and of codes of communication speaking through their users are very close, even to sharing the difficulty of explaining why behavior changes. For example, one explanation might be that a culture conquers and absorbs another, as in "The May-Pole of Merry Mount," and in the process is itself transformed from "within." In this view, Puritan and Merrymounter have different "psychologies" simply because they have different cultures. Furthermore, the mutual influence of their cultures is possible because human nature is so malleable: even "the iron man" Endicott "was softened," while the captive May Lord and Lady became Puritans and "never wasted one regretful thought on the vanities of Merry Mount." The ending to this tale, however, seems to add a progressive (though conservatively so) view of change as well, for when the young couple eschew vanities they go hand in hand "heavenward." This progress away from vanity has here a decidedly Christian emphasis, but it incorporates elements of what we may call developmental psychologies, "history" on the individual level. The development need not be happy: Endicott almost sighs "for the inevitable blight of early hopes." In his eyes, maturity is a tragic renunciation of selfishness, the acceptance of "reality." Freud seems the representative psychologist for this vision of human nature and history, one frequently present in Hawthorne's writing as was persuasively demonstrated by Frederick C. Crews some twelve years ago.[2] But there is a tragicomic psychology hinted at as well: "in the tie that united them, were intertwined all the purest and best of their early joys." In this psychology the healthy person progresses toward self-fulfillment by keeping intact the best visions of childhood. This more romantic concept of development comes to the fore when Hawthorne writes about persons—usually heroines—whose progress in maturation is thwarted by social pressure from without and within (often in the form of internalized moral codes). In its vision of human nature, or man's potential for perfectibility (the unfortunate contemporary term for realization or actualization), this psychology accords well with progressive versions of history.

Hawthorne studies generally have emphasized the conservative rather than this progressive psychology (and history), partly because it is the more explicitly expressed in Hawthorne's work, partly because critics of Lionel Trilling's generation created in their own image what he called "Our Hawthorne," an ironist with a tragic imagination.[3] This New Critical Hawthorne figured in the cultural histories that subsequently were written, and even Crews's psychoanalytical reading, although it did the most to establish Hawthorne as *homo psychologus* rather than as sad moralist and prose poet, did not alter much the view of history or human nature imputed to him in the preceding decades. Since Crews wrote, however, a great deal has changed. Although the reliance of Hugo McPherson's *Hawthorne as Myth-Maker* (Toronto: Univ. of Toronto Press, 1969) on Jung, the Cambridge anthropologists, and Northrop Frye has kept McPherson and his work from exerting much influence upon the main body of Hawthorne scholarship and criticism, he was in one sense like the other writers then setting out to define their Hawthorne: he too displayed the instinct of the literary historian by drawing on the mythological explanations given in Charles Anthon's *Classical Dictionary*, Hawthorne's source when he had reworked classical myths into children's books. John Caldwell

Stubbs (*The Pursuit of Form: A Study of Hawthorne and the Romance* [Urbana: Univ. of Illinois Press, 1970]) and Michael Davitt Bell (*Hawthorne and the Historical Romance of New England* [Princeton: Princeton Univ. Press, 1971]) looked carefully at what the genre of the New England historical romance was like, what generic rules and expectations Hawthorne had to work with and within. Bell's interests were historical in yet another way, for he also wanted to trace what he saw as Hawthorne's changing awareness of time and the past. In other words, Hawthorne not only worked with historical materials but developed in consciousness as well, so that a history of change as well as of continuity can be traced through his works. Such an argument had formerly been invoked only to explain the failures at the end of his career, as in Rudolph Von Abele's psychoanalytic *The Death of the Artist: A Study of Hawthorne's Disintegration* (The Hague: Martinus Nijhoff, 1957). One of Hawthorne's own fascinations thus came to be played upon him, after decades of relatively ahistorical or even antihistorical study at the hands of New Critics. Almost simultaneously John E. Becker (*Hawthorne's Historical Allegory: An Examination of the American Conscience* [Port Washington, N. Y.: Kennikat Press, 1971]) and Robert Fossum (*Hawthorne's Inviolable Circle: The Problem of Time* [Deland, Fla.: Everett/Edwards, 1972]) studied Hawthorne's peculiar apprehension of time and its child, history. In only four years the study of Hawthorne had undergone an astonishing transformation.

The four books to be reviewed here constitute the major part of two further stages in the transformation. Nina Baym's *The Shape of Hawthorne's Career* and Richard Brodhead's *Hawthorne, Melville, and the Novel* are literary-historical studies that extend work already done, although Baym's book can seriously be considered revolutionary, while Brodhead's admirably attempts to reconcile older New Critical and newer ways of reading. Kenneth Dauber's *Rediscovering Hawthorne* and Edgar Dryden's *Nathaniel Hawthorne: The Poetics of Enchantment* announce a new turn: these writers, as students of structuralist and phenomenological methods and poetics, take for granted that we must construct our own ways of reading Hawthorne, that we can never establish these as definitive, but that we should try to justify them by creating an interpretive structure that encompasses the whole of Hawthorne's literary production. Dauber is especially audacious, for while the idea of *rediscovering* Hawthorne suggests that he is faithfully recovering Hawthorne's way of writing (hence the "proper" way of reading him), he is also, perhaps "really," trying to show how to read literary fictions in a way used by Hawthorne but since largely lost owing to the intervention of the novel and its poetics. Dauber is not alone in trying to make the romance central to American literature — it probably has been the interpretive string most often harped upon — but he realizes more than most that the romance may be central to fiction itself and, whether central or not, that reading it is an art all its own. Hence the need to rediscover. Hence, too, the sense of a new *we* with new (or revived) and fuller ways of reading.

These ways are not full enough, however, to do justice to Hawthorne's sense of history and psychology as sketched above. To be sure, all four writers see other sides of these matters than did most of the writers of the forties, fifties, and even sixties, but none ranges so widely as Hawthorne. Dauber and Dryden are really "beyond history," more concerned with describing the structures that consciousness takes than with explaining how consciousness changes — except in combination "within" their structures. Nor are they holist historians, for even Hawthorne's interest in history interests them principally as a subject to be structured by his and their consciousnesses rather than as something different in kind and degree from the "contents" of "our" consciousness. Dauber finds Brodhead to be an ally in this effort to move beyond the consideration of history, a reader who knows that "the work . . . actualizes its own conventions. It says nothing we do not already know, but makes manifest man's ways of saying, the conditions by which he 'knows' in the first place. The reader becomes aware of the process by which ideas of reality come into being. He is made conscious of the conventions writer and reader share, made conscious of his own criticism, the limits within which writing and reading must operate."[4] This is true, but it is phrased as it is to bend Brodhead's analyses to Dauber's ends. Brodhead's real interest is "the novel," the history and poetics of a literary form, for which the creation of readers who are conscious of the artifice of their joint enterprise is an important component rather than the whole story. He too has doubtless read structuralist and deconstructionist critics and theorists, but he has bought only what he needs for his own ends—all that Dauber says that he does, to be sure, but he has bought from other stores as well. Baym buys nothing at all from structuralists, for by her lights they have nothing she needs. Had her ends been a little grander she might well have profited by using them. But her achievement is substantial without them, and of these four books hers is the easiest to appreciate for anybody skeptical about the newer methods of analysis grounded in linguistics.

Baym writes a history of Hawthorne's career, which she sees as developing along certain lines that follow closely the development of literary fiction in England and America. It is a progressive history, as literary histories go, not because it posits the more recent as better but because it tries to explain how change occurs, because is assumes that change is directional (even if not necessarily "progressive") and can be understood. As with all attempts at explaining change, Baym's has the problems of periodization and causation (or, in literary terms, emplotment): on the one hand, what were the times of relative stasis and what were their characteristics, and, on the other hand, why did one period change into another? This is the problem, writ small, of the relationship between synchronic description and diachronic explanation, the question of how what is becomes something else. Biographical history poses this question perhaps the most sharply of all, because in it we can observe continuity as well as change: the "new" man or woman is also in many ways the old. A common solution is to assume that the unchanging aspects are the real, the changing merely superficial. A pervasive platonism in our culture lends impetus to this denigration of change. So it has been in Hawthorne studies. Roy R. Male, whose *Hawthorne's Tragic*

Vision (Austin: Univ. of Texas Press, 1957) has been one of the most influential of the new critical works that argue for an ironical Hawthorne possessing a conservative vision of history, rejects outright Baym's thesis. The "major problem" with her book, he writes,

> is simply that Hawthorne's development was rather technical and unspectacular. Its major stages are familiar: his decision after the failure of *Fanshawe* to write short pieces, his abandonment of short fiction in the late 1840's, and his physical and artistic decline between 1860 and 1864. Because of his early decision to be a writer, his life lacked the dramatic conversions we find in the careers of Melville, Conrad, and Twain. Hawthorne's style was perfected by 1835 and did not change. Nor is there evidence of radical improvement in his work. Early stories like "Young Goodman Brown" are at least as good as his late ones. Thus any effort to discover more change than continuity in his career is bound to produce some distortion.[5]

Without mutually acknowledged standards, it is, of course, impossible to prove that Hawthorne's work did or did not improve, and it may or may not be that Hawthorne's style did not change, but there is much more which can and which makes these criteria inadequate for measuring change. How, after all, does one decide whether a full-length romance improves upon a sketch of a day at the seashore, or whether a change in persona is a change in style? Baym surveys Hawthorne's entire career as a man of letters and can in some instances identify the very occasion on which he first took up the moralized fiction, say, or the sketch, when he laid down and took up again gothic or sentimental devices. Sheerly as description, hers is the most complete account of Hawthorne's career that we have. Moreover, because Baym looks at the events in Hawthorne's life that accompanied these literary decisions, her book can be read as a skeleton critical biography of great worth.

To develop her thesis, however, Baym must do more than simply describe. That thesis is an explanation containing several explicit, visible strands and several more implicit but unseen strands that make it strong but uneven as well. Hawthorne became a writer because he had loved reading Scott and the gothic novelists, found other professions unsympathetic, and was taken by the idea that he could make money by writing the sort of thing he loved to read. From the outset, then, he had his eye on the market and wrote for it gladly. (It seems to have taken him a while to learn it, and even as a mature man he failed to foresee the shift in the public's taste from sentimental and gothic romance to domestic realism.) Superadded on this practical thesis is the more idealistic one that Hawthorne sought to embody and, in his writing, to justify the imagination to an audience of skeptical, practical-minded shopkeepers. This is a charmingly bourgeois combination of "literary Realpolitik" (p. 102) and romantic pride in one's powers or mission, yet it has the ring of truth to be heard in the feedback from the first thesis onto the second—Hawthorne's frequently expressed concern that the imagination is diseased, a curse rather than a gift. So long as Hawthorne's attitude toward literature was largely commonsensical, however, little difficulty ensued, for both his wish to succeed and his sense of mission could be satisfied by adapting to prevailing standards of taste. But when Hawthorne's attitude began to change (and Baym has trouble explaining why it changed), adaptation was not enough, a conclusion which Baym reaches but does not work into her thesis. It emerges implicitly, however, as when, apropos *The House of the Seven Gables*, she remarks on the conflict that emerges "between the writer Hawthorne wants to be and the writer he has discovered himself to be" (p. 153). This essentially psychological thesis muddies the clarity of her explicit theses, but it has the virtue of reaching deeper and explaining, although darkly, why Hawthorne's work became "romantic." Unfortunately, she leaves this thesis largely implicit, as she does the idea that there is a dialectical mode of change in Hawthorne's career, an interplay of motive and material that has its own generative logic. In discussing *Tanglewood Tales*, for example, Baym remarks that here "once more Hawthorne has pursued a literary intention to a point where its inadequacies overbalance its uses" (p. 212). Such a system of change with its own internal dynamics, together with the shadowy figure of the real but buried artist, is necessary to explain why Hawthorne changes after he no longer simply tries to adapt his wares to the market. Yet although Baym seems to find these ideas necessary, for polemical reasons she cannot admit them to the status of explicit theses, as they would blur the clean lines of the radical argument she is conducting. For that purpose she insists at every opportunity that Hawthorne's "deepest, and most sincere, literary feeling was the drive to be a successful author" (p. 87).

At the outset, she argues, Hawthorne, content to be guided by commonsense ideas about the function of art and artists, "put forth very modest claims for literature and for himself" (p. 8). This early period subdivides into three fairly distinct subperiods, depending upon how he felt about the imagination: a beginning (1825-1834), the period of *Twice-Told Tales* (1834-1839), and the Manse decade (1840-1849). During this time Hawthorne tried out many literary forms, subjects, and personae. In his earliest writings, for example, the imagination seems at times too dangerous, at others too trivial. As a consequence, he tried to steer a middle course during the middle 1830s, developing two "new" forms, the moralized fiction and the sketch, both of which require an "authorial presence," a sensibility "visibly at work": "a modest man who makes a modest claim for literature as a reinforcer of social values and an enhancer of our perceptions of life" (p. 52). (It was this persona he bade farewell in the 1851 preface to *Twice-Told Tales*.) Perhaps his dissatisfaction with the constraints of this persona, and certainly the new stimuli of the Boston Custom House, Brook Farm, and his subsequent marriage, gave impetus to the creation of a new persona, "a man of opinions, a critic, and commentator" who in his "worldly, self-assured, and ironic" voice (p. 99) addresses a particular audience, "literate Bostonians and New Yorkers attached to the Democratic Party" (p. 101). In this guise Hawthorne wrote *Mosses from an Old Manse* (1846), and it was this persona that he abandoned when he became the romantic artist capable of creating *The Scarlet Letter* (1850) and other romances. Baym is equivocal on why Hawthorne changed: either he discovered the buried artist or he cynically played to an audience ready for romantic artists. In either case the results were the same—he created a richer art that in turn helped justify his chosen profession. This "major phase" is the brief second period (1850-1853), during which he "found a position that released his greatest burst of creativity: the idea of the artist as a chronicler of the hidden life and representer of repressed but necessary emotions" (p. 275). Its history is well known, as are the essays by Baym that she reworks in her account of these years.[6] Even here she remains attentive to Hawthorne's strategies for capturing readers, as when she remarks that when Hawthorne set out to make *The House of the Seven Gables* "sunnier," he reverted to the types of writing he earlier had been successful with, blending together gothic romance, sketches, moralistic interludes, comic and sentimental touches. The succeeding English and Italian years (1853-1859) and the "last phase" (1860-1864) are periods of experimentation with realism and new personae—for instance, the Victorian sage in *Our Old Home* (1863). Instead of gradual decline, Baym thus traces further development in Hawthorne's last years, finding *The Marble Faun* (1860) "by far the most complex and ambitious of Hawthorne's mature romances" (p. 229). As a description of Hawthorne's career this is eminently satisfactory. Yet the explanations built upon the description cost Baym a great deal, and they fail, at the crucial point, to be very helpful.

The problem can be stated simply: how did *The Scarlet Letter* come about? As we have seen, Baym finds her explanation for change throughout in Hawthorne's attempts to adapt to or attract an audience and sometimes to justify himself to that audience—without boring it, to be sure. In conclusion Baym puts the matter a little differently: "Except for the decade of the major romances, Hawthorne's career developed as a series of tentative solutions to the question of the social significance of the artist" (p. 275). But that decade, especially its early years, is a major exception, a damaging one. Part of the trouble lies in how Baym treats the period she calls the Old

Manse decade. There, if anywhere, will be the signs of change, and in it she finds Hawthorne behaving in strangely contradictory ways. He is both negotiating in a worldly manner between "opposed positions with an eye to attracting the largest audience" (p. 103) and permitting, among other things, "an obtuse narrator" to "undermine the persona of the speaker in the Manse sketches" (p. 106). Baym rightly notes that these sketches and tales are among the most puzzling that Hawthorne ever wrote, but she will not modify her thesis to solve the puzzle. The probable solution lies on one hand in greater attention to psychology, both Hawthorne's and his characters' (Baym opens that door by speculating on the pressures exerted by his "frustrated and embittered imagination" [p. 83]), and on the other hand in Hawthorne's more complex sense of his relation to his audience. Surely his readers cannot simply be defined by the categories Boston, New York, and Democrat. Which of these is addressed in "Rappaccini's Daughter"? The readers of the *Democratic Review*, to be sure, for the story first appeared there, but few of those readers would have been ready to follow the twists and turns of that tale. Baym is not either and would rather call the tale "too rich," because it "seems to evade any single wholly satisfactory reading" (p. 107), than to conclude that Hawthorne's sense of meaning and audience might be quite complicated indeed. This period, along with the early years of Hawthorne's career, seems the most experimental and the most demanding on his ideal audience as well. Baym, however, prefers to conclude that Hawthorne has failed than to modify her thesis concerning what she calls Hawthorne's search for "audience tolerance" (p. 54). Quick to point out that "Drowne's Wooden Image" foreshadows the romances in proposing passion as the root of art, Baym will not conclude that the demands made upon Hawthorne's audience in *Mosses*—or Hawthorne's strategy of talking through some audiences—also anticipates them. Yet, as Brodhead points out, throughout *The Scarlet Letter* Hawthorne often gives his readers broad latitude in deciding just what happened and why, nowhere more so than at the climax, when we may stigmatize Arthur Dimmesdale or not, as we think appropriate. Were this a tale from the Manse period, Baym would explain that this freedom to choose is a means of attracting the largest audience, but here (and there too, in reality) there are better and worse ways of reading, and probably a best, that adopted by those members of Hawthorne's audiences most alert to alterations in the codes of communication. That separation of the audience, and the elaborate game of "The Custom-House," are as radically romantic as is the theme of passion creating art. But, just as Baym is largely silent on Hawthorne's psychology and interest in psychology, so she is usually unwilling to consider complicated states of consciousness. She comes as close as she can in her treatment of "The Old Manse," the prefatory essay that exhibits so beautifully what has come to be called the problem of the preface—that it is written last yet is to be read first. "The Old Manse" is a decidedly romantic work that "makes the highest demands on the literary artifact" (p. 116)—and, one could add, on the reader, who must match its atmospheric shifts and meandering structure with an alert consciousness. But it is more typical of the period than Baym admits, a period which as a whole should have been searched for the gradual and fitful change that prepared the way for *The Scarlet Letter*. (Stressing the tentative nature of these writings would also help overcome a problem of periodization, the fact that some works do not "fit" well Baym's description of the period and so must be "explained" as anachronistic.) Baym is correct in saying that Hawthorne's sense of his audience is a key to understanding the changes in his art, but she has not looked deeply enough, or with the right interests in mind, at how he imagined and addressed those audiences during this pivotal decade. Her explanation improves decidedly upon others made of Hawthorne's career, however, and the ground she has cleared now stands ready to be cultivated.

Kenneth Dauber, like Baym, is interested in tracing the shape of Hawthorne's career. He also assumes that the way toward apprehending it can be found in Hawthorne's sense of audience, his attempt to "open an intercourse with the world," as Hawthorne put it. This is Hawthorne's *purpose*—a word that has special meaning for Dauber. Dauber is like Baym in yet another way, for both assume that many elements of Hawthorne's works serve primarily to engage the reader, that their meaning is not to signify but rather is to provide an occasion for intimacy, for being a *we* together. For example, the familiar form of allegory, like Hawthorne's "familiar kind of preface," is a gambit to involve the reader rather than a pattern to be searched for its significance. (Baym sometimes assumes this, sometimes not. The apparently radical and especially feminist meanings of the romances are urgently significant to her—and, she argues, to Hawthorne as well. She is quite right.) Hawthorne thus becomes "Melville's opposite number," neither symbolist nor visionary but a writer deeply "realist" according to this useful, structuralist-derived definition: "he objectifies his culture's attitude toward the world, however demonic or angelic those attitudes are, without com ment" (p. 19). To put the matter another way, Hawthorne uses the conventional signs of his society's codes both to achieve intimacy with his audience (to say, in effect, "we are all users of this code") and to call their attention to these signs as the bearers of attitudes. In turn, this strategy should make the reader aware that his attitudes are merely that, states of mind at least in part engendered by the code. In both the objectivity of presentation and in the resulting awareness that we live not directly in "reality" but within and through codes, Hawthorne's vision and method are "realistic."

To manipulate the codes of communication with such wide-eyed deliberation requires Hawthorne's intense awareness that culture is artifice, a tissue of assumptions. In literary terms Hawthorne and his audience, like a speaker and interpreter in other discourse, must know what genre is being invoked, what functions one should perform on the linguistic act. These will vary widely among cultures, since a genre is confined specifically to a code—although the action of thinking with and through generic conventions is universal. (A genre is a species of generic thought, that is. In Paul Hernadi's homely phrase, all thinking is genre-alizing—which is not the same as saying

Reconstructing Hawthorne

that any genre is universal.)[7] This unmistakably holist view makes communication of what is known eminently possible within a social system or culture (though there will be interference, mixed or dropped signals, even in the best of systems among even the most skilled at using the code). But, in a familiar romantic argument, writers live what Dauber calls "marginal lives." They find themselves using modes of fiction, genres which "never quite express" them and which are addressed to "readers who never quite hear" (p. xi). In other words, the conventions of each literary work exercise such power that the reader interprets them to mean what the conventions invoked conventionally mean, not what their manipulation expresses about the possibly unique self or vision of the writer. Like Eliot's Sweeney, the writer can complain that "I gotta use words when I talk to you" even though the word in question strictly "dont apply." In this pressure for uniformity we can see exhibited the problem of change, the question of how to alter or manipulate the code so that new meanings can come into it. Dauber's answer is that the writer uses works in a sequence: the individual work, particularly if generically unified, is almost hopelessly bound to conventional meaning, but a patterned series of works provides spaces between where the writer and meanings "are" and can exercise counterpressure on generic meaning. Hawthorne's *purpose*, then, is to create a literary world of genres that, by their configurations and the course of his progress through them, will express him. Coincidentally he also exposes the conventions as conventions, shows them to his audience for what they are, the necessary but tragically limiting matrix of "our" world.

This exciting approach to Hawthorne reveals a great deal. In some works, for example, Hawthorne tries to do within the work what he tries to do among his works: he creates several different generic patterns that, by existing together, direct our attention between them rather than at them. As we have seen, Baym shows Hawthorne combining literary genres in *The House of the Seven Gables*, and indeed the presence of apparently conflicting genres has long been recognized as typical of modern romances. This practice of presenting the reader with works (or a pattern of works) uninterpretable in conventional ways creates active readers, aware that when all is merely, though necessarily conventional, a reader must be artful and aggressive in his interpretations if he is to escape banality. Closer attention by modern readers to Hawthorne's contrapuntal use of this generic pressure, to the purposeful exploitation of generic differences so as to admit as yet unconventional meaning and feeling, promises a rich harvest. Dauber justly remarks "that Hawthorne's wisdom, that curious ambiguity which has so often been remarked, is his understanding of the incompleteness of vision" (p. xi). As it is through and because of genre that vision is both possible and is rendered incomplete, the enterprise that Dauber begins is eminently worthwhile.

But two serious mistakes vitiate Dauber's reading of Hawthorne, mistakes worth dwelling upon because the virtues of Dauber's book and the intelligence manifested there will rightly recommend it to many. These mistakes derive from the assumption, common today, that historical research will produce nothing more of value. We already know too much, Dauber argues: instead of more facts, we need new ways of ordering what we already know, a method of reading commensurate with what the *we* now reading Hawthorne knows about language and literary motivation. Hence a view of art as active, purposive, performative rather than as an object; hence too, we are told, Dauber's attempt to trace the progress of Hawthorne's effort at communicating his purpose, at performing the valuable act of prying conventions slightly ajar. (Curiously, Dauber for the most part claims that Hawthorne is not expressing himself but rather locating himself within the convention-manipulating community. He thus "expresses" only his awareness of the codes.)

Dauber's first mistake is in selecting works to be sorted out into a pattern rather than sorting all—or making his principle of selection clear. To order temporally is not necessarily to order historically, and Dauber's is such a nonhistorical although temporal ordering—a myth, really. He wants to have it both ways, to be free from the drudgery of establishing

Hawthorne's efforts as truly his and emanating from his condition, yet to claim historical reality for what he describes. This is not merely Dauber's reading, in other words: Hawthorne actually had the purpose Dauber ascribes to him. To be convincing, however, Dauber must be more than merely interesting and consistent—the usual constraints accepted by the deconstructing "writerly" reader; he must also be relatively immune to challenge from other evidence. He needs to survey Hawthorne's career with the care that Baym has expended.

Dauber's second mistake is his failure to pay close attention to the generic conditions, the conventional expectations or pressures among which Hawthorne published his works. Given the importance accorded generic pressure in Dauber's explanation, this fault is especially shocking. We do not know too much about these conditions; we know far too little, although Baym, Bell, and Stubbs, with others, have recently increased the sum of our knowledge. If one considers how we respond to the welter of generic pressures in a novel by Thomas Pynchon, the parodies and other takeoffs and sendups that require of us a reservoir of information from the recent past as well as our present, we can see how complicated responding to generic pressure can be. Dauber, however, would have us accept a word here and there about gothicism and romance as being an adequate description of the genres exerting pressure on Hawthorne. In this light he would have been better off calling his book *Kenneth Dauber on Hawthorne*, for he has shirked the work of "rediscovering Hawthorne." Nonetheless, he has pointed the way toward combining structuralist and historical study. If only literary historians will be guided in their searches by what Dauber has shown is needed (though he has not, for the most part, provided it), we will be the better for it. It remains for the structuralist and deconstructing readers to make a similar accommodation, to be true to the insight that coded structures, especially in literary works, are so rooted in the code systems of their creators that a careful description of those systems is a precondition to criticism.

As noted above, Edgar Dryden has little use for historical

modes of thought. His method is basically phenomenological of the kind (domesticated by J. Hillis Miller) that seeks to describe the writer's mental "world." Melville, Poe, Stevens, and Faulkner have already been read in this fashion, and we can look for many other such readings. Dryden's own *Melville's Thematics of Form: The Great Art of Telling the Truth* (Baltimore: Johns Hopkins Univ. Press, 1968) is one of the earliest, and the polemical chapter with which it begins is an excellent starting place for thinking about the theory of the novel. Whereas Dauber had set out to write "the poetics that Hawthorne might have written" (p. ix), Dryden, although he writes in this new book a "poetics of enchantment," is much more interested in the question "Who is Nathaniel Hawthorne?" (p. 9). In answering this question he describes a Hawthorne even more bent than Dauber found him to be on making his reader active, an aggressive and unmystified co-creator of significance. Hawthorne disenchants the reader, that is, frees him from the tyranny of the author's control of meaning, grants him his rightful status as subject rather than as vibrating mechanism in some kind of wireless receiving set. (This is far from Dauber's claim that the code and generic pressure are in control, that the writer is the one set vibrating by the reader's expectations.) Hawthorne's prefaces, for example, both attract the reader by hinting that writer and reader can truly know each other and confuse him by holding him at a distance, with the result that the reader learns not to trust the writer's blandishments. In this and other ways Hawthorne creates "a suspicious, probing reader who will carry out in reverse the author's work of falsification," meet guile with guile, and counter fascination with "its opposite, interpretation" (p. 126). This strategy in turn is motivated by a conflict within Hawthorne: "Hawthorne's conception of romance might be said to develop from a tension formed, on the one hand, by his dreams of a 'Gentle Reader,' who in his innocence and simplicity will accept at face value and be enchanted by the beautiful web woven by the romancer, and on the other by a knowledge that such a dream represents an impossible ideal since understanding and appreciation depend

Reconstructing Hawthorne 157

upon deciphering and interpreting, and those acts are necessarily violent ones" (p. 127).

This sample is sufficient to give a sense of the whole. Dryden works with a romantic psychology of self in relationship with other, assuming a self that wants to be loved yet protected from violation and disappointment, that opens itself yet mystifies the other. Fear rules Hawthorne, fear that is the sign of his refusal to know himself deeply, so that his characteristic action is to deceive. There is thus at work a dialectic that generates other dialectical relations, those of the self in its relations to others, as involved in the special relationships of love and reading, and as caught up by the relation of self and present to time and the past. Enchantment and disenchantment have two meanings, two dialectical relationships: enchantment is how the self tries to protect itself by gaining power over the other, disenchantment how the self is rendered both open and vulnerable, but any belief held too firmly or course of action followed unquestioningly (including a disenchanted one) can become an enchantment. Change is thus dialectical but not progressive, one oscillates rather than moves forward. The happiest state is in between, the moment when one has the advantages of both polar states of being without the danger of enchantment engendered by either.

Romantic fascination with history, however, plays little part in Dryden's scheme except as an enchantment, perhaps the most powerful of all. This fascination with origins is a subject to be explained rather than an explanation in its own right. For it is an enchantment to believe that we can live better by returning to the past, even in sympathetic imagination. Not only is the past dead, it is merely a myth that past times were simpler and better. Eden is a lie, an enchantment that keeps man from living in the present, and history, it would seem, is a substitute lie. It is surprising, therefore, to see Dryden conclude his book by turning Eden on its head and positing a myth of modernity, a state which Hawthorne found his way to in the late, unfinished romances and which we occupy today, thanks to our demystified sense of reality. We have moved, with Hawthorne, beyond romance as well, that mediating strategy for spanning the distance "between the self and the other by mediating those polarities that constitute for him a matrix of human relationships" (p. 171). Instead of romance's holding sway in the house of fiction, a potent and quasi-magical force at the center, we now envision a web of fiction, "the product of will and desire rather than a reconstruction of tradition or a representation of qualities that lie beyond the senses" (p. 171). This web figures our condition, one in which we construct local orders out of materials at hand. In this assumption Dryden is decidedly a man living beyond history and without a belief in centers of value. All interpretive structures are ours, all codes of communication manufactured rather than given. Babel never was: we have always been prisoners of language, and we have only just matured enough to accept the fact.

It is not clear why this is the ultimate disenchantment, why it alone is not subject to becoming an enchantment itself, indeed why it is not already one. By invoking a myth to conclude his book, Dryden stays the dialectic by which it has been driven. Perhaps he does so in imitation of the conclusion he has reached, perhaps it is simply an ending imposed out of the necessity of ending. If the latter, there is much else in the book of the same kind, for throughout one has no sense of what is coming next: one is caught in an argument that takes apparently arbitrary turns. In retrospect this turns out not to have been so—the chapters are fitted together quite cunningly when seen in final perspective, and the order of each chapter mimics the movement from enchantment to disenchantment to enchantment described. Yet retrospective admiration does not cancel the sense felt while reading. It simply mollifies it. This may seem a minor flaw, but given the nature of the argument it takes on greater proportions than it would in most other books.

For Dryden must convince the reader that he is sensitive enough to have perceived correctly all that he describes. His assumptions, that there is "Hawthornian man" (p. 39) who appears everywhere and is everywhere the same and that all Hawthorne's works are equally valid and useful sources of insight and evidence, permit Dryden to choose from wherever he likes the evidence to support his perceptions and arguments. One must grant these assumptions, at least for awhile, but it is hard to continue in good faith when one finds the evidence often wrenched and torn from context as well as willfully rearranged. This happens throughout, as checking the sources quoted on almost any page will demonstrate—provided the quotation is to be found on the page cited, which it also all too frequently is not.[8] Such carelessness breeds suspicion, disenchants the reader in a way Dryden can ill afford. For however responsive to human psychology the phenomenological method used may be, it will register as successful only if the analyst has opened himself fully to the subject or text and apprehended the forms of consciousness there. This process is inevitably impressionistic, and the signs that seal the validity of impressionism are the tact and sensitivity of the interpreter.

Consider this opening to the chapter on reading, which in many ways is powerfully argued and well presented. Septimius Felton handles an old manuscript in which "there was a sort of spell and mystic influence imbued into the paper." It magnetizes him, enchants him. Well and good. But Dryden goes on to say, "It is not simply the text that fascinates him. It is the author who is present in the text as in ' "Arabian Nights" ' a 'demon' is present in a lamp or 'copper vase.' " Dryden then develops a comparison between the writer and demon, as well as between the reader and Aladdin, to the effect that "once the demon is released . . . he is the one in control." This curious interpretation of "Aladdin" is worth considering at one's leisure, but here it draws one up short. The genie is usually obedient in that tale, or, more precisely, the genies, as there is a genie of the ring as well. If one turns to the page cited in *Septimius Felton*, however, it is clearly not Aladdin who is referred to but rather a "story in the 'Arabian Nights' where a demon comes out of a copper vase, in a cloud of smoke that covers the sea shore." These details sound more like "The Story of the Fisherman and the Genie," where an Afrite, quite menacing, comes from the unstoppered vase but is tricked into returning ("How did you do that?" the fisherman slyly asks) and must do a favor to earn his second release. Here magic is overcome by common sense and simple cunning, a conclusion contradicting Dryden's present point, although potentially useful later in the chapter when he considers disenchantment. The attentive reader, however, may not read farther. It would be a mistake not to, but the provocation to abandon the book is powerful.

It may be unfair to complain that Dryden has not done what he never promised to do, but one kind of omission raises a final question about his method. The literature of enchantment is vast, and Hawthorne wrote at a time of belles dames sans merci, Loreleis, Runenbergs, and Venusbergs. If *The Arabian Nights Entertainment* can find its way into Dryden's book, it would seem they could too. But there is virtually no context at all: Hawthorne's mind seems empty of other art from his time and incapable of manipulating allusion to it. Poor Peter Schlemihl appears several times in Hawthorne's writing, but his shadow darkens no pockets in Dryden's. Dryden's narrow method is not without its justifying precursors, but there are contrary examples as well. As Robert R. Magliola points out, by the 1950s the Geneva phenomenologists had begun to consider historical influence and draw cultural inferences: "After all, without a consideration of literary history, how can one distinguish unique style from convention? Without reference to environment, how can one even understand the cultural elements that are embedded in literature?"[9] Hawthorne's attitude toward history was complex and even contradictory, as argued above, but it certainly held greater interest for him than as a substitute for a mystifying myth of origins. It is hard to trust a reading that does not take that fascination more fully into account.

Richard Brodhead's book is a happy combination of historical interest and recent thought on language and other codes, especially literary ones. Like Dauber he is interested in literary process, not only that obtaining between works, but more especially that generated between readers and works. The *liveliness* of Hawthorne's and Melville's novels, their possession of what Yeats called the "emotion of multitude," derives from the act of representing rather than from what is represented: "It exists not in the novel's created world but between the reader and that world; or, more accurately, it comes into existence in the author's act, joined in by the reader, of calling that world into being, of sending to his objects different sorts of what Keats calls greetings of the spirit in order to constitute them to himself as real and meaningful" (p. 17). The romance form was Hawthorne's and Melville's chief means of effecting this liveliness. Joined to the novel, it had the power in contrast to call attention to itself as a fiction, a construction of interlocked and overlapping systems of perception and interpretation. In Hawthorne's hands the romance thus imports to the dominant form (the novel) those truths about language and other coded structures that the *we* of which Brodhead is a member understand and accept as normal. Yet Brodhead does not jettison history as a meaningful concept. He is more cautious than Dauber and Dryden, more "realistic" if less consistent. He has some of Hawthorne's own sense that, although the truth must be pursued radically, it has many roots, that for some purposes we must think synchronically, holistically, structurally, while for others we must seek historical causes for change, create narrative fictions that embody them, and represent as well the inconsistencies of life, the brute facts that no coded structure, no language or myth, can reconcile for long. Dauber remarks admiringly on Brodhead's civility, which he finds to be partly a matter of his critical generosity but also bespeaking "a reluctance to bend all that is in his book to his own meaning."[10] This reluctance in turn derives from the sense that explanations are necessary but finally inadequate, that the vitality of history and psychology, and of the fictional art celebrating that vitality, triumphs over the conservative force of all structures. The growing orthodoxy that all is as it is structured is only part of the truth; the deforming pressures of what structure tries to order always are the greater, and we still have no substitutes for the twin romantic fascinations, history and psychology. These studies, these provisional explanations, try to account for the deforming pressure of the unconventional. That is why

Hawthorne is still a writer for our time, for mine as well as for Baym's, Dauber's, Dryden's, or Brodhead's, for he was as canny about the processes of these fascinating powers as about the workings of linguistic and other codes. He provides good common ground for effecting compromises of the sort he imagined playing on his carpet in the moonlight. These may yet be good times for readers. Most of us may no longer believe that there is a center of truth from which we best perceive and judge, but we need not abandon as a consequence the attempt to create a center. That was the effort of romance, and if the center usually turned out to be diffuse, it incorporated all the more for its very indefiniteness. A new *we* may indeed be forming, born, like the generation of the 1840s, with knives in their brains, hence keenly analytical and attentive to method, but not slavishly so, not encumbered with a foolish consistency. The romantics should have taught us how that stone can quickly dull even the sharpest of analytical tools.

Notes

1. Henderson, *Versions of the Past: The Historical Imagination in American Fiction* (New York: Oxford Univ. Press, 1974).

2. Crews, *The Sins of the Fathers: Hawthorne's Psychological Themes* (New York: Oxford Univ. Press, 1966).

3. Trilling, "Our Hawthorne," *Partisan Review*, 31 (1964), 329-51.

4. Kenneth Dauber, "Criticism of American Literature," *Diacritics*, 7 (1977), 63.

5. Male, rev. of *The Shape of Hawthorne's Career, American Literature*, 48 (1977), 599.

6. Nina Baym, "*The Blithedale Romance:* A Radical Reading," *JEGP*, 67 (1968), 545-69; "Hawthorne's Holgrave: The Failure of the Artist-Hero," *JEGP*, 69 (1970), 584-98; "Passion and Authority in *The Scarlet Letter*," *New England Quarterly*, 43 (1970), 209-30; "Hawthorne's Women," *Centennial Review*, 15 (1971), 250-72; "The Marble Faun: Hawthorne's Elegy for Art," *New England Quarterly*, 44 (1971), 355-76; "The Romantic Malgré Lui: Hawthorne in the Custom-House," *ESQ*, 19 (1973), 14-25.

7. Hernadi, "Why We Can't Help Genre-alizing and How Not to Go About It: Two Theses with Commentary," Special Session "Genre as

Knowledge," MLA Convention, Chicago, December 1977. Forthcoming in *Centrum*.

8. On p. 112, for example, Dryden mistakenly encloses the word *illustrates* within the quotation cited from III, 206, of the Centenary Edition—which is not there but on page 198. The speaker is "a pale man in blue spectacles," an unlikely spokesman for Hawthorne, although that is not an important question at this point. It is on pp. 148-49, however, where Dryden makes Clifford Pyncheon, during his and Hepzibah's "escape" from the house of the seven gables, a figure who explains why Hawthorne must escape the Old Manse. The assumption here, as throughout, is that all Hawthorne's characters are "Hawthornian man." Similarly, in arguing that Hawthorne erects a "house of words . . . between himself and 'this transitory world which is not our home,'" Dryden quotes what will serve his purpose but omits the more cheerful conclusion that the person in question has "a home everywhere or no where, just as you please to take it" ("Passages from a Relinquished Work"). Also on these pages is another miscitation, this time of II, 265, but I cannot find the correct page. These are two of only four or five places where I checked Dryden's quotations and citations. It is a nuisance often encountered in scholarly writing, but in this book especially irritating, that only volume and page are cited—one must read with the edition at hand. The better alternative would consume more ink and paper, but it would be easier on the reader if short titles were also used as a general practice where questions of accuracy and appropriateness are likely to arise.

9. Magliola, *Phenomenology and Literature: An Introduction* (West Lafayette, Indiana: Purdue Univ. Press, 1977), p. 43.

10. Dauber, "Criticism of American Literature," p. 63.

"Learning to be Joyce's Contemporaries": *Ulysses* in the Mid-1970s

Michael Groden

C. H. Peake. *James Joyce: The Citizen and the Artist*. Stanford: Stanford University Press, 1977. x, 369 pp.

Marilyn French. *The Book as World: James Joyce's* Ulysses. Cambridge, Mass.: Harvard University Press, 1976. 295 pp.

Suzette A. Henke. *Joyce's Moraculous Sindbook: A Study of* Ulysses. Columbus: Ohio State University Press, 1978. xi, 267 pp.

James H. Maddox, Jr. *Joyce's* Ulysses *and the Assault upon Character*. New Brunswick, N.J.: Rutgers University Press, 1978. xi, 244 pp.

John Henry Raleigh. *The Chronicle of Leopold and Molly Bloom:* Ulysses *as Narrative*. Berkeley and Los Angeles: University of California Press, 1977. xi, 282 pp.

Hugh Kenner. *Joyce's Voices*. Berkeley and Los Angeles: University of California Press, 1978. xiii, 120 pp.

Robert Martin Adams. *Afterjoyce: Studies in Fiction after* Ulysses. New York: Oxford University Press, 1977. xiii, 201 pp.

Robert H. Deming, comp. *A Bibliography of James Joyce Studies*. Second edition, revised and enlarged. Boston: G. K. Hall, 1977. xii, 264 pp.

"We are still learning to be James Joyce's contemporaries, to understand our interpreter," Richard Ellmann wrote some twenty years ago.[1] Despite great advances in our understanding of Joyce's works since then, we still have much to learn and, with no abatement of effort, we continue to try. Much of the effort has always centered on *Ulysses*. Compared even to the usual large output, the number of books dealing wholly or primarily with *Ulysses* (not to mention books on other aspects of Joyce's career) published between late 1976 and early 1978 was very high. These studies invite us to consider the state of *Ulysses* criticism in the mid-1970s as we begin the second half century of trying to understand Joyce's masterwork.

Ulysses criticism conveniently divides into two camps. The followers of Ezra Pound and Frank Budgen, on the one hand, emphasize the book's realistic, novelistic dimension, while those of T. S. Eliot and Stuart Gilbert insist on the primacy of the Homeric, mythic elements. The assumptions behind the two approaches were clearly stated long ago by Budgen and Gilbert. Budgen wrote, "It seems to me to be significant that Joyce should talk to me first of the principal character in his book and only later of the manifold devices through which he presented him. If the two elements of character and material can be separated this is the order in which he would put them." At the same time, however, Stuart Gilbert was writing that "the meaning of *Ulysses* . . . is not to be sought in any analysis of the acts of the protagonist or the mental make-up of the characters; it is, rather, implicit in the technique of the various episodes, in nuances of language, in the thousand and one correspondences and allusions with which the book is studded."[2] And Joyce encouraged both statements.

The mythic-symbolic approach dominated the criticism of the 1950s, but there was a strong reaction against this in the studies of the 1960s that concentrated on the novelistic aspects of Joyce's work. Attempts at the inevitable synthesis also began in the 1960s, as critics argued that Joyce's vision encompasses both poles and that neither view alone can hope to deal fully with the complexity of *Ulysses*.[3] It is against this background that we must look at more recent criticism.

Here I am considering seven studies of *Ulysses* (plus the newest full-length bibliography of Joyce studies) in an attempt to discern recent trends. I should mention that even these seven critical books present an incomplete picture of *Ulysses* studies during this period — missing are works by Bernard Benstock, Robert Boyle, S. J., Richard Ellmann, Michael Groden,

Phillip F. Herring, Matthew Hodgart, and Stanley Sultan (besides several books on Joyce that do not deal directly with *Ulysses*), and these works range from introductions for students to general reappraisals of Joyce's works to comprehensive treatments to studies and editions of Joyce's manuscripts.[4] Nevertheless, seven books are reasonably exhaustive (and exhausting), and from them several patterns emerge regarding *Ulysses* criticism in the mid-1970s.

Four of the authors—C. H. Peake, Marilyn French, Suzette A. Henke, and James H. Maddox, Jr.—offer full readings of *Ulysses* that attempt to show the unity of Joyce's achievement. These critics have assimilated the work of the past decade as they seek to find unity without ignoring the contradictions that Joyce built into the book. C. H. Peake, for example, argues that Joyce viewed human experience as "the product of interacting polar opposites" (p. 170) and that the structure of *Ulysses* directly reflects this view; Marilyn French discusses "a multitude of polarities throughout the novel, on every level" (p. 33); James Maddox speaks of "opposed ideas" versus an "essential identity" (p. 29). Suzette Henke places her study in a different relationship to past work; granting the well-known "innovative nature of Joyce's stylistic experiments," she sets out on a revisionist course as she emphasizes the "radical content of *Ulysses*" and "the revolutionary view of consciousness implicit in the novel" (p. 10).

All four studies rest firmly in the Budgen-Goldberg tradition of seeing *Ulysses* as a novel concerned primarily with representative human beings. Some recent studies (my own included) have tried to show how Joyce moved away from and ultimately discarded the concept of "character" and hence how *Ulysses* goes beyond the genre of the novel. These four critics do not confront this argument directly, but all implicitly counter it by assuming that the nonnovelistic elements—the elaborate surfaces, the mythic correspondences, the increasing self-reflexiveness—can be subsumed into a novelistic framework. The authors present their cases with great subtlety and insight; what I find most valuable (and slightly surprising) is their success in incorporating a great deal of Joyce's book into their different critical frameworks without any apparent discomfort. (In contrast, S. L. Goldberg had to reject at least seven of *Ulysses*'s eighteen episodes as insufficiently uniting form and content.) If I cannot quite let go of the conviction that an approach that holds *Ulysses* within the realm of the novel is incomplete, I am convinced by these studies that such an approach can carry us a great way toward an understanding of Joyce's book.

C. H. Peake's *James Joyce: The Citizen and the Artist* is the most basic study in the group and also the one comprehensive treatment of Joyce's career. Peake begins with discussions of *Dubliners* and *A Portrait of the Artist as a Young Man* that, besides offering solid, concise analyses of the two early works, serve to set up the citizen-artist dualism. *Dubliners* is the book of the citizen and *Portrait* the book of the artist, while *Ulysses* sets the two elements in opposition and finally links them. Peake devotes two-thirds of his book to *Ulysses*; he offers a quick plot summary, a discussion of the relation to the *Odyssey*, a column-by-column discussion of Joyce's notorious schema, an episode-by-episode treatment of *Ulysses*, and a concluding chapter on Joyce's moral vision.

Such an approach smacks of a "reader's guide," and Peake describes his intended audience as "interested readers rather than specialists" (p. vii). But his further claim that his book "has new emphases, views and interpretations of interest to the specialist" is also justified. His original contribution develops from his application of the citizen-artist pattern, which he uses to demonstrate that the profound dualities that critics have always argued about or attempted to synthesize (heroic/mock-heroic, sympathy/irony, comedy/satire, "yes"/"no") are basic to Joyce's conception of humanity and hence infuse every level of *Ulysses*. Joyce believed that human beings are "composed not of a set of characteristics, but of interacting forces" (p. 77) or "coexisting opposites" (p. 336)—terms often applied to *Ulysses* itself—and that human life is "the product of interacting polar opposites" (p. 170). Bloom is primarily the "citizen" and Stephen the "artist," though each man's character contains elements from the other type, and the movement toward their intersection is the "organic" principle of *Ulysses*, both thematically and structurally (p. 119). The kaleidoscope of styles with their increasing artificiality and the anticlimactic meeting and separation of Bloom and Stephen reflect Joyce's view of opposing forces behind human life, and they function (as Peake insists they must) as necessary forms for Joyce's vision.

Peake's basic dualism is neither original nor profound, and it does not operate as consistently in *Ulysses* as he would have it. But it provides a useful entry into Joyce's world, most useful because it allows Peake to move easily from the technical and stylistic to the thematic and realistic, since it makes the frequent clashes between style and content an integral part of the subject.

Both in argument and method, Peake is a model of common sense, with all attendant strengths and weaknesses. He risks little, and his insights and readings are less provocative than those in the other three books. On the other hand, his approach manages to assimilate much of *Ulysses*, and that is a major accomplishment. Peake's most valuable trait is his unwavering inquisitiveness and curiosity. He begins his discussion of each of Joyce's works exactly where, after fifty years of argument and analysis, one would think no critic would dare start: with Joyce's own descriptions of his intentions in the letters about *Dubliners*, Stephen's aesthetic theory in *Portrait*, and most startling of all, the schema for *Ulysses*. Because Peake refuses to gloss over complexities or to take any interpretation for granted, he can redirect our attention to Joyce's words in the letters and schemas and in the texts.

The Citizen and the Artist is not dramatically new; in fact, in many ways it is quite old-fashioned. But it is a fine attempt to demonstrate that Joyce's styles and structures are embodiments of his themes and visions. It is somewhat too long, and the discussions of individual *Ulysses* episodes are not always worth the length. But it is a solid book and an especially useful one for students looking for a first book on Joyce.

Like C. H. Peake, Marilyn French sees in *Ulysses* a world of opposing forces. Peake locates these forces within individuals and between people within societies, but French goes farther. In *The Book as World* she quotes Joyce's remark that "life is suspended in doubt like the world in the void";[5] she argues that the void lies in the external world behind all conflicting forces, and in *Ulysses* behind the many styles of an episode like "Oxen of the Sun" and of the book itself (p. 17). A critic perceiving only satire and irony, like Ezra Pound or Hugh Kenner in *Dublin's Joyce*, would stop here, but French continues: "Although *Ulysses* reveals the void in all its manifestations, . . . it simultaneously builds a bridge across or founds a world upon that void" (p. 36). For the characters, especially for Bloom, the bridge is *caritas*, freely offered love; for the reader, it is the recognition of the positive values in Bloom and the other characters and ultimately the ability "to extend *caritas* to Bloom, to allow him and the other characters to breathe and to live in their own space, without judging them. If we, the readers, do this, we are participating, whether or not we are conscious of it, in the morality advanced in the novel" (p. 53). This participation in the book's moral life (rather than in the narrative life, as is usually emphasized) constitutes a journey for the reader, who, French insists, is the modern Odysseus. With this argument that the reader is the true hero of *Ulysses*, French offers the first of several attempts we will see to free a definition of heroism from the straitjacket of the Bloom-Odysseus parallels and to show this heroism in operation within a novelistic framework in *Ulysses*.

French argues that we seek certitude to counter what the questioner in "Ithaca" calls the "void incertitude,"[6] but instead we constantly find a truth far less comforting (pp. 17, 184). The truth is the void, the incertitude behind all the details in *Ulysses*'s relativistic world. As *Ulysses* progresses from a basic style emphasizing the characters to an increasingly larger scope encompassing the city, the world, and the universe, the void is revealed in one manifestation after another. So the interpolated passages in "Wandering Rocks" show the "gap in human relations" (p. 123), and the overture to "Sirens" reveals "the arbitrariness of language, the void at its core" (p. 128). To counter the incertitude, the reader must act. As we watch the characters struggle to survive in a hostile world ("The anatomy of the human condition that appears in *Ulysses* shows it to be a miserable trapped state" [p. 39]) and face a series of hostile narrators (French regularly refers to the narrator as a "*dio boia*"), we actively resist the narrators and support the most positive value in the book, the characters' basic humanity. "The dehumanizing techniques . . . force the reader to reject those techniques and to assert with increasing intensity the humanity that is being so battered and choked" (p. 208). This assertion—"We affirm, whether we intend to or not, human value in the very midst of nihilism" (p. 232)—is the ultimate act of heroism; in recognizing Bloom's moral stature, we share in it. Thus, French deals with the stylistically elaborate episodes in the second half of *Ulysses* by insisting that we react against them, affirming what the words on the page seek to deny, Bloom's humanity.

French sets up her argument and then traces it through each episode. Many of the analyses are less impressive in their details than in the overview, and they suffer somewhat from repetition as French reminds us often of the void and incertitude. But French is convincing where it matters most, at the beginning and end. (See especially her discussion of "Ithaca," where she emphasizes Bloom's and Stephen's limited triumphs on the level of the plot, their greater triumphs on the moral level, and the relationship between the two.) Like Peake, though much more boldly, French has developed a unified approach to *Ulysses* that can deal with the stylistic extravagances while holding firmly to a novelistic reading. She offers a convincing and humane reading of *Ulysses*, one that asserts as equally important the humanity of the characters and the reader.

Suzette Henke would fully agree with Marilyn French's statement that Joyce's characters are trapped, and she too sees a recognition of this condition as the beginning of heroism. She outlines her argument in the opening pages of *Joyce's Moraculous Sindbook*: "In full recognition of the limitations that bind his life, [Bloom] manifests charity, sympathy, and the wisdom of self-control. He creates hope out of despair and presents the twentieth century with a model of contemporary heroism" (p. 7). For French, heroism involves a bridge of *caritas* over an all-encompassing void; for Henke, it is a recognition of and willed escape from an all-encompassing prison. For both critics, Joyce forces the reader to participate in the process and to share in the heroism.

Henke sees *Ulysses* as a "book as world," but it is the mental world, consciousness, that is Joyce's main concern. She claims allegiance to the methods of phenomenological criticism and seeks to analyze not only the consciousness of the characters but also that of the "implied" or "incarnate" author (p. 11) and the reader experiencing the work.

In Henke's reading, Joyce's characters, trapped by various internal and external forces, free themselves by acts of will; they "move from a world of psychological enclosure to an existential liberation of consciousness" (p. 12). So, in the impressive opening discussion of "Telemachus," Henke sets up Stephen's initial condition through her repetition of words like *alienated, bound, engulfed, immersed*. Crucial for Stephen is the active decision to challenge and transcend the nets that bind him (his old *Portrait* proclamation, now directed inward): "In a moment of self-determination, he can choose his own existence and break free of the paralyzed environment that threatens to destroy him" (p. 42). In "Proteus" he takes a crucial step by going beyond the intellect into the more disturbing areas of the subconscious, and in "Scylla and Charybdis" he presents a Shakespeare who creates art as "a constant attempt to gain control over psychological and emotional turbulence" (p. 70). The climax occurs in "Circe," where, smashing the chandelier after the vision of his mother, he "attempts to annihilate history by making it a controllable object of personal consciousness" (p. 200). As a result, his misunderstood words to Private Carr, "In here it is I must kill the priest and the king," take on added resonance as a willful assertion of freedom.[7]

For Bloom, the situation is different, since the causes of his dilemma are more direct and his approaches to them less intellectual and abstract: "With little erudition and with less philosophical training, he intuitively searches for a humane solution to the dilemma of personal freedom" (p. 75). Moving through the day, Bloom faces and deals with (and so frees himself from) his past and the social and emotional burdens of the present. He meets the dilemmas one at a time: the funeral involves the inevitability of personal annihilation and the demons of his own past; the encounter with Gerty MacDowell and his masturbation free him from sexual frustration and erotic obsession; and the apparition of Rudy at the end of "Circe" releases him "from the neurosis of guilt and impotence he has so long associated with the child" (p. 202). Finally, at the end of "Ithaca," in his mental slaying of the suitors, Bloom can will the crucial act: "Only by transcending the desire for possession can human beings get beyond the ever-present threat of amorous betrayal. Hence Shakespeare's mature wisdom in 'Scylla and Charybdis,' Richard Rowan's acceptance of conjugal ambiguity in *Exiles*, and Leopold Bloom's cosmic equanimity in 'Ithaca.' By conquering the 'pain of loss,' Joyce's cuckold achieves the freedom of non-possession" (p. 228). Henke sums up the process and Joyce's radical redefinition of heroism: "Each individual has within himself . . . the 'moraculous' potential of the psyche to absorb, transcend, and recreate experience through the artistic capaciousness of the intellectual imagination. The human mind can shatter the nightmare of history and challenge the specters of psychological enclosure" (p. 205).

Like Peake and French, Suzette Henke argues that a consistent view of human nature and heroism unifies the entire novel. She has isolated a specific process that defines heroism, and not all parts of *Ulysses* reveal the process equally well. But there are many places in *Joyce's Moraculous Sindbook* where the critical method and Joyce's text converge in truly illuminating ways, and Henke wisely directs most of her attention to these sections. Her discussions of the "Telemachia," "Hades," "Nausicaa," and "Ithaca," and of Molly as an abstraction rather than a realistic character are impressive. If *Ulysses* embodies the modern novel's change from external to internal action and from event to consciousness, we are unlikely to receive a stronger case for the possibilities for heroism inherent in the new emphases than Henke has provided.

The title of the fourth study, James H. Maddox's *Joyce's Ulysses and the Assault upon Character*, suggests the connection between this book and the other three. Like Marilyn French, Maddox discerns a pattern of contradictory impulses covering an unnamed center. But, whereas French constantly refers to this center as the void, Maddox talks less specifically about Joyce's technique of "implying and evoking but never naming the center" (p. 12). The result is an "art of surround and periphery" (p. 12), a "collocation of details which point toward an unnamable center" (p. 15).

Maddox finds this technique throughout *Ulysses*, in small details, methods of characterization, and the structure of the book as a whole. Since the book lacks a namable center, he argues that "character is the closest thing to a constant" (p. 16), and it is from this statement that the analysis proceeds. Not surprisingly, with his interest in character, Maddox claims strongest allegiance to S. L. Goldberg; despite limitations (more, I think, of overview than of detailed analysis), Maddox joins with C. H. Peake to reveal Goldberg's continuing power to inspire strong, valuable interpretative studies of *Ulysses*.

Like Suzette Henke, Maddox sees both Bloom and Stephen in a struggle. For Maddox, each character tries in his own way to hold to a continuous center despite a set of peripheral details that constantly change. In his discussion of Stephen, he refers to different though related dualisms to suggest the nature of the struggle; these include change/stability, multiplicity/unity, temporal changes/constant self, poses/essential self, phenomena/order. Each of the first three episodes offers a variation on the pattern, a struggle that Stephen recognizes intellectually. Bloom faces similar, though not the same, conditions, and his recognition of and reaction to them is less defined, more intuitive. Maddox's terms here include changes/ fixed points and phenomenal change/enduring self. Several of *Ulysses*'s key concepts, such as Proteus, metempsychosis and parallax, nicely support Maddox's periphery/center model.

In contrast to Marilyn French (and Hugh Kenner to come), for Maddox there is indeed something in the center. "Joyce tries the mettle of his characters by testing their ability to hold together opposed ideas without losing their sense of an essential identity" (p. 29). That such an identity exists, along with a reality at the center in the world and in *Ulysses*, is essential to Maddox's argument, for it is this essential identity that is the target of the "assault" of his title. *Ulysses*, he says, "assaults, flays, claws at Bloom in an attempt to know him, to pin him wriggling to the wall—or, if it cannot do that, at least to humiliate him" (p. 203). The characters' resistance to the assault is itself the mark of their heroism, though it is a far less triumphant heroism than Henke attributes to the characters or French to the reader. For Maddox, "thus does Bloom drift off to sleep, his mind having categorized and (at least for today) rendered neutral the unhappiness of his own existence" (p. 200); this represents "the logical and conservative statement of a man satisfied only to have survived" (p. 201).

As in the readings we have already observed, Maddox argues that the reader actively opposes the narrator who comes to dominate *Ulysses*. The process he outlines is less radical than French's or Henke's, but it is parallel nevertheless: "Style and narrative perspective gradually diminish the individual importance of character in *Ulysses*, but there is an underground current—the reader's own interest—running counter to this diminishment" (p. 17). The reader's continuing interest in character pervades Maddox's vocabulary, since for him character provides not only a constant in *Ulysses* but a standard. Thus, he refers to violations of the limits of realistic characterization in "Circe" as "psychological seepage" (p. 137), while the stylistic developments in the late episodes are "bizarre stylistic mutants" (p. 93). Maddox's devotion to character leads him to reorganize the episodes (he discusses them all but in a thematic sequence), a technique that allows him to concentrate on the characters but to de-emphasize the styles. For example, by linking "Lestrygonians," "Sirens," and "Nausicaa," he discovers intriguing and valid similarities in Bloom in the three episodes, but he does this by nearly ignoring the diverse methods of presentation. A conventional arrangement might have been more successful, since we might then have followed the process of narrative assault through the course of *Ulysses*.

Maddox's accounts of the individual episodes, even those where he seems to ignore or evade the problems raised by the styles and techniques, are fresh and full of insights, always gracefully expressed. Like the other critics, Maddox is especially strong in his treatment of the first six episodes, which he discusses in sequence, and the end. (See also his analysis of "Oxen of the Sun.") If the conceptual framework is limiting, the individual analyses are more than sufficiently rewarding to produce a valuable study.

We are thus offered four ways of seeking Joyce's meaning in *Ulysses* through his characters. C. H. Peake isolates a citizen/artist polarity and shows how, first embodied separately in Stephen and Bloom and then in their meeting, it serves as a basic and essential link between content and form. The other three critics argue that we actively resist the implications of the form and style to discover the characters' heroism. For Marilyn French, we extend *caritas* to fallible characters to construct a bridge over the void; for Suzette Henke, we recognize and share in the triumphant escape from traps and prisons that the characters will and achieve; for James Maddox, we hold to the characters as they struggle to maintain their sense of identity against assaults by an array of external forces. In some ways these views represent variations on a common approach; in other ways they are unique and incompatible with each other. Together they offer a rich, provocative set of approaches to *Ulysses* as a novel.

The four remaining books are too diverse to be grouped together. John Henry Raleigh's *Chronicle of Leopold and Molly Bloom* is yet another character-based study; in fact, it represents one extreme limit of the approach. Forty years ago Frank Budgen offered a brief reconstructed "biography" of

Leopold Bloom, which he introduced by noting that "if any ingenious writer liked to change the mode of narration adopted by Joyce in *Ulysses* and turn his book into a Bloom saga in many volumes with an eventual omnibus, the material for that exercise is to hand" in *Ulysses* itself.[8] Raleigh has responded to such a challenge, though instead of a saga he has produced a one-volume, year-by-year account of the Blooms' lives. He offers a brief list of eighteenth- and nineteenth-century events in their families, the Chronicle itself from 1865 to 16 June 1904, and summary accounts of "Sixteen Years of Marriage for the Blooms," "The Immediate Future for the Blooms," and "Future Possibilities, Intentions, and Fantasies." A prefatory section discusses the characters' genealogies, and appendixes list Bloom's addresses and jobs.

Such a project—to exhume "the chronologies of the lives of the Blooms which Joyce had scattered—and thus in a sense buried—throughout *Ulysses*" (p. 1)—necessarily ignores stylistic and technical matters as it tries to illuminate previously unnoticed facts in the text's naturalistic layer. Raleigh presents much of his evidence by quoting the Blooms, usually Bloom's interior monologues and Molly in "Penelope," though there is also much from "Circe." Typical entries are of two kinds: a short description of an event followed by a substantial quotation from *Ulysses* (often with an editorial note placing the passage in context), or a gathering of attitudes, statements, and other information regarding a single topic, such as Molly's father, Major Brian Tweedy. The first, more mechanical kind of entry represents the core of the Chronicle. Readers experienced with *Ulysses* have already reorganized much of Joyce's material in some folder in their mental *Ulysses* file, though, of course, not always accurately (Raleigh's efforts will surely help to reduce subsequent factual errors) and certainly not as systematically as in the Chronicle. The second type of entry is more flexible because it deals less with facts than with speculations and tentative conclusions that can be drawn from the incomplete evidence Joyce has provided. Unfortunately, the results are not always illuminating.

Raleigh makes several valid claims for his book's usefulness.

He wants to offer evidence to answer questions of fact about the Blooms' lives that have plagued readers of *Ulysses* and to highlight "the immense and detailed naturalistic base upon which *Ulysses* is constructed" (p. 6). He has accomplished both of these goals admirably. His most important purpose, he says, is to show that "Bloom takes on new dimensions when viewed chronologically" (p. 7), and his rearrangement certainly proves that the Bloom we usually talk about is only the last of six Blooms. This discovery adds a permanent new perspective on Bloom and in itself provides a strong reason to read the Chronicle. Finally, Raleigh's attempt to order Molly's thoughts, and a chronological order can work as well as any, sheds important new light on the contents of her monologue and her character.

Despite these achieved aims, though, Raleigh's book is in many ways an unsatisfactory, even annoying, production. If the compiler had limited himself to brief summaries of information and page references to *Ulysses*, the Chronicle might have been a neat, compact reference tool of 100 to 150 pages. But Raleigh or his publisher had loftier aims in mind. So the basic facts are buttressed with long quotations, and usually with editorial interpolations that fill in the context and seek to make the Chronicle resemble a self-contained narrative. We repeatedly find information that we already know or can easily look up. For example, Raleigh cites a passage from "Hades" in this way: "Mine [his own grave plot which he has purchased] over there toward Finglas, the plot I bought. Mamma poor mamma, and little Rudy [his dead son]."[9] And he offers standard historical facts about such people and events as Parnell, the Invincibles, and the Gold Cup Race, mostly cited from the readily available accounts in Weldon Thornton's *Allusions in Ulysses* and Don Gifford and Robert Seidman's *Notes for Joyce*.[10] Raleigh provides all this information because he wants the book to serve as a guide for newcomers to *Ulysses*, a "skeleton key" to the events of the Blooms' lives rather than to *Ulysses*'s page-by-page developments. This aim leads to his most inflated claims for the book: "It is meant to serve as an introduction to Joyce for the uninitiated who are, understandably, intimidated by the bulk and complexity of *Ulysses* in toto" (p. 5); "the Chronicle is no substitute for the novel, merely an introduction" (p. 10). Few readers confused by *Ulysses* itself will feel reassured by an artificial reconstruction of the book's factual information.

Raleigh's subtitle, Ulysses *as Narrative*, clearly announces his high intentions. Yet Raleigh never discusses "*Ulysses* as narrative"; even though his subject is a book that sets out to upset traditional notions of what narrative had to be, he assumes that the facts of the Blooms' lives constitute the narrative. He locates his book within a spectrum of previous criticism, but his view is troublesome; he says that "ever since [*Ulysses*'s] publication . . . it has been its Blakean or symbolic side that has attracted the attention or concern of both readers and critics," and he claims that he is redirecting us to "the Defoe-esque or narrative side" (p. 6). A critic might have talked like this in the 1950s; to do so in 1977 makes no sense. Finally, in an apology the ironies of which Raleigh seems to miss, he admits that his Chronicle "distorts the meaning of the novel" (p. 10). He makes the statement, however, only because Molly's affirmation from the end of *Ulysses* must appear near the beginning of the Chronicle. That the distortion is of a far more profound kind is a possibility he chooses not to pursue. Of course, no one would care about the distortions inevitable in such a project did the compiler not introduce the subject only to evade it.

There are a few problems in the details themselves. Raleigh's project necessarily entails a nearly exclusive concern with the content of the passages he cites, but it also requires careful discrimination between passages that can be trusted and those that cannot. Too often Raleigh relies on information from episodes where the style casts doubt on the literal accuracy of the content; this is especially true of "Circe." In general, Raleigh is too willing to trust surface statements and to assume that, when the words cannot be trusted, they hide the true novel that Joyce let slip away. (He says that the style of "Eumaeus" "is so cunningly wrought as almost to defy any attempt to set forth the real meaning of its serpentine and booby-trap laden sentences in any other kind of prose conveyance than that of the original" [p. 111].) And, if Raleigh trusts Joyce too much, he becomes blinded by his own evidence as well, as in his attempts to show that Joyce placed a special emphasis on the month of May by demonstrating that sixteen references are more than the seventeen he notes for June (pp. 97–98).

Raleigh's reconstruction of the events of Bloom's and Molly's lives, even if it does not reproduce the "narrative" of *Ulysses*, will be of lasting value. His book could have been a major addition to the group of reference works for *Ulysses*; as it is, it reads like a reference work looking enviously over its shoulder at nearby critical studies.

Hugh Kenner's *Joyce's Voices* is in many ways diametrically opposed to the five studies considered thus far. Suzette Henke, James Maddox, and John Henry Raleigh all discover *Ulysses*'s meaning in its characters and the events of their external and internal lives. Marilyn French argues that, because we alone can recognize Joyce's moral vision, *Ulysses* happens to us and not to the characters. Kenner, too, implies that the book happens to us, but because all is surface, words on a page rather than characters and events. French's distinction between certitude, which Joyce refuses to give us, and the less comforting truth he does offer, does not go far enough for Kenner. He says, "We may suppose that there is after all a 'truth' recoverable from beneath all these surfaces, a truth the writer could put straightforwardly if he wanted to. There is not" (p. 91).

Kenner's book originated as a lecture series called "Objectivity and After." He begins by recalling the common assumption, which he traces back to T. S. Eliot, that *Ulysses* at first holds to the principles of objectivity that form the basis of the novel as written by Defoe, Swift, and Flaubert. (Eliot, Kenner says, argues that Joyce's use of the Homeric myth forms "a grid on which to locate contemporary particulars, observed with an objectivist's eye" [p. 2].) He defines objectivity as "the outer world conceived as a sequence of reports to someone's senses, and a sequence occurring in irreversible time" (p. 4); we are told only what the observer could have experienced as the author attempts to "evade rhetoric and make the facts effect their own declaration" (p. 14). Yet even where it appears most objective, Joyce's narration sounds slightly like a character it is describing. Kenner quotes passages of narration from "The Dead" and *A Portrait of the Artist as a Young Man*: "Lily, the caretaker's daughter, was literally run off her feet"; "Every morning, therefore, Uncle Charles repaired to his outhouse but not before he had greased and brushed scrupulously his back hair and brushed and put on his tall hat."[11] Such statements are not as objective as they might appear, since "the normally neutral narrative vocabulary" is "pervaded by a little cloud of idioms which a character might use if he was managing the narrative" (p. 17); examples are "literally," "repaired," and "scrupulously." Kenner finds that this practice is directed by what he calls the Uncle Charles Principle, a term that has already entered the Joycean critical vocabulary. The principle entails "writing about someone much as that someone would choose to be written about" (p. 21); the broad implication is that "the narrative idiom need not be the narrator's" (p. 18).

From its opening pages, Kenner argues, *Ulysses* shows this principle in action. In "Telemachus," for example, the narration is tinged with the idioms and vocabulary of either Stephen or Mulligan, whoever happens to be nearer. These intrusions on an ostensibly objective narrative technique, at first subtle, become increasingly blatant. At the beginning Joyce divides duties between two narrators, "one voice perhaps better informed about stage management, the other a more accomplished lyrical technician" (p. 67); the first is responsible for the external world, the other for the internal. Eventually, the external narrator takes over more and more, and Kenner's vocabulary echoes French's and Henke's in his description of this narrator as ironic, malicious, insolent, usurping.

Kenner resembles French and Maddox in his emphasis on the multiple surfaces produced by Joyce's narrative techniques, with his Uncle Charles Principle serving as a reminder that we should look for variations even in the relatively homogeneous early episodes. However, Kenner finds no center that exists unnamed and no bridge to be built; for him the meaning is in the void. In the Dublin Joyce knew, he says, there existed "a nearly perfect Pyrrhonism: . . . no one at the bottom knows what he is talking about because there is nothing to know except the talk" (p. 53). For Kenner the aesthetic corollary in *Ulysses* lies in the fact that "when statements can have no substance they can only have style" (p. 55). *Ulysses* is all style; the substance has been imposed on it by the critics, commencing with the studies that Joyce himself encouraged Valery Larbaud, Frank Budgen, and Stuart Gilbert to write.

Kenner believes that, as he worked on *Ulysses*, Joyce came to realize that " 'outer' and 'inner' are artifacts alike, artifacts of language" (p. 89), and, in language's many embodiments, "memory is tricky, notation can be ambiguous, styles are provisional systems of consistency" (p. 88). So there can be no truth behind the surfaces, whether the surfaces represent the external world or the world of Bloom's thoughts, because ultimately the words refer only back to themselves. With objectivity eliminated in this way, Joyce can then introduce mythic parallels, since objectivity's adherence to verifiable sensual experiences precludes the introduction of correspondences and counterparts behind the characters' backs.

Twenty-two years separate *Dublin's Joyce*, Kenner's first book-length study of Joyce, from *Joyce's Voices*. The two works share Kenner's close attention to Joyce's words and to the ironies he sees thoughout *Ulysses*. Beyond this similarity Kenner has moved far away from his earlier view of Joyce as the great nay-sayer, and he has become a delight to read, not least because of his own obvious pleasure in reading and talking about Joyce and in playing Joyce's narrative, structural, and verbal games. In *Dublin's Joyce* he insisted too much on Bloom's descent from Bouvard and Pécuchet; in *Joyce's Voices*, after dismissing Bloom as an objective observer, Kenner is perhaps too willing to let him disappear into Joyce's words. But Kenner is one of the few critics who consistently causes us to see Joyce's words anew, and for this reason alone we should be grateful for *Joyce's Voices*.

Like so many of the other critics, Robert Martin Adams presents a *Ulysses* of many sides and angles, an "arrangement of emerging and retreating images" (p. xiii). But Adams's viewpoint is special. In *Afterjoyce* he sets out to study the impact and influence *Ulysses* has had on subsequent fiction, and he presents the sides and angles as perceived by the later writers who were affected by Joyce's work. Adams has tackled an immensely difficult project; on the one hand, he risks overemphasizing the importance of *Ulysses*, and on the other, even though *Ulysses* links all the discussions, he can never let the book come fully into focus, since it never did for the other writers who used only what they saw or wanted to see.

Working from the assumption that *Ulysses* "is infinitely more complex now than it was in 1922" (p. xiii), Adams tries to recreate the impact *Ulysses* had on its first readers. Doing so entails rehearsing some well-known facts about Dublin in the early twentieth century, the state of fiction at the time, and Joyce's own life because all these topics concerned his earliest readers. Adams discusses the relative lack of response to *Dubliners* when it appeared, the attention given to the prose style of *A Portrait of the Artist as a Young Man*, and, in much greater detail, the early reactions to *Ulysses* and *Finnegans Wake*. Then he considers three "devices-patterns-structures" (p. 36) in *Ulysses* that have been used by other writers: (1) paradigms and grids. He distinguishes between a paradigm ("a foreknown outline-image of a main plot-configuration") and a grid ("a formal configuration applied to a basic narrative but not integrally or expressively connected with it" [pp. 44, 45]). An example of the first for Joyce is Homer; of the second, Vico. Later users of such devices include John Updike, Iris Murdoch, and Vladimir Nabokov. (2) Surfaces, holes, blurs, smears—"devices for making surfaces as such the objects of deliberate consciousness" (p. 51). Adams sees two trends in Joyce's work: "the rejection of representation in favor of overt artifice" and "the rejection of artifice in favor of vision" (p. 56). Later examples include Beckett, Robbe-Grillet, and Nabokov. (3) Language, especially "artfully composed prose, . . . writing that seems aimed at rousing admiration for itself rather than attracting sympathy to the characters or opening a clear window on a scene" (p. 62). Joyce influenced later writers most dramatically through his precision and economy, the widened range of his fictional language, and the disintegration of language.

Following this topical chapter, Adams looks at Woolf and Faulkner, Beckett, Carlo Emilio Gadda, Alfred Döblin and Hermann Broch, Nabokov, and such contemporary writers as Lawrence Durrell, Anthony Burgess, Thomas Pynchon, José Lazama Lima, John Barth, Flann O'Brien, and Jorge Luis Borges. His one major omission is the French New Novelists, whom he chooses not to treat because Joyce's influence on them has already been considered in Vivian Mercier's *The New Novel*.[12]

With each of these writers Adams faces a double problem, since he must consider only the narrow part of *Ulysses* that each writer used and the narrow part of each writer's work influenced by Joyce. Such problems are not entirely surmountable in a book aimed at a general readership, as this one is, but Adams does quite well. There is too much plot summary (even if we allow for the need to summarize the novels unknown to English-speaking readers), and the book will not fully please specialists on any of the novelists, including Joyce. However, Adams clearly recognizes these problems, and he has organized his study to deal with them. For one thing, he adopts a loose and informal style and format. The book eschews the appearance of formal scholarship; there are no footnotes, for example, and Adams argues his cases through readings of the novels rather than through bibliographical research. The tone suggests an inquiry, as Adams tries to show how influence works and how it can be discussed. He is flexible enough to redefine "influence" as he moves along. In this way the role of *Ulysses* unfolds and evolves as *Afterjoyce* proceeds.

Adams begins with an open mind: "Let the word 'influence' mean whatever its various appearances will justify" (p. xii). Early on he rephrases this directive into questions—"Joyce lives. . . . Where? and How?" (p. 35). Along the way the term takes on more precise connotations. Woolf represents "one author making use of fictional dimensions first occupied by another" (p. 77); Faulkner's *The Sound and the Fury* is an example of "Joyce's liberating effect on an indigenous and independent inspiration" (p. 88); Beckett is "the chief post-

Joycean novelist to throw away his predecessor's machinery and concentrate on the attempt at vision" (p. 112); Broch was not influenced by Joyce but links up with him "in the hazier fields of affinity" (p. 145); Durrell "is a superior entertainer, who has found various elements of Joyce's composition useful in putting together his kaleidoscope" (p. 166); and, in the last and perhaps most useful formulation, José Lezama Lima's *Paradiso* is one of "the books that have fulfilled and extended lines that Joyce first began to trace" (p. 184).

These statements are all general, and some of them border on the obvious, but they represent both the Protean nature of the topic and the difficulty of pinning down one book's influence on several writers (rather than the more common problem of studying the cluster of influences on one writer). Adams has succeeded to a large extent in painting a sketch (he has not tried for more) of modern fiction as seen from one very precise viewpoint, the example and presence of *Ulysses*.

One more comment about the format: Adams's informal style and structure might appear to be products of hasty writing and production, but I think they ultimately work far better for such a project than would a weightier, more scholarly approach. However, for a book with such a wide range of reference, much of it not systematically arranged, I would have appreciated a bibliography of primary and selected secondary materials, a list of editions cited (page numbers are supplied but not editions), and an index. Informality has its limits.

Finally, in a period during which so many studies of Joyce have appeared, it is fitting that we have also been given a new bibliography of criticism. The revised and enlarged second edition of Robert Deming's *Bibliography of James Joyce Studies* lists secondary materials that were published through the end of 1973. The first edition, which went through the end of 1961, contained over 1,400 entries (there are 770 pre-1961 entries added to the new edition); the second edition notes 5,885. Everything about the volume suggests the quantity of materials, from the price ($45.00) to the oversized, double-column format.

Deming organizes the studies into several categories. Section

I — Bibliographical, Biographical, and General Treatments — includes milieu studies; studies of provenience, reputation, and influence; comprehensive treatments of Joyce's works; reviews; dissertations; and musical settings, theatrical productions, radio and television broadcasts, films, and recordings. Section II contains studies of the separate works, and an index to the entries closes the volume.

It is nearly impossible to review such an endeavor, except to welcome its existence, praise its comprehensiveness and general accuracy, and complain about its apparent shortcomings. Inevitably, I found errors in individual entries simply by glancing through the pages. Misspelled names (Archie Liss for Loss, John Middleton Murray for Murry, Mark Schechner for Shechner) made me worry, as did my difficulty in locating two classic studies that I expected to find with the reviews, Pound's "James Joyce et Pécuchet" and Eliot's "*Ulysses,* Order and Myth." (Deming lists the former under "*Ulysses:* Studies of Influence and Comparison" and the latter under "*Ulysses:* Studies of Technique and Structure.") Studies of the major works are subdivided; for *Ulysses* there are groupings according to individual episodes and general topics. But the choices for the latter are curious; for example, "Studies of Technique and Structure" and "Allusions" flank "*Ulysses* in Court: Censorship." There is also a problem in the cross-referencing of books and articles that belong in two or more categories. Deming provides such a service, but his lists are undigested alphabetical collections. A more topical arrangement would better serve the reader. And since there are no cross-references for the individual *Ulysses* episodes (unlike the valuable lists in the checklist of criticism that appeared in *Modern Fiction Studies* in 1969),[13] we must find our own way in all the items listed in the twenty-four-page section of general studies for *Ulysses* and the eighteen pages for general studies of Joyce's works. More sophisticated cross-referencing together with other improvements, would certainly have added work to an already Herculean task, but such efforts seem not too much to ask from a volume that simply by its existence becomes a standard reference tool and cannot be redone for at least another decade.

Although, of course, a bibliography exists for its entries, I must make a few comments about the brief preface included here. These four pages serve only to make a fairly simple, self-explanatory arrangement appear needlessly complicated. In explaining his divisions, Deming at times becomes virtually opaque (see "I. F Dissertations" [p. viii]) when the arrangement itself is perfectly straightforward. He includes a complicated coding system for his divisions that he uses throughout the preface and carries over into the table of contents, but after the reader has begun to learn the system, it does not appear in the bibliography itself (nor is its absence felt). Why introduce it at all? Errors are inevitable in a book of this kind, and so are some inconveniences, but Deming and the copyeditors at G. K. Hall should have done a better job on the mechanical details of the book. These criticisms aside, I, like most other Joyce scholars, will refer to the *Bibliography* frequently, and I expect to find it useful and solid. I wish it were better; I'm glad it is as good and comprehensive as it is.

The past few years have been exciting and stimulating times for Joyce studies. The proliferation documented in Deming's *Bibliography* is not disturbing when the quality turns out to be as high as in the studies considered here. If we have not yet caught up with Joyce our "contemporary," studies like these are taking us closer. After all, it is only his hundredth birthday that we will soon celebrate.

Notes

1. Ellmann, *James Joyce* (New York: Oxford Univ. Press, 1959), p. 1.

2. Budgen, *James Joyce and the Making of* Ulysses (1934; rpt. Bloomington: Indiana Univ. Press, 1960), p. 17; Gilbert, *James Joyce's* Ulysses: *A Study* (1930; rpt. New York: Vintage, 1952), pp. 8–9.

3. Examples of the mythic-symbolic approach: T. S. Eliot, "*Ulysses*, Order and Myth,"*The Dial*, 75 (November 1923), 480-83; Gilbert, *James Joyce's* Ulysses; William York Tindall, *A Reader's Guide to James Joyce* (New York: Noonday, 1959). Realistic-novelistic approach: Ezra Pound, "James Joyce et Pécuchet," *Mercure de France*, 156 (June 1922), 307-20; Budgen, *James Joyce and the Making of* Ulysses; S. L. Goldberg, *The Classical Temper: A Study of James Joyce's* Ulysses (London: Chatto and Windus, 1961); Stanley Sultan, *The Argument of* Ulysses (Columbus: Ohio State Univ. Press, 1964). Synthesis: Arnold Goldman, *The Joyce*

Paradox: Form and Freedom in His Fiction (London: Routledge and Kegan Paul, 1966); Peter K. Garrett, *Scene and Symbol from George Eliot to James Joyce: Studies in Changing Fictional Mode* (New Haven: Yale Univ. Press, 1969).

4. Benstock, *James Joyce: The Undiscover'd Country* (Dublin: Gill and Macmillan; New York: Barnes and Noble, 1977); Boyle, *James Joyce's Pauline Vision: A Catholic Exposition* (Carbondale and Edwardsville: Southern Illinois Univ. Press, 1978); Ellmann, *The Consciousness of Joyce* (New York: Oxford Univ. Press, 1977); Groden, Ulysses *in Progress* (Princeton: Princeton Univ. Press, 1977) and General Editor, *The James Joyce Archive*, 63 vols. (New York: Garland, 1977-1979); Herring, *Joyce's Notes and Early Drafts for* Ulysses: *Selections from the Buffalo Collection* (Charlottesville: Univ. Press of Virginia, 1977); Hodgart, *James Joyce: A Student's Guide* (Boston: Routledge and Kegan Paul, 1978); Sultan, Ulysses, The Waste Land, *and Modernism* (Port Washington, N.Y.: Kennikat, 1977).

5. French, p. 42; quoted from Ellmann, p. 568.

6. James Joyce, *Ulysses* (1922; New York: Random House, 1961), p. 734.

7. Joyce, *Ulysses*, p. 589.

8. Budgen, p. 270.

9. Raleigh, pp. 72-73; Joyce, *Ulysses*, p. 111.

10. Thornton, *Allusions in* Ulysses: *An Annotated List* (Chapel Hill: Univ. of North Carolina Press, 1968); Don Gifford with Robert J. Seidman, *Notes for Joyce: An Annotation of James Joyce's* Ulysses (New York: Dutton, 1974).

11. Kenner, pp. 15, 16-17; quoted from James Joyce, *Dubliners*, ed. Robert Scholes with Richard Ellmann (New York: Viking, 1968), p. 175; James Joyce, *A Portrait of the Artist as a Young Man*, ed. Chester G. Anderson and Richard Ellmann (New York: Viking, 1964), p. 60.

12. Mercier, *The New Novel from Quineau to Pinget* (New York: Farrar, Straus and Giroux, 1971).

13. Maurice Beebe, Phillip F. Herring, and Walton Litz, comps., "Criticism of James Joyce: A Selected Checklist," *Modern Fiction Studies*, 15 (1969), 105-82.

To Teach and to Please: The Literary Achievement of Nicholas Rowe

Richard H. Dammers

Annibel Jenkins. *Nicholas Rowe*. Boston: Twayne Publishers, 1977. 167 pp.

J. Douglas Canfield. *Nicholas Rowe and Christian Tragedy*. Gainesville: The University Presses of Florida, 1977. x, 212 pp.

With the appearance of these two long-awaited books evaluating the literary achievement of Nicholas Rowe, it is appropriate as this point to examine the state of Rowe criticism.[1] Other scholars, such as Richard Sherry and Alfred Hesse, have worked strenuously to evaluate Rowe's achievement and to unearth information about his life.[2] But as scholarly research on Rowe is completed and published, it becomes increasingly clear that even more remains to be done. These two books are a sign of things to come, of an interest in Rowe's achievement, an understanding of his plays, and a particular direction in Rowe scholarship. Canfield's and Jenkins's books are vastly different, the first proposing the thesis that all of Rowe's tragedies are dramatic theodicies, and then testing that thesis against each of Rowe's plays, and the second offering a general introduction to Rowe's literary achievement, his favorite themes, and his relation to historical events. Both Canfield and Jenkins approach the Rowe canon play by play, although Canfield does group the plays according to religious theme. Jenkins, by contrast, adopts a chronological format in order to facilitate the rather large bulk of historical information she places in tandem with Rowe's life and plays. It is curious that these two books rarely intersect. The authors discuss the various plays on separate levels, and they focus upon different concerns — though their disagreement about Calista's repentance in *The Fair Penitent* is a striking exception. Jenkins's book opens with a chapter entitled "Early Life and Times," which is a general treatment of Rowe's friendships with other authors, and moves to a brief biography together with a presentation of history primarily from George M. Trevelyan. In contrast, Canfield opens with a preface and an introduction, which pugnaciously announce his theses; his combative tone is unfortunate and unnecessary, for his theses and his presentation are sound and well reasoned. The remainder of Jenkins's work is divided chronologically play by play, whereas Canfield's is in two parts, "The Trial of the Innocent," which includes five of Rowe's seven tragedies, and "The Trial of the Sinner," on *The Fair Penitent* and *Jane Shore*.

The Ambitious Stepmother, says Canfield, is a dramatic theodicy, and his careful analysis of both the action of the play and Rowe's Epistle Dedicatory argues his theses convincingly. Canfield takes great pains—his thoroughness is appreciated—to remove a potential stumbling block, the deaths of Artaxerxes and Amestris, from a theodicean reading. Rowe appears concerned in his prefatory comments about objections to this apparent breach of poetic justice: "Some People, whose Judgment I ought to have a deference for, have told me, that they wish'd I had given the latter part of the Story quite another turn; that Artaxerxes and Amestris ought to have been preserv'd and made happy in the Conclusion of the Play."[3] Rowe's concern is not, however, that strict poetical justice has been frustrated in *The Ambitious Stepmother*, but rather that the deaths of his two leading characters achieve a greater affective response from his audience than could be realized by their happiness. In fact, Rowe claims that poetical justice is strictly observed "because the two principal Contrivers of Evil, the Statesman and Priest, are punish'd with death, and the Queen is depos'd."[4] But this claim ought not surprise the perspicacious reader; Canfield notes that "indeed, the usual practice in English Renaissance tragedy . . . provides a punishment for the wicked but not a temporal reward for the innocent" (p. 29). The solution to the apparent dilemma is of course clear and perhaps obvious: death, even

The Achievement of Nicholas Rowe

death for Amestris and Artaxerxes, brings with it a reward for the just, a Christian poetical justice. "So, in the Christian vision, death becomes—not an indictment of Providence—but rather a *proof* of Providence" (p. 36).[5]

Jenkins's chapter on *The Ambitious Stepmother* examines not its theme so much as its source, suggesting that the "initial situation . . . [is] suggested by the biblical account of the story of David and the succession of his son Solomon" (p. 34).[6] But Rowe's concern, like Dryden's in *Absalom and Achitophel*, is primarily topical and political, though religious as well; in fact, suggests Jenkins, "the topic of the problems of the succession . . . was of special interest to Rowe's audience in December, 1700" (p. 36).[7] As earlier, Jenkins is especially interested in historical parallels.

Surprisingly, neither book suggests Dryden's *Aureng-Zebe* as a source for Rowe's first play, although James Sutherland led Rowe scholars to Dryden years ago.[8] A juxtaposition of the characters of Rowe's play with the characters in *Aureng-Zebe* reveals numerous similarities and some interesting contrasts: Nourmahal to Artemisa, Indamora to Amestris, Melesinda to Cleone, Aureng-Zebe to Artaxerxes, Morat to Artaban, and perhaps even Arimant to Memnon. Rowe has reworked the plot considerably, but such similarities in convention and characterization should not go unnoticed. Rowe is drawing on literary wealth in the heroic drama which extends to the conventions of the French heroic romance, and this heritage is not insignificant.[9] Seeing Rowe's play against this background helps one perceive the tradition for Rowe's emphasis upon the female protagonist. Dryden's virtuous female characters were preceptresses instructing male protagonists in the maintaining and balancing of love and honor in a male-dominated world; by contrast, Rowe's preceptresses actively guide men to virtue through not only instruction but also imitation. The world of Rowe's plays is focused on women and marriage, not love and honor. No scholar can ignore the importance of marriage in any of Rowe's tragedies.

In her second chapter Jenkins suggests that "the emphasis [in Rowe's plays] has been shifted, at least slightly, toward the role of women and love and away from the men and valor" (p. 28). In fact, this important shift of focus to women and *marriage* is repeated in all seven of Rowe's tragedies. Frederick Gilliard has noted the reduced dimensions of Rowe's male protagonists, accompanied by larger roles for his female characters.[10] But the shift in focus also involves a departure from courtship, observed and analyzed with precision in Dryden's heroic drama, to marriage; Rowe's constant theme, in all of his tragedies, is the importance of marital responsibilities, the sacredness of the marriage bond, and the dangers of disregarding matrimonial vows.

Religion and marriage are inescapably woven together in Rowe's plays, and much of Rowe's homiletic lesson is directed at the young, as he displays the newly married couple struggling with fear, despair, and temptation, and threatened with the destruction of the marriage covenant. For example, see *The Ambitious Stepmother, The Royal Convert,* and *The Tragedy of the Lady Jane Gray.* To a greater or lesser degree, every virtuous female character in Rowe's plays acts as a religious preceptress, guiding her husband to a greater awareness of morality, to a resistance of despair, and to an unselfish devotion to religion.[11] But *Jane Shore* and *The Fair Penitent* concentrate on the destruction of the marriage vow through female infidelity. In *Jane Shore*, Rowe explicitly states his theme lest the obtuse miss its full import:

> Let those who view this sad example know
> What fate attends the broken marriage vow;
> And teach their children in succeeding times,
> No common vengeance waits upon these crimes.[12]

The vengeance is not from Shore, who forgives her. Jane must die for breaking the vow of marriage—a religious vow—and though she repents, suffers, and prays, she regains equanimity only after her death. Any lighter punishment would not be adequate retribution. Yet in this same play Rowe portrays the beauty of the marriage convenant, what *could* have been for Shore and his wife, as an ideal to be desired:

> My arms, my heart are open to receive thee,
> To bring thee back to thy forsaken home
> With tender joy. [p. 69, V.i., 325-27]

A more problematic presentation of infidelity and ruined marriage appears in *The Fair Penitent*. The penitence proposed in the title is doubted by some scholars, while others make an excellent case for a religious meditation concluding in repentance and forgiveness. Canfield and Jenkins are divided over this question, a problem resulting from Rowe's delineation of Calista's extremely complex and thereby fascinating character. Jenkins denies Calista true repentance, allowing her only regret, and she has company in this view.[13] But Canfield and others such as Lindley Wyman argue convincingly that Calista undergoes a true and deep repentance.[14] Canfield makes Calista's repentance central to his reading of *The Fair Penitent*, and he is right to do so: "The lesson of the scene is, as it has been throughout the play—and throughout Rowe's tragedies—trust in Providence. . . . Calista's final plea, 'Mercy, Heav'n,' becomes at once a mark of her complete repentance and of its efficacy. Calamitous as the ending of the play is, the final note is one of hope and reconciliation" (p. 137).

At the other end of the marital spectrum in *The Fair Penitent* are Lavinia and Horatio, who represent the ideal marriage.[15] Once again Rowe depicts the religious preceptress about her business, leading her husband to salvation. Lavinia exemplifies the innocent, forgiving, loving, and honest wife; she guides the hot-tempered and hasty Horatio to Christian forgiveness and charity. She has a sister in every Rowe play; especially close in temperament and religious devotion are Ethelinda in *The Royal Convert* and Jane in *The Tragedy of the Lady Jane Gray*.

Lady Jane Gray focuses not on sin, as is the case in *Jane Shore* and *The Fair Penitent*, but rather on virtue and sacrifice. The matter of Jane's stalwart self-sacrifice and unflagging virtue appears to have bothered later audiences and was consequently dropped from acted versions of the play.[16] In 1715, however, the succession was omnipresent to the English people, and, as Jenkins says, a play based on "a story wholly involved with church and state" and the Protestant Succession was bound to have especial interest (p. 121). "Rowe's purpose in his last play was two-fold, first, to create a patriotic Protestant character willing to die for her country and religion. To that extent his aim is propagandistic and topical and ceased to matter when the political conflict itself was over. Second, he created a genuinely admirable and pathetic heroine who is victimized by her family's ambition."[17] In the midst of personal and national catastrophe, Jane Gray maintains the role of religious preceptress as she reinforces Guilford's moral courage and prevents him from acceding to despair. "Guilford needs Lady Jane to 'teach' him what 'energy divine/Inspires' her with 'such unshaken courage.'"[18] Perhaps more than in the earlier plays, the love relationship here is subordinated to a higher theme, providential justice—both personal and national.[19] Canfield delineates the theodicean nature of Rowe's last play and thereby demonstrates that it is not a weak final effort but rather a capstone to a major career. Rowe sees precisely what he is about in *Lady Jane Gray*; through Canfield's careful and sound analyses modern readers are also better able to perceive the nature of this and all of Rowe's tragedies. Canfield's book should dispel the critical confusion of some readers who approach Rowe with affective responses gained from post-Romantic theory and without a requisite knowledge of religion and history.[20] Both Canfield's and Jenkins's books provide accessibility to Rowe and his tragedies and through him to drama of his age. With Sherry's editions and Hesse's biography under way in addition, Rowe scholarship is alive and well indeed.

Notes

1. For an evaluation of Rowe scholarship published during the first half of the present decade, see my essay "Recent Scholarship on Nicholas Rowe," *British Studies Monitor*, 5 (Summer 1975), 24–27.

2. See Richard Sherry's unpublished dissertation, "Nicholas Rowe's *The Tragedy of the Lady Jane Gray*: A Critical Edition with Introduction,' " Diss. Univ. of Illinois 1978. Sherry plans a complete edition of Rowe's plays. See also Alfred Hesse's superbly researched articles in *PBSA* and *Notes and Queries*. Hesse plans a biography of Nicholas Rowe.

3. Nicholas Rowe, *The Ambitious Stepmother*, 3d ed. (London: J. Darby, 1720; rpt. Westmead, England: Gregg International, 1971), p. v.

4. *Ibid.*, p. vi.

5. Claiming that the "metaphor of death as rest for the just is a traditional theodician answer to the problem of death," Canfield lists a number of works, among them *Gulliver's Travels*, without explanation. Such an assertion requires documentation. See Roland M. Frye, "Swift's Yahoos and the Christian Symbols for Sin," *Journal of the History of Ideas*, 15 (April 1954), 201-17.

6. She refers to "The *Bible*, 2 Samuel 11-12; I Kings 1:5-49" (p. 153).

7. Unfortunately, numerous printing errors mar Jenkins's book. No list of corrections is presented.

8. J. R. Sutherland, *Three Plays by Nicholas Rowe* (London: The Scholastic Press, 1929). Sutherland says that *The Ambitious Stepmother* "owes a good deal to the work of Rowe's immediate predecessors. The tricks and conventions of the heroic drama are all here—the heroic blasphemy, the apostrophe, the habit of flattering self-description, the air of conscious worth in the heroes, the lengthy simile, the oaths, the conflict between love and honour" (p. 22).

9. See Leslie Howard Martin, Jr., "Conventions of the French Romances in the Drama of John Dryden," Diss. Stanford Univ., 1967, pp. 195-203.

10. Frederick William Gilliard, Jr., "Nicholas Rowe's Men: A Playwright's Dramatic and Thematic Approaches to Characterization," Diss. Univ. of Utah, 1971, pp. iii-v, 1-154. Although his initial premise that Rowe's men are reduced in importance and stature is correct, Gilliard's analytic methods, his argument, and his conclusions are weak.

11. Canfield's discussion of Ethelinda's guidance of Aribert in *The Royal Convert* from despair to faith is admirable. See p. 84.

12. Nicholas Rowe, *The Tragedy of Jane Shore*, ed. Harry William Pedicord (Lincoln: Univ. of Nebraska Press, 1974), p. 73.

13. She quotes Samuel Johnson's *Life of Rowe*. Sophie Chantal Hart in her 1907 edition of *The Fair Penitent* and *Jane Shore* also denies Calista

"any inner regeneration" (p. xiv). Malcolm Goldstein avoids the problem in his introduction to *The Fair Penitent* ([Lincoln: Univ. of Nebraska Press, 1969], p. xviii).

14. See Lindley A. Wyman, "The Tradition of the Formal Meditation in Rowe's *The Fair Penitent*," *Philological Quarterly*, 42 (1963), 416. Wyman claims that "Rowe attempts to show the depth of contrition which his heroine feels." Rejecting Donald B. Clark's suggestion that Calista feels no remorse, Wyman claims that "Clark assumes that when Calista tosses away the book of instruction she also tosses away her repentance. She tosses away the book, however, not because she does not want to take her medicine, but because the medicine is not strong enough" (pp. 415-16). The book is a contritional prayer book, not the Bible. Frank Kearful, in "The Nature of Tragedy in Rowe's *The Fair Penitent*," *Papers on Language and Literature*, 2 (1966), says: "Calista's scorn for the artificial means of penitence forced upon her is, in fact, a measure of the depth of her interior realization of the state of her own soul" (p. 360).

15. See Canfield, p. 124, and Kearful, p. 359.

16. Sherry, Introduction, pp. cvii ff. Professor Sherry has very kindly allowed me to read his dissertation in its unpublished form.

17. Sherry, p. vii.

18. Canfield, p. 95.

19. *Ibid.*, p. 89: "Lady Jane is the suffering innocent par excellence, who never loses trust in Divine Providence and who acts with complete submission to God's will throughout. . . . And despite her suffering and that of England to follow her death, the play ends with the promise of ultimate providential justice for both Lady Jane and her country." Geoffrey Marshall comments in *Restoration Serious Drama* (Norman: Univ. of Oklahoma Press, 1975): "At the end of the seventeenth century, partly in response to Hobbesian psychology, the notion began to appear that self-sacrifice could be self-satisfying and that a man could best serve himself by serving others" (p. 61).

20. For example, see Eugene Hnatko, "The Failure of Eighteenth-Century Tragedy," *Studies in English Literature*, 11 (1971), 459-68. Hnatko says: "That eighteenth-century tragedy is poor theater is evident to all readers." Hnatko reveals his preconceived notions when he remarks that "it was with the Romantics that intelligent and sensitive understanding was born."

Mirror Tricks: An Interdisciplinary Exercise

Carl Ficken

William Mallard. *The Reflection of Theology in Literature: A Case Study in Theology and Culture.* San Antonio: Trinity University Press, 1977. xi, 271 pp.

Interdisciplinary study is exciting, but difficult. The excitement comes from the juxtaposition of two subject areas that on the surface appear unrelated. Such placement brings new insights, expands horizons, and occasionally offers correction to the limited vision of a single field; the historian or sociologist or literary critic or philosopher is allowed a brief escape from his or her specialization and may even dream, for a moment or two, of a Renaissance breadth of knowledge. The difficulty of interdisciplinary study, however, comes precisely as a result of specialization: the wealth of literature in each field seems to prevent most mere mortals from approaching omniscience in more than one discipline. When we get far away from the puddle of our own presumed expertise, we find ourselves treading very deep water indeed. Only a few giants in our time seem to have the breadth of vision and the intellectual scope to engage two different academic fields in a thorough, professional, scholarly fashion.

William Mallard's *The Reflection of Theology in Literature* provides an illustration of both the attractiveness and the arduousness of cross-disciplinary work. Trained at Duke University as a church historian specializing in the Medieval and Reformation periods, Mallard teaches in the Candler School of Theology, Emory University, and in the university's Graduate Institute of the Liberal Arts. His courses are in church history or the history of Christian thought, but he offers several graduate courses in the area of literature and theology. His previous writing has been in church history and contemporary theology.[1] He brings to this volume, then, a broad background in theology, a career in the church, and experience in the study of literature. The book itself is the fourth volume to be published in Trinity University's monograph series in religion and is a handsome publication, beautifully bound and clearly designed.

The purpose of the book is, at a minimum, twofold. Mallard wants to explore and describe the state of contemporary theology, and he wants to investigate the relationship between theology and imaginative literature. More broadly, he wishes to offer some analysis of the connections between theology and modern Western culture—thus the subtitle of the book, "A Case Study in Theology and Culture." In order to cover such an ambitious agenda, Mallard must also, along the way, range over linguistic problems, the meaning of metaphor, various theories for relating literature and theology, epistemology by way of Heidegger, process theology, novels by Faulkner and Kafka, and modern New Testament studies. To his credit, Mallard guides the reader through this territory by plotting his course in an introductory chapter and by providing well-spaced signposts in the form of careful recapitulations of his argument. Further, it is fair to say that despite the considerable ground to be covered, the two basic directions are clearly staked: contemporary theology and the relationship between theology and literature. For the purposes of this review, I am more interested in discussing the interdisciplinary dimension of the book; but Mallard's two aims do bear on each other, and his general approach should first be outlined.

Another way of putting Mallard's objective would be to say that he wishes to distinguish between what he calls "reflected theology" and "theology proper." For Mallard "theology proper" is based on the New Testament narratives about Jesus of Nazareth and offers explicit statements related to a classical Christian confession (p. 239). "Reflected theology," on the other hand, has to do with culture's way—as opposed to the church's way—of transmitting and implying, with varying degrees of accuracy or even irony, the theology proper (pp. 109-14, 150-54). A major thesis is simply that there does exist

Mirror Tricks: An Interdisciplinary Exercise

a reflected theology. Building toward a theological criticism of literature, Mallard seeks the shape of reflected theology and finds it—in Part I of the book—in language: first in the function of language to present "the true reality of things" (p. 27); then in the powers of metaphor, narrative, and the work of art as a whole to offer "a 'world,' or a perspective on *the* world" (p. 93): "If language in general, if metaphor and symbol, if the literary work of art can to some degree illumine the world, then a theological suggestiveness is likely present. Theology is concerned to make some sense of the world vis-a-vis God, the world's foundation or creator. Very broadly speaking, literature effects a grasp of that world with implications for its ground and goal. That there would seem a theological dimension within literature is no surprise" (pp. 93-94). More specifically, Mallard argues that "literature and theology have a formal link in and through the Christ story, which heavily influenced the shape and substance of them both" (p. 105). Having made that kind of case for the reflection of theology in literature, Mallard goes on in Part II to discuss the movement of theology in Western culture, its dissolution on the one hand, its reflected influence on the other. Arguing that "certain prominent theological motifs find strong analogues within the act and the results of literary creation" (p. 160), Mallard looks at William Faulkner's *The Sound and the Fury* and Franz Kafka's *The Trial* to find the theology reflected in those two novels. Then, in Part III, he is ready to talk more explicitly about the shape of theology proper by examining the New Testament narratives about Jesus and by placing his own two types of theology side-by-side in order to extend his theological reading of imaginative literature. One result of his inquiry is that "if . . . theology proper implies reflected theology or suggests the latter as already implicated within a classical Christology, then we must draw the surprising, if not disturbing conclusion that all Western literature of aesthetic merit belongs finally within the sphere of the Christ. The theologian must admit that statement, while knowing that it cannot be defended with clarity" (p. 253). After surveying very briefly three types of literature—aesthetic failures, works of both artistic excellence and Christian viewpoint, and apparent opponents of Christianity — Mallard concludes by acknowledging the difficulty of holding theology proper and reflected theology together conceptually but finds hope in the "continuing conversation of confession and quest" (p. 262).

This summary is too brief to do justice to Mallard's complex arguments, but it nonetheless highlights some of the problems that beset his work. To be sure, behind this general argument lies an analysis of works by Erich Auerbach, Hans Frei, Martin Heidegger, Paul Ricoeur, and other significant thinkers.[2] If, however, one finds some of the passages quoted above to be vague or unacceptable, then the summary has adequately revealed troublesome undertones of Mallard's work. Not only is his own language imprecise at points, but his use of his sources is questionable, his attention to earlier literature in his field is insufficient, and his own theory for relating theology and literature is problematic. Still the book is engaging enough that it asks not to be put aside cavalierly but rather to be brought into dialogue.

A point at which discussion is desirable, and in fact needed, lies exactly within one of Mallard's essential concerns, the relationship between literature and theology. As he seeks an appropriate method for relating the two disciplines, Mallard notes and dismisses what he considers the two prevailing approaches: the confessional view, represented by T. S. Eliot's assertion that literature should be judged from a specific theological standpoint (pp. 18, 100-101);[3] and the apologetic view, represented by Paul Tillich's correlation of culture and theology which, according to Mallard, addresses a theological answer to problems held in common by both literature and theology (pp. 19, 101). One brief paragraph is given to each of these positions. Although he quickly summarizes and criticizes Tillich's views, Mallard makes no specific reference to Tillich's own writing; Tillich, in fact, said very little about literature, but he did make observations about the visual arts, and his ideas there have some bearing on issues in literary criticism and have been seminal for scholars in the field of literature and theology.[4] In an additional three paragraphs Mallard re-

Mirror Tricks: An Interdisciplinary Exercise

views and faults the work of John Killinger, Sallie McFague TeSelle, and William Lynch (pp. 101-3).[5] One major problem with all of this is that Mallard is able to move so easily over a considerable amount of scholarship: he does not really engage the ideas of the three men who perhaps have done the most important work in the area of literature and theology: Stanley Romaine Hopper, Nathan A. Scott, Jr., and Amos N. Wilder.[6] Nor does he even mention a host of other scholars in the field whose thought may well have strengthened—or corrected—his own thinking.[7] Now obviously Mallard could not thoroughly examine this whole body of criticism without having a very different kind of book; and I would not suggest that he should have padded his footnotes just to show his familiarity with the field. The point is simply that if one proposes to move beyond existing theories for relating theology and literature, one might well present a more substantive analysis of the previous positions.

All the same, Mallard's invitation to a new approach is a serious one. Despite his own failure to enter earlier discussion, he presents his readers with an alternative that deserves attention. Indeed, we can hope other scholars will debate Mallard's theory on the reflection of theology in literature. He has an appropriate concern for the integrity of literature; he raises basic issues regarding the influence of language and culture; he respects the tensions and ambiguities inherent in the theologian's reading of literature; he encourages a sensitive address to the questions of literary criticism. He also knows—and this is important for the tone of the work—that he has not reached a "final solution" (p. 253), and he admits the tentativeness of his approach (p. 252).

Having acknowledged these contributions, I must confess that I find the basic direction of the book unsatisfactory for at least two reasons. In the first place, Mallard's view of a theology reflected in literature comes close again to the very objection he raised about other approaches to the issue: that is, the critic, under Mallard's view, comes to the literature with a distinct presupposition about finding a reflected theology. Perhaps Mallard does not intend to fall into what he knows is a pitfall, but when he talks about a "formal link in and through the Christ story" (p. 105), and when he concludes that "all Western literature of aesthetic merit belongs finally within the sphere of the Christ" (p. 253), and when he categorizes literature in terms of its affirmation or denial of Christian theology (pp. 254-60) — when he brings all this to his reading of literature, he has already determined what he wishes to find. Mallard does seek to be objective, and when, as in the case of Kafka, he finds no clearly reflected theology, he acknowledges the impasse. The problem is that his effort to view literature through the Christ story betrays his critical concern for objectivity.

A second difficulty is that the very term, *reflected theology*, does not seem especially helpful. It must be fairly obvious, as Mallard himself argues at perhaps too great a length, that theological ideas — notions about God, the nature of humanity, the end of time, the possibilities of human well-being — work their way into many expressions of the culture, including literature. Whether one likes those ideas or not, whether one affirms or denies them, they cannot possibly remain enclosed in heavy theological tomes or in cathedral walls. The influence of the Jewish and Christian traditions on Western civilization is abundantly clear. What are we, though, to make of that influence on literature? To say that it provides images and symbols and moral values is one thing; to claim that the literature thereby represents the theology is quite another.[8] Several related questions arise. Does a mirror show what is really there or can it twist and invert? Is irony really a reflection? If grace is reflected as "forgetful indifference" (p. 112), how is it still grace? If reflected theology's definition of God is "the general process of things in time" (p. 161), can it still be counted as theology? Why exactly is "the 'move' of the world toward renewal in the aesthetic act" an "analogue of Christ's resurrection and the end-to-come, glory following upon upheaval" (p. 105)? Indeed, is there apparent in the world a movement toward a renewal in aesthetic acts? Is there not often movement toward confusion? And what of literary critics who do not share Mallard's view about the pervasive reflection of theology

Mirror Tricks: An Interdisciplinary Exercise

in literature? Must they be converted, or are they doomed to ignorance? These questions are not at all derisive but are born of Mallard's category of reflected theology and suggest basic problems in his approach.

Still another difficulty stands in the way of this book's success. For all his concern with the relationship of literature and theology, Mallard deals only slightly in the book with specific literary works, and when he does he speaks without the benefit of previous criticism of the literature. This is the same pattern of operation Mallard followed regarding the special field of literature and theology, but perhaps here his failure to consult critics is even more damaging. In his chapter on *The Trial*, Mallard refers only to a *New York Times Book Review* essay (pp. 203, 207);[9] in the chapter on *The Sound and the Fury*, he apparently uses only Walter Brylowski's study of myth in Faulkner's novels (p. 183).[10] The impossibility of this method is easily illustrated in the Faulkner chapter. As most students of American literature know, we have an enormous body of criticism on *The Sound and the Fury*—much of it not very good, but some of it quite perceptive. Mallard interprets the novel by seeing Caddy Compson as its center (p. 176); surely he would have profited from reading the fine studies of Caddy by Catherine Baum and Eileen Gregory.[11] Might not Mallard's discussion of the reflection of God in the novel have been sharpened by John Hagopian's analysis of the nihilism there?[12] Certainly in a study of this kind reference to John Hunt's *William Faulkner: Art in Theological Tension* was essential, to say nothing of essays of Cleanth Brooks and Carvel Collins and Michael Millgate.[13] Mallard's treatment is not without value: he recognizes ambiguity and does not try to derive from the novel a Christian statement of faith, and he has some interesting comments on levels of time.[14] This chapter would surely have been better, however, had Mallard consulted the criticism.

Mallard's way of dealing with the literary work, though, seems not atypical in interdisciplinary study. All too often the specialist in one field feels exempt from doing homework in another field. That practice prevails frequently among theologians who manage to comment on a novel or a poem without the slightest acquaintance with the existing criticism; the same habit may be found among literary critics who consider themselves authorities in religion and theology without background in the scholarship of those areas. A given theologian may well be a perceptive reader of literature, and, for sure, any reader is entitled to make a response and form judgments without checking in with the critical establishment. But when a person prepares to enter scholarly discussion of a work, he must expect to undertake the full rigor of conscientious study. If interdisciplinary work is ever to be helpful and productive, its laborers will have to demonstrate competent scholarship in each of their fields, not in one only.

If Mallard's approach to the relationship of theology and literature is not entirely satisfactory, we might well ask what methodology would be helpful. Such a question would prompt a longer discussion than this review can provide or perhaps a longer book than Mallard's. What is needed is a careful analysis of the options that have already been proposed by the critics: TeSelle has laid a good foundation for that analysis, but her important study was published in 1966, and Mallard and many others have added new material since then. We have theoretical studies and we have practical criticism of specific writers or works, but we could benefit from a survey of how critics in the field actually go about their task. Theologically oriented readers might also pay more attention to how other critics deal with religious imagery and symbolism.

While I would not presume to outline a new theory here, I do want to make two suggestions in response to Mallard's work.[15] One is that whatever methodologies are finally developed for this cross-disciplinary study, the theologian's primary task in approaching a work of literature is to be a first-rate literary critic. A person with theological background comes to the critical task no differently than does a person who is uninterested in theology: he or she must still do solid literary criticism, must practice those skills of analysis and interpretation, investigate the previous criticism, and deal honestly with the work itself. The critic will strive for objectivity but will also

Mirror Tricks: An Interdisciplinary Exercise

attempt to enter the world of the novel or story or poem and be sensitive to what is happening there, as indeed Mallard would have it (p. 230). The requirement that a critic be scholarly and professional is unaffected by that critic's theological — or philosophical or psychological or scientific — persuasions.

A second suggestion is more theological in nature: the study of literature might better be viewed under the realm of creation than under the realm of redemption. As I have already noted, Mallard sees literature belonging "within the sphere of the Christ" (p. 253). That assumption raises continuing problems because it seems to demand that literature at its best will exalt Christian values, or that is must be judged finally on Christian terms. To see literature, on the other hand, as belonging to the realm of creation is to allow it a place in a pluralistic society and to accept its integrity. This way we need no special treatment for a literary work that is somehow more affirmative or redemptive than another; we may evaluate a work on its literary merits rather than on its philosophical stances.

A few other matters in *The Reflection of Theology in Literature* need mention. Mallard has a few annoying stylistic habits: what must be an irresistible urge to emphasize words by placing them within quotation marks; a practice — all too common in speech patterns today — of letting "hopefully" dangle; a tendency toward abstractions; some curious logic where words like "presumably" and even "therefore" bear a tremendous weight. The text of the book has been printed with care; the only errors I found appeared in the quoted material (omission of commas, use of parentheses when brackets should have been used, the dropping of italics when italics were in the original text). The footnotes are, for the most part, quite accurate: I found only five printing errors and two instances where a book's publisher is incorrectly given.[16] The index, on the other hand, has a few wrong page assignments and is inconsistent and incomplete; for example, it notes single allusions to Dylan Thomas and George Bernard Shaw but neglects multiple references to Milton and Shakespeare. More disturbing than these mechanical errors is Mallard's own use of his sources. He has a footnote early in the text that includes notice of Robert W. Funk's *Jesus as Precursor* (p. 23); I cannot help but wonder why Funk's chapter there on *The Trial* is not helpful to Mallard when he begins his own discussion of Kafka's novel. Mallard's use of Brylowski's study is also instructive: although he led Mallard to certain passages in *The Sound and the Fury* and to interviews with Faulkner (p. 183), Brylowski seems to have been less persuasive with his general thesis. Mallard argues, for instance, that "the biblical, 'mixed' style and the Christian tradition have had the greater impact upon *The Sound and the Fury*, though classical tragic themes are present" (p. 174), whereas Brylowski's position is that "*The Sound and the Fury* illustrates very early that although Faulkner makes much use of the images associated with Christianity he offers no great allegiance to their mythic content. The Christian myths are useful tools, he admits, but they are subordinated to larger mythic ideas, such as the scapegoat and the earth mother images."[17] Mallard might at least have argued a little when his only source among the Faulkner critics disagreed with him so completely. His practice, at several spots, hints at a questionable selectivity and perhaps some missed opportunities.

William Mallard's study must rest in that danger zone of all interdisciplinary work. The book is thoughtful and stimulating; it explores some new ground; it invites dialogue. But it also runs into some of the hazards that seem inevitably to loom up at those who attempt to relate separate disciplines. Literary critics will find the work short on attention to the details of criticism; theologians will find the theological development limited. Still, the book should be examined by those who are interested in literature and theology; and it deserves a place on reading lists in that field. Mallard has tackled a difficult task, and he has shared his excitement about its possibilities.

Notes

1. A biographical sketch at the end of the volume (p. 271) includes, for example, notice of Mallard's "Method and Perspective in Church History: A Reconsideration," *Journal of the American Academy of Religion*, 36 (1968), 345–65, and "A Perspective for Current Theological Con-

versation," in *Toward a New Christianity: Readings in the Death of God Theology,* ed. Thomas J. J. Altizer (New York: Harcourt, Brace and World, 1967), pp. 321-41. He has also written "Transcendence and Mystery in Modern Literature," *IDOC/International Documentation,* No. 71 (March-April 1976), 89-105.

    2. Mallard is especially indebted to Auerbach's *Mimesis: The Representation of Reality in Western Literature,* trans. William R. Trask (Princeton: Princeton Univ. Press, 1953) and Frei's *The Identity of Jesus Christ: The Hermeneutical Bases of Dogmatic Theology* (Philadelphia: Fortress Peess, 1975).

    3. The reference is to Eliot's "Religion and Literature," which Mallard quotes from Nathan A. Scott, Jr., ed., *The New Orpheus: Essays toward a Christian Poetic* (New York: Sheed and Ward, 1964), p. 223. The essay was collected in Eliot's *Essays Ancient and Modern* (New York: Harcourt, Brace, 1936).

    4. See Tillich's *Theology of Culture* (New York: Oxford Univ. Press, 1959) and his "Existentialist Aspects of Modern Art," in *Christianity and the Existentialists,* ed. Carl Michalson (New York: Scribners, 1956), pp. 128-47.

    5. Killinger, *The Fragile Presence: Transcendence in Modern Literature* (Philadelphia: Fortress Press, 1973); TeSelle, *Literature and the Christian Life* (New Haven: Yale Univ. Press, 1966). From TeSelle, Mallard quotes Lynch's "Theology and the Imagination, II: The Evocative Symbol," *Thought,* 29 (1954-55), 529-54; his *Christ and Apollo: The Dimensions of the Literary Imagination* (New York: Sheed and Ward, 1960) is another valuable study.

    6. Hopper, ed., *Spiritual Problems in Contemporary Literature* (New York: Harper, 1952); Wilder, *Modern Poetry and the Christian Tradition: A Study in the Relation of Christianity to Culture* (New York: Scribners, 1952) and *Theology and Modern Literature* (Cambridge: Harvard Univ. Press, 1958). Scott has written extensively, e.g., *The Broken Center: Studies in the Theological Horizon of Modern Literature* (New Haven: Yale Univ. Press, 1966) and *Negative Capability: Studies in the New Literature and the Religious Situation* (New Haven: Yale Univ. Press, 1969).

    7. The list might be very long. These few titles should suggest some of the opportunities: Norman Reed Cary, *Christian Criticism in the Twentieth Century: Theological Approaches to Literature* (Port Washington, N.Y.: Kennikat Press, 1975); Helen Gardner, *Religion and Literature* (New York: Oxford Univ. Press, 1971); Wesley A. Kort, *Narrative Elements and Religious Meanings* (Philadelphia: Fortress Press, 1975); Gerardus van der Leeuw, *Sacred and Profane Beauty: The Holy in Art,*

trans. David E. Green (Nashville: Abingdon, 1963); Brian Wicker, *The Story-Shaped World: Fiction and Metaphysics* (Notre Dame: Univ. of Notre Dame Press, 1975); James B. Wiggins, ed., *Religion as Story* (New York: Harper, 1975). Mallard does mention briefly the valuable anthology edited by Giles B. Gunn, *Literature and Religion* (New York: Harper, 1971).

8. Mallard notes that "either Christ is an *a priori* reality setting the shape of culture, or he is merely a paradigm of culture, produced and governed by it" (p. 139). Those need not be the only alternatives. In a classic study of this issue — *Christ and Culture* (New York: Harper, 1951) — H. Richard Niebuhr has analyzed five patterns in which Christianity and culture have been related throughout history (Mallard makes no reference to this work). One reviewer of Mallard's book has noted that Mallard's position falls within Niebuhr's category of "Christ and Culture in Paradox" (Ralph C. Wood, *The Christian Century*, 1 March 1978, p. 219); although I recognize Mallard's sensitivity to the ambiguities involved in any discussion of literature and theology, I rather think he would be more sympathetic toward Niebuhr's fifth and more Calvinistic category, "Christ the Transformer of Culture."

9. A parenthetical sentence refers to Leonard Michaels, "Life, Works, and Locus," *New York Times Book Review*, 21 November 1971, p. 1.

10. Brylowski, *Faulkner's Olympian Laugh: Myth in the Novels* (Detroit: Wayne State Univ. Press, 1968).

11. Baum, " 'The Beautiful One': Caddy Compson as Heroine of *The Sound and the Fury*," *Modern Fiction Studies*, 13 (Spring 1967), 33-44; Gregory, "Caddy Compson's World," in James B. Meriwether, comp., *The Merrill Studies in* The Sound and the Fury (Columbus, Ohio: Charles E. Merrill, 1970), pp. 89-101.

12. Hagopian, "Nihilism in Faulkner's *The Sound and the Fury*," *Modern Fiction Studies*, 13 (Spring 1967), 45-55.

13. Hunt, *William Faulkner: Art in Theological Tension* (Syracuse: Syracuse Univ. Press, 1965). See also chapters in Brooks, *William Faulkner: The Yoknapatawpha Country* (New Haven: Yale Univ. Press, 1963), Millgate, *The Achievement of William Faulkner* (New York: Random House, 1966), and Collins, "The Pairing of *The Sound and the Fury* and *As I Lay Dying*," *Princeton University Library Chronicle*, 18 (Spring 1957), 114-23. Even if Mallard had looked only at studies dealing specifically with Faulkner and religion, he would have found useful material from Wilder and Hunt in J. Robert Barth, ed., *Religious Perspectives in Faulkner's Fiction: Yoknapatawpha and Beyond* (Notre Dame: Univ. of Notre Dame Press, 1972). André Bleikasten's major study, *The Most Splendid Failure: Faulkner's* The Sound and the Fury (Bloomington:

Indiana Univ. Press, 1976) probably appeared too late for Mallard to know of it.

14. This discussion of time, however, fails to note the essays of Jean Pouillon, "Time and Destiny in Faulkner," and Jean-Paul Sartre, "On *The Sound and the Fury:* Time in the Work of Faulkner," both in Robert Penn Warren, ed., *Faulkner: A Collection of Critical Essays* (Englewood Cliffs, N.J.: Prentice-Hall, 1966), pp. 79-86, 87-93.

15. As I have indicated above, Mallard is certainly aware of the difficulty of relating literature and theology, and, in his last chapter, observes that "no conceptual model of the link between them is possible, and if such were to appear, finally it would belong to one side or the other" (p. 252). One has to wonder, then, if all the conceptualizing about reflected theology is really worth the exercise? I suspect that it is, since it leads to some interesting issues; Mallard must think so too since he still published his book even after coming to that conclusion about the impossibility of linking the two fields.

16. One of these is *The Sound and the Fury*: Mallard uses the 1946 Modern Library edition—a notably poor text—but identifies it as a Vintage Book (see p. 183); the other is *The Martin Luther Christmas Book,* which was published by Muhlenberg Press, not Westminster (see p. 69).

17. Brylowski, p. 85.

Editorial "Jamming":
Two New Editions of *Piers Plowman*
David C. Fowler

    A. V. C. Schmidt, ed. William Langland, The Vision of Piers Plowman: *A Complete Edition of the B-Text*. London: J. M. Dent & Sons; New York: E. P. Dutton, 1978. xlvii, 364 pp.

    Derek Pearsall, ed. William Langland, Piers Plowman: *An Edition of the C-Text*. London: Edward Arnold (York Medieval Texts, second series, I), 1978; Berkeley: University of California Press, 1979. 416 pp.

Students of *Piers Plowman* and indeed all lovers of early English poetry should be grateful for the recent appearance of excellent new reading editions of two versions of that great medieval poem. The B text, edited by A. V. C. Schmidt, and the C text, edited by Derek Pearsall, are both compact, learned, and skillfully arranged for the purpose of "enabling the text to release its original power" (Schmidt, p. xvi). It is difficult to choose between them, unless one already has a literary preference for one version over the other. The B text is cheaper (in its paperback form less than one-fourth the price of C), but the C text is more handsomely printed and easier to read. The quality of editing is very much the same, though I would have to give the edge to Pearsall, the more experienced of the two men. My main point, though, is that the reading public is fortunate to have the services of two such talented scholars dedicated to the task of editing a sometimes intractable poem. Before looking at their work in detail, we need to consider some of the difficulties they have had to face.

    While it is true that *Piers Plowman* exists in three related versions, one might think it the better part of valor for an editor to concentrate entirely on the single version that he has chosen to edit. Yet this is really impossible, because the other versions are often important sources of information for use in solving both textual and interpretive problems. Fortunately both editors have realized this fact, and both seem to have a good grasp of the complex relations of all three versions. Only occasionally, as we shall see, was I able to detect lapses in this regard.

In addition to holding three versions in his head, so to speak, the editor must take a stand on certain basic issues of textual criticism that have plagued students of the poem ever since W. W. Skeat's edition appeared in the late nineteenth century. The textual problem has many facets, but it finally comes down to this question: among so many different manuscript readings, how does one identify or reconstruct the author's original words? Considering the stubborn nature of the textual problem in this poem, one might expect that some of the legion of scholars who have devoted themselves to it would have published textual studies, but such is not the case. Textual critics of *Piers Plowman* are few in number, and barely exist at all outside the team of scholars who have been and are now working on the Athlone edition. Very little help is coming from American graduate schools, where textual criticism has virtually vanished from the English curriculum. Under these circumstances the courage of Schmidt and Pearsall in undertaking their respective editions should be recognized and commended.

If each of these editors could proceed as if he were the first to grapple with the text, the problems would be formidable enough; but the task is now complicated by the fact that several modern editions of *Piers Plowman* have appeared in the last three decades, not all of them pointing in the same direction. The edition of the A text that I brought out in 1952 (in posthumous collaboration with Thomas A. Knott) was based on the genealogical method of determining manuscript relationships; in 1960 George Kane, continuing the work of R. W. Chambers and J. H. G. Grattan, published his A text, in the introduction to which he rejects the genealogical method in favor of an ad hoc approach that treats each problem separately, relying on information about scribal tendencies of substitution in order to identify the reading of the text most likely to have given rise to existing variants. Kane employed this technique with great restraint, and I for one found the resulting text very persuasive.[1] Meanwhile E. Talbot Donaldson had joined forces with Kane in the enormous task of editing the B text. But, for whatever reason, this new edition, when it appeared in 1975, differed in many ways from Kane's A text, both in its method and in its resulting form, so much so that the senior editor found it necessary to refer in footnotes to his change of heart since he edited A. My own objections to the methodology and radical reconstructions of the Kane-Donaldson B text are a matter of record.[2]

It is perhaps inevitable that Schmidt and Pearsall should feel the influence of the Kane-Donaldson B text, the most significant and weighty editorial work on *Piers Plowman* in this century. And yet I find that both editors, though they freely acknowledge their indebtedness to their predecessors, nevertheless display unquestionable independence in their editorial decisions. Of course Schmidt is more directly under the gun, so to speak, since he also is editing B, and hence it is not surprising that he seems the more thoroughly indebted to Kane-Donaldson. Despite this, Schmidt disagrees with their conclusions quite often. But influence can sometimes be more subtle: I suspect that the example Kane-Donaldson set in freely emending the text many hundreds of times has had its effect on Schmidt. He remarks: "As well as fourteen emendations from Skeat and one each from Wright and Bennett, I have adopted 260 of Kane and Donaldson's reconstructions and conjectures and added 163 of my own" (p. xxxviii). Before 1975, who would have dared make over 400 emendations? But in comparison with more than 1,600 questionable "corrections" of the base manuscript by Kane-Donaldson, Schmidt's 439 emendations could almost be called conservative.

Going back to the appendix to my review of Kane-Donaldson,[3] I did my own rough calculation of the extent to which Schmidt seemed to follow their lead, and came up with these numbers (omitting Parts I and II of the appendix):

III. Emendations for which justification is insufficient: Kane-Donaldson, 273 cases; Schmidt, 123 cases.

IV. Unjustified emendations that have the effect of harmonizing the B text with one of the other versions:
   a. Harmonized with the A text: Kane-Donaldson, 684 cases; Schmidt, 152 cases.
   b. Harmonized with the C text: Kane-Donaldson, 236 cases; Schmidt, 102 cases.
V. The unacceptable practice of emending to produce regular alliterative patterns:
   a. First half of B text, Prologue, and Passus I-X: Kane-Donaldson, 160 cases; Schmidt, 95 cases.
   b. The B-Continuation, Passus XI-XX: Kane-Donaldson, 256 cases; Schmidt, 125 cases.

Schmidt's much greater restraint is clearly evident, but what these numbers fail to show is that in some of the above categories (particularly V.a. and V.b.) very nearly half of the cases represent instances in which Schmidt agrees with Kane-Donaldson as to the need for emendation but differs in what that emendation should be. I see a potential danger here for the future. If the editorial philosophy espoused by Kane-Donaldson continues uncriticized, successive generations of editors, each with his own opinions, will continue to an eventual state of anarchy regarding the text that will be much worse than the mere problem of manuscript variants. The poet's voice will come to resemble not so much the sound of many waters as a broadcast signal subjected to editorial jamming. The only thing worse than no guide is too many guides.

When we turn to the C text the case is very different. Pearsall has essentially printed a single manuscript (Huntington Library MS HM 143) with corrections from a few others and an occasional emendation. His procedure in fact is very much in the manner of Skeat, but Pearsall has chosen a better manuscript and therefore gives us a text that is often superior to Skeat's. The irony is that this simple editorial procedure which I praise is a feature for which the editor apologizes in his introduction (pp. 20 ff.), deferring to the forthcoming edition of C by George Russell, which will complete the three texts of the

Athlone edition under Kane's general editorship. Nevertheless, one can only hope that Pearsall's example will act as a restraining influence. We need a C text with complete corpus of variants, such as Russell's edition will provide; what we do *not* need is a C text with radical reconstructions like those of the Kane-Donaldson B edition.

Dealing with all three versions of the poem simultaneously, and listening to conflicting signals from a small number of textual scholars, the prospective editor faces also a third challenge: he must make up his mind about the authorship of *Piers Plowman*. Of course some students of the poem have been saying that the problem of authorship is an illusion of earlier scholarship and that what we need now is a gentleman's agreement to the effect that the problem no longer exists. George Kane published an appeal to this effect more than a decade ago, and most scholars, though not all, have accepted this "final word" on the subject with an embarrassing alacrity.[4] Studies of *Piers Plowman* published since 1965 usually refer approvingly to Kane's manifesto and regularly exclude from their bibliographies books and articles, past or present, that deal seriously with the authorship question. The two editions under review here are no exception to this rule.

If Kane is right in saying that the single-authorship hypothesis works best in the study of the poem, then of course the sooner we are rid of the vestiges of that old controversy, the better[6] But if he is wrong — and I venture to say that he is — then the artificial constraints which the present gentleman's agreement imposes on all of us will be very damaging to future study of the poem. My purpose in these remarks is not to offend anyone (I am automatically a friend of all who admire this poem and devote themselves to the study of it) but rather to encourage a more open attitude toward this important question than seems in evidence at the present time. I bring it up here because I believe that the editors of the two editions under consideration are to some extent victims of the constraints mentioned above and that in a freer atmosphere they could have avoided certain lapses to which I shall call attention from time to time in the following commentary on their work.⁵

Schmidt's B Text: Textual and Lexical Commentary

IV.158 [Kynde] Wit acorded therwith and
        comendede hise wordes.

Here Schmidt follows Kane-Donaldson (hereafter K-D) in substituting *Kynde* for *And*, the reading of the manuscripts, adding that "K-D's conj. seems necessary if confusion with Wisdom's crooked companion Witty (27 above) is to be avoided." Despite the agreement of these editors, I am convinced that they are wrong. Why shouldn't this reaction be Wit's hypocritical acceptance of the (perhaps temporary) victory of Reason? (Note that he is sometimes called Witty, e.g., in lines 27 and 67; and elsewhere called Wit, e.g., in lines 81 and 91). Wit(ty), like his companion Waryn Wisdom, is an ancestor of the Vicar of Bray: Wisdom winks at Meed and says, "I am youre man, what so my mouth jangle" (155). The same applies to the sentiments attributed to Wit in line 158. In A, these two are speechless (A IV.141-43), but in B they are allowed to speak and reveal their hypocrisy (B IV.152-60). The revisor is enlarging the reaction of the Westminster crowd in order to suggest that the victory of Reason is precarious at best. An editor might wish to take issue with this interpretation, but he should not try to rewrite the passage to fit his own conception of its meaning.

VIII.70 That ever dremed [dr]ight in [doute], as
         I wene.

Schmidt follows K-D in making B conform to A, but admits that "the absence of C evidence makes determination of originality difficult here." This is merely one of many cases where the editor's difficulty arises from his authorship assumption. The word *driʒt* is indeed "rare," occurring only in the A text. The change to "wyʒte" in B and the removal of the line altogether from C are the work of a reviser whose vocabulary simply did not include the word "driʒt."

VIII.102   That if Dowel or Dobet dide ayein
           Dobest.

K-D add a line here from MS F, modified to match A IX.93, but Schmidt does not agree, arguing that Langland could have revised from a MS of A lacking the line or that he may have omitted it deliberately as useless. In my opinion there is nothing scribal or casual about these revisions. The A text describes an arrangement whereby the power of the king is to be put at the disposal of the bishop (Dobest) for disciplining the commons and the clergy (Dowel and Dobet) whenever they "were unbuxum at his bidding, and bold to don ille" (A IX.93). The reviser is by no means willing to let this stand (on his attitude toward bishops compare B X.256-88 and C IX.255-81). In B the first step in toning it down is the removal of A IX.93; but notice especially what happens in C X.99-101:

> Thus Dowel and Dobet demede as Dobest
> And crounede oen to be kyng, to kull withoute synne
> That wolde nat do as Dobest deuinede and tauhte.

The discipline to be exerted by the king is now specifically said to include the death penalty, but the particular estates in need of his discipline are no longer specified! This is *not* the work of scribes; this is the reviser engaged in aiming the heavy artillery of the A text in a new direction (some years after the Peasants' Revolt). It is probably not an exaggeration to say that about half of the problems discussed by Schmidt under the rubric of "textual and lexical commentary" are in fact cases of authorial revision.

IX.26-48

In this passage the poet makes a distinction between the creation of man and that of other creatures which is skillfully explicated by Daniel M. Murtaugh.[6] K-D emend the passage rather freely (26, 27, 33, 39, 40, 42); Schmidt accepts none of these: lines 26 and 27 he retains as in Skeat (and the MSS); 33 he rejects (an A line imported into B by K-D); and the remaining three lines he emends, but differently. This is a good example of editorial "jamming." Even where the editors agree that emendation is required, they disagree on what it should be. Schmidt's argument from the text is not strong here. He speaks of B as "doctrinally superior to A" and indeed calls A itself "near-heretical," whereas Murtaugh, speaking of the K-D text (with its A readings) in comparison with Skeat's B, remarks that "the influence of Christian exemplarism, discussed here, is clear in both" (16 n.22). The analogy of the lord wishing to write a letter (K-D 39–41; Schmidt 38–40) is provided with alternative solutions in the two editions when in fact no emendation is needed: "If a lord skilled in writing wished to write a letter but lacked parchment or pen, I dare say that letter, for all his lordship, would never be written!" Editors should leave passages of this kind alone; they are there to test the reader, and should not be subjected to paternalistic "correction."

X.61, 69

Two more rare words found in the A text only (*honesshen* XI.48 and *kete* XI.56) are lost or replaced in revision (cf. VIII.70 above). K-D restore the A word in both cases; Schmidt restores the first (*hunsen* 61), but not the second (*othere kynnes men* 69). Surely both are words deliberately removed in revision (*kete* is removed again from X.455), either because the reviser did not have them as part of his own vocabulary or because of a desire to soften the harshness of this picture of loveless clerks and aristocrats expelling the poor and hungry. This scene returns to haunt the reviser frequently in his continuation. It would be interesting to compile a list of words unique to A to see whether they all fit into a definable region or dialect area.

X.73 And prechen at Seint Poules, for pure envye of clerkes.

Schmidt concedes the natural sense of line 73b to be "because of pure ill-will *towards* the clergy," but goes on to point out that since the friars themselves are clerks we perhaps should read "out of sheer clerkly [i.e. intellectual] malice [*sc.*, against the unlearned, the 'simple faithful']." But surely the "natural sense" is intended (clerkes = secular clergy).

X.78-79 For God is deef nowadayes and deyneth noght his eres to opene,
That girles for hire giltes he forgrynt hem alle.

These two lines are in RF only, an important pair of manuscripts representing an independent line of transmission. K-D concluded, wrongly I believe, that their departures from the other MSS are not revisions but the result of scribal activity in one group or the other. Schmidt evidently accepts their verdict. Concerning the above lines he remarks: "Omission from β through censorship is an interesting possibility." On the contrary, these lines may well be an addition expressing the poet's pained reaction to some recent events; note that they are preserved in C with a notable change (*good men* replaces *girles*). RF additions of this type may well prove to be important for dating the poem more precisely (i.e., later) than it is now. It would be a shame if editorial presumptions of this type were to hide this evidence from the eyes of future historical critics.

X.139 And as doumb as a dore nail drough hym aside. Skeat: And as doumb as deth and drowe hym arrere.

K-D restore from A XI.94, and I think this is what Schmidt meant to do, but he seems to think that the A text agreed with MS F (*dore nail*), whereas in fact A reads *doumb as a dore*. But again no emendation is necessary because we are dealing here with another revision. The reviser did not like or did not understand the expression "dumb as a door" (I'm not sure I do either; could it be for "dumb as a deer [= beast]"? cf. A IV.141-43), and so he changed it in B to "dumb as death." As frequently happens in such cases, he then deletes it completely in revising to C. Once again we have revision—not scribal activity.

XI.338-39   Males drowen hem to males amornynge by hemselve,
And [femelles to femelles ferded and drowe].

With a slight modification (*amornynge*) Schmidt accepts the reconstruction of K-D, who envisage the male animals as mourning post coitum (Pearsall finds their reading "attractive" but does not adopt it.) I rejected the K-D reading without elaboration,[7] but in view of Schmidt's acquiescence, perhaps a further comment is in order. The original reads (Skeat XI.330-31): "Males drowen hem to males • a mornynges bi hem-self, • And in euenynges also • ȝede males fro femeles." The only thing unusual about these lines is the alliteration of 331 (aaxy), regularized in C (which the editors then use to reconstruct B XI.339). There is certainly no "defective sense." Males consistently (morning and evening) stay apart from the females. The passage illustrates the reasonableness of animals by describing a phenomenon Aristotle calls "herd shunning" ($ἀτιμαγελεῖν$): "And generally, we may say that all, or most, wild male animals do not graze with the females before the season for pairing, but go off on their own once they have reached maturity, and the males and females feed apart" (*Historia Animalium*, VI, xviii, Loeb ed., trans. Peck). Not only does Aristotle not mention the "ancient notion" invoked by K-D, but his words make it evident that the phenomenon of herd-shunning has nothing to do with that idea. The text of the poem shows the same thing, unless we are to suppose that the alleged *tristitia* of the males lasts through an entire season. But the author makes it clear that the behavior he is describing does not occur during *rotey tyme* (line 337).

XIV.23   Shal nevere my[te] bymolen it, ne mothe after biten it.

There is no need to repeat my criticism of K-D, who also emend.[8] There is absolutely nothing wrong with archetypal *myste*. We now have a *myte* to add to K-D's *myx*.

XV.237   In court amonges japeris he comeþ
          but selde.

Schmidt here follows Skeat, while K-D emend so as to produce regular alliteration and harmonize with C: "In court amonges [þe commune] he comeþ but selde." Here is K-D's comment: "Deliberate alteration through misconception of the kind of court in question." Schmidt, on the other hand, has this to say: "K-D's plausible conj. makes *court* the manor-court; but *Iaperis* is more easily seen as a visual error or visually motivated substitute for *carperis* (unrecorded before C 15th)." (But note that Schmidt does not actually emend.) Both of these editorial comments, taken together, offer an interesting insight. K-D's scribe tends to be *cerebral*; Schmidt's scribe is more *visual*. A careful study of cases where they agree on emending, but differ in their emendations, would, I believe, bear this out. In this particular case Schmidt overlooks the fact that K-D are emending by the use of C XVI.359. But he is right not to emend.

XV.502-8 ff.

Schmidt reluctantly goes along here (and see also his note to XV.566) with K-D's theory that there has been a major dislocation of the text in B XV, doing so apparently because he lacks "an alternative explanation." None is needed. The line-order of the B text is entirely satisfactory as it stands in the MSS. This is one instance where the influence of K-D on Schmidt is particularly unfortunate, and the effect on future generations of readers will be especially disruptive. But I am glad to report that Pearsall, at least, has not let this theory affect his editing of the C text.

XV.527

Schmidt clearly perceives that line 526 contains a "pointed personal allusion" (Skeat), but he is misled in what he says by K-D's disruption of the text (above) and their new theory about MSS RF. Here is the way I think his note should read: "The original passage (XV.505-8, 527-30, 568-76) was an angry exhortation to bishops to abandon their corrupt practices and to begin dispensing bodily as well as spiritual food. Later the poet adds a more positive appeal (XV.509-26), recounting the history of episcopal heroism, and referring to some action of which Abp. Thomas was an exemplar — presumably risking his life in salvation of men's souls." *That β* represents the form of the text before the later insertion (written in a very different spirit) required changing it to read: *and naught to.* (The allusion in line 526 is no doubt to the murder of Archbishop Simon Sudbury in June 1381.) When I see an editor as skilled as Schmidt being misled (note how one must look ahead to pick up the rest of the bishop passage in lines 568-76 because of K-D's theory of dislocation), I can't help feeling a certain outrage on his behalf.

XVI.115   Ac a[r] he made the maistrie, *mestus cepit esse.*

Schmidt cites John 11:35. More precisely, as Pearsall indicates (C XVIII.146n), the words are from Matt. 26:37, but here applied to the action of John 11:35.

XVI.198-201

Schmidt makes a bold effort in his note to these lines to deal with a difficult passage. I prefer to keep the punctuation of Skeat (and K-D), translating as follows: "Patriarchs and prophets and apostles were the children, / and Christ and Christendom and all Christians (are) Holy Church. / To signify that man must believe in one God, / If there it pleased him (to do so) and (if it was someone) he loved, he showed himself in three persons." (The latter reference is to Gen. 18:1 ff., made explicit in XVI.225 ff.) The danger in trying to use the C text here (as Schmidt does) will be seen when we notice that C has suffered a dislocation (perhaps attributable to the author himself in the process of revision — cf. K-D ed., p. 125 n. 55). As Schmidt points out, C XVIII.211 is identical in form to B XVI.210, but he fails to notice the repetition of "bileve" at the end of lines 200 and 210 responsible for the dislocation. This slip apparently triggered a thoroughgoing revision of the entire comparison of the Trinity with mankind (C XVIII.212-40). But the original error remains uncorrected: line C XVIII.211 follows 210 as if it were intended to complete the sentence begun in line 209. The difficulty of making sense out of C XVIII.209-11 can be seen in Pearsall's note to these lines (C XVIII.208-9n). He calls his 210 "a new line in C," when in fact it equals B XVI.210. There are hundreds of textual problems like this in editing *Piers Plowman*, any one of which is enough to make a scholar's head swim.

XVIII.31

Apparently Schmidt takes *likthe* (LRF) to be a form of *liketh*, but surely Skeat is right in classifying it in his glossary with the verb *liȝen*. The preservation of this form in RF, a MS tradition very close to the original, may even preserve here the author's own dialect (southwestern).

XVIII.394   And my mercy shal be shewed to manye of my bretheren.

K-D emend from C to read [*halue*]*breperen*, but Schmidt is right to reject it, seeing C as a revision. But where is "the (implied) distinction between pagans / prechristians and Christians"? Jesus has brothers "in blood" (all men) and "in baptism" (Christians). In B the latter are "hole bretheren" (line 378), but in C this designation is revised to read "half bretheren" (line 422), perhaps after second thoughts about the theological daring of "hole bretheren" to describe the relation of man to God-man. (For the problem of C's reading here, see my comment on Pearsall's edition below, XX.436).

XVIII.406   They dorste noght loke on Oure Lord, the [lothli]este of hem alle.

All manuscripts read *boldeste*; K-D read *leeste*, after C. Schmidt makes a better case for his emendation than K-D do for theirs, but no emendation is needed (the line alliterates *aaxy*). Yet Schmidt's note leaves me wondering about the validity of C's *lest* (Pearsall XX.448). It looks like revision to improve alliteration, but would the poet be willing to weaken a line so, just for the sake of the metre?

XIX.90   And Reson to riche[ls] — To right and to truthe.

K-D emend using a sophisticated reading from MS F. Schmidt plausibly conjectures *richels* for *riche golde* (BC), a conclusion arrived at independently by Pearsall (XXI.90n). This is one of a very few emendations which I think may well be correct.

XIX.410

This line, according to Skeat, is identical in both versions (Skeat B XIX.405, C XXII.409): "But Conscience the comune fede • and cardynale vertues." But according to K-D, Schmidt, and Pearsall (in that order) it should be read as follows:

But Conscience [be þi] comune[s] and Cardinale vertues.
But Conscience be the comune fode, and Cardinale Vertues.
Bote Consience thy comune fynde and cardinale vertues.

A good illustration of editorial "jamming."

XX.367   And make yow [and] my Lady in masse and in matyns.

Schmidt inserts *and*, but otherwise lets this line stand. K-D read: "And make [of] yow [*memoria*] in masse and in matyns," explaining *my lady* of the MSS as misreading of the contracted form of *memoria* (p. 160). When their edition came out I was impressed by this emendation and grouped it with those I classified as "justifiable." Now Schmidt calls it "quite unconvincing," disagrees also with Pearsall's solution (C XXII.366n), and explains his line as follows: "The solution here adopted depends on remembering Flatterer's way with women (line 346 above). He is offering membership of the fraternity to both master and mistress." This is very impressive indeed. I still say that K-D's solution is ingenious, but my confidence in it has certainly been shaken. Trying to decide which editor to follow is an exhausting business.

Schmidt's B Text: Literary and Historical Commentary

II.211   Falsnesse for fere thanne fleigh to the freres.

To say, as the editor does, that "this is the first of the attacks on the friars which run through PP" is misleading at best. In the A text (from which this line comes) the friars receive no more and no less criticism than other groups. In B, of course, the story is quite different: there they hold positions of leadership in the army of Antichrist (XX).

III.128   And hath apoisoned popes and peired Holy Chirche.

I do not share the editor's confidence that this line (= AIII.115) alludes to the Donation of Constantine. Conscience is showing how Meed (bribery) can be used to commit murder: the preceding line alludes to the murder of Edward II in 1327. (In a note to line 127 the editor professes certainty that this king "was not destroyed through avarice"; how does he know that?) Hence I see no reason why Conscience should not then allude to the poisoning of Benedict XI (1306) in line 128. But the main point is that we have here an example of Langland harmonistics: Schmidt is obviously influenced by the fact that there is a passage on the Donation in B XV.555-59 (written some two decades later).

IV-VI.   Further examples of Langland harmonistics.

IV.172: If "Reason's actions accord with his nature as later defined at XV.27-28," it is after the fact, since they stood for years in the A text without benefit of that definition.

V.45-47: The editor here seeks to harmonize Reason's exhortation of the regulars (= A V.37-39) with Clergy's prophecy concerning the Abbot of Abingdon (B X.314-27) in order to reach the conclusion that "Langland advocates not suppression but right observance." But see my comment below on Pearsall, V.168-71.

V.61: Schmidt dissents from Bennett's characterization of "Wille" in this line (= A V.44) as "a momentarily personified abstraction of the human will" in order to suggest that the sins here confessing are the dreamer's, who elsewhere is called Longe Wille (B XV.152), and who seems to be addressed by Repentance at the close of the confession of Wrath (B V.184-85). Whose sins were they during the time that these "clues" did not exist? The editor might reply that this is none of his concern, but elsewhere he does take A into account in seeking to understand B (e.g., III.127n).

V.514: "*beestes* was perhaps suggested by *iumenta* 509a above." But *bestis* stood in the text (= A VI.2) long before B V.478-509a was added to it.

V.632: The wafer-seller (= A VI.117) may have *suggested* the creation of Haukyn (B XIII.226); but it is misleading merely to say that he "anticipates" him.

VI.75-77, 226: Of the former passage (= A VII.67-69) the editor remarks, "Langland seems certain about the fate of such characters"; of the latter line (in B only) he says that it "urges charity without regard to desert." Such a difference of opinion must surely be worthy of note. The explanation is that A advocates severe treatment of sinful and uncooperative members of the community, while B urges charity regardless of the sinful state of the needy. But the attitude in B is not so clear-cut as this simple opposition would suggest. In this passage he may be obliquely acknowledging the role of some of the poor in the violence of 1381, while at the same time urging that this not lead to a backlash against all of them, a withholding of charity to the poor. Schmidt's reconstruction of lines 223-24 (following K-D) somewhat obscures the nature of the B-revision here.

VI.307: What possible connection is there between this line (= A VII.291) and B XV.534?

VII.44-59a

There is no "digression on law and lawyers"; this is a mandate for lawyers (excepting lines 44-45) which exactly parallels the mandate for merchants just concluded. There *is*, however, a digression on beggars (lines 71-87) added by the reviser. Hence to perceive the original form of this "absurd" pardon the editor would do well to glance back at the A-text, where it is presented intact and without digressions (A VIII.9-88).

VII.85-86

The editor remarks that "the *solas* comes from the accounts of God's direct provision for his saints (see XV 269ff)." But if God's provision for Mary Magdalene is at all representative (XV.294-95), the particular beggars being addressed would find little solace indeed. No doubt the poet recommended the lives of the saints in the perhaps naive hope that their ascetic example would shame beggars into a more austere or less clamorous attitude toward the securing of their next meal. But whatever may be the true meaning of Psalm 36, it is clearly being used here to warn beggars that "the Book banneth beggerie."

VII.98-104

"The operative idea is not the suffering of the physically handicapped but the patience and humility with which they bear it; this is what wins God's favour." No doubt this is the operative idea in the B text, which commends the reading of Saints Lives to the hungry (above); but these are lines carried over intact from A (VIII.82-88), where they express a compassion that is not strained and communicate an anguish in the presence of human suffering that is both unmistakable and unqualified by the fact that the meekness of the sufferers is also affirmed.

VII.122-24

In a note to line 123 the editor remarks: "The relevance to this of Ps. 33:20, which SkBn quote, is not clear." To see why

Skeat referred to this psalm, we must look at the lines involved (= A VIII 104-6):

> The prophete his payn eet in penaunce and in sorwe,
> By that the Sauter seith—so dide othere manye.
> That loveth God lelly, his liflode is ful esy:
> *Fuerunt mihi lacrime mee panes die ac nocte.*

Obviously the only certain biblical reference we have here is the Latin verse (Ps. 41:4), which Schmidt (accurately) translates as follows: "My tears have been my bread day and night." But it is evident that the poet reads the verse in a slightly different way: the prophet may eat tearfully, but the point is that he *eats*, he does not starve. Skeat, who seems to have felt that the author was on shaky ground in basing his argument on this text, has rushed to the rescue with Ps. 33:20 for line 123b (*iustorum* [plu] accounting for *othere manye*), and Ps. 33:11 for line 124, despite the fact that the Latin quoted immediately following is from Ps. 41:4. Perhaps it is best simply to accept the author's somewhat strained interpretation of this verse and set aside the props offered by Skeat and Bennett.

VII.154

This line (= A VIII.134), says the editor, "explicitly makes the dream Nabuchodonosor's (Dan 2:36ff), but it is his ?son Baltasar (Belshazzar) who 'lees his lordshipe' (Dan 5:30)." But the dream *is* Nabuchodonosor's, who is here (i.e., in the A text) taken as representative of the Babylonian dynasty. In this sense he did lose his lordship, and *"lower men* (plu) it hadde" (Dan. 2:39). The reviser, failing to perceive this, later made a "correction" (C IX.306-9) which incorporates both predictions (Dan. 2:39 and 5:30).

IX.35   For he was synguler hymself and seide
Faciamus.

Another example of Schmidt's brilliant reading. In an eleven-line note he explains clearly and concisely a passage (B IX.26-48) to which Daniel Murtaugh devotes seven pages.[9] The only flaw in these explanations comes from the fact that both Schmidt and Murtaugh base their explication on an emended text. Both critics agree, in dealing with the analogy of the lord who wishes to write a letter (IX.38-40), that the parchment, like the earth from which Adam was made, renders visible his word (or wit), while the pen is the instrument of his effort (= God's power). Murtaugh, following K-D's emendation of these lines, supposes that the lord lacked parchment but had a pen; Schmidt, following his own emendation, supposes that the lord lacked a pen, but had ample parchment. But as their own explanations make clear, the poet wishes to say through this analogy that God "needs" both power *and* wit to create man. (Hence the plural *faciamus* as opposed to the singular *fiat* used earlier: see Murtaugh, pp. 19-20, where one finds a slight corrective to the opening sentence in Schmidt's note.) *Ergo* the lord will be frustrated if he lacks *either* parchment *or* pen. There is no need for emendation (see above, textual and lexical comment on IX.26-48).

IX.95-98a   Dowel, dobet, dobest:

The editor provides a good, concise description of the ensuing definitions of the triad. It would clarify matters, I think, if he had pointed out that although Wit's emphasis is indeed on inward dispositions, the three social classes are still to be kept in mind: the commons (dowel), the clergy, secular and regular (dobet), and bishops (dobest). The reader will then more readily understand why at line 108 the mention of *dowel* triggers a discussion of marriage.

X.117   Ymaginatif herafterward shal answere to youre purpos.

The "striking reference to Ymaginatif" is striking because the B poet rarely uses this direct method of alerting the reader to the corrections of A-text opinions to be provided in the B-continuation. Furthermore it is not Study's reference but rather the intruding voice of the B poet himself, promising a *reply* to Study, whose intent is clearly to demonstrate the corruption and uselessness of learning (however shortened and blurred the B form of her speech). Ymaginatif (XI.408 ff.,

XII) "does not explain why men suffer death" because Study does not raise that issue (X.107-10 is simply an illustration of the adverse effects of learning). The lay "maistres" (X.115) do not attack learning but themselves illustrate its adverse effects (blasphemy and lack of charity toward the poor). Finally, learning is not attacked by Will in XI.367-73, where he simply asks why reason does not govern men's behavior. The attack on learning in the A text is directed by the poet himself, who uses Study as his main spokesman, but who also permits the dreamer to attack it in the epilogue, A XI.250-303 (preserved in blunted form in B X.369-72). It is this assault that Ymaginatif "answers" in B XII (see Schmidt's note to XII.157).

X.118

This line, and the cross-references given in the note (VIII.58, 111) are all A lines preserved in B. In A, Will constantly (and at times ironically) seeks a commonsense understanding of things, not the intellectual gamesmanship which Augustine condemns. When Study aggressively misunderstands Will's intent in A XI.86-91 (somewhat obscured in B X.131-36), the effect is comic (B X.137-48).

X.259-327

Clergie's "diatribe," which is not a digression, is directed first against unworthy bishops (X.256-88, corresponding to A XI.192-95), and only then (adopting and expanding the A text) "against unworthy religious" (X.289-327 = A XI.196-227).

X.264   I rede ech a blynd bosard do boote to hymselve.

The "blind buzzard" addressed here is not "the ignorant priest" suggested by the editor, but a bishop charged with the function of *correcting* the priesthood (256, 281, etc.), and his blindness is a moral failure, not the result of ignorance. The B poet includes parsons and priests in his exhortation (265) in order to show the bishop being addressed that he does not hold to a double standard in thus singling out bishops for criticism. Priests who correct their flocks must likewise set an example of integrity in their own lives. See also the comment just below on X.278-80.

X.278-80

The editor's interpretation of the story of the capture of the ark of the convenant and the death of Eli and his sons (1 Sam. 4) fails to call attention to Clergie's main point (spelled out in X.281-88), namely, that Eli (the "bishop" in this case) broke his neck and died because of his failure to correct his sons (1 Sam. 3:13). Eli thus stands as a biblical warning to those "dumb dogs that cannot bark" (X.285). The point is made quite explicit in subsequent revision (C Prol.95-127).

X.284

The *burel clerkes* referred to in this line are those who have been critical of bishops for their failure to serve as watchdogs in the public interest. If bishops led holy lives and fearlessly denounced corruption in high places as they should (and not themselves become instruments of the establishment), their critics would be less disrespectful and more likely to respond to their public and pious exhortations. *Burel clerkes* is a pejorative phrase, used here ironically by the poet: "those critics whom *you* call *burel clerkes* when they speak out against you fearlessly and honestly."

X.301-3

The editor remarks that "Clergie contrasts unfavorably the lax monasteries with the rigorous universities." I do not see such a contrast in these lines. The poet is speaking of life "in cloister or in school" (line 298) in a passage of his own, which is then followed by a passage carried over from the A text critical of the life of those who leave cloister (or school) to go out into the world (A XI.208 ff.). The B poet rarely (if ever) revises in such a way as to allow the kind of reading that the editor attempts here: interpreting a passage consisting of old and new lines as if they had all been composed consecutively on a single occasion.

X.371-74

Will is not "oppressed." He is angry, and his attack on learning has the full backing of the author (of the A text).

X.452a

The "distortion" of Augustine's words (if such it be) was not "meant to be recognized" in the A text, where the meaning of the Latin text as quoted is passionately affirmed. In B, the entire condemnation of learning is carefully refuted (B XI-XIV), without the slightest hint that Augustine's words implied anything other than the meaning assigned to them in the A text (B X.450-57; C XI.288-95). The argument that, since the Latin of the poem differs from that of the modern text of Augustine, it must have been "doctored" is precarious indeed. The chances are much greater that the author saw it, for example, in a collection such as the *Legenda Aurea* (ed. Graesse), CXXIV, p. 551: "Surgunt indocti et coelum rapiunt et nos cum doctrinis nostris in infernum demergimur." This passage does not match the Latin of our text, but at least it lacks *sine corde*, and it has *in infernum*. Yes, the author of A *does* "attack learning as dangerous in itself" (but without doctoring his texts): it is this idea that the reviser meets head on and refutes, with all the skill at his command, principally in the urgent arguments of Imaginatif (XII), though also in his carefully drawn distinction between Clergie (learning per se) and the friar doctor (William Jordan, the embodiment of corrupt learning).

XI.166 ff.

For reasons already given (see X.452a just above), there is no need to try, as the editor does here, to harmonize what is said in these lines with the teachings of Scripture in the A text (B X.344 = A XI.230). The strategy of the reviser (quite evident here) is to place love above learning and by this means to bring the dreamer gradually around to his new attitude. Schmidt rightly points out that "Trajan's argument that learning without love is valueless does not *condemn* learning *per se*," but precisely the *appearance* of that idea in this strongly worded afterthought (preserved in RF only) may be what decided the author to cancel it when revising to C.

XI.185 In a povere mannes apparaille pursueth us evere.

This beautiful line (as Skeat calls it) may also owe something to the traditional depiction of Christ as *peregrinus* (Luke 24:18; cf. B XI.232-34). But lines 198-203, far from developing this theme, introduce an entirely different issue: it is God's will that there be rich and poor in society, and *both* were redeemed by Christ. This idea is directed against the numerous denunciations of wealthy men (all originating in the A text, e.g., II.149-61, VIII.162-75), for which the dreamer is now being held responsible, despite his ironic defense of them (B X.341-43 = A XI.228-29. The other passages cited by Schmidt (VI.207-9, XVIII.376-79) have nothing in common with this passage except the general idea of blood brotherhood. Piers applies the notion to beggars (*never* to the rich!), and Christ promises mercy to his bretheren at the Last Judgment (to those at least who have themselves been merciful — cf. XVIII.394-96).

XI.357 And some briddes at the bile thorugh brethyng conceyved.

Skeat identified the bird here as the partridge, noting that Aristotle, in his *History of Animals*, says that "if the hen stands in the way of the breath of the male she conceives" (trans. Cresswell). But Schmidt, consulting the Loeb ed. (trans. Peck), finds the same sentence rendered differently: "when the hen partridge stands to windward of the cock, she conceives" (p. 231). From this he concludes that the description of the partridge "does not seem the source of the passage." But the point is not how the sentence is now understood by modern scholars but how it was read in earlier times. The key phrase of the original is κατα πνευμα, which can mean "downwind" (I assume Peck's translation "to windward" is a slip for "leeward") or it can mean "from the breath." Our two translations illustrate these two possibilities. At the moment I do not have access to Latin translations in manuscript, but on consulting early printed editions I find (in *De Animalibus, Interprete Theodoro Gaza,* Venice, 1495): "Nam si contra marem steterit foemina, aura ab eo flatem, sit pregnans," which I take to mean that she conceives by means of a "breath blown from him." But even without resorting to Latin translations, there is evidence that Aristotle himself intended "breath" rather than "wind." In an earlier passage of *Historia Animalium* (V, v; Loeb ed., p. 111) he observes: "When female partridges stand to leeward of the males, they become impregnated; they often do so too when they hear the voice of the male, if they are on heat, or when the male flies over them and breathes down (καταπνεῦσαι) on them." Here the verb can *only* mean "breathes down." Turning once more to the Latin we find: "Videlicet dum mas ipse in foeminam foetificium spiritum demittet." The phrase *foetificium spiritum* can only be translated "fertile breath." Hence I think it is safe to say that Skeat was correct in his citation of Aristotle, and that the bird in question is the partridge. Should anyone wonder why I am so passionate in defense of the partridge, the explanation is simple. I already knew that the bird was the partridge, but I knew it from a source that others might not accept: the Cornish *Ordinalia*, a fourteenth-century biblical drama. In the *Origo Mundi* (lines 123-34), Adam names the animals, including a list of birds that matches almost perfectly the birds whose habits are described in this passage of *Piers Plowman* (B XI.350-61). When the names are all matched with the descriptions in the poem, the one and only bird in the drama that fits line 357 is the partridge (grvgyer). But some might object that Langland would not have known Cornish, and so I had to find a different kind of proof. For another instance where my "honor" is at stake, see below, commentary on Pearsall's C text, XVI.271.

XII.40-41

The editor's suggested answer to the rhetorical question in these lines seems wide of the mark. Ymaginatif here drops his perfunctory definition of the triad and launches into his real subject: the value of learning. In fact, he answers his own question in line 45, where the surprise ingredient is "kynde wit," a faculty which is destined to be downgraded in B (from its lofty position in A) and equated with worldly wisdom.

XII.146-47a

Schmidt comments: "Ymag. means that the statement 'there was no room in the inn' implies that Joseph and Mary were seeking a room at an inn and therefore cannot have been beggars." But in fact Ymaginatif says: "Ne in none beggers cote was that barn born, / But in a burgeises place, of Bethlem the beste." That is, he does *not* make the inference that the editor attributes to him, but rather denies flatly that the Child was born in a "beggers cote." Skeat calls this a "strange version" of Luke 2:7. But see the Wycliffe Bible, Early Version: "for ther was not place to hym in the comyn stable." (The Later Version reads: "for ther was no place to hym in no chaumbir.")

XIII.83   I shal jangle to this jurdan with his juste wombe.

The editor cites XI.101-6 to cast doubt on the punning reference in this line to William Jordan. But those earlier lines have nothing to do with "Langland's methods and views as a satirist." In them Lewte is assuring the dreamer that it is quite all right to denounce "thyng that al the world woot" as long as one is not overhasty in assigning blame or too eager to make public what is private: all criticism should be dispassionate and restrained. Fortunately for the dreamer (and thus the poet) the main point is that "al the world woot" the corruption of the friars, so that in fact Lewte's carefully worded proviso serves mainly to reassure potentially hostile colleagues that the poet is not irresponsible (for the poet's sensitivity to audience reaction see B XV.91, 381, 412, 487). There is nothing to indicate that the shortcomings of Friar William Jordan so brilliantly depicted here were anything other than a matter of common knowledge, at least among Oxford faculty and students.

XIII.108-9

The reference to "yonge children" is a passing thrust at recruiting practices of the fraternal orders, particularly at Oxford. Archbishop Fitz-Ralph in his sermon against the friars, *Defensio Curatorum*, complains that the friars beguile children into their order and then keep them there by force, not allowing them even to communicate with their parents. "In euydence herof, þis day as ich come out of myn Inne, come to me a good man of Englond þat is comen to þis court for socour and remedye; and he tolde me þat anoon after Ester þat last was at Oxenford, freres byname hym his sone þat was nouȝt xiii ȝere olde, & he came þider to speke wiþ his sone, & moste nouȝt speke wiþ his sone but vnder warde & keping of freres."[10]

XIII.119-29

It is true that Piers himself did not attack learning, but the B poet is aware that the attack on learning in the A text was conducted on the plowman's behalf, as a result of his clash with the priest in the pardon scene (A VIII.89-121). It is therefore to be expected that if the plowman is to be given a second life (in the B text), honesty requires that Piers be represented as in essential agreement with this main thesis of the A poet, articulated by Will in the Epilogue (A XI.250-303). The fact that this sharply worded conclusion grows out of antagonism toward the priest in the pardon scene is evident in the poet's expansion of Mark 13:9: "Whanne ye ben aposid of princes or of *prestis of the lawe*" (A XI.289). It is thus not necessary to assume that Clergy's comment on Piers in this passage "presupposes knowledge of the latter ulterior to that supplied in the text." It is indeed appropriate that Clergy speak with particular hesitancy: not only has he suffered embarrassment because of the behavior of the learned doctor, but he has also personally been the target of the slings and arrows of the A poet.

XIII.136-38

Patience does not "set science at a sop" because the author does not either. For the reason that Piers is said to do so, see comment just above on XIII.119-29.

XIV.208-9

The different value assigned to wit and riches by Ymaginatif (XII.45) and Patience (XIII.208-9) is more apparent than real, and it is determined by the context. Ymaginatif wished to persuade the dreamer of the value of clergie (learning), and one of his devices to this end was to cast doubt on the reliability of kynde wit (= common sense), for which the dreamer has shown (in the A text) a high regard. Patience, on the other hand, here wishes to persuade Haukyn (and the dreamer) that poverty is to be preferred to riches, and hence stresses wit and wisdom (*not* kynde wit) as a potential attribute of the poor much more acceptable to God than wealth.

XV.561

More precisely this line indicates that worldly preoccupations prevent prelates from *praying for peace*. The poet is writing in a time of *war and woe* (XV.540). These are not routine doctrinal statements.

XVIII.109a   *Cum veniat sanctus sanctorum cessabit unxio vestra.*

On page 223 the editor refers to Dan. 9:24, the ultimate source of this quotation, but in his note (p. 350) reports that "the exact source is untraced." Pearsall traces it to the pseudo-Augustinian sermon *Contra Judaeos* (PL 42: 1124) as used in one of the lessons for the fourth Sunday in Advent (C XX.113an). Schmidt in his translation (p. 223) takes *unxio* to refer to kingship; earlier in a previous occurrence of the same quotation (XV.598), he understands *unxio* to refer to "the special relation of the Jews with God" (p. 197).[11]

XVIII.396a

Concerning this abrupt quotation of 2 Cor. 12:4 the editor remarks, "This is Langland's boldest claim for the value and validity of his own 'visions and revelations.' " On the other hand Pearsall believes (C XX.438an) the poet applies Paul's words to the dreamer, "suggesting that he is aware of the limits to which his vision of Christ's promise of mercy can be taken." In this case, considering the anguish that lies behind this entire speech by Christ (on which hinges the fate of all participants in the violence of the early 1380s), I am convinced that Pearsall's interpretation is the right one.

XIX.189-91

The editor apparently takes these lines to refer to the pope's power only, whereas surely they apply to the power of the priesthood in general. The confessional is being invoked here, and the implication is that the priest-confessor has the power to *require* the penitent to "pay what he owes." The purpose of this line of argument in the poem is to urge use of the priest's power as confessor to compel reconciliation of the warring elements in contemporary society. The poet was living in a time of violence (XV.355, 540). In Passus XVIII he saw hope of reconciliation through mercy of Christ (see comment just above on XVIII.396a); in XIX, for those perhaps not yet persuaded, he holds out the iron rule of *redde quod debes*.

XX.10-11

To his remarks here the editor should have added: "according to Need, whose teachings are not to be trusted."[12] This comment also applies to Schmidt's notes to lines 18, 23, 35, and 43.

XX.135 And overtilte al his truthe with "Tak this up amendement."

The editor translates 135b as "Take this (bribe) to amend

your judgment [in my favour]." On the other hand I suggest: "Take this (small amount) until (I can) improve (on it)." In other words: "There is more where this came from." Cf. GGK 897-98.

Pearsall's C Text

Pearsall treats his text very conservatively and does not have (like Schmidt) a separate section of textual notes or commentary. Hence in what follows I am simply calling attention to certain textual problems which I noticed in passing, before turning to Pearsall's explanatory notes.

I.97-101   *lineation disordered* XUIP
  The editor is probably right to leave these lines in manuscript order (= Skeat). But this passage includes more jumbled lines than he has indicated (I.94-102). Moreover, there are many other examples of this kind of disordering that all the editors (not just Pearsall) seem to ignore.[13]

IV.23   Forthy lat peytrele wil and pole hym with peynted withes. withes] XUIP wittes.
  Here is one of Pearsall's rare emendations, and I regret to say I believe it unnecessary. The reading of the MSS (wittes) should be retained and the line translated: "Let Wil [the name of Reason's horse in C only] be armed with a pectorale and let him be restrained [by means of a martingale] [as protection] against [an attack by] painted wits." The attack by painted wits (waryn wysman and wyly-man) occurs almost immediately (IV.27 ff.). The purpose here is not visual (withes) but allegorical.

V.158   Ledares of lawedays and londes ypurchaced. lawedays XU] I ladies; P louedaies.
  AB: A ledere of love-daies and a lond biggere.
  In this case the A MSS are seriously divided (H_2ChURI *love-*

daies, TDAWMH₃Di *ladies*) while the B MSS are unanimous in reading *lovedayes.* Yet Pearsall chooses a third variant *lawedays,* despite the fact that C MSS MIFSG (Skeat) read *louedaies* (Pearsall gives this as the reading of P, but according to Skeat P omits this line). I am inclined to think *lovedaies* should be retained in C. For a similar but more difficult case, compare the variants in all three versions for the second stave word in C VI.402: *wexid / wipyd / waschid.*

VI.173   with þat at y shal," quod that shrewe, "Saturdayes, for thy moder loue.

Pearsall has no textual note here, but Skeat (P) reads "for thy love," which makes sense since Lechery is here addressing the Virgin (VI.170 ff.). I assume that *for thy moder loue* means "for thy mother's love," but I suppose the editor could be understanding it to mean "for thy mother-love."

VII.261   Ac be war thenne of Wrath, þat wikkede shrewe. þat I] XU nat þat.

The editor corrects his base manuscript to conform to the readings of Kane's A text and the K-D B text. I still think that the line should read: "Ac be war thanne of Wraththe-nought, that wykkide shrewe" (Knott-Fowler A VI.95). *Wrath-not* is the harder reading in context and conforms to the negative pattern of the decalogue in C VII. 205 ff.

XV.106   Of Dowel and of Dobet, and yf Dobest do eny penaunce. Dobest B] XUITP Dobet.

This might be a case of error in the B archetype, which Pearsall uses here to correct his C text against the readings of the MSS. The easier reading is *Dobest,* since in a line referring to Dowel and Dobet the scribes would naturally expect the third stave to read *Dobest.* But Patience has a reason for prompting the dreamer to ask the doctor if *Dobet* does any penance: because the friar-doctor belongs to the regular clergy who in A were associated with the life of Dobet (A XI.

Two New Editions of *Piers Plowman* 241

196–215), and he has thus far shown no inclination to deny himself or do penance of any kind. Hence the question asked by the dreamer (XV.111, which should read, "Is Dobet eny penaunce?" as in Skeat) is designed to find out what the doctor will say about the rules that should govern *his own* way of life (Dobet), *not* the life of bishops (Dobest).

XVI.166, 167

Pearsall transposes second half-lines, following K-D (pp. 209–10). But see Schmidt, pp. 288 ff. B XV.16–17n.

XX.182   Moises and many moo mery shal synge.
         mery B] XUITP mercy.

Pearsall follows K-D (p. 208). But see Schmidt, p. 297. B XVIII.178n.

XX.208   "And y shal preue," quod Pes, "here payne
         moet haue ende." preue B] XUIPT preye.

Pearsall follows K-D (B XVIII.203). But see Schmidt, p. 297, note to B XVIII.202n. These editors are all agreed (apparently) that they must choose one or the other. In my opinion the poet first wrote "preue" (in B), and then revised to "preye" (in RF, retained in C). Not much is at stake here, but the cumulative effect of ignoring the literary character of RF readings may, in the long run, have a damaging effect on future study.

XXII.236 And sethen thei chosen chele
          and cheytyftee. cheytyftee] XU
          cheytyftee pouerte; TP chaitif
          pouerte.

Pearsall follows K-D (p. 117). But see Schmidt, p. 303, XX.236n.

Pearsall's Explanatory Notes

Prol. 2   Y shope me into shroudes as y a shep were.

I cannot see that Langland "associated himself elsewhere with 'ermytes' of dubious vocation," or that there is "a persistent hint of self-criticism" anywhere in the text. The author does say that the dreamer, while living like a lollard in Cornhill, incurred the wrath of lollards and hermits because of what he said about them in his verses (V.1-5). But the supposition that this is intended as autobiography (which I hesitate to attribute to Pearsall, since he elsewhere appears to concede the fictitiousness of the dreamer's wife and daughter) or that it somehow conveys authorial self-criticism is nowhere substantiated.

Prol. 35

I question the accuracy of the editor's comments on the treatment of minstrels in the three versions. In the A text, good minstrels are commended (Prol. 33-34) and bad minstrels are denounced (Prol. 35-39). In the B and C texts nothing good is said about the minstrels at all (other than what is held over from the A text), and instead lords and ladies are warned against supporting entertainers at the expense of poor men, who are likened to God's minstrels (B XIII.421-56; see also a similar passage in C IX.126-38 cited by Pearsall). The differences in attitude therefore divide A/BC, rather than AB/C as the editor suggests. The treatment in BC does not "clarify the problem"; it simply expresses a different attitude.

Prol. 95-124

Much more than "false priests," this biblical exemplum is concerned with "prelates" (101), who are being warned by the example of Eli to speak out against corrupt practices in the church (96-102) or suffer the consequences. The passage is moved here by the poet from its earlier position in B X.277-80 (where it was part of a long critique of bishops) and considerably expanded; but its appearance here is not as "abrupt" as the editor seems to indicate, since Conscience is using it to criticize those bishops (line 85) who are enriching themselves in government service and ignoring the spiritual condition of their flocks.

I.136

"Kynde knowyng," or "kynd wit" (actually the same thing) cannot be successfully defined without taking into consideration the sharply different values assigned to it in A (very high) and BC (very limited).

II.243-48

These lines are not "added in C": they are an expansion of A II.165-66, lines absent from B, though they are "restored" by K-D, II.204-5 (Schmidt omits).

III.14

Pearsall translates the *iustices somme* as "the justices, some of them." I question whether this is good Middle English, and I certainly would not give the words that meaning in the A text, where such qualifications are not in the author's style: "Thei that wonith at Westmenstre worsshipeth hire *alle*" (A III.12; for *alle* C has "monye"). In this context of sweeping condemnation, the following line should be rendered, "Gently with joy the justices *together*" (ysomme, OE æt-somne). It is perhaps a moot question whether the altered C context would justify the editor's (awkward?) translation.

III.68-72

This passage is "totally intrusive" only if we disallow the poet's frequent spontaneous excoriations of immorality. Even Chaucer is occasionally given to this kind of outburst (CT Gen. Prol. 659-62).

III.408-41

The story recounted here of Saul versus the Amalekites (1 Reg. 15 = 1 Sam. 15) is said by the editor to be "not intrinsically a very good one for the illustration of meed, since Saul's purpose in keeping back the best of the spoil was to offer it in sacrifice to God; Samuel's point was that God prefers absolute obedience (1 Reg. 15:21-2)." But the biblical narrative makes it clear that Saul and his men were motivated by greed in their selective "devotion" of the enemy and his possessions (1 Reg.

15:9; cf. Jos. 7); it was only after being challenged by Samuel that Saul invoked the pious motive of sacrifice (15:15), and under pressure from the prophet he later confesses this to be a fraud (15:24). Nothing is said explicitly in the Bible about the monetary benefits of sparing the king, but it is surely a legitimate inference that these would be considerable (A III. 245-46; C III.408, and cf. III.233-34 and note).

III.451-81

It is misleading to say that "this prophecy of the golden age is not in A." The first two lines *are* from A. In fact, these are the final two lines of Conscience's prophecy in A III.257-73, and what follows is not so much a "prophecy of the golden age" as an apocalyptic expansion of such a prophecy in the A text. (The biblical reference should read Isa. 2:2-5.)

IV.51

The first mention of robbers lying in wait for people on their way to the St. Giles fair at Winchester is made by Patience (B XIV.301; preserved in C XVI.138). In the C text two new references are added, the one here by Peace, and another by Recklessness (XIII.51). Such insistence on the dangers of the London-to-Winchester road suggests that the author may be recalling some painful experience of his own. Even Chaucer was not immune to assault by robbers.

IV.71, 72

These two notes lack precision. Line 71 simply points out that Meed was manifested in the efforts of Wrong to buy his way out of trouble. The names of the legal officials (Wisdom and Wit) are used with complete consistency throughout the passus in A, and, with one exception (B IV.67), also in B; it is in the C text that the names differ, and for a recognizable purpose. In the original (A) text, the corrupt nature of the two officials is hinted at in their names, *Waryn* Wisdom and *Witty,* and made clear in their behavior. But in C the author wishes to make quite explicit the "painted wits" (IV.23) of the Westminster crowd, and so he increases the number of lawyers and gives them more obvious names: Wareyn Wisman and Wilyman (27), Witty-man and Wareyne Wryng-lawe (31), Wyles (77), and "a wise one" (83), in addition to the original Wisdom and Wit (66, 72, 77, 87, and 96). Of the editor's cross-references, only XXII.133 (a reprise of the Westminster scene) has a real bearing on this passage.

V.2

The editor cautiously suggests that Langland (in his use of the term *lollere*) "had little sympathy with the Wycliffites." Later, in a note to XVII.220, however, he remarks that "Langland shows in this passage how close he is in spirit to many of Wyclif's ideas and to Lollardry." The latter opinion is, I think, closer to the truth.

V.36

The editor is normally careful in making inferences, but he here speculates on the author's schooling, based on the words of the dreamer to Reason. He concludes that the poet attended a university but had to drop out "half-trained for a clerical vocation." This is certainly an improvement over the popular image of Langland as a rail-splitter from Malvern Hills, but it falls far short of my impression (from the whole poem) that the author (of the B and C texts) is a highly educated member of the secular clergy who worries about such things as the inability of Masters of Divinity to respond to a *quodlibet*, assuming there were faculty capable of examining them (XVIII.114–16), and the integrity of the teaching profession (XVI.241 ff, XVII.76–84, XXII.120, 302).

V.163

The note to this line is a fine example of the editor's ability to explain a passage in depth and show its connection with other passages in the poem importantly related to it. The subject here is the endowment of the regular clergy by secular lords and the corruption that ensues from this practice. I trust Pearsall will forgive me if I offer as a further illustration of this theme the teaching of John Trevisa, who seems to have prompted his patron, Thomas IV, Lord Berkeley, to withhold the customary lavish bequests to monasteries that had been a tradition in the family for years.[14]

V.168-71

The editor disallows Skeat's acceptance of this passage as a "prediction" of the Reformation. But Skeat knew that "it was merely due to the prevalent views as to the supreme power of the king." And Pearsall has difficulty relating the phrase "incurable þe wounde" to "the idea of monastic reform" (177a*n*). The standards invoked here to rule out the predictive element in this passage would discredit perhaps all of the forecasts (e.g., regarding the Babylonian exile) made by the Old Testament prophets. In this case I believe common sense is on Skeat's side.

VI.37

Here and in a few other places the editor corrects what he takes to be an author's error: the occasional failure to convert from masculine third person to first-person pronoun after moving the Haukyn passage back to the confession of Pride, spoken by Purnele (a woman). Making such changes is a precarious business: where do you stop? Should we emend, for instance, when Purnele speaks of herself as "strengest uppon stede and styuest vnder gyrdel" (43)? But in this case I am not sure that the discrepancies are in fact authorial, since (a) they are not present in MS P (Skeat VII.14-60), (b) there are signs of revision (of the relocated passage) toward feminization of the speaker (see esp. lines 44, 46-47), and (c) the "errors," including one which Pearsall lets stand (60), occur in passages *that have been revised* (51, 59-60). Hence I think it would be appropriate to adopt the pronouns from MS P throughout (lacking a full corpus of variants on which to base a judgement).

VI.206

If the "circumstantiality" of this passage seems "trivial," that may be because it is inherited from the A text (A V.113-40) and is here imbedded in a confession of a very different order (C VI.196-349). Circumstantial detail in A (e.g., A V.71-72) often becomes allegorized in BC (B V.119-20; C VI.86-87 and Pearsall's note). Whether this is an improvement or not is a matter of taste, but I for one do not find A's circumstantiality trivial, and I doubt that John Ball did either.

VI.246   And with Lumbardus lettres lene gold to Rome.

One may wonder how Langland, "a half-trained cleric in minor orders" (see notes to V.2, 36), would be aware of the inner workings of the international monetary exchange while living like a loller on Cornhill. Either he must have supplemented his income with a clerical job (despite his protestations to Reason) or perhaps had at some time traveled abroad. The relevance of the latter possibility can be seen in the life of John Trevisa: on 29 Jan. 1387 a license was granted to Angelus Christifori, a Lombard dwelling in London, to make a letter of exchange for 20 marks (provided no gold or silver in the lump or in coin be sent over by color of this command under pain of forfeiture of the same) payable to Master John Trevysa clerk, possibly in preparation for a journey to Italy (Calendar of Close Rolls 1392-96, p. 524).

VII.82-119

It seems misleading to speak of this passage as "developed from the suggestion of 75-80" when the latter is itself part of the whole passage moved here in revision from B XIII. If we look back at the B original, we find it further complicated by revision in RF (B XIII.436-53) and ultimately inspired by the angry fulminations of Dame Study (A XI.5-92). This is a good example of the difficulty of using the C text as the starting point for study of *Piers Plowman*.

VII.252   And she hath þe keye and þe clycat, thow þe kynge slepe.

To clarify *thow þe kynge slepe* the editor adds "i.e. in her womb." This clause occurs in C's three-line expansion (251-53) of A VI.91 (B V.604), where, attracted by the mention of keys, the revisor transforms Grace, the "good man" (line 243), into "a ful leel lady" (line 251), i.e., the Virgin. But I cannot see that this affects the meaning or function of our Lady here, who is able to admit a penitent sinner to the court "though (the justice of) the king sleep" (line 252), the point so frequently made in traditional miracle stories. We should not overload the allegory with a reference to the Incarnation. The Virgin is here serving in her capacity as Queen of Heaven.

IX.3

The editor's contention (e.g., here and in VIII.2n) that the final two passus provide a spiritual commentary on parts of the *Visio* frequently seems dubious when applied. Here XXI.182-90 (the definition of Dobest in Conscience's sermon on the Ascension) is said to explain the nature of the Pardon granted to Piers by Truth. Conscience's reference to Piers's pardon is tied to the theme of *Redde quod debes,* which seeks to invoke the power of the confessional to heal a society torn by strife and hatred. But Truth's pardon to Piers is an instrument of satire, parodying and ironically differing from "a conventional indulgence."[15] Hence in this case it is difficult to see how the one passage can be used to explain the other. The thing that makes Truth's pardon "superior to the usual kind of indulgence" is precisely what makes it no pardon at all: if you "do well" there will be no punishment *and no guilt*. But Piers's pardon *Redde quod debes* (XXI.187) assumes the widespread presence of guilt and prescribes the only permissible remedy: satisfaction.

IX.5

The editor's reference to "Peres's impatience with the pardon (291, below)" must be a slip. The speaker in line 291 is the priest, and we know the reason for *his* impatience: he expected to find a conventional indulgence, but all he sees is a doggedly simplistic excerpt from the Athanasian Creed.

IX.255-81

Bishops are treated with restraint *only* in the A text, where they are encouraged to correct the clergy (A VIII.16–17; cf. B VII.15) and, if necessary, to use the royal power to discipline them (A IX.90–96). They are the flower that grows out of the root and briar of society (A X.117–24), they abase the proud (A X.211–12), and serve as princes over God's people (A XI.194–95). The B reviser keeps most of these passages intact, except the last: here he inserts an abrasive denunciation of bishops, especially with respect to their corrective function, warning them to set their own house in order before presuming to correct others (B X.264–96). Skeat calls attention to the fact that lines 285–88 were shifted in C to the Prologue, forming an expanded critique of worldly bishops (and their clergy) put into the mouth of Conscience (95–124); apparently he did not notice that the rest of this B passage was completely rewritten and inserted here as C IX.255–81. But the most interesting point is the radical change (from B to C) in the poet's attitude toward bishops: whereas in B X he warned them sharply against correcting others without first correcting themselves, here in C IX he demands that they exercise their power of correction and lays squarely on them the responsibility for "al this caytiftee" (line 255). The reason for this striking difference in attitude is attributable, perhaps, to a change in bishops. There is no room here to go into detail, but I have long believed that the poet's anger in B was directed at Bishop Thomas Brinton (for his role in the "correction" of Wyclif's opinions),[16] and I now think that in C his somewhat different exhortation is intended for the ears of the new archbishop of Canterbury, William Courtney, whose predecessor, Simon Sudbury, had been assassinated in 1381 ("ho-so durste sygge hit, Simon *quasi dormit*" [C IX.257]). For an allusion to Sudbury's death in the B text (in an RF passage), see XV.525–26 (Skeat XV.555–56).[17]

IX.265–66

The editor translates the Latin, "Under a weak and negligent shepherd the wolf befouls the wool," no doubt with an eye on line 268b. But surely the translation of *lupus lanam cacat* in line 264 is better: "the wolf shiteth woolle" (Skeat).

Pearsall emends to read "þe woole," no doubt to accommodate his interpretation of the Latin; but if we let the line stand it makes perfectly good sense. The editor says that *cacat* "has no literal sense," but it clearly does if we understand the wolf to have eaten the sheep. Furthermore it is also good allegory: for the notion of predatory officials *eating* their victims, see Micah 3:1-3.

IX.318

I question the change to "Israel" here; it is doubtful that the author, anxious as he is to make everything clear, would use the name "Jacob" (line 312) and then a few lines later speak of "Israel." Why not simply adopt the reading of P (Iacob)? But the most notable thing in the line is the reviser's deliberate introduction of the idea that Rachel ("his dame") went with the family to Egypt, when in fact she died years earlier giving birth to Benjamin (Gen. 35:16-20). This variation also occurs in certain other forms of the story, e.g., the Middle English *Iacob and Iosep* (ca. 1250), apparently out of a desire for the mother to participate in the joyous reunion or perhaps from a concern that Joseph's prophetic dream (in which the sun and moon represented his parents) be exactly fulfilled. It is worth pointing out that the A poet carefully modifies Jacob's response ("I my self and my sones" [A VIII.143; cf. Gen. 37:10]) to conform to the event. The reviser retains this line (C IX.314), but then in line 318 deliberately puts Rachel back into the story, thus giving us, in the space of nine lines, contradictory versions of the biblical narrative.

X.20, 21, 28

The comments in these notes calling attention to the shortcomings of the dreamer do not fit this passage, carried over as it is with little change from the A text, where the dreamer is being allowed a little fun at the expense of the friars. The BC context may affect the way we read these lines, but any notes calling attention to the dreamer's need for reform are best restricted to passages added in revision, where his recalcitrance is unmistakably dramatized. In this scene the dreamer's "trappings of scholarly disputation" (line 28n) are donned strictly for the occasion, as a satirical mimicking of the friar's absorption in matters scholastic.

X.56

The dreamer's farewell to the friar is ironical, though not in the sense intended by the reference to Davlin. See comment just above on X.20, 21, and 28.

X.76

The view of the dreamer's development expressed in this note no doubt represents majority opinion. The same view may be seen in chapter 4 of Elizabeth Kirk, *The Dream Thought of* Piers Plowman.[18] In a review article devoted to the book I tried to show why I believed this depiction of the dreamer's development to be mistaken.[19] The matter is important enough to justify alerting the reader to the existence of a difference of opinion.

X.78-98

The editor here provides some valuable observations on the organization of the *Vita* in relation to the triad of Dowel, Dobet, and Dobest. When one thinks of the vast and complicated differences in the three versions of this section, it is remarkable if any statement on the subject can stand scrutiny. But I do think it would be wise, even in an edition of the C text, to point out that in A Dowel is the commons, Dobet the clergy (secular and regular), and Dobest bishops or high ecclesiastical office in general. Even though the reviser (in B and C) drastically changes the context of the passus corresponding to the A *Vita*, he never loses sight of these definitions in the process of rewriting.

X.88

This note is replete with problems—largely because the lines discussed here derive (with few changes) from the A text (A IX.82-85). First, *is ronne into religioun* does mean " has entered a religious order," because Dobet stands for the clergy, both secular and regular (see comment just above on X.78-98). There is, moreover, no special animosity toward friars in the A text, such as we find in BC; but even if there were, the technique of satire in A would not dictate their exculsion from Dobet. It is true that the three terms represent progressive ideals of the good life, but they are applied ironically in the case of Dobet. When the A poet, for example, likens society to a plant, the commons (Dowel) are the root, the bishops (Dobest) are the flower, and the clergy (Dobet) are the briars (A X.119-24). In the present case Dobet's choice of text shows him to be condescending toward those for whom he is spiritually responsible (the "unwise"). A similar thrust will be found in virtually every definition of Dobet in the A text. Second, the phrase *rendred þe bible,* whether or not *rendred* means "translated" (in this instance I think not), cannot be associated with the Wycliffite translation of the Bible, because the text in which that phrase appears was composed about a decade before the Bible project was begun. Third, the passage as a whole (lines 88-91) depicts Dobet as a member of the religious orders, engaged in preaching condescendingly to the people. This is not much of a definition of the good life, but then it was not meant to be.

X.100

I do not see why "we should not interpret 'king' literally." Surely he is not "the principle of order and stability, upon which the good life depends." Here he is defined as the bishops' enforcer.

X.281

Surely *secular man* means "layman"; Wit devotes most of his attention in all three versions to the commons (Dowel) and its most troubled institution, marriage. There is no indication of a digression here from the main topic.

X.31-34

This "brief reference to a favourite theme" (support of

bawdy entertainers at the expense of God's minstrels) is in fact all that is left of a much longer passage in A (XI.24-37), leading me to wonder whether it is in fact a "favourite theme" (in B and C). There *are* new passages on this subject in BC, of course, but I would describe them as conscience-striken responses to Dame Study rather than something introduced spontaneously as a favorite theme of the reviser.

XI.81-83

The editor quotes from a 1929 article by H. W. Wells, informing us that "the A text breaks off," an opinion with an amazing vitality, going all the way back to the earliest of the polemical articles of R. W. Chambers. The idea persists in the book by Elizabeth Kirk already referred to (see comment above on X.76). The same criticism applies to XI.163n.

XI.97   And ouer Skripture þe skilfole and screueynes were trewe.

I question whether the poet means that clergy is "superior in authority to Scripture," though some MSS read "ouer" (P has "of"). The line seems overcrowded with ideas. To whom does "skilfole" refer? What does the second half of the line have to do with the first? The idea of scribal fallibility appears abruptly, reminding us of the "much travail" of the Wycliffite translators in seeking "one Latin bible somedeal true." Perhaps this is what Dame Study says (94-97): "I shall direct you to my cousin Clergy, who knows all sciences and the fundamentals of Dowel, Dobet, and Dobest, for he is recognized as a teacher of all these, and skilled (in the interpretation) of Scripture, as long as scribes are accurate." If the editor's reading of line 97 is correct, we are left wondering why the poet would say that "Clergy is superior in authority to Scripture" and immediately thereafter declare that she (Scripture) is "as wise as himself (Clergy) in lore and in letters, in law and in reason" (99-100).

XI.166

The only thing that Study and Scripture have in common is

scorn. Study aggressively identifies the dreamer with the clerks who have God in their mouth (A XI.5-12, 86-91, partly surviving in C XI.5-10, 81-83), but when he defers graciously to her viewpoint (C XI.88-92), she commends his meekness and directs him to Clergie and Scripture. Scripture, on the other hand, is blunt, brief, and entirely serious as she accuses the dreamer of not knowing himself (C XI.163-66), and we are to understand that this flaw entirely invalidates his conclusions (A XI.250-303; completely removed from the C text at this point and reassigned to Recklessness in XI.196-298). Scripture's accusation, of course, was originally the opening salvo of the B-continuation (B XI.1-2).

XI.168

Again I must disagree with the editor's account of this important transition to the BC-continuation (see above comment on XI.81-83). The dreamer is not seeking "an escape from despair of salvation." He is rather being driven into a dream of corrective self-examination (Scripture's "know thyself"). The twelfth passus of A referred to is entirely without authenticity from the point of view of textual criticism (which is why both Kane and I separated it from the main body of the text) and is clearly the work of someone other than the original author (from the point of view of style). Doubt on this point survives because it is thought to lend credence to the erroneous idea that the A text ends inconclusively.

XI.178 And bade me for my continence counte clerkes techyng lihte.

The editor offers alternative meanings for the phrase *for my continence:* "for the sake of my looks" or "as far as self-restraint was concerned." But there is a third possibility, on the analogy of the phrase *In continance of clothyng* (Prol. 26), where *continance* means an "appearance," "show," or "front" that conceals the true nature of the person (cf. AB Prol. 24b, *comen disgisid*). The dreamer here is advised to disparage the teaching of clerks for the sake of appearances, to persist in his view so as not to have to admit he is wrong.

XI.196

Notice here the very perceptive note by the editor on the role of Recklessness in the C text: "The immediate purpose of extending his role in C is so as to allocate to him the intellectual questionings concerning learning and salvation attributed to the dreamer of AB, and in so doing to discredit them explicitly, or at least to withdraw from them any hint of authorial sanction." It is precisely this problem (that the dreamer's conclusions in A had "authorial sanction") that the reviser attempted to solve in B by means of the elaborate interrogation of the dreamer that begins in Passus XI. But until now I had not realized that the expanded role of Recklessness in C constitutes a further strategy toward that same end and goes a step nearer to making the poem as a whole more fully in harmony with the purposes of the reviser. What an unsurpassed guide to this poem Pearsall could be for all of us if he were freed of the constraints of his authorship assumption!

XI.221

Here is another valuable observation by the editor, in this case on the introduction of the "righteous heathen" problem: "It is worth noting that Rechelesnesse introduces the question, not out of any concern for Aristotle and Solomon, but in order to prove that learning is of no use in winning salvation." It is likewise worth remarking that the dreamer in A, when he introduced this question, had precisely the same motive and also had authorial sanction behind it.

XI.298

This line corresponds to the last line of the A text (A XI.303). The editor observes: "The orthodox view was that purgatory might be by-passed by those who led devout ascetic lives of penance and self-denial and by baptized children who died young (*Prick of Conscience* 2637–42, 3286–3349). The views expressed throughout this passage are, of course, those of Recklessness." But the editor also cross-references IX.185, a line expressing the same idea in a passage which he characterizes as "authorial exposition" (IX.159n). In fact both lines are inherited from the A text (A VIII.88, XI.303) and express the passionately held opinion of the author (whether orthodox or not). The reviser was not without human sympathies, but his remarks on this subject are not so much an affirmation as a prayer (B XIV.164-65, C XVI.17-18).

XII.87

The editor plausibly attributes this speech (XII.87 -XIII.127) to Recklessness and then adds that "his interpretation is recklessly simple, and has later to be qualified (XIV.204)." Yet in B this speech is attributed by Skeat to Loyalty, hardly the kind of spokesman to be considered reckless (others suggest that the dreamer is the speaker). It seems to me that whoever may be the speaker, the poet in these lines is setting forth his own ideas. If they are now (in C) to be seen as somewhat reckless, this should be shown to be the case by reference to new or revised lines. If for correction of Recklessness we are to rely on Imaginatif (as suggested by the editor's reference to XIV.204), I am afraid we may be left unsatisfied. Imaginatif's handling of the "righteous heathen" issue at best walks the edge of a cliff, and his *vix* leaves us admiring his sense of balance but wondering whether he has in fact come up with a satisfactory solution to the problem (cf. XIV.204*n*).

XII.98

I doubt that the poverty theme "is being exploited by Recklessness as part of his strategy to discredit learning and prove it unnecessary to salvation" (see comment just above on XII.87). In B a careful distinction is made between poverty as a state and poverty in relation to a spiritual condition in order to undercut A's comparison of rich and poor (always to the disadvantage of the former). Though now assigned to Recklessness, the speech seems in its theme completely unchanged (e.g., C XIII.25 ff.). The only time Recklessness uses the argument attributed to him here by the editor is in those lines transferred to him from the dreamer of the A text (XI.205 -305). This argument has been such a problem for the reviser (its refutation requiring much of Passus XI–XIV) that it seems unlikely he would voluntarily introduce it anew in his own part of the poem.

XIV.90–91

For the idea that Christ's birthplace was not in a stable, see Wycliffite Bible, E.V. Luke 2:7. The editor emphasizes Matt. 2:11, but note that in the parallel passage in B, it is Luke 2:7 that is quoted. (See comment earlier on Schmidt, Literary and Historical Commentary B XII.146–47a.)

XV.33

Patience is cast in the role of the poor who cry at the gate mentioned by Dame Study (A XI.45; cf. C XV.186–89). It is noteworthy too that Patience, in being likened to Piers the Plowman, is also said to resemble a "palmer" (and cf. XV.131). This would appear to be the earliest reference in the poem (it is not in B) to suggest what is later made explicit: the identification of Piers with Christ (see XVI.337n). The image of Christ as pilgrim (see XII.130–31) derives from his post-resurrection appearance on the road to Emmaeus, when Cleophas calls him *peregrinus* (Luke 24:18). In this connection we may recall that the ballad on Christ's meeting with the woman at the well is entitled "The Maid and the Palmer." The hooded figure of Patience-Piers-Palmer is presented enigmatically, but our hearts are meant to burn within us as he speaks to us on the way (Luke 24:32).[20] This delicate transformation of the character of Piers from angry advocate of social justice (A text) to the embodiment of patient poverty (in BC) is a tribute to the skill of the reviser and a major instrument in changing a radical poem of the 1360s into a conservative poem of the 1380s.

XVI.1

Another of Pearsall's fine perceptions: "It is interesting to see that poverty, which was the worst of the world's problems in the *Visio* (= A), is now the solution to them."

XVI.211

Surely our "sympathy" for the dreamer's intellectual curiosity is not entirely anachronistic (the editor attributes it to "a changing view of the Faust-story"). After all, the dreamer prefaces his desire with a proviso: "by so no man were ygreued." Besides, the whole passage (XVI.201 ff.) is composed in a comic spirit: the dreamer has entered the last phase of his education, and his mentors (here, *Liberum Arbitrium*) are much more relaxed in their treatment of him.

XVI.271

The editor suggests "an intermediate source" for this text from pseudo-Chrysostom on Matthew, but I am convinced Skeat is correct in asserting that the quotation was made from memory. The evidence for my support of Skeat is as follows. On 13 May, 1378 Edmund de Stonore, sheriff of Oxford, prepared an indenture listing (among other items) twenty-four books that a faction of scholars in Queen's College (including John Trevisa) were ordered to turn over to the sheriff. Among these books was *Crisostomum super Matheum*, which J. R. Magrath identified as the Homilies of St. John Chrysostom on Matthew.[21] But a check of the second folio reading, which is fortunately included for each book on the list, proves that the work in question was pseudo-Chrysostom, or *Opus Imperfectum*. Exactly when the sheriff recovered these books is not known, but the fact that pseudo-Chrysostom is quoted from memory (in B XV.118) suggests that it must have been not too long after the date of the indenture.[22]

XVII.117

The editor's comment on this line sounds legalistic, if not unfeeling. Freewill is speaking for the author, who is deeply worried about the lack of spirituality in his society, and not merely indulging in the "world upside down" topos (XVII.85n), or engaged in refuting a Wycliffite position. He is trying to be honest with himself and with his audience, and for this we should be grateful.

XVII.124

I do not see the reason for the editor's skepticism here. Surely Russell is correct in seeing a reference to the opinions of Uthred of Boldon. Of course this *does* suggest that the author is perhaps learned, or at least that he spent time at Oxford: but there is no need to resist such inferences.

XVII.220

On the poet's closeness to Lollardry, compare the editor's note to V.2. It might have been well to point out that this story was not the sole property of Lollards. When Ralph Higden (a monk) uses it in his *Polychronicon*, for instance, the speaker prophesying ruin was not an angel but *hostis antiquus*, "the olde enemy" in Trevisa's translation (V.131), although some Trevisa MSS read "aungel of heuene."

XVII.278-80

A very misleading note: the failure here is attributable to the editor's acceptance of the notion that RF passages do not represent authorial revision (contrary to Skeat's opinion). Lines 279-80 do in fact refer to the lucrative activities of titular bishops, but line 278 is the final line of a passage (262-78) added to the original B text and is on an entirely different subject. Skeat perceived that there was a "pointed personal allusion" in this line, and elsewhere I try to show that the reference is to Simon Sudbury, archbishop of Canterbury.[23] The editor's faulty note here, among so many excellent ones, is a painful reminder of the critical importance of leaving no assumption unexamined.

XVIII.66

It is difficult to see that the contradiction between the fruit described in line 60 (early ripe, early rotten) and that described in lines 64-66 (the sooner ripe, the sweeter and more savory) is "resolved" by line 100 (= B XVI.72). Rather it seems to me that the problem is confined to the new C passage itself (C XVIII.53-84, 91-99, 101-5), which replaces the dreamer's frivolous question about the three piles and Piers's abrupt reply (B XVI.53-66, and incorporating 67-72 in C XVIII.85-90, 100). The problem is in fact confined to line 60 in C, where the author, while describing "real" apples, slips into a proverbial phrase which he has used elsewhere (XII. 222), forgetting momentarily that it will not suit the application to follow. No such problem exists in B.

XVIII.76

The poet's association of widows and religious with the contemplative life does not seem "confusing" except perhaps when viewed against the ambiguity of tradition mentioned here by the editor. What widows and religious have in common is the fact that they have "here owere wil forsaken" (line 76).

XVIII.199

It seems an exaggeration to say that "Abraham's explanation of the Trinity is here much abbreviated from B" when a passage of some eighty-four lines is reduced to seventy-six. Nor do the editor's reasons for the revision seem satisfactory. Especially compare B XVI.191-224 with C XVIII.201-39, where the revison seems to spring at least in part from an initial copying error (C XVIII.208-10 = B XVI.198, 199, 210: from repetition of *bileue* in B XVI.200, 210), which explains the syntactical problem discussed by the editor in his note to lines 208-9 (210 is not "a new line in C"; it corresponds to B XVI.210).

XVIII.202-3

After puzzling over these lines, one is tempted to say, with the dreamer, "This is myrke thyng for me" (line 197). Pearsall has obviously given them much thought, and he has provided the best explanation that I have yet seen. If K-D and Schmidt are right about the prose order of Bx (and they agree here), and if we apply the same reasoning to C, then line 202b would read: *his owne myhte to se*. Construing *to se* as a passive infinitive, we would then achieve, without further emendation, the same result for this line that the editor seeks in suggesting the substitution of *shewe* for *se*: "Power, and a mediator (through whom) his own power (is) to be seen." But the real puzzle is 203b, *and what soffreth hem bothe*. Admirable as is Pearsall's explanation, I have a modification to suggest. Presumably this half-line gives us the third person of the Trinity as well as (by analogy) the third ingredient necessary for a lord who claims allegiance (line 201). Therefore I take it that in the case of the worldly lord this third ingredient is someone to be on the receiving end, someone to endure (suffer) the exercise of his power. The third person of the Trinity, as we already know, is the Holy Ghost, but in terms of the secular analogy being employed, the unidentified subject that *soffreth hem both* (*hem* = Father and Son) must be Holy Church or, collectively, the "children of Charity" subsequently referred to (line 207), who have experienced (suffered) the Spirit of God descending mightily upon them (Acts 2).

XVIII.215

I doubt that Augustine's comparison is being used to depict "the limited understanding of Abraham" (see my comment above on XVIII.199). The author appears to be expressing his own thoughts (as often) through Abraham, and it is interesting to note that in B he seems to share Augustine's uncertainty about the validity of the comparison (B XVI.212 "telle if I dorste," line 214 "if I dorste seye").

XIX.90

Surely the line means, "No man ever went this way without being robbed." This explains why the wounded man, even after taking communion, will have to be plastered with patience: robbers will continue to provide "fondynges" (line 89). Long after the advent of Christianity, it will still be "a jungle out there." It is interesting that B XVII.105–26 is more optimistic but is deleted in revision. Could the deletion have occurred after a particularly bad experience on the road to Winchester? (See comment above on IV.51.)

XIX.161a

The editor informs us that the rest of the passus (i.e., over half of it) is occupied with the sin against the Holy Ghost and its relation to "wanhope." If this were indeed the case, then the Samaritan's disquisition on the Trinity would no doubt be the dull affair that many critics apparently think it is. But this entire passus, particularly lines 167-331, was written in an agony of spirit that is only partly hidden behind the theological language. The poet's emotional crisis was brought on by the spectacle of society divided against itself, seeking to solve its problems by rioting, destruction of property, and murder. The subject is so fully in the foreground of this passus (and indeed the one following) that critics have apparently been unable to see it. Yet it is the poet's agony in the face of these events (the London riots of 1381) that determines the Samaritan's doctrinal emphasis. Rich men are denounced because of their covetousness and their consequent failure to be generous and thus close the gap between rich and poor which lies behind the violence (lines 223-49); the poor who rioted and destroyed property (e.g., the burning of the Savoy in London) are warned that God's forgiveness is contingent on repentance *and* restitution (lines 196-208); churchmen (meaning the friars) who encouraged the rioters by taking Acts 2:44 as their text in sermons (cf. XXII.275-76) are warned that they are guilty of murder by mouth if not by hand (lines 250-56); those who actually committed murder are said to have committed the sin against the Holy Ghost (lines 257-73); and the Samaritan comes within an ace of saying that these latter will *never* be forgiven—so nearly so that the dreamer rushes to the rescue (lines 274-77).

XIX.278

Pearsall says: "It is the capacity of the hardened sinner to repent that is in question, not God's willingness to grant forgiveness." No doubt. But the poet here is invoking the power of the confessional to compel a reconciliation of the warring elements in his society (a second attempt at reconciliation in XX.370-478 is more positive and, I believe, more effective), and he comes very close to denying the possibility of forgiveness despite the dreamer's carefully worded question (see comment just above on XIX.161a).

XX.53

In B the drink offered to Christ on the cross was meant to shorten his life; in C its purpose is to lengthen it. Despite the editor's speculations on the significance of the C revision (a macabre joke, or perhaps the torturers' acting as instruments of the devil's purpose expressed below in line 335), I am inclined to believe that the change was made because the author was wrestling with a genuine crux of biblical interpretation. To this day commentators disagree on how to reconcile gospel accounts of the incident (Matt. 27:34, Mark 15:23, Luke 23:36, and John 19:28-30).

XX.113a

This is another case of authorial uncertainty about the interpretation of a biblical text. One should remember that Trevisa at this time was at work on biblical translation.[24]

XX.278   And lede hit þer lazar is and lihtliche me bynde.

A puzzling reference, if indeed Lazarus the brother of Mary and Martha (John 11) is meant. Certainly he is the one mentioned above in line 275. But since *þer Lazar is* represents an RF revision,[25] (see Skeat B XVIII.267: *ther hym lyketh*), the poet may have introduced here a reference to the beggar Lazarus (C VIII.279; Luke 16:22), not noticing that confusion might result from mention of the two Lazars in close proximity. If the above is correct, then *þer Lazar is* would be merely a satanic euphemism for "in bliss" (XVIII.273).

XX.299

To the editor's references add Robert Longsworth, *The Cornish Ordinalia: Religion and Dramaturgy*, (Cambridge: Harvard Univ. Press, 1967), Ch. 4.

XX.420

The editor cites the *Prick of Conscience* as background for this passage. Much more to the point, I believe, is John Trevisa's note on "tweie manere helles" in his translation of Higden's *Polychronicon*, Rolls Series, Vol. VI, p. 461. After all, the problem in this line is knowing in what sense a person can be said to come out of hell, and his note is precisely on this point, consisting of an explication of Psalm 85:13 (V); "thou hast delivered my soul out of the lower hell." It is perhaps not coincidental that Trevisa also uses the analogy of the felon reprieved at the last moment from death on the gallows (cf. C XX.421-25). One need not accept my hypothesis of Trevisa's authorship of BC before using the evidence of his writings to illuminate passages in *Piers Plowman*.

XX.430   Be hit enythyng abouhte, the boldenesse of here synne.

The editor renders the first half-line as follows: "If it be at all adequately paid for (i.e. by Christ's sacrifice)." He then goes on to suggest that the passage expresses the doctrine of universal salvation. I fear both the translation and the doctrine are based on a mistaken idea of the purpose of this passage (lines 415-44). It is true that the hope of universal salvation is expressed, but the possibility is made contingent, not only on universal repentance, but also on universal satisfaction (line 430). Christ will be merciful to *many* of his halfbretheren (line 436), but not all, because "bloed may not se bloed blede, bote hym rewe" (line 238). Anyone who regarded the taking of a human life as a righteous act, and therefore not requiring repentance, will be damned by Christ on the Day of Judgment (see my comments above on XIX.161a). Of course I have deliberately exaggerated for clarity's sake what must be to some extent read between the lines. This passage is actually much more positive and hopeful in tone than the warnings of the Samaritan in Passus XIX. But it is just as rigorous in the final analysis.

XX.436

Pearsall perhaps should have pointed out that the compound *halue-bretherne* in C replaces *hole bretherne* in B

(Skeat C XXI.422, 438). But apparently (no variants are given) all the C MSS used by the editor except P read *hole brethrene* in C XX.419 (Skeat XXI.422). Still, I take it that the reference here (436) is to the same group: those who are kin to Christ both in blood and in baptism. The use of *halue bretherne* in C, I suppose, indicates a retreat from the theological rashness of *hole bretherne* in B.

XXI.6

The editor fails to note that the "Christ of the winepress" (Isa. 63:1-7), in addition to being a text for Wednesday of Holy Week, is the basis for depictions of the Ascension (notably in medieval drama). It is doubtful that we are meant to turn back the calendar to the middle of Holy Week after having just heard the bells of Easter morning at the end of Passus XX. Indeed the vision here emphasizes what was a main theme of Ascension sermons: the exaltation of human nature as a result of the victory of Christ. Conscience's sermon (XXI.26-198) is then followed, as should be expected, by Pentecost (199 ff.), since the poem is and has been moving through the feasts of the Church calendar, as Pearsall elsewhere points out (e.g., XX.6*n*).

XXI.187 *Redde quod debes*

The editor remarks: "Restitution is not to be understood solely or primarily in material terms." But I have to say that these are precisely the terms intended here. See above, comments on XIX.161a, XX.430; and see the later passage on this same theme: XXI.389-95.

XXI.308

Why the reference to "prinses lettres" (cf. IX.281)?

XXI.394

It is not that the communicants have no debts to pay but that they forgive each other their debts (as the quote from the *pater-noster* indicates) before taking communion. The choices are to pay or to be forgiven the debt. The latter alternative, of course, is entirely dependent on the good will of the person to whom the penitent is indebted. But even with this possibility in mind, the rigorous standards of Conscience are too much for the brewer (396 ff.).

XXI.477

Criticism of the king is obliquely presented, but it is just as surely in these lines as it is, more directly, in the case of the brewer, the clergy, and the lord already presented. The literary source for this sequence is a doomsday drama such as that of Chester, with its sequence of lamentations spoken by representatives of the estates of society, presented there *in bono* and *in malo*, rather than as here in single human representatives of these estates before the crack of doom. This was a popular theme in medieval art as well as drama, as can be seen, for example, in the wall paintings of the parish church of South Leigh, near Oxford.

XXII.37

Although he wavers a bit (in notes to XXII.15 and 23), Pearsall finally seems to acknowledge the force of R. W. Frank's interpretation of Need's speech as expressing the friars' defense of their theoretical poverty, something which the poet of course rejects absolutely. One only need compare the counsel of Patience (XV.255-61) with the contrary advice of Need (XXII.10-15) to know which side the author is on.

The experience of reviewing these two editions has left me in a state of some uncertainty. On the one hand, both editors have done a professional job for which we should be grateful. On the other hand, I find myself so often in disagreement with their conclusions that I am discouraged to think that the poem is now to be read in a form that will so often be misleading to the unschooled reader. To some extent this may be due to the inherent difficulty of the poem; but this difficulty is exacerbated by the unfortunate influence of the flawed Kane-Donaldson B text, particularly evident in Schmidt's edition. To the many variants of the medieval manuscripts are now added the unwarranted reconstructions of modern editors, who often disagree not only with unanimous manuscript readings but also among themselves. Small wonder, then, if this editorial "jamming" of the voice of the author results in a crisis of confidence in the "authority" of the text of the poem. But the blame for this state of affairs should not be directed principally at these two editors. On the contrary, my heartfelt thanks go to both Schmidt and Pearsall for the remarkable success of their editions, achieved despite formidable obstacles, both in the difficulty of the poem itself and in the assumptions concerning it which they share with the great majority of *Piers Plowman* scholars.

Errata

Below are listed errors noted in both editions by page and line number (e.g., xxx.3) or page, note, and line number in note (e.g., 268.298n.4), or by page number, passus, and line number of text, and note or variants (v) to the line on same page (e.g. 21.II 135v). Each correction is separated by a slant sign.

Schmidt's B Text

xxx.3 worldly / xlvii.2 XI 51 / 21.II 135v lawe *om* / 23.II 202v lat *om* / 31.III 229 is wel worthi / 36.IV 15v hym *om* / 45.V 102v I wolde . . . evere] god woot my wille *All* B MSS *om* / 54.V 334v the *om* / 56.V 392v Raxed *om* / 57.V 428v is *om* / 62.V 541v sowe and *om* / 62.V 559v after *om* / 68 VI 87v ha*p* deserved *om* / 74.VI 236v wolde *om* / 76.VI 288v while *om* / 96.IX 145av *for* 145a *read* 146 / 103.X 94v to (2) *om* / 104.X 124v whyes *om* / 104.X 135v I *om* / 104.X 139 *for* A (*foll.* a.d.n.) *read* nail *om* A (*so* K-D) / 107.X 215v Founded *om* / 108.X 249v thi *om* / 112.X 348 any man Cristene / 112.X 348v any man / 117.XI 2v sette *om* / 125.XI 202v gentil *om* / 128.XI 276v begge *om* / 131.XI 362v on (1&2) *om* / 133.XI 418v wi*p om* / 142.XII 195v amenden *om* / 143.XII 230v *read* And Kynde kenned *and correct v* / 145.XII 278v to *om* / 145.XII 282v seith *om* / 158.XIII 345v som *om* / 205.XVI 216 *read* As / 249.XIX 432v *omission of sigla* W (*twice*) / 250.XIX 467v *read* I w. L *& r* (I w. after W) / 263.XX 361v chaunge *om* / 268.298n.4 cf. X 86 / 270.266n.3 censorship / 272.114n.1 (*MED s.v.*(c)) / 277.31n.5 XIII 296   / 279.60n.1 *hym yn* / 289.115n.1 *read* I do not follow K-D / 290.388n. K-D p. 194 / 293.201n.1 XV 392 / 303.307n *read* 308 / 315.11n.3 Burrow, 'Action' *is not in bibliog. p. xliv, but see p. xliii n.16* / 318.396n.2 Child *not in bibliog.* / 320.585-608n.8 *read* echoes I 163-4 / 322.133-8n *out of place;*

insert above 148n / 329.124-6n.6 *read* pp. 88-92 / 330.118n.5 VIII 58 and 111 / 336.357-8n.4 *read* (VI, ii, end, p. 233) / 336.410n *read* elements of Wit's at IX 95-8c (*C*) etc. Will has not yet / 336.1n.6 senses and the / 338.95n.2 (see also XI 9) / 339.45-5an.4 may come from / 343.300an.2 VI 269-70 / 350.111n.1 Mt 27:45 / 353.62n.4 27-30 above /

Pearsall's C Text

56.39n.1 see I 82n / 75.235-57n *read* 235-56 / 84.451-81n.3 (Isa. 2:2-5) / 104.140n *read* 139a / 109.3n.7 *delete* 3n / 117.196n.2 see XVI 86n / 123.310n.1 cf. IV 17n / 161.5n.1 (see VIII 111n) / 178.2n delete 2. / 178.2n.8 XIII 79n / 179.21n.4 (cf. III 485a) / 190.234an.3 he contrasts with / 191.254-69n *read* 254-67 / 196.53n *in her herte* / 196.53n.1 (cf. VII 188n) / 216.108n VIII 217 / 217.135an.3 XVII 21n / 220.210n *gyueth hym foel to name*: "calls (him) by the name of fool" (i.e., *stulte*, 214a), lit, "gives him fool / 241.132n.2 nice play on / 246.5-24n.4 202-4 / 247.30n.1 *doctour*, 66 / 262.32an *read* 32. / 265.114n.3 223) / 281.58an.6B XV 308 / 285.150n.3 XIV 205n / 304.248n *read* 247 / 363.37n.6 XII 98n / 394 fare *n.* add V 8 / 403 mete *n add a meles mete* enough food for one meal VI 289 /

Notes

1. *Modern Philology*, 58 (1961), 212-14. Hereafter *MP*.

2. *Yearbook of English Studies*, 7 (1977), 23-42. Hereafter *YES*.

3. *YES*, pp. 39-42.

4. Kane, Piers Plowman: *The Evidence for Authorship* (London: Athlone, 1965); for a dissenting voice see *English Language Notes*, 3 (1966), 295-300.

5. Unless otherwise indicated, I cite the A text from Thomas A. Knott and David C. Fowler, Piers the Plowman: *A Critical Edition of the A-Version* (Baltimore: Johns Hopkins, 1952); the B text from Schmidt; and the C text from Pearsall. The others cited are W.W. Skeat, *Piers the Plowman* (parallel text edition), 2 vols. (Oxford: Clarendon Press, 1886); George Kane and E. Talbot Donaldson, Piers Plowman: *The B Version* (London: Athlone, 1975).

6. Murtaugh, Piers Plowman *and the Image of God* (Gainesville: Univ. Presses of Florida, 1978), pp. 16-22.

7. *YES*, p. 35.

8. *YES*, p. 36.

9. Murtaugh, Piers Plowman *and the Image of God*, pp. 16-22.

10. *EETS, OS* 167, p. 56.

11. See *YES*, p. 38.

12. See R. W. Frank, Piers Plowman *and the Scheme of Salvation* (New Haven: Yale Univ. Press, 1957).

13. See *MP*, 50 (1952), 5-22.

14. See *Traditio*, 18 (1962), 314 and n. 99.

15. *MP*, 71 (1974), 397.

16. See my Piers the Plowman: *Literary Relations of the A and B Texts* (Seattle: Univ. of Washington Press, 1961), pp. 173-74, 237-38.

17. See also *MP*, 77 (Nov. 1979), 158-59.

18. Kirk, *Dream Thought* (New Haven: Yale Univ. Press, 1972).

19. *MP*, 71 (1974), 398-400.

20. See F. C. Gardiner, *The Pilgrimage of Desire* (Leiden: Brill, 1971).

21. Magrath, *The Queen's College*, 2 vols. (Oxford: Clarendon Press, 1921), I, 127.

22. See *MP*, 58 (1960), 94, item 7 and n. 68.

23. *MP*, 77 (Nov. 1979), 158-59.

24. See *YES*, p. 38, and *MP*, 58 (1960), 81-98.

25. *YES*, pp. 34-35.

Letters, Parables, and Guides: Some Recent Work On Flannery O'Connor

Diane Tolomeo

Sally Fitzgerald, ed. *The Habit of Being*. New York: Farrar, Straus, Giroux, 1979. xix, 617 pp.

John R. May. *The Pruning Word: The Parables of Flannery O'Connor*. Notre Dame: University of Notre Dame Press, 1976. xxv, 178 pp.

Robert E. Golden and Mary C. Sullivan. *Flannery O'Connor and Caroline Gordon: A Reference Guide*. Boston: G.K. Hall and Co., 1977. 342 pp.

Since her death in 1964 the popularity of the stories of Flannery O'Connor has increased so that she is no longer regarded as "Ferocious Flannery" with a style "as balefully direct as a death sentence."[1] The "dry withered prose" which according to one critic struggled from sentence to sentence is now seen to comprise some of the finest examples of the art of the short story in contemporary writing.[2] Her stories appear in new anthologies regularly, and her name is no longer greeted with quizzical looks in academic circles. Thanks to the recent publication of many of O'Connor's letters, as well as a new critical study of her works and a thorough bibliography of criticism of her stories, it is now possible to know her better and understand her writing more clearly than ever before.

Introduced and edited by her friend Sally Fitzgerald, Flannery O'Connor's letters are collected as *The Habit of Being*. The title derives from Maritain's concept of the "habit of art," a virtue which sharpens the intellectual faculty and which Fitzgerald attributes to O'Connor. To this, however, she adds that "the habit of being" was also present as "an excellence not only of action but of interior disposition and activity that increasingly reflected the object, the being, which specified it, and was reflected in what she did and said" (p. xvii). The letters bear witness to this judgment and are also perhaps the closest we will ever get to a formal biography of her. They convey the dry humor, deep faith, and clear eye for observation of herself and others that are also the unique mark of her stories.

It is to our advantage that O'Connor was such a prolific letter writer: "Mail is very eventful to me," she wrote in 1951 (p. 29), and several years later in 1957 she wrote, somewhat sarcastically, "I am learning that I had better be careful what I say . . . as the simplest things are going to be repeated" (p. 203). But they are generally very much worth repeating, and from her correspondence with friends and with unknown readers who became friends we learn her literary tastes and her attitudes toward her own writing as it progressed. Her motivation for writing never wavered: "You do not write the best you can for the sake of art but for the sake of returning your talent increased to the invisible God to use or not use as he sees fit" (p. 419). One of the earliest letters in fact explains to a publisher who wished to change the direction of her work that "I am amenable to criticism but only within the sphere of what I am trying to do; I will not be persuaded to do otherwise" (p. 10). Fortunately for us, she remained firm.

O'Connor received numerous letters from students, teachers and would-be writers. Some of these persons she described as "people I might have created myself" (p. 82). And her replies to them reveal that she too was not entirely separate from the characters she created. To an admiring single gentleman she wrote "that I didn't think I'd like him a bit but he would be crazy about me as I had seven gold teeth and weighed 250 pounds" (p. 87).

Similarly, her letters reveal a preoccupation not only with literary and theological matters but also with the anecdotal side of daily life on the farm, so that we often forget we are reading her letters and not her fiction: we receive word of the election of Miss Gum Spirits of Turpentine, learn about the tastes of peafowl, and get a running commentary on the comings and goings of the farm help, who could easily be dropped into one of her stories without anyone's being the wiser. Fitzgerald has helped capture this sense by preserving many of O'Connor's spelling and grammatical "errors" (most of them intentional) which add to the informal tone and liveliness of the letters. Thus we find words such as "yestiddy," "Sareday," "bidnis," "simmernarians," and "Evalin Wow" (the English novelist). The letters reveal a personality which took delight in the natural world and its daily events and to which the trivial often concealed the divine.

But there is a more serious side to these letters, even if it is sometimes presented in a lighthearted manner. In the early days when her disease, lupus epizooticus, began to interfere with her writing, O'Connor explained that she was nevertheless able to continue because "what you have to measure out, you come to observe closer, or so I tell myself" (p. 57). Her keen observation often led to the creation of "grotesque" characters and situations, and she wrote as early as 1955 that she was "interested in making up a good case for distortion, as I am coming to believe it is the only way to make people see" (p. 79). Thus characters such as Enoch Emery (in *Wise Blood*), Hulga (in "Good Country People"), and Tarwater (in *The Violent Bear It Away*) appealed immensely to her. She wrote of them as if they were real: "Me and Enoch are living in the woods in Connecticut with the Robert Fitzgeralds. Enoch didn't care so much for New York. He said there wasn't no privetcy there. Every time he went to sit in the bushes there was already somebody sitting there ahead of him" (p. 21). These three characters in particular seem to have been extensions of herself. She was very fond of them and even signed her name as various permutations of Tarwater's name in her letters to Maryat Lee. And of Hulga she wrote, "My heroine already is, and is Hulga. . . . Hulga in this case would be a projection of myself into this kind of tragic-comic action" (p.106).

These letters reveal an honest sense of herself and her writing, and while O'Connor often sounds as if she were not sure of her own abilities ("my talent lies in a kind of intellectual vaudeville" [p. 80]), we are misled if we take such comments very seriously. More revealing are her discussions of matters of faith, which also shed light on her writing. A good deal of this material is found in her letters to "A," an unidentified woman with whom O'Connor shared books and clippings, encouragement and criticism in writing, and ideas on religion and belief. She sponsored "A" at her confirmation after being received into the Catholic Church and grieved at her leaving it five years later. The friendship sparked some of O'Connor's most serious and enlightening comments, such as this indication of where she thought her work might be headed: "If I were to live long enough and develop as an artist to the proper extent, I would like to write a comic novel about a woman — and what is more comic and terrible than the angular intellectual proud woman approaching God inch by inch with ground teeth?" (pp. 105-6).

Throughout the letters, Sally Fitzgerald has used tact and judgment both in what she omits and in the information she adds for the benefit of the reader. None of the daily letters which Flannery wrote to her mother while she stayed with the Fitzgeralds in Connecticut is included, since these were personal and private. But in the rest of the letters Fitzgerald has clarified references to characters and events by including (in brackets) titles of the stories to which they refer. She has briefly introduced new correspondents as they appear and has supplied appropriate footnotes where the subject under discussion is not immediately apparent or where extra information is required. The index is comprehensive.

These letters prove that O'Connor was wrong when she wrote that "lives spent between the house and the chicken yard do not make exciting copy" (p. 291), for the letters are delightful and provocative, moving and inspiring. They will be of immeasurable value for those seeking further insights into the stories but are also worth reading solely on their own merit. They bring Flannery O'Connor very close to us indeed.

While the letters emphasize the personal, most of the recent critical work on O'Connor leaves behind her daily life and places her in her newly accepted position as a widely known writer who has finally acquired the distinction of being "respectable." But whether respectability is something O'Connor would herself have desired is not at all certain. Her stories were intended to shout to the hard of hearing.[3] They were not intended to lull her audience into an oblivious trance in which detached criticism could be carried out while a person's spiritual core remained untouched. She wanted her stories to be subjected to the same four levels of exegesis used by medieval commentators on the Scriptures: besides the literal, there was "one they called allegorical, in which one fact pointed to another; one they called tropological, or moral, which had to do with what should be done; and one they called anagogical, which had to do with the Divine life and our participation in it."[4] It is this kind of vision, she insisted, which produces and increases the meaning of a story. Thus it is not at all inaccurate to see her stories as modern day parables that on the one hand capture the audience with their literal level of plot and dialogue and at the same time concern themselves primarily with spiritual truth and man's response to it.

This is the stance adopted by John R. May in *The Pruning Word: The Parables of Flannery O'Connor*, a significant study of all of O'Connor's works, something none of her other critics have attempted. May's introduction recapitulates and amplifies many of the ideas he presented earlier concerning the integrity of criticism and the way in which the consensus in interpretation is best achieved, namely, through scholarly dialogue that interprets, evaluates, and then reevaluates.[5] May's work is one of the few books on O'Connor that falls readily into his third category. Earlier critics disagreed violently amongst themselves and gave evidence of the difficulty of attaining objectivity in viewing O'Connor's stories. Such objectivity is especially difficult when one considers fiction that excites as much religious and psychological response as O'Connor's does. Her stories invite enthusiastic comment from both religious fanatics, who ignore their literary merit, and from literary critics, who deny their religious implications. A longtime friend of O'Connor's, John Hawkes, maintained, despite her efforts to convince him otherwise, that she was of the devil's party ("Flannery O'Connor's Devil," *Sewanee Review* 70 [1962] 395-407); while *Time* magazine called her characters "God-intoxicated hillbillies" (29 February 1960, p. 118). It is only within the past decade that full length books on her life and art have appeared. May's work takes a solid stand on the side of those who see her theology as an essential element in her art. His arguments reflect his rigorous thinking as a Jesuit who is at home with literary criticism as well as with theological precision. Yet his strong theological bias does no violence to O'Connor's stories. On the contrary, it enhances our understanding of them. One can hardly begin to attempt an evaluation of any of O'Connor's work without first accepting *her* world. For some readers this will mean a willing suspension of their disbelief: they must put on the minds of impassioned believers in God, believers, moreover, in orthodox Catholic doctrine, to apprehend fully much of what she writes. This is not the world of critics such as Josephine Hendin, who, in *The World of Flannery O'Connor* (Bloomington: Indiana Univ. Press, 1970), would exclude religious belief from critical discussion of the stories and would focus primarily on them from a psychological or secular perspective.

On the other hand, neither is May in sympathy with critics such as Martha Stephens (*The Question of Flannery O'Connor* [Baton Rouge: Louisiana State Univ. Press, 1973]) who see O'Connor's faith as a block to our appreciation of the stories. May is much closer to Preston M. Browning, Jr.'s, *Flannery O'Connor* (Carbondale: Southern Illinois Univ. Press, 1974) and to Carter W. Martin's *The True Country* (Nashville: Vanderbilt Univ. Press, 1969), both of which sense a deliberate balance in O'Connor's work between the material and spiritual worlds, thereby creating a sacramental view of life.

But May goes further than these earlier critics. He proposes that her "structural aesthetic principle" is the " 'word' as interpreter of human existence" (p. xxiv). Language, the word, is the common denominator between theology and literature: the word interprets the characters within a story as it also interprets the reader of that story. Its judgment of the reader is based on its ability to lay bare our own folly of trying to impose our ideas on reality rather than discovering the order that is already there. It is in this sense that the word becomes the "pruning Word," an image drawn from the Gospels (John 15:3) to describe the action of Christ's word on his followers.[6] This pruning word in O'Connor's fiction either converts or condemns her protagonists and gives her stories their meaning.

This argument is the basis of May's most interesting and challenging chapter, in terms of its literary and theological insights. The title of this first chapter, "The New Hermeneutic and the Parables of Jesus," while not seeming to deal with O'Connor's fiction, does in fact have a direct relationship with it. In calling O'Connor's stories "parables," May defines a parable as a story in which religious meaning comes from human conflicts that echo man's relationship with God: "If their meaning is fundamentally religious, it is because they confront man with his radical poverty in the face of reality" and "startle him with the suddenness of the sacred in the midst of the ordinary" (p. 13).

It is this approach, both literary and theological, that sustains May's readings of the individual stories. He discusses them in three separate chapters: "The Uncollected Stories" (those not included in the two original collections), "The Collections" (stories in *A Good Man Is Hard to Find* and *Everything That Rises Must Converge*), and "The Novels" (*Wise Blood* and *The Violent Bear It Away*). May's approach to the stories will appeal to both the student and the more advanced scholar of O'Connor's works: there is some plot summary, but not enough to substitute for a reading of the text. For May, plot summary never becomes a means of evading analysis.

While the power of the word is not seen to be especially strong in the uncollected stories, May argues that it is nevertheless significant as a "unique aesthetic principle" toward which O'Connor was building (p. 60). It can be dangerous to conclude retrospectively that there was a particular early tendency in an author's work, but one is on fairly safe ground here since O'Connor's theological view of fiction was from the beginning the very essence of her view of the writer's role. May examines the early stories in terms of their language and the role of words and communication, or lack of it. The four stories that were later incorporated into *Wise Blood*[7] are examined for their own merits as well as in their roles as precursors of that novel. May's analyses are generally convincing, though there are curious omissions: for instance, he notes such changes as the name of Hazel Wickers in "The Train" (p. 35) to Hazel Weaver in "The Heart of the Park" (p. 41) and ultimately to Haze Motes in "The Peeler" and *Wise Blood* (p. 41), but he does not attempt an explanation of such variations from either a literary or theological point of view. Possibly the names "Haze" and "Motes" are too obviously metaphorical to require any glossing, yet some readers might not be aware of the biblical allusion suggested by the "mote" which, in a man's eye, can prevent him from seeing properly, even as Haze Motes eventually blinds himself in order to right his "hazy" vision.

Similarly, in the early stories "The Barber" and "The Turkey" we encounter characters named Rayber and Mason, names later given to main characters in *The Violent Bear It Away* who are not entirely removed from their earlier namesakes. It may be argued that to explore the significance of every proper name is just one detail of many which an author is forced to ignore for the sake of concision. Yet in a book of only 178 pages, which deals rather heavily with the significance of language and the word, it would be proper to examine naming as a function of character. May in fact does this in his perceptive interpretation of "Parker's Back," where he discusses the names "Obadiah Elihue" and "Sarah Ruth" to help establish a "subtle pattern of biblical allusions" (p. 117). Naming in that story is seen as a fundamental role of language, but this is also true of other O'Connor stories.

In the collections of stories May sees language used both in its "conventional role" of dialogue and as a process by which words "take physical shape and function as separate dramatic entities; they are forces to be struggled with at least in the mind of the protagonist" (p. 70). There are, for instance, the words of revelation that gradually make Ruby aware of her pregnancy in "A Stroke of Good Fortune," the transforming (to the child) word of the hermaphrodite in "A Temple of the

Holy Ghost," and the final words spoken to the Misfit by the Grandmother in "A Good Man is Hard to Find." While it is difficult to find fault with May's readings, the concept of the "word" is so broad that it at times becomes diluted and seems to be used simply to mean the narrative or dialogue of the story itself (e.g., pp. 69, 70, 142-43). In such instances it ceases to be an aesthetic structural principle and becomes a too convenient, overgeneral way in which one could talk about any story.

Nevertheless, May offers many valuable insights into the nature of the stories. He is undoubtedly correct to see "A Circle in the Fire" as a story that deals with the nature of stewardship, and he explicates with clarity and accuracy the reference to the book of Daniel that concludes the story (p. 82). Likewise, the "heart-mind dichotomy" in "Good Country People" is surely crucial to the meaning of that story (p. 87), and the explanation of Mrs. Shortley's death at the end of Part I of "The Displaced Person" is totally convincing as we realize she has not in fact undergone any conversion or "spiritual renewal" (p. 92). "A View of the Woods" receives a mythic reading, establishing it as an Edenic allegory (p. 102).

There is, however, a group of stories that May treats with more specific references to language and the word than those already mentioned. The role of sound and of listening is of primary significance in "Greenleaf"; the "word approximates meaning" in the final accusation spoken by Sarah in "The Comforts of Home" (p. 109); the very title of "The Lame Shall Enter First" can be equated with the pruning word of judgment (p. 110); and the title of "Revelation" reflects the divine nature that can be present in words spoken in ordinary human speech (p. 113).

A final and extremely valuable contribution to a number of the stories is provided by May in his notes to Chapters 2 and 3. He reprints at length earlier versions of significant passages from the stories and uses them to defend some of his more theological interpretations. He has thereby made available material from the manuscripts of the O'Connor Collection (in Milledgeville, Ga.) which is of considerable interest and which contributes to what we already know of O'Connor's proclaimed intentions. For "The Partridge Festival" we are given the beginning and ending of the earlier and inferior version, "The Partridge Pageant," in which the characters seem unaffected by the events of the story. The earlier ending of "The Artificial Nigger" was expanded to provide the blunt religious imagery of the final version. Two final paragraphs added to "Good Country People" provide a clearer frame of reference for the reader. An earlier version of "Revelation" alters the nature of Ruby Turpin's vision; a number of significant verbal revisions in "Parker's Back" are supplied; and the ending of "Judgment Day" is given in its earlier "transitional" versions.

The chapter on the two novels comes at the end of the book. By delaying his discussion of them, May is able to incorporate into his final chapter many of the arguments presented in earlier chapters. While he thus violates the chronology of O'Connor's works, he also makes his task simpler: because they are novels, the two works are necessarily more complex in their structures and linguistic patterns than the short stories.

May uses the motif of "going home" as a basis for his discussion of *Wise Blood* and sees it at work in Haze's "converting," or turning around (p. 133). This concept unites O'Connor's first novel to her last story, "Judgment Day," which also deals with a man's going home in a spiritual sense, and one wonders why May did not explore the relationship between these alpha and omega points of O'Connor's work. Dealing with each story in isolation, he often ignores such overlapping themes, whereas the stories can often serve to gloss one another.

Nevertheless, May meticulously (and convincingly) charts a tripartite pattern of statements, assertions, and actions in *Wise Blood* which unify it, though he does not look beyond this pattern to connect the novel to O'Connor's evolution as a writer. On the other hand, while his treatment of the stories that later became part of *Wise Blood* established the presence of the themes of mortality, concupiscence, and the natural man, May does expand these themes to describe Haze's realization of and response to Original Sin. The theological implications underlying the plot and character are admirably unveiled and explicated in keeping with the sense of both mystery and manners that O'Connor sought to convey.[8]

May also discusses O'Connor's second novel, *The Violent Bear It Away*, in isolation. While he sees it as containing O'Connor's "most sustained and compelling use of interpretive language" (p. 137), he does not relate it to the stories she wrote after it, most of which are more mature artistically as well as theologically. His assertion thus remains undefended. Yet it is here that the concept of story as parable gets its fullest rendering. May uses the Gospel's Parable of the Sower to provide the basic metaphor of the seed that is sown as the Word of God. The parable is entirely appropriate in explaining much of the novel's imagery: Tarwater's unremitting hunger, which can only be satisfied by allowing the seed to bear fruit; Rayber's suppression of the seed sown long ago as he struggles to control his strong urge to love his idiot son; and that same son whose name, Bishop, means "overseer" (p. 145). But the novel is far more complex than the simple parable of the Gospels, as May recognizes when he deals with much of the remaining imagery of the novel. He is in fact quite correct to emphasize that the story is meant to judge *us* in terms of how we respond to Mason and Rayber. May thus gives a clear example of how both the reader and the characters are "pruned" by O'Connor's words. In fact, some experience in teaching this novel has made me accept this last point without dispute. Today's readers almost invariably tend to support Rayber's actions and intentions and see Mason as a distasteful and narrow-minded old man. And they believe this to be the attitude O'Connor intended them to have. When confronted with her statement that "Old Tarwater is the hero of *The Violent Bear It Away* and I'm right behind him one hundred percent," they are baffled, disbelieving, and outraged.[9] Such reactions support May's assertion that the pruning word still judges us, even though we may not be fully aware of its action when it confronts us in the guise of a modern short story. He has chosen an apt title for his book because the book has appeal for the theologian, the academic, and the literary critic. May deals with all of O'Connor's stories in this concise study and offers some answers to the problems raised by attempting to reconcile belief with art.

At the other end of the spectrum is Robert E. Golden's exhaustive and praiseworthy annotated bibliography of reviews, articles, and books about O'Connor and her work. I do not intend to consider here the second half of the volume, which is a bibliography of Caroline Gordon compiled by Mary C. Sullivan. Golden's share of the reference guide is almost totally complete through 1974. While much of importance has been written in the years since then, bibliographies must end somewhere. If any updating is planned, a high standard has been set by this work, which ought to challenge future bibliographers to meet its level of competence.

The annotations are detailed and to the point, avoiding such unhelpful phrases as "an important study" or "a negative review," which often plague the researcher desiring more specific information. The listing has been arranged chronologically, a distinct advantage with O'Connor since it reflects clearly the rapid growth of her reputation from the sparse reviews of 1952 to the copious number of items listed for the past decade. The index provides detailed listings by both author and title, though unfortunately does not include a listing by journal. While this feature would seem to demand a tedious lengthening of the index, it nevertheless would have been useful to see at a glance what periodicals reviewed O'Connor's works and in what years.

Another useful principle adopted by Golden is to cross-reference replies made to articles and reprints of articles at a later date. The only omissions I could discover in this regard were the reprint of Maurice Edgar Coindreau's 1959 introduction to *Wise Blood* as "Preface to *Wise Blood*," in *The Time of William Faulkner: A French View of Modern American Fiction*, edited by George McMillan Reeves (Columbia: Univ. of South Carolina Press, 1971), and Eileen Baldeshwiler's "Thematic Centers in 'The Displaced Person,'" in *The Process of Fiction: Contemporary Stories and Criticism*, edited by Barbara McKenzie (New York: Harcourt, Brace, Jovanovich,

1969). The latter item is further confused by another kind of cross-referencing that is not provided: Golden unfortunately does not include cross-references where the author (in each case a woman) has written under more than one name. Thus we have no way of knowing that Sister M. Joselyn and Eileen Baldeshwiler are the same writer. There are other cases where different names conceal a single identity: Dorothy Nyren and Dorothy Curley, Patricia Dinneen and Patricia Maida, and Joyce Carol Oates and J. Oates Smith.

Another omission is a listing of where O'Connor's stories and nonfiction essays first appeared in print. This information is provided for the first editions of her novels and story collections, and it would not have been a long or tedious process to indicate as well original publication information for the individual stories. Such information, though available elsewhere, would have been convenient to have here as well.[10]

While it was undoubtedly a policy decision to exclude poems of tribute to O'Connor, these are few enough that they would not have added noticeably to the bulk of the book, and they are of some interest in assessing O'Connor's reputation. These are included in the addenda below. Students of O'Connor iconography might also have welcomed an indication of articles that included pictures of O'Connor and her environment.

These minor flaws, however, do not mar the high quality of this reference guide. Golden has managed to locate and annotate several articles and reviews in obscure or minor periodicals. Such items in the *Atlanta Journal,* the *Jackson Daily News,* the *Milledgeville Union-Recorder, Nexus,* and *Phoenix,* while not unobtainable, surely required much time and patience for their inclusion here. The oversights given below are not to be considered a list of errors so much as a further contribution to an already valuable guide for anyone who has an interest in O'Connor studies.

Addenda

1960. Amis, Kingsley. "Assassin's Progress." *Observer,* 11

September, p. 26. A mixed review of *The Violent Bear It Away* (reviewed with four other novels).

Curley, Dorothy Nyren. *A Library of Literary Criticism.* Vol. 2. New York: F. Ungar. 1960; 4th ed. 1969, 432-37. Excerpts of critical articles ranging from 1952 to (in the 4th ed.) 1966.

Gilman, Richard. "Critics' Choice for Christmas." *Commonweal,* 73 (9 December), 284. Of the four books recommended, *The Violent Bear It Away* was the most satisfying and makes Graham Greene look like a "con-man."

1964. Agnes, Sister. "In Memory of Flannery O'Connor." *America* 111 (17 October), 455.

A 23-line poem.

1966. Hicks, Granville. "A Holy Kind of Horror." *Saturday Review* 49B (2 July), 21-2.

An essay-review of Stanley Edgar Hyman's *Flannery O'Connor* and Robert Drake's *Flannery O'Connor* which necessarily includes some of Hicks's own responses to and readings of several of the stories. While agreeing with the basic interpretations of images and symbols, he also discusses the problem of readers who do not agree with O'Connor's outlook.

1969. "Close-ups." *Times Literary Supplement,* 3515 (10 July), 745.

A review of *The Violent Bear It Away* in its English edition. It places the novel in the tradition of the New England trancendentalists as well as of orthodox Catholicism. "All are batty, all bats" here, where the pattern of symbols at times seems to dominate all else.

Driskell, Leon V. "To Flannery O'Connor (1925-1964)." *Southern Humanities Review,* 3 (Spring), 145.

A 24-line memorial poem.

1974. Klevar, Harvey. "Image and Imagination: Flannery O'Connor's Front Page Fiction." *Journal of Modern Literature,* 4 (September), 121-32.

An informative essay which documents the "sources" of two

of O'Connor's stories, "A Late Encounter with the Enemy" and "The Displaced Person," by reprinting and examining articles and photographs from the *Milledgeville Union-Recorder,* the local newspaper of O'Connor's hometown. Gen. George Poker Sash is seen to be derived from a 106-year-old Gen. William J. Bush, who attended his wife's graduation from college and is pictured in a rocker and holding a cane, flanked by his wife and his niece. The "Displaced Family" which arrived in Milledgeville was named Jeryczuk, had two small children (a boy and a girl), had come from a camp in Austria, and settled on a dairy farm. They entered the country under the Catholic Resettlement Commission and did not speak English. O'Connor expanded the material in each case to give it larger and more spiritual dimensions.

1975. Gossett, Thomas F. "No Vague Believer: Flannery O'Connor and Protestantism." *Southwest Review,* 60 (Summer), 256-63.

This item goes beyond the dating of the bibliography, but it complements Gossett's earlier article "Flannery O'Connor on Her Fiction," item 1974. B10.

Dissertations:

1973. Vest, David Carl Quentin. "Perpetual Salvage: The Historical Consciousness in Modern Southern Literature." Vanderbilt University. Discusses Faulkner, Tate and O'Connor.

1974. Hiers, John T. "Traditional Death Customs in Modern Southern Fiction." Emory University. Discusses O'Connor as well as ten other writers.

Errata

1955.B27 for "Wylie" read "Wyllie"
1960.B10 for "Balliff" read "Ballif"
1964.B18 should be listed under "1963"
1968.B14 should be listed under "1969"
1970.B27 for Flannery O'Connor's *Wise Blood:*'Unparalled Prosperity and Spiritual Chaos'" read "Flannery O'Connor's

Wise Blood: 'Unparalleled Prosperity' and Spiritual Chaos"

Dissertations:

1966. "Blackwell, Annie Louise" should be listed under "1967"

Notes

1. "Such Nice People," *Time*, 6 June 1955, p. 114.

2. Rev. of *Wise Blood*, *New Yorker*, 14 June 1952, p. 118.

3. Flannery O'Connor, *Mystery and Manners* (New York: Farrar, Straus and Giroux, 1961), p. 34.

4. *Mystery and Manners*, pp. 72-73.

5. "Of Huckleberry Bushes and the New Hermeneutic," *Renascence*, 24 (Winter 1972), 85-95; "Flannery O'Connor and the New Hermeneutic," *Flannery O'Connor Bulletin*, 2 (1973), 29-42; and "Flannery O'Connor: Critical Consensus and the 'Objective' Interpretation," *Renascence*, 27 (Summer 1975), 179-92.

6. See also May's earlier article, "The Pruning Word: Flannery O'Connor's Judgment of Intellectuals," *Southern Humanities Review*, 4 (Fall 1970), 325-38, much of which is reworked into the first chapter of the present work.

7. "The Train," "The Peeler," "The Heart of the Park," and "Enoch and the Gorilla."

8. O'Connor, *Mystery and Manners*, p. 103.

9. Quoted in John R. May, *Toward a New Earth: Apocalypse in the American Novel* (Notre Dame: Univ. of Notre Dame Press, 1972), p. 136.

10. At the end of *The Complete Stories* (New York: Farrar, Straus and Giroux, 1971), p. 551-55.

Dickens and the Business of Authorship
Peter L. Shillingsburg

Robert L. Patten. *Charles Dickens and His Publishers.* Oxford: The Clarendon Press, 1978. xvi, 502 pp.

What a fine irony that Dickens, who lamented Thackeray's public attitude about literary work (that it was a trade, like a cobbler's, without special mystery or sanctity and with only the "dignity" of working men)—what a fine irony that he should be so neatly caught in the act of conducting the business—the trade—of authorship. This book is the first of its kind in nineteenth-century studies—at least one would hope other similar efforts in the field will follow. Its primary focus is the professional life of Charles Dickens. But it goes beyond mere biography, for it gives a view of the relationship between a nineteenth-century author and his publishers: the business of authorship, its contracts, its proofings, its profits, the effects of marketing on structure and format, and the effects of popularity and slumps on incomes and tempers.

To be sure, we have had investigations into the field before. There are general studies like J.W. Saunders's *The Profession of English Letters* (1964), which presents an overview derived almost entirely from secondary sources. There are more specialized approaches, such as Royal Gettmann's *A Victorian Publisher: A Study of the Bentley Papers* (1960), which concentrates on the business of a single publisher, or Ben Harris McClary's *Washington Irving and the House of Murray* (1964), which, though less detailed in its treatment of commercial aspects of authorship and publishing, concentrates on an author and one of his publishers. And perhaps more to the point, there is John Sutherland's introductory and eye-opening *Victorian Novelists and Their Publishers* (1976), which combines original research in various specific author/publisher relationships with an attempt to synthesize the prevailing business trends as they affected authors in their choice of subject, format, length, frequency of appearance, and, of course, income.

Reading Patten's *Dickens and His Publishers* leaves one with the sense that Sutherland has perhaps oversynthesized, that he has assumed prevailing methods or customs where the facts are very complicated and where variety is more striking than similarity. This is not to detract from Sutherland's ground-breaking contribution, but only to say that Patten's is the first sustained concentration on one author's business and professional career. Patten shows us what we have only guessed at, and sometimes missed, about author/publisher relationships, their variety, complexity, and unpredictability. Though *Charles Dickens and His Publishers* is readable and well organized, the most important fact about it is that its material is original. Based largely on the half-yearly reports Dickens received from Bradbury and Evans and Chapman and Hall (now preserved in the Forster Collection in the Victoria and Albert Museum), Patten's research extends also to the publishers' own records for Bradbury and Evans and for Bentley (those for Chapman and Hall no longer survive). The raw materials—ledger books which record copies printed, stitched, given, sold, remaindered and discounted, sums spent on advertising and producing books, sums realized by publishers and author—are augmented by relevant information about Dickens's personal life and by secondary sources on the Victorian economic and book-trade world. All is woven into a narrative revealing the business of book production. But the book is not given to generalizations; it is, rather, a narration of facts. And it is packed—464 densely printed pages plus a selected list of references and an index.

Of course, Patten is not the first Dickensian to use this material, nor does he pretend to be. But his study is broader and more detailed than any previous work in the field and, giving credit where it is due, he also corrects errors in the work of his predecessors—including on occasion the editors of the new Pilgrim edition of Dickens's letters (see p. 108).

Dickens and the Business of Authorship

Patten's approach is chronological, dividing Dickens's professional life into four segments: "The Rise to Fame," "The Anxious Forties," "Fortune with Fame," and "The Man of the World." Each segment corresponds roughly to Dickens's primary association with a different publisher: Bentley and Macrone in the early years, Chapman and Hall during the forties, Bradbury and Evans during the lucrative though darkening fifties, and a return on new footing to Chapman and Hall for the remaining years. Each shift in publisher shows Dickens gaining ascendancy in the power struggle between author and publisher as his known worth and bargaining experience increase. (Or so goes Patten's argument. But one might ask a question that apparently cannot be cleared up by reference to the material in this book. Patten argues that Dickens's greatest success in forcing a publisher to accept his terms came in the arrangements with Chapman and Hall in the 1860s. And the contracts certainly bear out that opinion, as does the fact that Dickens enjoyed his greatest income in the sixties. However, analysis of the figures on profits in Appendix C seems to indicate that from 1846 to 1850 Dickens got 42% while Chapman and Hall got 58% — including commissions — of the income from Dickens's works. From 1855 to 1861 Dickens seems to have gotten 77% and Bradbury and Evans only 23% of the profits from books issued by that publisher. From 1862 to 1866 Dickens got, apparently, 49% while Chapman and Hall got 51% of the profits. Though Chapman and Hall worked the copyrights so vigorously that Dickens's income from them increased in the sixties, it appears that the publisher still profited more than the author in that last "most advantageous" arrangement. But perhaps the statistics are misleading.)

A summary chapter, "The Audience Widens," contains, offhandedly, the justification for this kind of literary research and demonstrates the common sense underlying this prodigious assembly of facts: "*As You Like It* need not be played in a replica of the Globe, any more than Dickens need be read in parts. But a fuller understanding of the opportunities and constraints that shaped each work may be gained from an awareness of the circumstances of their first appearance" (p.

336). The final 120 pages are devoted to appendixes summarizing the contents of the publishers' ledger files: A—"Sales and Profits of Dickens's Works, 1846-70"; B—"The Printing History of Dickens's Monthly Serials, 1846-70"; C—"Income from Dickens's Works for Dickens, Bradbury and Evans, and Chapman and Hall, 1846-70"; and D—"Income from *Household Words* and *All the Year Round.*"

The high ratio of appendixes on matters of income to those on production and printing history is indicative of Patten's tendency to chronicle the commercial and to slight compositional and textual matters. The reason is not hard to find. The records provide as much information as we are likely to get about the commercial successes and failures and their effects in sales, reprints, choice of subjects and formats for future books. But to pursue the textual significance of reprints would have required a tremendous additional research effort, and it is not surprising that this pursuit was largely foregone—though Patten knows more than most scholars about the textual history of Dickens's works.

This book is of course not a bibliography, but its importance to textual scholars, editors, and bibliographers of Dickens's works is hard to overemphasize. The textual and bibliographical scholar working on Dickens without access to the information laid out here is wandering blindfolded in a mine field. *Charles Dickens and His Publishers* makes the data available to all. The student of *Dombey*, for example, now knows that there are eight printings of the first edition. Whereas in the past a collation of three or four copies of the first edition might satisfy the would-be bibliographer in his search for an undetermined number of reprints, the publisher's records now make his search less of a blind fishing expedition.

That such a pursuit may be worth undertaking is not much emphasized by Patten, but if *Dombey's* contemporary, *Vanity Fair*, can be taken as an indication, then the search certainly is worth undertaking. The first edition of *Vanity Fair* reached six printings (some parts being printed more often) during Thackeray's lifetime. Over 200 significant textual changes were introduced after the first printing, and most of these were introduced after stereotyped plates had been cast and used. *Vanity Fair* is unique, but its method of production and publication is shared by lesser works.

The commercial story is probably as fully presented by Patten as it needs to be, but his book is also a seedbed for further serious scholarship. A look at the material on *Nicholas Nickleby* (1838-1839) will illustrate the point as well as reveal some minor flaws in Patten's book. For some undisclosed reason (that is, the explanation is not given in the logical places, though I may have missed something in the narrative portion of the book), the records on *Nickleby* begin in 1858, though other Chapman and Hall publications are reported from 1846 on. However, the surviving material is rich enough for our purpose. In three full pages Patten reports the following facts: *Nickleby* first appeared in twenty numbers (nineteen parts) from April 1838 to October 1839. The records, beginning in 1858, indicate six printings as follows: June 1858—250 copies of each number; December 1862—500 copies each; December 1863—750 copies each; December 1865—750 copies; December 1867—750 copies, and June 1870—500 copies of each number. An additional printing of unknown size may have been run off in 1867.

We know, therefore, of six, possibly seven, printings of *Nickleby* between 1858 and 1870 besides the undisclosed number of printings between 1838 and 1857. Yet John Eckel in 1932 calls *Nickleby* an uninteresting collector's item and records only one textual variant (*visiter* for *sister* at page 123, line 17). Hatton and Cleaver in the next year added paragraphs and pages on variant plates (full-page illustrations) and variant advertisements, but only one more textual variant (*latter* for *letter* at page 160, line 6up). E.H. Strange in 1937 shifted the interest from the covers and inserts to the text, but found only three or four typos corrected. He did carefully note instances of printing space-quads, but he assigned an inordinate significance to them from his failure to realize that they might appear and disappear within a single printing from type or be retained from one printing to the next as a flaw in stereotyped plates. Finally, in 1973, Michael Slater had the opportunity to set the record straight. He had the example of Hinman's work on the Shakespeare folio available to him; he had fine collections of Dickens's works with multiple copies of *Nickleby* to choose from; he had the best facsimile printers in the business working for him—but he did not use the Forster collection records on *Nickleby*, had no idea of the complexity of the book's printing history, and merely followed Hatton and Cleaver, and Strange, for the *visiter* and *latter* readings and for his comparatively extended commentary on the advertisements.[1] Would access to the information in Patten's book have changed Slater's attitude, or the selection of text to reproduce, or the research expended on the text? One cannot tell, but there is now no excuse for the oversight. *Nickleby* was an early novel; it was reprinted at least seven times and probably ten to fifteen more times over the nineteen years after first publication for which there are apparently no records. Its printers were Bradbury and Evans, who expended unexpected energy correcting, from printing to printing, the works of Dickens's contemporary, Thackeray. Furthermore, Dickens revised the book for new editions at least twice. In the face of this circumstantial evidence, what is the likelihood that the first edition of *Nickleby* contains only two substantive variants and three corrected typos? It could well turn out to be one of the most, rather than the least, interesting collector's items.

A few specific aspects of *Charles Dickens and His Publishers* deserve special notice. The publishers' records are deceptive: not only does Dickens on occasion find errors in the reports made to him, or throw up his hands in despair at understanding the accounts, but there are also postponements of charges from one year to the next and conflation of costs in a single entry, and other more or less complicated doctoring of the records to make totals square at the end of accounting periods. Patten is very careful to detect these problems and is good at articulating the pitfalls in the use of the records (see especially pp. 3-4, 176-79, 283, and 346). Patten also has a particularly succinct introduction to the Victorian publishing scene (pp. 18-27) reminiscent of and complementary to Suth-

Dickens and the Business of Authorship

erland's *Victorian Novelists and Their Publishers*. And there are occasional instances of historical information, such as those on advertising duties (p. 221) and on the court's definition of *edition* (p. 291), which are of general interest and usefulness to the study of other authors as well.

Charles Dickens and His Publishers is marred by a few errors—though to indicate them in so masterful a book is more a service or even a compliment than a detraction or warning. On page 10 a comparison is made between Thackeray's, Trollope's, and Dickens's incomes, demonstrating Dickens's greater earning power. In its effect the argument is right, but in method it is misleading and inaccurate. The figure on Thackeray is his own estimate of his annual income from all his copyrights (not new works).[2] The figure on Trollope represents the initial payment for each of two new works (not their annual rate of income nor the accumulated annual income from his various active copyrights). And the figure for Dickens includes the initial payments and subsequent profits from a single book over a two-year period. Again, on page 226, a technically accurate statement gives a slightly skewed impression. The decline in sales of *Bleak House* is inferred from a decline in the stitching orders from "34,000 for Number IV to 31,500 for Numbers XVII–XX." In fact, the stitching order stayed at 34,000 through Number VI and the decline began with Number VII. On pages 229–30, Smith, Elder and Company is credited with publishing Thackeray's *Pendennis* (1849–1850), and the impression is given that *The Newcomes* (1854–1855) was the first Bradbury and Evans book-publication for Thackeray, though there had been the *Punch* connection earlier. But in fact Bradbury and Evans had been Thackeray's main publisher commencing with *Vanity Fair* (1847–1848), and they were the publishers of *Pendennis*. It might be useful, furthermore, to mention that Thackeray's *Life of Tallyrand*, mentioned as announced for publication by Chapman and Hall, was never written, let alone "not apparently issued" (p. 279).

A few other matters, though not errors, do raise questions: The speculation about the relation between the profits (or lack thereof) from *Master Humphrey's Clock* and the expense of including illustrations in the type-pages with the need to wrap type around them is not supported by facts. Nowhere is any indication given about the relative cost of including or not including inset illustrations. Again, on pages 111 and 112, references are made to the cost of woodcuts, but no figures are given from the publisher's ledgers. Similarly, the remark that "the *Clock* was not making money, and its sale had fallen to 30,000 copies" is difficult to comprehend. Almost no publication other than Dickens's recorded in the Bradbury and Evans ledgers reaches so high a figure as that. Robert Smith Surtees, who did not lose money for the publishers, seldom reached initial print runs as high as 5,000. Many books were manufactured and sold at a profit with circulations of 2,000. What can it mean when the *Clock* makes no money at 30,000? Too bad the Chapman and Hall office ledgers are lost. Is there a connection between the *Clock's* high sales (compared to non-Dickensian titles) but low profits and the question about the author's percentage of the income which I raised earlier in this review? That Patten tends to compare Dickens's successes and failures with Dickens's own best performances more than with those of other professional writers of the time causes him, I believe, to lose some perspective. For example, he speaks of the effects of the "disappointing sales of *Chuzzlewit*" and the "modesty of *Copperfield*'s reception" (p. 208), but the figures in Appendix B show that roughly twice as many copies of *Copperfield* were sold as of Thackeray's most successful novel, *The Newcomes*. "Which of us," asks the clown narrator of *Vanity Fair*, "has his desire? or, having it, is satisfied?"

Patten's work may have errors I have not detected, and it may have some flaws of presentation. But it stands as a milestone in Dickens scholarship, making way for new developments and trends in investigating Dickens as well as other authors of the period, and it suggests tacitly at every turn the outlines of specific textual and bibliographical studies to be undertaken. This book is indispensable to the student of Dickens and of the Victorian publishing scene.

Notes

1. Eckel, *The First Editions of the Writings of Charles Dickens, Their Points and Values* (New York: Maurice Inman, 1932); Thomas Hatton and Arthur H. Cleaver, *A Bibliography of the Periodical Works of Charles Dickens* (London: Chapman and Hall, 1933); Strange, "Notes on the Bibliography of *Nicholas Nickleby*," *Dickensian*, 33 (1937), 30-33; Slater, "The Composition and Monthly Publication of *Nicholas Nickleby*," in Charles Dickens, *The Life and Adventures of Nicholas Nickleby*, a facsimile reproduction with introduction (London: Scholar Press, 1973).

2. Thackeray was writing in April 1858. The publishers' records (at the *Punch* Office, London, and John Murray, Publishers, London) indicate that in 1858 Thackeray's income from copyrights with Bradbury and Evans was £557.13.4, and from Smith, Elder was £49.3.6. He may have received a small additional sum from his copyrights with Chapman and Hall. So his guess was pretty accurate. In addition, of course, Thackeray earned £3,000 in 1858 from *The Virginians*—still not the equal of Dickens by a long shot.

Elizabeth Bowen: A Portrait
E. C. Bufkin

Victoria Glendinning. *Elizabeth Bowen.* New York: Alfred A. Knopf, 1978. 331 pp.

In *Pictures and Conversations,* published two years after her death, Elizabeth Bowen wrote: "One of my reasons for wishing to write this book . . . and one, also, why I think it should be a fairly good or at least an engaging book, is: books, lengthy critical studies, theses are perpetually being written about writers, novelists in particular. I, inevitably, have been the subject of a certain number of these. While appreciative of the honour done me and of the hard work involved, I have found some of them wildly off the mark. To the point of asking myself, if anybody *must* write a book about Elizabeth Bowen, why should not Elizabeth Bowen?"[1] She did not live to complete that good and engaging book about herself, but a biography of her, the first, has now appeared. Responding to the self-posed question, "Why a life of Elizabeth Bowen?" (p. xv), Victoria Glendinning states without qualification that Elizabeth Bowen is a major writer, one of "the ten most important fiction writers on this side of the Atlantic in this century" (p. xv). She is "what happened after Bloomsbury; she is the link that connects Virginia Woolf with Iris Murdoch and Muriel Spark" (p. xv); moreover, "when she died the Anglo-Irish literary tradition died with her" (p. xvii).

Born in 1899 in Dublin, Elizabeth Bowen was reared in that city and in the country at Bowen's Court, the ancestral home in County Cork, which she, an only child, inherited upon the death of her father in 1930 and which she was the last Bowen to own, having been compelled to sell it in 1959. It was soon afterwards demolished. The outstanding fact in her life doubtless was her heritage as a member of a family of the

Protestant Ascendancy, and she lived after the age of seven both in Ireland and in England. (She used to say that the Anglo-Irish "were really only at home in mid-crossing between Holyhead and Dun Laoghaire,"p. 13.) Members of that class possessed "great style" and "verbal fluency," both of which, Glendinning tells us, Elizabeth Bowen "had in full measure" (p. 14) — and both of which served her well in her writing, as her readers know. The Anglo-Irish also had "a natural warmth and gregariousness that lead to a great sense of hospitality and a liking for celebrations of all kinds" (p.16), traits that Elizabeth Bowen inherited and exhibited, generously, all her life. She was, as Glendinning demonstrates, "an overwhelming personality": "vital, indefatigable, sociable, independent, extremely hard-working, brave, kind-hearted, perceptive" (p. xvi). Physically striking, she was a confessed romantic. According to her friend Eudora Welty, "she was a prime responder to this world. It was almost as if she'd been *invited* here."[2] In 1923 she married and also published her first book, a gathering of stories called *Encounters.* This volume was followed by six more collections and by ten novels as well as by several works of nonfiction, perhaps the most notable being a history of Bowen's Court. She lived her last years in England and died, in 1973, in Hythe, Kent. She was buried, however, in Ireland in the churchyard that faces where Bowen's Court had stood since the eighteenth century.

Victoria Glendinning has told the story of this accomplished and distinguished woman with considerable skill and charm; she has shaped it, fittingly, by starting and ending with that churchyard where Elizabeth Bowen is buried. The English edition of *Elizabeth Bowen* quite cogently carries as subtitle *Portrait of a Writer.* Not a full biography for obvious reasons of consideration and decorum, the book may therefore be premature. But to depict Elizabeth Bowen as the subject of a portrait is eminently suitable; for in so doing Glendinning has in effect made her narrative what Elizabeth Bowen called her own writing: "verbal painting" (p. 49).

Elizabeth Bowen once declared that she was a writer before she was a woman. As critic of the writer, Glendinning is, on the whole, less pleasing than she is as portraitist of the woman. We have a much more vivid impression of Elizabeth Bowen the woman than of Elizabeth Bowen the writer. Her career, as recounted, seems to have had little existence or dramatic conflict of its own, and the advent of one work seems to have been very nearly uniform with that of every other.

The first novel, *The Hotel,* was published in 1927. Glendinning finds it "on every level a very good novel" (p. 76), but not everybody's estimation is likely to be so charitable. Although its inspiration was a stay on the Italian Riviera, the work seems more to derive from other fiction—in particular, E.M. Forster's *A Room with a View,* as has been observed more than once. Glendinning's description of *The Hotel* as "a study in immature sexuality" (p. 65) is more to the point; for it identifies that preoccupation with the subtle yet unmistakable ambiguities and ambivalences of character—what Glendinning calls the "fantasies, fears, and manipulations that underlie social behaviour" (p. xvi)—which define a Bowen novel and constitute one of her more conspicuous technical contributions to the art of narrative. People in her best-realized novels are not mere bodies; they are bodies with fine-wrought nervous systems. Thus in the characters lies the source of the tension and highly charged atmosphere in her novels—which, excepting a couple of instances, are lacking in conventional "action." No other novelist since Henry James has been able to handle character in just this fashion to this degree. D.H. Lawrence of course knew how to do so; but, whether unable or (more likely) unwilling, he never sustained the tension.

The particular trouble that Elizabeth Bowen had in writing *The Hotel* as well as the two novels that followed, *The Last September* (1929) and *Friends and Relations* (1931), was locating a narrative center. These three are "group" novels. The author seems to have feared, or perhaps felt uncongenial with, the single protagonist. Consequently, the reader at the outset of these novels, and occasionally for an extended while thereafter, feels unsettled, unsure of himself; he does not know, with confidence, whose story he is reading. Indeed, Bowen's preference for the group over the single individual runs through all her novels (the group sometimes yielding to paired individuals and doublings) until the final one, *Eva Trout*. Only that novel among the ten has a character's name for its title.

The Last September, "the classic Bowen novel of arrivals and departures" (p. 80), is easily the best of the first three; but many critics, following Elizabeth Bowen's own persuasive opinion, tend to overrate it. Her affectionate regard for *The Last September* — "this, of all my work, is nearest to my heart" — resulted from personal experience in Ireland during her youth, and the heroine, she wrote, "derives from, but is not, myself at nineteen."[3] Yet the work falls short of complete success despite numerous excellences, like the satirical picture of the English in Ireland and the scene of the Anglo-Irish Naylors viewing their great country house, Danielstown, set aflame by the Irish raiders during the Troubles, its front door "open hospitably upon a furnace."[4]

In *To the North* (1932) Elizabeth Bowen showed a mastery of form at once more sophisticated and less schematic than in the preceding novels. "Shape," she believed, "is possibly *the* important thing" in writing;[5] and her attention to form must surely have come from her expressed interest in design and architecture. Houses figure prominently in her narratives as they did no less in her life. Bowen's Court was a lifelong concern; and Clarence Terrace, Regent's Park, one of the most beautiful residences in London, where she lived for seventeen years, appears importantly in two of her novels.

Elizabeth Bowen had a special liking for tripartite structures in her works. She first used that arrangement of material in *The Last September*, but only arbitrarily since it does not match the arrival-departure scheme of the novel. She best used it in *Friends and Relations,* "the Elizabeth Bowen novel that even Elizabeth Bowen enthusiasts tend to forget about" (p. 98); but there it serves no discernible purpose except that of division, a period of ten years separating the opening from the middle and closing sections. *To the North* falls into no such blocking: its narrative rushes forward in straight lines connecting three structuring episodes. The novel opens at night with a train trip: "Towards the end of April a breath from the north blew cold down Milan platforms to meet the returning traveller"; reaches a contrasting and literal peak at almost midpoint with a daytime airplane trip, a brilliant setpiece; and finishes at night with an automobile trip:

> Recollecting herself, she glanced at the clock on the dashboard, they gathered speed and went forward, uphill, then down. He saw "The North" written low, like a first whisper, on a yellow A.A. plate with an arrow pointing: they bore steadily north between spaced-out lamps, chilly trees, low rows of houses asleep, to their left a deep lake of darkness: the aerodrome.
> "Hendon," he said. "I wish we were still flying."
> "So do I," she said with an irrepressible smile. "I wish it were still that day."[6]

The form is absolutely right for theme and plot; not only does it embody these, but it comments incisively upon them and upon the characters. The lines lead swiftly and inevitably to a final catastrophic point at which the symbolic meaning and import of the title are manifest, everything being shaded and rounded off in a brief ironic coda. Such command having been attained, Elizabeth Bowen was now to produce her best-known and most skillful novels.

The House in Paris (1935) and *The Death of the Heart* (1938) have long been acknowledged as masterpieces. The first (based, we learn, on a love affair the author began in 1933 with a "brilliant, highly sexed, introspective, susceptible" man, p. 106) was one of Elizabeth Bowen's favorite works just as the second was, surprisingly, her least favorite—"it was really an inflated short story, that thing" (p. 156). These two novels she also built in three sections. The chronological arrangement of material in *The House in Paris* is indicated by the names of its parts—The Present, The Past, The Present; the thematic concerns of *The Death of the Heart* are indicated by the names of its parts—The World, The Flesh, The Devil. These novels are almost inexhaustible sources for studying how to design and build narrative structures for maximum effect. This formal aspect has been too much taken for granted and slighted, and thus some of the importance of these two works has been lessened. The shift of point of view to the maid Matchett at the conclusion of *The Death of the Heart*—frequently mentioned by commentators but hardly discussed or analyzed for itself—is psychologically, thematically, and structurally very daring; but the maneuver "makes" the novel in much the same way the time shifts "make" *The Secret Agent* and *Under Western Eyes*, in whose company the stature of *The Death of the Heart* is in no way diminished.

War followed soon after the publication of *The Death of the Heart* and interrupted the writing of Elizabeth Bowen's next novel, *The Heat of the Day*, which was not published until 1949. Criticism, academic and journalistic, has turned this into the most controversial of her novels. It received much attention and was financially successful, 45,000 copies selling almost at once. Nonetheless, hardly anybody was at the time entirely pleased with it, including its author's friends Rosamond Lehmann and Edward Sackville-West. Elizabeth Bowen herself said that it was the most difficult novel to write she had yet undertaken and that it presented "every possible problem in the world" (p. 187). There were objections to the character of Robert, the traitor-lover of the protagonist Stella; to the use of what Elizabeth Bowen herself acknowledged as "pointblank melodrama" (p.187); and vigorously, to the style.

"Further development of her supple and expressive style," wrote the reviewer in the *Times Literary Supplement*, "may commit Miss Bowen to charges of over-developing it; there are passages here which remain obscure after a second reading."[7] The style, however, has since been seen to be not rococo but functional, making the texture itself representative of the time, place, and atmosphere concerned—wartime London. Obscurity and complexity are the essence of the matter, and the narrating voice abjures omniscience. Hence, some of the obscurity is deliberate and remains, regardless of the number of rereadings. To illustrate: Robert's death is caused by a "fall or leap from the roof."[8] The reader never learns which.

Obviously the famous Bowen style was deliberately developed and practiced, and as a device it is indispensable. In *The Heat of the Day* the following sentence, which Glendinning terms "contorted, maybe, but effective" (p. 191), tells what happens just after Robert's final departure from Stella — he is either falling or leaping: "In the street below, not so much a step as the semi-stumble of someone after long standing shifting his position could be, for the first time by her, heard."[9] The sentence is more than contortion and effect. Its compositional design diffuses meaning into atmosphere and emotion, themselves the equivalents of the atmosphere of the nocturnal scene and of Stella's emotional state. Alliteration and spare punctuation hold, loosely, the elements of the sentence together. Within, the subject is secured by the "not so much . . . as" formula. The voice is passive, and the predicate is interrupted by two prepositional phrases ("for the first time" and "by her"). Not until the very last does the main word come, its dental exploding and completing predicate and thought: "heard." Significance is reinforced by the juxtaposition of "her" and "heard" (repetition of the same word or, as here, near-same words being one of Elizabeth Bowen's stylistic habits). The result is startling; proof of which can be ascertained by recasting the sentence into normal order and by changing the voice from passive to active. But abnormality and passivity (in the sense of being acted upon by an external force) are conditions of war, the enveloping subject and action of the novel. *The Heat of the Day*, "the classic novel of London in the war" (p. 193), is a virtuoso's piece. It has for almost thirty years remained unforgettable, invulnerable to critical belittlement.

After it, Elizabeth Bowen published only three more novels. The received opinion is that they are less distinguished than the others; indeed, are decidedly less so. Glendinning reports that Elizabeth Bowen "was happy" (p. 252) about the first, *A World of Love* (1955), and that she "was satisfied" (p. 285) with the last, *Eva Trout* (1968). *The Little Girls* (1964) is, of all her novels, the only one that, to a marked degree, contains sentimentality; though in it, perhaps to lessen that sentimentality, she attempted to emulate the manner of Evelyn Waugh by presenting the characters solely from without, omitting all reports of thoughts and feelings. Elizabeth Bowen could not, Glendinning says, "at the end keep to her policy of not giving the characters' thoughts" (p.277). To have made the attempt was artistically and tempermentally wrong for her; her way of writing was, as much as her themes and subject matter, incompatible with Waugh's.

Glendinning believes that it is too soon "to assess precisely" (p. xv) Elizabeth Bowen's place among the twentieth-century novelists. But is it? Her last novel was published a decade ago, and, as Francis Wyndham asserted in his review of *Pictures and Conversations*, the revived recognition of Elizabeth Bowen's greatness was, even then, overdue.[10] She has, after all, long since become an Influence. Iris Murdoch found precedent in her for certain stylistic excesses and bizarreries; Muriel Spark, for quaint obscurities and obliquities.

In calling attention to a major writer and her world, Glendinning has performed a worthwhile task, and her book is important for being the first biography of Elizabeth Bowen. As Vladimir Nabokov pertinently remarked about the first book about his life, "The first biography, no matter what comes after, casts a certain shadow on the others."[11] Glendinning is sympathetic with her subject, and she is not naggingly tendentious, as is Catherine Dupre, for example, in her recent biography of John Galsworthy. Glendinning offers the kind of information that to a later biographer (though he may be able to give more factual information and to do so in greater, and less considerate, detail) would be unavailable — information obtained from living friends and acquaintances of Elizabeth Bowen. Glendinning has also quoted from Elizabeth Bowen's unpublished correspondence, which illuminates both her personality and her attitudes toward her writing. These passages complement Bowen's more public and formal statements in books like *Collected Impressions, Afterthought,* and *Pictures and Conversations;* and the quotations contribute colorfully to the total portrait of the artist.

This book is thus useful and helpful. But it is not comparable in achievement to recent literary biographies on the scale of Quentin Bell's *Virginia Woolf* and P.N. Furbank's *E.M. Forster*. Clearly, Glendinning's goal was more modest, and she would surely not claim for hers their definitiveness. Her book contains at the end a section that includes notes to the text, a select bibliography, and a listing of Elizabeth Bowen's books. By American, as opposed to English, scholarly standards, this apparatus is inadequate. For instance, the first note to Chapter 1, which is typical, reads: "From E.B.'s *Bowen's Court*. Unless otherwise indicated in text or notes, all quotations from E.B. in this chapter are from *Bowen's Court*" (p. 305). Since it gives neither page number nor edition, the note is only partially functional. The impression is one of hurriedness, of half-doing the job, and the serious reader becomes uncomfortable. Understandably. For such briskness can cause inaccuracies, as an obviously symptomatic example indicates. In discussing *The Hotel*, Glendinning associates its principal male character, the clergyman James Milton, with John Anderson, a lieutenant in the British army with whom the young Elizabeth Bowen was in love. Occurs a *lapsus calami* that confuses and commingles these two men with a great English poet: "John Anderson had had a primitive appeal for Elizabeth that both frightened and attracted her, though John Milton, the clergyman, is not John Anderson" (p. 75).

Glendinning's work should lead to a renewal of interest in Elizabeth Bowen's books. Moreover, it should prompt a really good study of them, not wildly off the mark, that will correct and counteract such evaluations as Martin Seymour-Smith's that Elizabeth Bowen "was a snob . . . who desperately wanted not to be " and that "she was good on the wealthy upper class, but always failed not only with the lower classes but also with the poor."[12] Although not itself a scholar's book, Victoria Glendinning's *Elizabeth Bowen* is a provocative book in whose shadow future scholars will indebtedly work.

Notes

1. Bowen, *Pictures and Conversations* (New York: Knopf, 1975), p. 62.

2. Welty, *The Eye of the Story* (New York: Random House, 1978), p. 272.

3. Bowen, Preface, *The Last September* (New York: Knopf, 1952), pp. vi, xi.

4. *Ibid.*, p. 303.

5. Elizabeth Bowen, Graham Greene, and V.S. Pritchett, *Why Do I Write?* (London: Marshall, 1948), p. 24.

6. Bowen, *To the North* (New York: Knopf, 1950), pp. 1, 298.

7. "The Climate of Treason," *Times Literary Supplement,* 5 Mar. 1949, p. 152.

8. Bowen, *The Heat of the Day* (New York: Knopf, 1949), p. 327.

9. *Ibid.*, p. 326.

10. Wyndham, "Between Living and Writing," *Times Literary Supplement,* 24 Oct. 1975, p. 1254.

11. Quoted in Andrew Field, *Nabokov: His Life in Part* (New York: Viking, 1977), p. 7.

12. *Who's Who in Twentieth Century Literature* (London: Weidenfeld & Nicolson), p. 50.

Medieval Texts and the Editor
Richard A. Dwyer

A.G. Rigg, ed. *Editing Medieval Texts, English, French, and Latin Written in England: Papers Given at the Twelfth Annual Conference on Editorial Problems, University of Toronto, 5-6 November 1976.* New York: Garland Publishing, 1977. 128 pp.

The University of Toronto has been holding annual conferences on editorial problems since 1965. After a dozen years they got around to the subject of editing medieval texts—from manuscripts written in England—in a conference held in November 1976. In spite of the exiguity of the scope, this was the first of their sessions to deal with medieval literature in any form. Thus, the collection of five papers read that weekend comes as a particularly welcome addition to the volume of helpful discussion generated by these Canadian conferences.

The last decade has seen a strikingly animated interest in medieval manuscripts. I recall vividly the UCLA Conference on New Techniques for the Appreciation of Medieval and Renaissance Literature, held in 1971. Organized by the late William Matthews, that meeting focused particularly on the relevance of textual work to literary criticism.[1] Since then, the St. Louis Conferences on Manuscript Studies have been held annually, and the yearly medieval roundups at Kalamazoo have featured whole sections devoted to manuscript studies.[2] All of this activity, in addition to the recent issuing of handsome facsimile editions by the Scholar Press and others, complements such venerable efforts as those of the Paris Institut de Recherche et d'Histoire des Textes and the gorgeous volumes of *Scriptorium* emanating from Antwerp, to mention only a portion of the expression of recent interest in medieval manuscripts.

At the Toronto conference the two British and three Canadian contributors and their topics were Malcolm Godden, Fellow and Tutor of Exeter College, Oxford, speaking on Old English; Anne Hudson, Fellow and Tutor of Lady Margaret Hall, Oxford, on Middle English; Ian Lancashire, of the Department of English, University of Toronto, on Medieval Drama; Brian Merrilees, of the Department of French, University of Toronto, on Anglo-Norman; and George Rigg, Acting Director of the Center for Medieval Studies at the University of Toronto, on Medieval Latin. Rigg also convened the conference and wrote a brief introduction to the volume under review. A panel discussion concluding the second day, chaired by Professor John Leyerle, is not presented here. Each speaker was asked to discuss the history of editing in his or her area, the present "state of play," specific editorial problems, and future needs and desiderata. Besides setting these guidelines, Rigg's introduction discusses the range of notions of what constitutes an edition and acknowledges as well a recent interest in discriminating among kinds of manuscript witnesses. These he sees as ranging from agents for the straightforward transmission of classical or sacred texts to the other extreme of idiosyncratic compilations for the pleasure of their makers.

Malcolm Godden stresses the limited number of surviving Old English texts and manuscripts and the resulting problems and opportunities afforded to editors by this circumstance. He surveys the history of the printing of Old English texts from the early appearance of prose as supporting precedent for Protestantism and the translation of the Bible. It was not until the nineteenth century that interest in Old English poetry began to develop. Prompted first by genteel antiquarians and more recently by university researchers, this interest has in its turn led to a neglect of prose in a pursuit of literary interest at the expense of other cultural concerns.

What seem to be needed, according to Godden, are editions of the remaining unpublished prose and improvement of the older editions by the addition of manuscript histories, commentaries on the meaning, and glossaries. Godden calls for shorter and less imaginative accounts of literary quality and for more discussion of cultural and intellectual background and the relationship of the texts to contemporary ideas. Godden cites the unclear identity and boundaries of individual works within the manuscript compilations that have fortuitously come down to us as the chief problem in the field. He also discusses the unclear motives for those particular compilations and, less excusably, the assemblages of some modern editors. I would recommend Godden's intriguing account of the so-called *Ælfric's Heptateuch* as a dramatic example of these problems.

The medieval and latter-day liberties taken with once unrelated pieces evoke from Godden a rebuke for unnecessary respect for the manuscripts.[3] He calls instead for author-based editions—to include Cynewulf and Ælfric—and subject-based collections of anonymous works. Fortunately, less remains to be desired in the technique of editing Old English texts or locating all the manuscripts and early modern transcripts. And, in spite of his distrust of scribal compilations, Godden is enthusiastic about the need to analyze later textual variants, glosses, and alterations—after the establishment of texts as close as possible to the original—for what they reveal about the historical reception of the works.

After some remarks on new techniques in dating texts, Godden observes that recent work on the sources of Old English literature has focused on the intermediate transmitters more than on the ultimate authorities, and he concludes by noting that the primary editorial contribution to Old English scholarship in the future is likely to be a historical one, providing material for a fuller understanding of Anglo-Saxon culture as a whole.

Anne Hudson's account of editing Middle English manuscripts is the only one to essay a definition of *edition*: "A printing of a text which, by virtue of its inclusion of commentary or collation, appears to be more than a simple reproduction of a single manuscript." Although this restricts the eligible candidates to those beginning with Thynne's 1532 Chaucer, Hudson does recognize and classify the types of medieval editing.

She observes that scribes altered their exemplars to suit new audiences and attempted relevant compilations, that authors reworked their own texts, and that many anonymous hands helped to produce ballad versions of earlier romances.

In her discussion of the later history of the editing of Middle English texts, Hudson gives high praise to Thomas Hearne's early eighteenth-century editions of some chronicles, an effort not essentially improved upon by the later activities of the clubs and text societies. She makes the point that the Early English Text Society at no time had either a monopoly on editions of Middle English works or any proclaimed policy on what ought to be published or how it should be edited.

Hudson turns next to those scholars who have had theories about editing, defining these theories by their extremes: "one reveres the least whim of the scribe, whilst the other, in seeking to get behind the individual manuscript to the lost hypearchetype, tends to see all scribes as interfering and incompetent dunces." In her examples, editors of the first persuasion—such as those who prepared the EETS *Ancrene Riwle* and Layamon's *Brut*, and A. J. Bliss's *Sir Orfeo*—sin somewhat less than the more vigorous stemmatic textual critics. Hudson singles out for criticism here M. C. Seymour's edition of Trevisa's translation of the *De Proprietatibus Rerum* of Bartholomaeus Anglicus. By printing only those variants that justify editorial departures from the base text, Seymour forces the reader to depend on his authority. Hudson places in a special category the Kane and Donaldson B-text of *Piers Plowman* (which has since been awarded the Haskins Medal by the Medieval Academy of America) and devotes a capsule review to contesting its "radical, if not revolutionary, claim," which is "that the modern editor has better means of determining the medieval writer's likely original text than any of the medieval scribes upon whose witness the editor is wholly dependent" (p. 42).

In the course of her discussion of what remains to be done, Hudson announces the "good news that a start is to be made on a prose equivalent to the invaluable *Index of Middle English Verse.*" Before turning to review the book at hand, I was able to attend the conference at Emmanuel College, Cambridge, in July 1978, coordinating the work of fifty or so scholars on this prose index. Organized by Derek Brewer, Derek Pearsall, and Anthony Edwards, this conference featured several speakers, including, once again, Anne Hudson. Her remarks on the special problems of untangling the strands of Wycliffite prose abounding in Middle English manuscripts may be said to reinforce her conclusions at the Toronto meeting. In particular, the "wretched indexers" will need to exercise special alertness to the fluid and allusive nature of these Lollard texts and the impossibility of making simple identifications on the basis of ordinary incipits.

The most entertaining of the papers in the collection is that on Medieval Drama by Ian Lancashire, and it contrives to be informative and erudite as well. Lancashire laments the trying duty it must have been to edit our early drama at the turn of this century in a milieu of Victorian skepticism, aestheticism, and delicacy. In tracing the checkered history of such editorial enterprise, he divides the practitioners of the art into Truemen and Lovewits, after the characters in the first anthology of medieval English drama: James Wright's *Historia histrionica* (1699). The former sort account for the best editions before 1864, while F. J. Furnivall is clearly a Lovewit in his appreciation of the medieval "steps" to the temple of Shakespeare. Lancashire's tale of the resulting muddle would be comic were it not for the pathetic result that now, "seventy-two years after every major medieval play reached print, no one has published in English a general critical study of any single English cycle" (pp. 62-63).

Lancashire turns to the many daunting, and as yet unsolved, problems in textual transmission offered by medieval English drama. The manuscripts we have all date from fifty to two hundred years after the plays were first written and represent "layers upon layers of accretions, alterations, and excisions by revisers, actors, or scribes from various regions and periods." Furthermore, none of the manuscripts is an acting text. Rather, they are civic registers, or worse still, compilations from different registers. Critical editions, facsimiles, and the medieval equivalent of the Arden Shakespeare have appeared at various times in an effort to cope with these problem texts, but there is still plenty of work to be done. Besides listing the texts that need better treatment, Lancashire suggests the kinds of editing needed and the tools editors will require for the job. All of this leads him into an absorbing account of his own specialty, the external records of dramatic activity—"the subject's last frontier." However, with the founding of an international editorial project, Records of Early English Drama, at Toronto in 1975, the conquest seems well under way, and in a fashion that challenges editors to master disciplines "that engage the whole mind rather than chain it to drudgery."

In surveying the editing of Anglo-Norman texts, Brian Merrilees contrasts the Middle English situation with that described by Anne Hudson. Whereas the EETS allowed its area to suffer from lack of policies, the field of Merrilees's interest has been rather thoroughly dominated by the activities of the Anglo-Norman Text Society, founded in 1937 and still going strong. What has characterized this series is the "remarkable uniformity of presentation" of the twenty texts issued so far, all edited "on what one might term 'modified' Bédier principles." The editors stick largely to one manuscript without attempting to reconstruct an archetype or regularize the linguistic features.

After observing the gradual emergence of Anglo-Norman studies from its tainted status among Romance philologists, Merrilees traces the development through four main periods, ending with the founding of the ANTS. This advent brought a virtual end to the earlier interventionist practices of editors and to the construction of stemmata. With the aid of this reassuring uniformity of approach, editors could turn to the vexing problems of insular departures from continental linguistic forms and, in particular, to the odd versificational structure of so many Anglo-Norman texts. Merrilees sketches the achievements and problems remaining in this area.

Finally, in his remarks on desiderata, Merrilees asserts that the degree of freedom left to the individual editors within the constraints of the Society's instructional brochure should be used to incorporate more descriptions of syntax and vocabulary and properly synchronic descriptions of the phonology lying behind texts. I might observe here that this does go exactly against the recommendations of such Middle English scholars as Angus McIntosh, who argue that editors should not attempt to reduce the informative variety of graphic forms to speciously systematic phonemic inventories. Last, Merrilees looks forward to future editions which will publish all or at least several manuscripts of a text so that readers can appreciate *la trace de l'oeuvre*, or compare short and long, or Anglo-Norman and continental versions.

Partly owing to the range and complexity of the field of writing in medieval Latin, George Rigg's essay on editorial problems there is perhaps the least thorough of this collection. Works written over a period of a thousand years in nearly every region of Europe have been edited to meet the needs of a great variety of interests, making the survey of something called Medieval Latin "unthinkable." Even the works of Latin written in medieval England are scattered through a diverse array of series and individual volumes reflecting the lack of cultural unity among works which may owe more to an Augustan milieu than a Norman one. Unlike the other areas surveyed in this volume, medieval Latin offers many yet unedited poems as well as many editions in need of replacement.

Rigg is led to comment on the economics of editing in the face of the amount of work still to be done, the small number of qualified readers, and the great diversity of their primary interests ranging from rhetoric to recipes. He makes the case for facing translations while medieval Latin studies remain a service industry for specialists in other fields. Orthography is one of the editorial problems Rigg finds central; he is dead against classicizing. More importantly, he argues that greater respect be paid to individual scribes and manuscripts. Although partly motivated by economic considerations too, his rejection of the critical edition and its customary costly apparatus is equally grounded in a sense that "a scribe of 1250 surely knew more about a text written in 1200 than I do." Rigg is also convinced that the medieval texts were living works subject to continuous interpretation in the hands of their copyists.

The most remarkable development emerging from this and other meetings, as well as from many recent journal studies, is the positive view of the activities of scribes. Quite apart from their only-too-well-known role in abetting the corruption of texts, the scribes are coming to be taken seriously as contemporary readers of books and as participants in a cumulative process of creation. It is as if scholars, if not critics, were beginning to realize that there are at least as many legitimate "Ideas" of the *Canterbury Tales* as there are manuscripts of it. In consequence of this new interest, those recent editions that obscure the activity of specific scribes in their manuscripts come in for some criticism from the conference participants. Malcolm Godden's almost isolated demurrer from this view derives from the unusual circumstance that so much Old English poetry survives in the fortuitous compilations of unique manuscripts. Thus we get editions of the *Exeter Book* as if it were an authorial collection comparable to the *Decameron*, or even the *Pricke of Conscience*. Nevertheless, even these latter-day compilations must be given their due consideration.

Although the convener of the conference had enjoined all the speakers to touch on the history of editing in their respective areas, only Anne Hudson was moved to give some attention to the "editing" that began within the Middle English period itself—the scribal alteration, compilation, and reduction to ballad form that constitutes contemporary intervention in texts transmitted manually and orally. Given the bearing these activities have on modern editing and interpreting of texts, I wish here to add a further desideratum to those of the speakers. In order to grasp firmly what medieval literature is, we need something that, for want of a better name, could be called a *history of editing* in the medieval period. The obvious defect of calling it by this term is that we thereby assume what the purposes of scribal intervention were, without leaving it an open, empirical question to be answered after sufficient data are in. It may very well be that some hardy scribe had the same self-image possessed by, say, Thomas Wright, but the studies of such scholars as Graham Pollard, R. A. B. Mynors,

A. I. Doyle, M. B. Parkes, and many others on the scrivening profession in the fifteenth century have already broadened our notion of the men and women who wrote the books. One of the more intriguing possibilities is that certain urban professional scribes intervened in their texts as an expression of resistance to the proletarianization of their craft by the merchant stationers who were monopolizing the sale of books. The hired interpolator thus reaffirms his connection with creativity and the other meaning of *writing*, that is, to compose as well as to copy.

If, as witness to contemporary interest and skill in the editing of medieval texts, we had only such effusions as Charles Moorman's *Editing the Middle English Manuscript* (Jackson: Univ. Press of Mississippi, 1975), then we might have to agree with E. J. Kenney, classical scholar and fellow of Peterhouse, Cambridge, in his resurrection of the following gloomy observation by George Thomson: "If we examine the record of bourgeois scholarship during the present century, we can trace, on the one hand, the decline of materialism into empiricism and eclecticism, and, on the other, a decline in technical skill, in the older branches of the subject, which have failed to develop in accordance with the possibilities created by the great bourgeois scholars of the last century."[4] But with the appearance of volumes like this one, making available to us all the fruits of a stimulating gathering in Toronto, we need not yet accede to such counsels of despair.

Notes

1. My own paper, "The Appreciation of Handmade Literature," later appeared in the *Chaucer Review*, 8 (1974), 221–40.

2. E.g., the session of Robert E. Lewis in 1977 and his earlier paper "The Scribe as Editor: Variation in the MSS of the Middle English *Pricke of Conscience*," *Manuscripta*, 20 (1976), 16.

3. This view goes back at least to Kenneth Sisam's "The Authority of Old English Poetical Manuscripts," *Review of English Studies,* 22 (1946), 258–68.

4. Cited in *The Classical Text, Aspects of Editing in the Age of the Printed Book* (Berkeley: Univ. of Calif. Press, 1974), p. 148.

Posterity's Stepchildren: Two Bibliographies of Living Authors

John Bush Jones

James L. W. West III. *William Styron: A Descriptive Bibliography*. Boston: G. K. Hall & Co., 1977. xxxviii, 256 pp.

Joe Maynard and Barry Miles, comps. *William S. Burroughs: A Bibliography, 1953-73*. Charlottesville: University Press of Virginia, 1978. xxvi, 246 pp.

Bibliographies of living authors are rather like dictionaries of slang: they are potentially obsolete from the moment of publication. The sources for obsolescence in living-author bibliographies are, quite obviously, two. First, it is always possible that the subject of the bibliography will continue to write new works. Second, even if no new writings appear, there is always the chance that new published forms of works already in print will be forthcoming during the author's lifetime. And since the full-scale bibliography is not just an enumeration of the author's titles but a recorded description of their physical manifestations as published books, articles, pamphlets, or whatever, and since any new publication of a book during the author's lifetime *could* introduce new authorial intervention in the text, it is important that all such publications be eventually described and reported. A simple case of this situation, affecting one of the two books presently under review, is the recent American Penguin paperback publication of Styron's *Lie Down in Darkness* since that company's takeover of the Viking Press. Whether the Penguin text contains any alterations (authorial or otherwise) from the Viking Compass impressions remains to be determined, but even without that knowledge the Penguin publication represents yet another stage in the publishing history of the novel and, as such, deserves to be recorded.

The potential obsolescence of a living-author bibliography can, however, be dealt with in one of two ways. The easiest — also the most mechanical, arbitrary, perhaps facile — solution is to set rigid parameters for the scope of the bibliography, whether or not these limits are logically conceived. Nowhere, for example, in the Joe Maynard and Barry Miles bibliography of William S. Burroughs do the compilers state why they have chosen the inclusive dates 1953-1973. As far as I can see, this is a purely arbitrary time span, a "neat" block of twenty years from the first publication of *Junkie*. While the cutoff date of 1973 does indeed prevent the kinds of obsolescence just discussed, the starting date of 1953 gives the perhaps dangerously erroneous impression that Burroughs never wrote a published word prior to *Junkie*. The open-ended treatment of Styron, on the other hand, allows for the inclusion of even quite ephemeral juvenilia and seems the more sensible route to take if completeness is to be one of the goals of a bibliography (and most bibliographers would undoubtedly concur that completeness *is* a desirable end for such a reference tool). If compilers do choose stringent parameters for what they include, however, they at least have the mandatory obligation of explaining the reasoning whereby those limits were set. But Maynard and Miles say nary a word.

The second way of coping with inevitable obsolescence is by facing it squarely and admitting it. In the introduction to his Styron bibliography, James L. W. West III defines his intention as "a thorough descriptive record of Styron's publications to date" (p. xii) and later goes on to recognize that

William Styron's career . . . is full and impressive. It is far from over: I expect to be busy, for many years, recording addenda yet to be published. I have attempted to compile an exhaustive listing of Styron's publications to date, but I am aware, as every bibliographer is, that certain items have eluded me — "Typhoon and the Tor Bay" and the *Stingaree* publications, for example. If Mr. Styron is correct in saying that I have located 99.44% of his published work, then I would surely like to find the other .56%. I trust that users of this bibliography will help me to do so by bringing to my attention any omitted items. [p. xxxii]

Acknowledging, then, temporal incompleteness as the single disadvantage of preparing a full-scale descriptive bibliography during an author's lifetime, West finds other positive virtues to this approach to his task: the advantage of consultation with the author himself; the advantage of examining publishers' records while still extant, and of interviewing editors and printers "while their memories are still fresh"; the stimulation a full-dress descriptive bibliography provides dealers and collectors "to pursue the publications of an author more aggressively"; the manageable number of documents to be dealt with before the reputation of an "institutionalized" author effects such a proliferation of publications that they cannot be dealt with in adequate detail; and the stimulation a complete record ("to date" seems implicit here) of an author's work has for critical study and scholarship (pp. xi-xii).

Not content, then, with the checklist approach some bibliographers take to living authors, West aims to record "the physical aspects of Styron's books and . . . their publication histories and textual transmission patterns" (p. xi) with the richness of detail accorded any full-dress descriptive bibliography. By contrast—and, as we shall see, perhaps by way of apology for their numerous omissions and shortcomings in recording important kinds of information—Maynard and Miles take a defeatist tone when they "recognize that the first edition of a bibliography can rarely hope to be much more than an introductory checklist" (p. xxiii). They need only compare their work with West's to see, in fact, that the case is otherwise.

Aside from the built-in obsolescence of the living-author descriptive bibliography, the only other drawback, and not a very serious one at that, to West's undertaking such a full-dress compilation during Styron's lifetime is the stylistic stance he must take when writing of his material and his study of it. Ideally, one would like to approach a descriptive bibliography as a permanent reference tool, one whose contents will be as detailed, as accurate, as complete—in short, as "definitively" useful—generations from now as at the time of publication. In his introduction, however, West is time and again compelled to use such phrases as "from his [Styron's] high school and prep school years to the present" (p. xi), "Styron's publications to date" (p. xii), and "Styron's current American reputation" (p. xv), all of which imply a use of the bibliography roughly contemporaneous with its publication rather than continuing utilization by generations of scholars and critics. This implicit contemporaneity of use is further reinforced by a section on "Recommended Texts" (pp. xxx-xxxii) that occasionally must resort to noting what impressions of the several novels are "currently in print" (p. xxxi). It is questionable whether such commentary on available texts rightly belongs in a descriptive bibliography, a work whose primary functions should extend beyond the temporal limitations implicit in such a discussion.

Strengths and weaknesses peculiar to the preparation, presentation, and usefulness of bibliographies of *living* authors aside, three basic criteria may be employed as standards of evaluation for all descriptive bibliographies: completeness with respect to the quantity of items described (or listed, in the case of undescribed items such as contributions to periodicals), the degree of accuracy, and the quantity of detail included in the descriptions of those items given descriptive treatment. That it is desirable for a bibliography to be as nearly complete a record as possible of an author's published writings goes without saying. But the matters of accuracy and detail deserve perhaps a few remarks, if only as a reminder of G. Thomas Tanselle's classic treatment of them in "Tolerances in Bibliographical Description" (*The Library*, 5th Ser., 23 [1968], 1-12; rpt. in *Readings in Descriptive Bibliography*, ed. John Bush Jones [Kent, Ohio: Kent State Univ. Press, 1974], pp. 42-56. Citations in this review are to the reprint.) This essay on the character of bibliographical descriptions has not been matched for soundness and common sense in the ten years since its first publication. Tanselle initially makes the distinction between accuracy and detail: accuracy is a relative term "which has a meaning only as it is defined for each specific purpose" (pp. 42-43)—hence, the system of measurement suitable for a cook might not be precise enough for a chemist; detail is a quantitative term referring to the kinds of information included in a description. From these definitions Tanselle constructs his main arguments: (1) a descriptive bibliography should contain that degree of accuracy and quantity of detail necessary to fulfill "the purpose for which a [given] bibliographical description is intended" (p. 49), and (2) whatever limits of accuracy and detail bibliographers decide upon for their particular purpose, they "should include a few paragraphs in their prefaces explaining exactly where they have drawn the line in regard to accuracy and detail. . . . No description, of whatever sort, can be comprehended unless the operating rules on which it is based are made known" (pp. 56, 44).

Implicit in Tanselle's arguments is the desirability for every compiler of descriptive bibliographies to include in his introductory matter not only his limits of accuracy and detail but also a statement of the specific purpose(s) of the particular bibliography and the reasons that the limits of accuracy and detail have been set as they have. Only if the purpose of the bibliography is clearly articulated, and only if reasons for the limits of accuracy and detail are stated (as, say, for a given author's publications the various impressions within an edition can be detected only by leaf measurements to the nearest quarter-millimeter), can a user of the bibliography properly evaluate whether a sufficient degree of accuracy and quantity of detail have been selected to provide the most useful descriptions and to carry out fully the purpose(s) of the given bibliography. It is with such criteria in mind, then, that one can begin to evaluate West's bibliography of Styron and Maynard and Miles's bibliography of Burroughs.

Before proceeding with a detailed examination of each of these bibliographies in turn, it may be helpful at the outset to record the general impression that each work left on this reviewer and thus to set out a framework or general context within which later specific observations on the books may be viewed. In brief, then, though not without flaws, West's Styron bibliography is patently the work of a trained professional who is precise in his theoretical knowledge of descriptive bibliography and meticulous in the application of its principles, except at those few points where, whether through oversight or carelessness, he seems to have fallen asleep at the proverbial switch. By contrast, the Burroughs compilation is by two admitted amateurs. In his section of the preface, a piece of writing almost embarrassing in its preciosity, Maynard alleges that by "reading all the textbooks and all the really good bibliographies . . . I had the knowledge without the college" (pp. xv-xvi), an allegation that the bibliography itself proves to be largely false. This amateurism, as will be explicitly shown later, reveals itself in every aspect of the book from the compilers' lack of informed knowledge of precisely what a descriptive bibliography is and does, through their scrambled use of technical terminology, to pure sloppiness in the physical presentation of the material. The only virtue of the book is its seeming completeness, down to quite miniscule ephemera, in listing William S. Burroughs's published writings during the arbitrary time frame set up by Maynard and Miles.

Easily rivaling the Burroughs bibliography for completeness (in the preface, William Styron himself compliments West on his thoroughness), the Styron is also in many ways a model of organization, clarity, and explicitness in a descriptive bibliography. Following an unusually long and detailed introduction and other preliminaries, the body of the bibliography is divided into ten lettered sections, each discreet and logical in the material it records, but with copious cross-references to related items in other sections. The subdivisions are: A—Editions in English; B—Editions in French; C—Previously Unpublished Contributions to Books and Other Publications; D—Republished Contributions to Books; E—Appearances in Periodicals and Newpapers; F—Published Letters; G—Blurbs; H—Non-French Translations; I—Interviews, Published Discussions, and Published Comments; J—Miscellaneous. The volume concludes with a General Index and an Index to Publishers.

The rationale and plan for each of the lettered sections are delineated in West's introduction together with, where appropriate, explanations of the systems used for describing aspects of the physical book and for recording other kinds of information. Abbreviated statements of the contents and plans of the subdivisions are repeated as headnotes to the lettered sections, a useful device that obviates the necessity of referring back to the introduction to discover the general character of the section one might be consulting.

It is clear from the fullness of his introduction that West aims to incorporate Tanselle's two desiderata of stating explicitly the purposes of his bibliography and delineating precisely the degree of accuracy and quantity of detail he has chosen as appropriate to his bibliographical descriptions. Though falling somewhat short of the ideal in the second of these, West's introduction is still meritorious for its recognition that the user of the bibliography has to know the ground rules in order to play the game.

West partly defines his purpose in terms of the potential user, or rather users, who fall into six groups ranging from "literary critics and scholars interested exclusively in Styron" through "scholars of the future who will study the twentieth-century book trade" to "book dealers and book collectors" (p. xviii). While recognizing that "not all data recorded here will be of interest to all of them" (p. xviii), West has wisely chosen to incorporate in his full-dress descriptions a wide range of information so that some parts of it will be of use and interest to various members of the broad spectrum of scholars, critics, historians, dealers, and collectors he envisages consulting his bibliography. To accomplish this end, sections A and B lay out in considerable detail "the physical aspects of Styron's books" and information illuminating "their publication histories and textual transmission patterns" (p. xi), while the remaining sections are more largely enumerative than descriptive since they only "list all other known publications by Styron" (p. xi; again "to date" is implicit in this statement). West's later restatement (p. xii) that "this compilation is intended to be a thorough descriptive record of Styron's publications to date" is somewhat inaccurate and misleading, since he has already acknowledged that only the sections covering Styron's English and French-language book-length publications would be fully descriptive, with the rest chiefly containing *listings only* of Styron's other published writings. I have no quarrel with West's decision to divide his work thus between descriptive and enumerative bibliography, but his introductory remarks should more consistently articulate this modus operandi.

The bulk of the introduction (pp. xix–xxix) is given over to a discussion of the ten lettered sections of the bibliography, their contents, their method of arrangement, and—for those that contain descriptions—a listing of those features of the book described and the methods employed in the descriptions. It is here that West seems to be striving for Tanselle's goal of fully articulated statements of the limits of accuracy and detail, and while his attempt is on the whole admirable, it is also here that the bibliography's few weaknesses most reveal themselves.

West's method of labeling entries is nothing short of superb; the combinations of letters and numbers used to designate each item show the reader at a glance precisely what form of a given title is being described and also what its place is in the printing and publishing history of that title, or, in a word, what its relationship is to other published forms of that title. In addition to the title being described in a given section of the bibliography, these labels indicate the edition, plating, impression, and—where applicable—issue. (West notes that there are no states described in the Styron bibliography, but presents a method for labeling them consistent with the rest of his system, in the event that any come to light and must then be recorded in a later revision of the volume [p. xx]. After thus declaring the absence of states, West on the following page makes an unfortunate slip of mind or pen when he writes of "each impression or state in Section A," where he clearly means to refer to *issue*.) West's introduction of *plating* between *edition* and *impression* is an especially valuable designation for seeing relationships among twentieth-century books that are often the products of duplicate plates and now, more and more often, of photo-offset replating. West's application of the term here is particularly revelatory of the relationships

Two Bibliographies of Living Authors 325

of numerous British publications of Styron titles to their American counterparts.

Following a thorough explanation of his labeling system (pp. xix–xxi) that includes bibliographically sound definitions of *edition, impression,* and *plating,* and some rather more tentative remarks on the still debated category of *issue,* West proceeds to a step-by-step outline of his full-dress descriptions in Section A, acknowledging his sources in Bower's *Principles* with additional material from Tanselle's several articles on typography, paper, patterns, and jackets. A full entry contains paragraphs for title page, copyright page, collation, contents, running titles, typography, paper, casing, and jacket (or wrappers in the case of paperbound publications), followed by a record of copies examined and numbered explanatory notes. Descriptions of first impressions of first editions also include a paragraph for the dedication page.

To delineate here what West intends to include in these several paragraphs and his methods for so doing would in large part be merely repeating standard practice in bibliographical description, but the presence of these discussions in a volume of descriptive bibliography is to be highly commended. Here, in large part, are those ground rules so necessary for a comprehension of the descriptions themselves.

And yet here too are those lapses, those omissions, those little unanswered questions that one would so like to have explained in order to comprehend yet more thoroughly West's methods and intentions. In his discussion of title page transcription, West properly informs the reader that "all measurements are in millimeters" (p. xxii) but neglects to say if these measurements are taken to a particular fraction of a millimeter or only to the nearest whole millimeter. Only by checking the descriptions themselves does a user discover that the latter is the case; a simple statement of limits here would obviate the need for such a check. (It also seems inconsistent that in a single instance of gutter measurements—a detail of description, incidentally, not discussed in the introduction— the measurement is taken to the nearest half-millimeter [see p. 6].

With no explanation of his use of gutter measurements in distinguishing a second impression, and with no limits of accuracy set for his measurements, West leaves the significance of this bibliographical detail unclear.)

One must also ask why West has chosen to indicate all rules, barring adjectives for thickness, with the single designation '[rule],' not even distinguishing between those that run the width of the type page as '[rule]' from all shorter examples as '[short rule],' let alone recording their actual length in millimeters. Perhaps such distinctions are not pertinent to the fullest bibliographical description of Styron's works, but if that is indeed the case a reader anticipating finer distinctions here deserves to know the reason for their absence. A similar argument can be made over West's '[logo]' sans measurements or descriptive detail for "any seal, device, symbol, or trademark that is used by a publishing house as its identifying sign" (p. xxii). Perhaps again such descriptions or measurements are not useful in identifying or describing the various published forms of Styron's novels, and yet a glance at the logos of Random House and Hamish Hamilton on several title pages reproduced in West's bibliography reveals considerable differences in both size and style.

A reader might also quibble with another of West's decisions, his choosing to use "admittedly impressionistic" color designations because of an inability on his part to use Tanselle's method with consistency. But one can at least respect West's detailed and reasoned explanation for making this choice (see pp. xxxii–xxxiii, n. 9).

Finally, respecting the introductory matter, no rationale is given for the number of copies examined in the process of preparing the individual descriptions. Even for first impressions of first editions the number is sometimes as few as two (though in other cases as many as six or more). If it is West's intention to describe the "ideal copy" of each form of publication (and he nowhere states this as his goal), is the inspection of so few copies sufficient? One might argue that since Styron's published writings are the products of mid-twentieth-century machine printing, comparison of large numbers of apparently identical multiple copies of a single impression is unnecessary since no concealed issues or states will be revealed, and therefore West has made a reasoned choice in holding the number of examined copies down to a few. Still, one can only come to such a conclusion through inference in the absence of a clear-cut rationale developed in the introduction.

I may seem to have dwelled at inordinate length on some seemingly minor omissions, inexplicit passages, and failure to explain methodology fully in the introduction, but I have done so chiefly to demonstrate that a statement as generally sound, meticulous, and complete as West's still may have some way to go to reach Tanselle's ideal of fully articulating the limits of detail and accuracy employed in a descriptive bibliography. Still, it is to West's credit as a bibliographer that these lapses are so few, and, more importantly, that the techniques for description he sets up in his introduction are applied with such consistency, precision, and meticulousness in the body of his work. West's collations and descriptions of contents, when joined with his distinctive labeling system, present a vivid picture of the printing and publishing history of Styron's novels to date. (Incidentally, West's eye for detail is amply demonstrated in the few examples of manifest error discovered in the text. See Section I of the Appendix to this review.)

The questions to be raised about material in the body of the bibliography are even fewer than those posed by the introduction. And since I have not, quite frankly, decided on answers to these questions myself, I will simply pose them as questions for readers of this review to contemplate further. First, at several points in Section A, West records numerous impressions of a title the existence of which are known from publishers records but which he as the compiler of the bibliography has not seen. The question thus becomes, should impressions not seen and examined be listed in the main text of a *descriptive* bibliography, or should such items be relegated to an appendix?

Second, there are several passages, such as one on p. 80, in which West engages in literary interpretation and critical commentary based on a preceding list of variant readings. As a reference tool, and, especially, as one that is designed to describe and record in an objective manner not only for the present but for future generations of scholars and critics as well, is a descriptive bibliography the proper place for such personal interpretive and judgmental remarks?

In the context of 237 pages of closely packed and elegantly presented bibliographical detail and related data, these questions become rather small indeed. In fact, in the entire body of the bibliography there is only one serious omission, an omission so obvious as to be downright amusing. Whether through modesty or oversight, West has left out from Section C— Previously Unpublished Contributions to Books and Other Publications—William Styron's Preface to the bibliography itself!

Would that some such single omission were the greatest fault of the Maynard and Miles bibliography of William S. Burroughs. If such were so, the second part of this review would be a pleasure to write. Regrettably, the task is more painful than pleasurable, for one is faced in this volume with—among other things—an entire fabric of omissions; not, it is true, omissions from the Burroughs canon in the designated period, but omission of the kinds of information one reasonably expects to find in a descriptive bibliography.

Now, the compilers of the Burroughs volume might say that such an expectation is invalid since their book is not explicitly a "descriptive bibliography" of Burroughs's works, but rather "*A Bibliography, 1953-73*." And they might remind the critic of their previously quoted disclaimer that "the first edition of a bibliography can rarely hope to be much more than an introductory checklist." But such possible defenses of the omission of many kinds of useful information can be negated by noting that the publishers designate the volume "A Linton R. Massey Descriptive Bibliography" (p. iv) and also by observing the fact that the entries for Burroughs's book and pamphlet publications do in fact contain a quantity of material, whatever the omissions, proper to a descriptive bibliography, the inclusion of this data quite belying the claim that the volume is but an "introductory checklist." To call it a halfhearted and ill-informed attempt at descriptive bibliography comes closer to the truth.

The plan of the book bears a superficial resemblance to West's organization of his Styron bibliography. That, and the apparent thoroughness in listing Burroughs's published work, are the best of Maynard and Miles's accomplishments. Following a Foreword by Burroughs himself, an Introduction by Allen Ginsberg, and a Preface and Some Notes on the Bibliography by the two compilers, the body of the text is divided into seven sections followed by a single general Index. The sections are: A—Books and Pamphlets; B—Contributions to Books and Anthologies; C—Contributions to Periodicals; D—Foreign Editions; E—Interviews; F—Miscellaneous; G—Records and Tapes. Maynard and Miles's categories do not make West's useful distinctions between previously unpublished contributions to books and republished contributions, and there is an inherent ambiguity in their Section D—Foreign Editions—since so many of Burroughs's writings were published in France and elsewhere abroad. A title for this section more accurately describing its contents would be Foreign Language Editions.

The single most serious omission from the volume is that of a coherent and explicit introduction setting forth the purpose of the bibliography and the methodology and principles employed in its preparation. Instead, a user of the Burroughs bibliography must content himself as best he can with the brief and uninformative Preface and Some Notes on the Bibliography. A reading of this introductory matter is, however, useful for revealing yet another shortcoming of the bibliography: the absence, in the compilers, of the kind of thorough theoretical knowledge of and technical skill in descriptive bibliography that would have enabled them to write the kind of introduction the volume lacks.

To cite but a few examples, the lack of precision in handling technical vocabulary is manifest evidence of the level of the compilers' knowledge of the subject. As a minor instance, there is Maynard's reference to the kind of book he is planning as a "full-scope analytical bibliography" (p. xvi) in seeming ignorance of the considerable differences between the "analytical" and "descriptive" branches of bibliographical study. Far more damaging to the reader's understanding of the Burroughs bibliography itself is Maynard and Miles's opening paragraph of Some Notes on the Bibliography, here quoted in full:

The books and pamphlets are arranged in chronological order. Each different book is numbered; under that number the first edition is lettered a and second or subsequent editions of the same book are assigned consecutive letters of the alphabet. Reprints are noted in the printing histories of the first edition. When the book has been re-released with revisions or even a new cover or when the same book [the same type-set, plating, or sheets seems implied here] has come from another publisher, the book has been considered another edition and is separately lettered. These minor editions have not been as fully described as their precursors as they usually — except for the new cover, publisher, etc. — are identical with the previous editions. [p. xxi]

Now, though I will not detail every misuse of terminology in this paragraph, it is still immediately apparent that *edition* has become the catchall word for every published form of a book from the actual thing to *plating, impression*, and *issue*.

The continued inaccurate use of this term in the descriptions themselves and the abreviated kinds of description the paragraph alludes to make it virtually impossible to discover with any degree of accuracy the publishing history of a given Burroughs title. Occasionally, one is fortunate enough to notice that the leaf size of, say, an American "edition" of an earlier published British "edition" is roughly the same and that their collational formulas match; in which case he might conjecture that the American item is a new impression (and most likely a photo-offset replating as well) of the British book, and not, of course, an edition at all. But too often the information is so scant that the reader is unable to make such inferences, since those very details of printing and publishing history that a true descriptive bibliographer would have made explicit from the first are missing. Consequently, too much is left up to the deductive powers of their readers. Far too often a true description is replaced by some variant of the following statement: "Collation (except for minor differences) and contents are the same as AlOd" (p. 51). There seems to be no recognition on the part of the compilers that just such "minor differences" are the stuff that significant bibliographical data are made of.

Other instances of the ambiguous use of terminology include "issues" used to mean "copies" of a book (p. 10), and on the same page "format" in its popular rather than bibliographical sense. An entire paragraph on page 52 speaks consistently of editions when what is being discussed is one of the few true cases of simultaneous issues. Finally, the reader becomes so caught up in an Alice-in-Wonderland world of jumbled meanings that he is hopelessly unequal to deciphering, on page 186, "This constitutes the first state of issue." Whatever the textbooks were that Maynard alleges to have read, it is clear he needs to read them again, or, better yet, have them explained to him.

That this is so in matters reaching well beyond the definition of terms is illustrated in Maynard's approach to the entire descriptive formulary (it was Maynard who was largely responsible for the sections on books and pamphlets). To begin with, in each description of any magnitude what is normally considered the contents note or contents description (the page-for-page statement of what is contained in the preliminaries, quasi-facsimiled where necessary, the inclusive pages of the text proper, record of blank pages, and so forth) is contained without break in the paragraph labeled "*Collation*" that contains the leaf measurements, collational formula, and pagination formula. A separate paragraph labeled "*Contents*" is a brief, and often redundant, listing of the literary works (text and any major preliminaries by Burroughs or others) contained in the volume. The explanation for this anomalous and somewhat repetitive system of description is found in a statement (p. 48) wherein Maynard unwittingly reveals his misunderstanding of what a *Collation* is and what it contains: "96 leaves, with last leaf glued to back cover; except for this and the wording of page 4, the collation is the same as A1Oa." For Maynard, then, the collation includes the material bibliographers normally consider proper to the statement and description of contents. It is necessary for a user of the Burroughs bibliography to understand this misunderstanding in order to make sense of numerous statements in the book.

Similarly, considerable work seems to have been done with little or no understanding of the reasons for recording certain kinds of data. This difficulty is most apparent in Maynard's attempts to present a statement of signing for books allegedly having signatures. For example, in his entry for the Olympia Press edition of *The Naked Lunch*, Maynard gives the collational formula as "1–14^8 15^4, 116 leaves; [pagination statement]. All gatherings signed '76'." This repeated 76 is, of course, no signature at all, but the number that *The Naked Lunch* was assigned in Olympia's Traveller's Companion Series. What we have here in fact is an unsigned book whose formula should have been written as "[1–14^8 15^4]" followed in its proper place by Maynard and Miles's usual "No sigs." indicating an unsigned book. Two similar instances (pp. 13, 23) mistaking abbreviations for titles or series numbers as supposed signatures further demonstrate the compilers' apparent lack of understanding of what signatures are, how to record them, and their significance in a bibliographical descriptions. It is data like these found in the description that compel one to conclude that much of the compilation was done by rote rather than reason.

But I began my remarks on the Burroughs bibliography by complaining of omissions, since which time I have been dwelling mostly on points of misunderstanding, inaccuracy, and error. Returning to those omissions now, it is simplest merely to list the kinds of information one might wish for but which are nowhere to be found in the descriptive sections of the Maynard and Miles compilation:

1. No system is included to indicate relationships among editions, platings, impressions, and issues.

2. No description of type, on any level, is included.

3. No description of running titles is included.

4. Though the total number of leaves is recorded, no total

number of pages is similarly given, though this would be especially useful since many of Burroughs's titles have complex or erratic pagination.

5. No rule measurements are given, only a statement of "long" or "short."

6. In the description of paper, no measurement of thickness or bulk is provided and no more sophisticated color statement than "white" if the paper falls within the general range of whiteness. (Attention to such details of paper most likely would have resolved conclusively this "either-or" statement on p. 99: "It either uses original sheets or is reproduced in offset from them.")

7. Perhaps most regrettably, there are no statements of the number or location of the copies examined in preparing the descriptions. Without such information a user has no way of telling whether the descriptions are based on the scrutiny of a perhaps imperfect single copy of a title or on a wider-ranging examination working toward the description of an "ideal copy." The absence of this single piece of information severely limits the usefulness of the descriptions.

Compounding the simple omission of these seven classes of information is the irregular, inconsistent, and incomplete treatment of other material included (or not) in the descriptions. Sources of blurbs and reviews are only irregularly given; cross-referencing is erratic and, when present, frequently in error (see Section II of the Appendix to this review); scant attention is paid to bibliographical details in impressions after the first, often with loose, vague statements substituting for precise data, e.g., "except for slightly larger leaf size" (p. 17); and, in general, the descriptions are inconsistent in the kinds and amounts of material recorded. Even the physical presentation of the descriptions has allowed the introduction of ambiguity: Maynard and Miles have permitted intrusive hyphenation at the line-ends of quasi-facsimile transcriptions, thus often leaving the reader to wonder whether hyphenated words in the transcriptions actually appear that way in the material being transcribed. The compilers should have insisted that their printers not permit any such hyphenation to intrude on quasi-facsimile passages.

Beyond omission, beyond irregularity, vagueness, and inconsistency, there is, finally, manifest error. Much of this, as the corrigenda list in my Appendix reveals, is the result of careless proofreading, but the errors so created are more often than not the kinds that could easily misinform a user of the bibliography, rather than being clearly nonsensical typographical errors. An example of erroneous quasi-facsimile transcription and another of incorrect collational formula will suffice to illustrate the kinds of manifest error in the descriptions not attributable to problems in printing and proofreading. The binding description of the Digit Books publication of *Junkie* records in quasi-facsimile that the lines 'CONFESSIONS OF AN UNREDEEMED DRUG ADDICT' and 'WILLIAM LEE' as well as six other lines or part-lines are, as reproduced here, in roman capitals. Fortuitously, page 4 of the bibliography reproduces the wrappers thus being described, revealing beyond question that these lines should have been transcribed as '*CONFESSIONS OF AN UNREDEEMED DRUG ADDICT*' and '*WILLIAM LEE*' since these and the six other lines erroneously transcribed are uniformly in uppercase italic.

The incorrect collational formula occurs on page 30 and is for the Olympia Press edition of *The Ticket That Exploded*. It reads: "1^4, $2-12^{16}$, 92 leaves;" a check of the collation against the total number of leaves shows the former to be an impossibility. Clearly, it should be rewritten "1^4, $2-12^8$". This tallies both with the "96 leaves" and with the pagination statement totaling 184 pages that follows.

My judgmental terminology may sound harsh, but, in making my concluding evaluation, I am sorely tempted to label the Maynard and Miles bibliography of William S. Burroughs *dangerous*. The defects of this book are such as to mislead and misinform not only the casual user but trained scholars and critics of literature as well—something no reference tool should be allowed to do. In my mind, the volume's errors, omissions, and other problems are analogous to the defects found in automobiles that precipitate a rapid recall to the factory of all models containing those defective parts. If such a thing were possible, as in fact it is, I would seriously urge the immediate recall of all copies of the Burroughs bibliography presently in the hands of libraries and private users for a thorough examination and overhaul by competent bibliographers before it is reissued in a thoroughly revised, corrected, clarified, and trustworthy form. In the event such a drastic measure is not feasible, the Maynard and Miles bibliography must stand as a permanent source of embarrassment to the distinguished and venerable institutions that are its respective sponsor and publisher, the Bibliographical Society of the University of Virginia and the University Press of Virginia.

Appendix

Corrigenda to Positive Errors in the Two Bibliographies

Note: Whereas no systematic effort at proofreading was made while reading the two bibliographies for review, nevertheless a considerable number of positive and manifest errors, especially in the Burroughs bibliography, immediately showed themselves. Hence, while the following lists do not claim completeness in their correction of such errors, they may in part aid users of the bibliographies in identifying errors that might otherwise mislead or misinform them. The numbers in the left-hand column are to pages and lines; where applicable, superscript [a] and [b] refer respectively to the left- and right-hand column of an index.

Section I

West's Bibliography of William Styron

	Published Reading	Corrected Reading
9.15,16,17	MacMillan	Macmillan
15.12	A 1.I.c.1	A 1.I.b.1
64.21,26	A 2.V.a.1	A 5.I.a.1
64.28	150x	1.50x
89.5	A 3.IIa.1	A 3.II.a.1
133.4	PS3569.T915	PS3569.T9I5
180.8	ˏ* *	'* *

Section II

Maynard and Miles's Bibliography of William S. Burroughs

	Published Reading	Corrected Reading
17.18	CROSO	CORSO

	Published Reading	Corrected Reading
28.11	bown	brown
30.6	advertisements	advertisement
43.19	blurb|	blurb]|
50.24	Aylesburg	Aylesbury
50.27	*1965*	*1964*
63.5	p. 10: blank˯	p. 10: blank.
73.17	half title,	~~.
78.10	Chopin˯	~.
81.29	Baby7"	Baby"
94.26	Marucie	Maurice
100.19	C142	C143
101.22	*Harpers*	*Harper's*
103.2	B23	B15
107.28	B57a	B58a
107.31	B51	B52
108.5	C226	C266
108.10	*Harpers*	*Harper's*
108.17	B13	B10
111.4	131. John	131. Ed. John
116.23	Thinking"'	~,'"
132.6	˯From	"~
147.1	Martins	Martin's
151.16	Bomb Culture	*Bomb Culture*
152.12	*Exploded*˯	~"
154.28	C57	C51
157.5	C57	C51
161.2	C158	C157
161.10	C24	C241
163.28	note which appear	notes which appear *or* note which appears
173.14	Calude	Claude
174.8	*Harpers*	*Harper's*
176.16	Neulenhoff	Meulenhoff
193.31	Mangonotti	Manganotti
210.19	A26	A2b
211.5	E5	F5
217.21	C117	C177
223.3[a]	˯Abstract,"	"~,"
223.30[a]	Need,˯	~,'
226.1[b]	Burroughs, Pélieu, Kaufman	Burroughs, Pélieu, Kaufman
227.6[a]	Chlorhyidrate	Chlorhydrate
227.39[a]	"The	'~

Women's Biographies of Women: A New Genre

Carolyn G. Heilbrun

Gloria G. Fromm. *Dorothy Richardson.* Chicago: University of Illinois Press, 1977. xix, 451 pp.

Cynthia Griffin Wolff. *A Feast of Words: The Triumph of Edith Wharton.* New York: Oxford University Press, 1977. viii, 453 pp.

Janet Hobhouse. *Everybody Who Was Anybody: A Biography of Gertrude Stein.* New York: Putnam, 1975. xii, 244 pp.

Phyllis Rose. *Woman of Letters: A Life of Virginia Woolf.* New York: Oxford University Press, 1978. xv, 298 pp.

Renee Winegarten. *The Double Life of George Sand: Woman and Writer.* New York: Basic Books, 1978. x, 339 pp.

Paula Blanchard. *Margaret Fuller: From Transcendentalism to Revolution.* New York: Delacorte Press, 1978. xii, 370 pp.

Nancy Cardozo. *Lucky Eyes and a High Heart: The Life of Maud Gonne.* New York: Bobbs-Merrill, 1978. 468 pp.

Until the last decade, a biography of a woman writer written by a woman was an anomaly. That most famous of anomalies, Elizabeth Gaskell's biography of Charlotte Brontë, paid for its uniqueness with its virtual invisibility, not to readers but to historians of biography. Thus A. O. J. Cockshut, in his highly acclaimed recent study *Truth to Life: The Art of Biography in the Nineteenth Century* does not even mention it, despite the fact that it is more widely read than most of the biographies on which he dotes.[1] More important, Gaskell's biography of Brontë was ignored by any possible female emulators. If women writers became the subjects of biography, men were the biographers. Indeed, it might have been argued by the subjects that this situation was quite proper since, as a writing woman once observed, when a woman "because of some chance or talent comes out of obscurity, she contracts, instantly, virile duties."[2] Perhaps only a man could understand such duties, or recount them in a female context without anxiety or embarrassment.

The "virile duties" inherent in the creation of fiction were, in fact, ignored by Gaskell. Her stated aim was to show "what a noble, true and tender woman Charlotte Brontë was," to "make the world honour the woman as much as they have admired the writer." She saw it as her task to rescue Brontë's "feminine" virtues from the shadow of "male" accomplishment. In the course of this endeavor she created a fine biography but repressed both Brontë's passionate and painful unrequited love for Heger and her no less painful and passionate search for selfhood. The truth of the love was early restored to us; the truth of the search we have only lately begun to learn.

The connection between fiction and biography, essential to an understanding of the life of any writer, is especially important in the case of a woman writer. And it was on this connection that female biographers of female writers faltered. The problem is a double one. Not only has biography tended to separate itself from fiction, so that biographers of writers considered the life apart from the work, but women themselves stood in a precarious relation to fiction.[3] Women have long declined, or have been unable, to make individual fictions of their lives, to ignore the general fiction inscribed for them, to contrive distinctive stories of which they, as individual females, are the protagonists. The reason is not far to seek: woman's destiny, an erotic one leading to marriage, depended wholly upon another's activity, another's pursuit, another's *speaking*. A woman remained the passive object of male activity, one event in the life of a man—a major event if the woman was fortunate, a merely conventional one if she was not. Were a woman sufficiently "unfeminine" to permit herself the contrivance of fiction, she could defend herself as a woman, and her biographers could defend her only by proving that her fiction-making talents had not desexed her, had not unfitted her for her erotic destiny. This was a task most women biographers found not only difficult but full of anxiety and confusion. Women biographers therefore preferred to make their reputations writing of male accomplishment that supported, rather than contradicted, the personal life. Brontë herself wrote about her fictions, "Unless I can have the courage to use the language of Truth in preference to the jargon of Conventionality, I ought to be silent."[4] Women biographers took, so far as women subjects were concerned, the suggested path of silence.

Are there no exceptions to this sweeping stricture? If we consider James Clifford's collection *Biography as an Art*, we discover that, in addition to some forty essays by men, there are six essays by women, biographers all.[5] These women have written biographies of men, or of royal women, or of women whose celebrity consists in their having been events in the lives of famous men—Carlyle's wife, for example, or Byron's daughter. Royal women such as Lady Jane Grey, Mary Queen of Scots, Queen Christina, or Eleanor of Aquitaine are comfortable subjects for the female biographer precisely because they have had fame thrust upon them; they did not seek it, and little that they did affected the destinies of ordinary women.

Catherine Drinker Bowen, a not atypical female biographer of six men (Tchaikowsky, Anton Rubinstein, Justice Holmes, John Adams, Sir Edward Coke, Francis Bacon) is particularly interesting because she has told us how she herself, as a child, took the annals of male accomplishment to heart. "The talks of heroism that my brother Cecil read aloud in the billard room at Bethlehem in some indefinable way showed me that dedication to work, with all the risks of complete immersion, could be a goal in itself, for girls as well as men." Yet she did not look for her subjects among "girls" who pursued such goals. On the contrary, Bowen revealed late in life that when people asked her, as they always did, why she had never written about a woman, she had to invent answers because the real one: "I have, six times," would have been incomprehensible.[6]

Easier, in short, to project one's own sense of selfhood onto a male creature who will embody one's own ambitions rather than involve oneself in the dark complexities of a female's "virile" goals.

Meanwhile, biographies of women writers continued to be written by men—perhaps because, as men, they did not need to identify themselves with the anxieties of a divided destiny, or perhaps because some aspect of their own selves found strange confirmation in the struggles of an accomplished woman. Whatever the reason, men gladly wrote the lives of those women writers and continued to dominate the field into the early 1970s. Thus since 1970 we have had James Woodress on Willa Cather, John Rosenberg on Dorothy Richardson, John Brooks on Rachel Carson, Gordon Ray on Rebecca West, R. W. B. Lewis on Edith Wharton, Joseph Barry on George Sand, James Mellow on Gertrude Stein, Quentin Bell on Virginia Woolf—one pauses only arbitrarily. Yet—and here the seventies mark themselves as a turning point—we have also had women biographers of women: Gloria G. Fromm on Dorothy Richardson, Cynthia Griffin Wolff on Edith Wharton, Janet Hobhouse on Gertrude Stein, Phyllis Rose on Virginia Woolf, Renee Winegarten on George Sand, Paula Blanchard on Margaret Fuller, Nancy Cardozo on Maud Gonne—again one pauses arbitrarily. Gaskell's followers had arrived.

George Steiner, reviewing Ruby Redinger's biography of George Eliot in 1976, commented somewhat patronizingly that the trap awaiting the woman scholar is her wish to be judged as a scholar while "she urges the authority of novel or particular insight." Yet, he concludes, the argument from "femininity does have autonomous things to say of art and the past."[7] With such recognition there could be no turning back.

Thus women biographers began to search out those female subjects whose lives could become fictions, biographical fictions, had indeed become fictions for the women living them. By writing these lives as the women had lived them, as fictions of female accomplishment, the biographers were reinscribing the role of female protagonist in a male world.[8] No longer assuming the desexing of a female subject, women biographers now reaffirmed her uniqueness in creating a fiction, and therefore the possibility, of activity, assertion, autonomy, selfhood. The "autonomous things to say of art and the past" to which Steiner referred in 1976 were, in that year, affirmed by at least four revolutionary biographies: Helene Moglen on Charlotte Brontë, Bell Gale Chevigny on Margaret Fuller, Martha Kearns on Kathe Kollwitz, and Yvonne Kapp on Eleanor Marx (Vol. 2).[9] Each of these biographies reinscribed the accomplished life of its subject, not to excuse but to exalt it.

All four of these women could be seen, in the new biographies of them, to have recognized their ambitions as intruding upon spheres conventionally reserved for men, and all saw these ambitions as directly conflicting with woman's expected erotic destiny. Each of them married even if, like George Eliot's, their marriages were sometimes factual rather than legal; each had known herself in childhood to have a boy's dreams, each struggled with what Woolf would call "the manliness of their girlish hearts," each felt, as Kollwitz put it, "the tinge of masculinity within me." Only Charlotte, the literary artist, created fiction of women seeking selfhood on their own behalf. For this reason, and because its subject was Gaskell's subject, Moglen's biography of Brontë stands as the paradigm of the new art of female biography.

Brontë transcended the conventional female condition through writing; Moglen's biography demonstrates how, in the development of her novels, Brontë accomplished this, even as Gaskell tried to deny the accomplishment.(Perhaps for this reason Gaskell ignored the tiny books of childhood fictions she had held in her hand: she was searching not for the fictions of selfhood but for the conventionalities of womanhood.) Because Brontë's life was so constricted, because, unlike Marx, Kollwitz, and Fuller, she found no sphere of revolutionary activity open to her, she was forced to create entirely through her fiction the revolutionary process by which female selfhood might emerge. Thus, between the life and the literature we can, under Moglen's guidance, watch the process of female self-creation as it occurs. If Brontë was original in being one of the few women writers in more than a century to create an autonomous female protagonist, Moglen has been original in her turn by describing that fictive process as it occurs. So Moglen traces Brontë's writings, from her early romantic heroines who fear to have autonomy thrust upon them, to the more independent heroines still enthralled by Byronic heroes, to her final, plain heroine, Lucy Snowe in *Villette*, who will discover her own worth, her own destiny, while overcoming all temptations to see herself as discarded by life because unsuited to the inscribed female destiny. Lucy Snowe, as Moglen shows, is established, like a male hero, in terms of her own interiority, which then finds external expression and a place in the larger world beyond domesticity. Over a century divides Gaskell, who ignored Brontë's writings and who was accused by the *Edinburgh Review* of writing a biography like a novel, from Moglen, who perceives in the writing of novels a biography. Perhaps the watershed for female biography is precisely here.

The following years brought many new biographies of women: Cardozo, for the first time, saw Maud Gonne in her own right and not as though she had lived only to be the woman Yeats loved. In Gloria Fromm, Dorothy Richardson at last found a woman biographer who could uncover the heart of Richardson's fictive ambitions. In her introduction to *These Modern Women*, a rediscovery of autobiographical essays of feminist women of the 1920s that originally appeared in the *Nation*, Elaine Showalter demonstrated not only these women's lack of followers, but, in the comments of the contemporary men who had been asked to respond to these women, the reasons why "growing up" meant finding the least painful compromise between their ambitions and their expected roles as wives and mothers.[10] Bereft of sufficient support in their own lives, these women could not inscribe for other women the possibilities inherent in the life they had themselves achieved. In that same year, Radcliffe sponsored a new biography of Margaret Fuller; Paula Blanchard could now frankly assert her intention of saving Fuller from the nasty public image her aggressiveness had provoked. As Chevigny had published the writings to demonstrate a coherence, Blanchard reinterpreted the writings and the life to make a biography.

In many ways Phyllis Rose's biography of Virginia Woolf, *Woman of Letters*, can be seen as marking the new, strong current in women's biography. Woolf is a particularly fine example—she may indeed be the unique one—of an outstanding woman writer whose contributions to literature and to new literary forms are the essence of modernism, yet who was for years acclaimed only for her sensitivity, her "mere femininity," or else dismissed for the same reason. With the insights now being offered us from France, by Derrida and Foucault especially, we may begin to admit that the revolutionary artist of modern British literature is not Joyce but Woolf.[11] Still, such great claims need not be insisted upon. For the present it suffices to notice the feeble criticism of Woolf we suffered with for so many years, and particularly to remark upon the lack of courage or originality in women's biographical studies of her—as though Woolf were a feminine sufferer like all women, a bit more talented, a bit more sensitive, luckier in her origins perhaps, but shakier in her psychic health. The important new critical works on Woolf now being issued at last honor her with the position to which she has long been entitled.

Rose's biography is the first to see Woolf's sense of her own displacement as a woman from the center of established institutions as essential to her achievement. Woolf, Rose shows us, saw herself rejected not only by the male patriarchy of her Victorian childhood but by the homosexuality of the young men who surrounded her in her youth. While that very homosexuality may have enabled them to offer her the companionship they themselves had found at the university (may, indeed, have enabled her to accept it), she discovered, as do all women whose male friends are homosexual, their profound distaste for womanhood. At the same time, Rose manages to cast new light on Woolf's marriage and on our conditioned judgments of it. From her parents Woolf learned that the giving necessary to marriage is in direct conflict with the nongiving necessary to art; it is Rose's great originality to have illuminated this, as well as the fact, not easily asserted, that a woman's frigidity in marriage may be a preservation of the self and that an equal marriage is not a partnership whose basis is, or pretends to be, sexual passion. Rose perceives, furthermore, that Woolf's feminism provided her with a channel for social concern, so that in protesting her female lot she was not merely defending her own weak ego. These, but a few of Rose's points, indicate the wholly new approach to a major writer who has been a best-seller for fifty years. Disagreements with Rose are possible—particularly, perhaps, on her view of Woolf's relationship with her father—but this biography, like Moglen's, gives us the woman's perspective, not her perspective of men's views of what her perspective should be.

Significantly, though less for their own sakes than for what they suggest about the connection between the lives of women, and the fictions that can be made of those lives, two novels have recently appeared based on the lives of two famous women: *Eleanor,* by Rhoda Lerman, tries to recreate the interiority of Eleanor Roosevelt in her search for an individual destiny, and *The Daughter,* by Judith Cherniak, makes fiction of the life of Eleanor Marx, particularly her bouts of despair and her ultimate suicide.[12] The use of biography for such a purpose is certainly questionable; but if women can perceive the fictions in biography, they may soon be able to make, for themselves, biographies—that is to say, lives—of their own fictions. The promise in such endeavors is therefore real.

Notes

1. Cockshut, *Truth to Life: The Art of Biography in the Nineteenth Century* (New York: Harcourt Brace Jovanovich, 1974). The Gaskell biography is also unmentioned in Leon Edel, *Literary Biography*, Paul Murray Kendall, *The Art of Biography*, and André Maurois, *Aspects of Biography*.

2. The woman was Marie d'Agoult (Daniel Stern). She is quoted in Nancy K. Miller, "Women's Autobiography in France: For a Dialectics of Identification," forthcoming in *Language in Women's Lives*. This ex-

cellent essay is essential to a study of the relation between women's biography and fiction.

3. See Robert Alter, "Literary Lives," *Commentary,* May 1979, pp. 56–62.

4. Quoted in Inga-Stina Ewbank, *Their Proper Sphere* (Cambridge, Mass: Harvard Univ. Press, 1968), p. 161. This early study of the three Brontë writers intelligently considers their relation to woman's "proper sphere" and makes intelligent use of the fictions.

5. Clifford, ed., *Biography as an Art: Selected Criticism 1560–1960* (New York: Oxford Univ. Press, 1962).

6. Bowen, *Family Portrait* (Boston: Little, Brown, 1970), pp. 124–25, xiii.

7. Steiner, "Woman's Hour," *New Yorker,* 5 Jan. 1976, pp. 71–74; Ruby V. Redinger, *George Eliot: The Emergent Self* (New York: Knopf, 1975).

8. See Miller, "Women's Autobiography in France," where this point is analyzed.

9. Moglen, *Charlotte Bronte: The Self Conceived* (New York: Norton, 1976); Chevigny, *The Woman and the Myth: Margaret Fuller's Life and Writings* (Old Westbury, Conn.: Feminist Press, 1976); Kearns, *Kathe Kollwitz: Woman and Artist* (Old Westbury, Conn.: Feminist Press, 1976); Kapp, *Eleanor Marx,* vol. 2 (New York: Pantheon, 1976).

10. *These Modern Women,* ed. with an introduction by Elaine Showalter (Old Westbury, Conn.: Feminist Press, 1978).

11. See Edward W. Said, "The Problem of Textuality: Two Exemplary Positions," *Critical Inquiry,* 4 (1978).

12. Rhoda Lerman, *Eleanor: A Novel* (New York: Holt, Rinehart, Winston, 1979); Judith Cherniak, *The Daughter: A Novel Based on the Life of Eleanor Marx* (New York: Harper & Row, 1979).

Old English Sermons
W. F. Bolton

Milton McC. Gatch. *Preaching and Theology in Anglo-Saxon England: Ælfric and Wulfstan.* Toronto: University of Toronto Press, 1977. xiv, 266 pp.

This book treats two aspects of the homilies of Ælfric and Wulfstan: "the question of the uses for which their homilies were prepared" and "the nature of the theological content of the homilies" (p. 119). The author concludes that the homilies were prepared not only for reading on liturgical occasions but also for extraliturgical public reading and for private devotional reading, and he shows that—in contrast with the anonymous homilies (such as Blickling and Vercelli) in Old English—Ælfric's and Wulfstan's were original in their striving "for greater clarity and consistency and stricter orthodoxy than their theological compatriots" (p. 120). This he believes was the result of the monastic reform or revival movement of the tenth century.

Following the usual preliminaries, the book falls into five parts: "Ælfric and Wulfstan: an Introduction"; "The Uses of the Old English Sermons"; "The Eschatology of Ælfric and Wulfstan"; "Ælfric and Wulfstan in Historical Perspective"; and, as an appendix, an edition of "Ælfric's Excerpts from Julian of Toledo, *Prognosticon Futuri Saeculi.*" The introduction is brief—the chapter on Wulfstan extends to barely four pages—and the last part before the appendix is a ten-page summary. The heart of the book, then, lies in the "Uses" and "Eschatology" parts that occupy about 92 pages (some of them entirely blank, others nearly so). But the bibliography, footnotes, and three indexes occupy 120 pages. The two central questions that the author treats are significant ones, and especially in the second part he treats them with originality and scholarship; but the proportions of the book seem wrong. It also seems to lack unity of argument and consistency of treatment, for a routine chapter on the life and works of Ælfric does not belong between the same two covers as a deft and erudite chapter on Ælfric's preaching materials.

In its present form, the study runs risks that it does not entirely survive. The notes, for example (gathered inconveniently enough at the back of the book in unsightly and hard-to-follow double columns), are unsatisfactory: inconsistent, sometimes inaccurate, often pointlessly full. The inconsistencies often involve the placement of the comma or period, especially with abbreviations and with the translations of Old English and Latin in the main text (Old English and Latin in the notes themselves usually go untranslated). Brackets and parentheses are now missing, now otiose. The abbreviation for manuscripts (in general) is sometimes MSS, sometimes mss, even in the same column (e.g., column 1 on p. 234). More seriously, the *Sammlung englischer Denkmäler* that appears as such on p. 182 turns up as *Sammlung Englischen Denkmäler* on p. 175; the reference to Cruel's *Geschichte der deutschen Predigt im Mittelalter* (1879, not 1897) on p. 191 contains two mistakes within three lines; *zugeschriebenen* (p. xii) appears as *zugeschreibenen* (pp. 161, 182); Jean Leclercq's best-known book is cited sometimes by its original French title, sometimes by the title of the English translation; German *Religion* gets a masculine definite article (p. 196); and in several places the type seems to have been disturbed, as on p. 184 where a title is reduced to ". . ." or p. 242 where two note numbers are missing. The desire to give encyclopedic references ("The best guide to patristic theology is . . .", p. 213) has hypertrophied the notes to a point where they are simply out of Gatch's control; that must be why he let slip forms he knew perfectly well were wrong, like *De Veteri Testamenti* (p. 221 bis; cf. pp. 78, 177) or "Caesarius of Arcles" (p. 235). These are difficult times for scholarly publication, and every line of type needs a justification. Too many in these notes do not have one.

The same may be said for the bibliography: it simply lists in alphabetical order the works that also appear, with full bibliographical details, in the notes. The bibliography is twenty pages long (it does not have all the problems of accuracy and consistency that plague the notes; the author had the assistance of Carey W. Kaltenbach with the bibliography). Again, it seems hard that twenty pages repeat information already given in full elsewhere. Why not, for example, reserve the full citation for the bibliography, and reduce the note reference "Jean Leclercq, *The Love of Learning and the Desire for God*, trans. Catherine Misrahi (1961; New York, 1962), pp. 168–70" (p. 197) to "Leclercq 1962, pp. 168–70"?

The three indexes are "Ælfric: Citations," arranged by categories and individual works; "Wulfstan: Citations"; and the general index. The idea of the first two was especially good, for they serve as handlists of the oeuvres under discussion and keep the general index from sprouting ungainly entries under the two homilists' names. The general index itself appears to have been well done, but it follows an unspoken convention of indexing medieval authors referred to in the notes (e.g., Bede or Alcuin) but modern authors only if they appear in the main text. The several note references to Gatch's own work thus go unrecorded in the index, as does most mention of Cross, Pope, and Clemoes.

Clemoes's name is misspelled in the list of abbreviations. Other misfortunes occur, sometimes in bunches: two errors in Old English within two lines on p. 42 (*magan* for *magon*, *scelolon* for *sceolon*), three within four lines on p. 97 (comma missing, *ungeripode* for *ungeripoda*, *geongun* for *geongum*), two within three lines on p. 99 (*halgen* for *halgan*, *dómstlum* for *dómsetlum*), as well as *deowað* for *ðeowað* (p. 96), *lichman* for *lichaman* (p. 98), *dá* for *ðá* (p. 99), *uriht* for *unriht* (p. 106); in modern English, there are two obvious errors within two lines in the last paragraph on p. 104, and the quotation ending "in the religious orders" (p. 56) appears on p. 49 (not p. 48 as the note to the later citation claims) with the ending "in the religious order." A less expansive work might have left the author time for more precision, so that errors and inconsistencies (Ecgbert or Egbert, for example) could have been spotted and avoided.

The style could also have been improved. Gatch very frequently employs the "*one* should not consider how *he* will die" sort of construction (p. 97, emphasis mine), always irritatingly and sometimes really ambiguously: "at the same time as one must acknowledge his celebrity, he must also observe that his standards . . . were not followed" (p. 121) is only one example out of many. Gatch is often wordy and awkward: "The fate of the works of Ælfric as a coherent corpus, despite all his cares to avoid such an eventuality, and the fact that Ælfric and Wulfstan left no worthy successors may indicate that the reformers never completely succeeded in purifying the intellectual life of the church" (p. 121). Gatch was not paying attention when he wrote that "Ælfric seems, in a rough way and in the First Series in particular, to be providing materials for roughly every other week" (p. 50). His wordiness allows him to write "The balance . . . were also reflected" (p. 123) because of the long prepositional phrase that intervenes between subject and verb; to put "collaterally, if not generically" (p. 124) where it seems he intended "genetically"; and to say, of his edition of Ælfric's excerpts, that "vocalic *u* is transcribed as *v*," where forms like *iuvenum* in the edition suggest that he meant "consonantal *u*" (p. 133).

The book makes a sound and valuable contribution, especially by its adept use of internal evidence in Old English homilies and its learned application of external evidence from Carolingian preaching. Without its wordiness, its routine surveys, and its redundant documentation, the study would have been — perhaps in the form of two or three substantial articles — a more accurate one, one that made more obvious the very considerable worth of its findings and their significance. As it is, the achievement is blurred and the reader is distracted, results that, in such specialized studies, are especially unfortunate.

Hemingway: The Writer as Researcher
Charles J. Nolan, Jr.

Michael S. Reynolds. *Hemingway's First War: The Making of* A Farewell to Arms. Princeton: Princeton University Press, 1976. xiv, 310 pp.

When Hemingway published *A Farewell to Arms* in 1929, firmly establishing his place in American literature and assuring himself financial security for life, he asked Scribners to downplay the autobiographical element. Early reviewers, however, insisted upon making the connection between Frederic Henry's experience and Hemingway's life.[1] Later, critics like Philip Young and Carlos Baker did the major interpretive work. Along with Audre Hanneman, they seemed to establish the various scholarly directions possible in Hemingway studies.[2] To be sure, sound articles and books continued to come out; but the major ground-breaking work appeared to be done. Then in 1976 came Michael S. Reynolds's *Hemingway's First War: The Making of* A Farewell to Arms.

Put simply, Reynolds's thesis is that, instead of transcribing his life onto the pages of *Farewell*, "Hemingway went back to someone else's front and recreated the experience from books, maps, and firsthand sources" (p. 15). Reynolds makes it clear that "Hemingway had never seen that bridge [at Codroipo] when he described it"; he "had never crossed the Tagliamento, had never been in Udine or Gorizia, had never seen the Bainsizza plateau. . . . The obvious conclusion is that Hemingway used secondary source material in writing the novel, and this is not the popular portrait of the artist that we have always been given" (p. 134).

To support this contention, Reynolds discusses what he believes to be the probable sources, generic and specific, that our most famous war novelist used. Thus, though he is always properly tentative, Reynolds makes a convincing case for such works as G. Ward Price's "The Italians at Bay," a detailed depiction of the retreat from Caporetto, which contains abundant information about the weather and road conditions, the stealing, the enemy airplanes, and the chaos surrounding the disaster. In addition to magazine articles like Price's, Hemingway also seems to have read several of the military histories that came out shortly after the war, possibly *Battle Fields of the World War* or *The Great Events of the Great War*. In the latter book, he evidently found essays by Perceval Gibbon and G. M. Trevelyan, both eyewitnesses, and drew especially from Trevelyan's account of the collapse of the Second Army. He may also have used Thomas N. Page's *Italy and the Great War*, which like the others portrays the retreat in full detail, and, for his description of Udine, even Baedeker's *Guide to Italy*.[3]

A more extensive source Reynolds tracked down is Bakewell's *The Story of the American Red Cross in Italy*, which contains especially good discussions of the executions at the Tagliamento and the story of Lt. Edward McKey, whose life and wounding parallel Frederic Henry's in important ways.[4] An artist living in France and Italy before the war, McKey, like Henry (who had been studying architecture in Italy), signed up to drive ambulances for the Italians. Both spoke the language well, and both resembled the founders of the Norton-Harjes ambulance corps in France. Like Henry too, McKey was blown up by an Austrian artillery shell, but unlike Hemingway's hero he was killed instantly, the first Red Cross casualty in Italy. Other printed sources Reynolds found are diverse: Hugh Dalton's *With British Guns in Italy*, from which Hemingway apparently took the description of Gorizia, the details of the Third Army's retreat from the Carso, and the name Rinaldo Rinaldi; *Reports by the Joint War Committee of the British Red Cross*, an unlikely source; Hemingway's own newspaper stories, especially "A Veteran Visits Old Front, Wishes He Had Stayed Home," for the first chapter of *Farewell;* and perhaps Stendhal's *Charterhouse of Parma*, which seems to have influenced the writing of the retreat from Caporetto.[5]

In looking for the biographical material that informed *Farewell*, Reynolds is again a good detective. Noting that Hemingway's most immediate biographical sources—the war memories of the soldiers and nurses whom the novelist met while he was convalescing in Milan—are virtually impossible to document, Reynolds is relentless in pursuing others. He shows that the mood of war-weariness pervading the book comes from Hemingway's fellow drivers, many of whom, before coming to Italy, had already been at the front several years as members of the Norton-Harjes group. He provides a brief sketch of the right Count Giuseppe Greppi (1819-1921); Baker had discussed the wrong one but graciously pointed Reynolds to the actual model for Count Greffi. And he makes clear exactly how much of Hemingway's own experience went into the novel.

Perhaps the most important discussion of biographical material, however, is the long chapter on "The Search for Catherine." In it, Reynolds makes use of a 1971 interview that he conducted with Agnes von Kurowsky, Hemingway's war nurse. He also brings to bear other pertinent material in examining the degree to which Miss von Kurowsky served as the prototype for Catherine Barkley. Interspersing sections of the interview with passages from the novel, data from Agnes's Red Cross file, snippets from her diary, and selections from letters by and about the principals, Reynolds presents a wide-ranging biographical sketch of Agnes that includes everything from her chest measurement to the reason why she never accepted any of the marriage proposals she got during the war: "I didn't meet anyone I cared enough about" (p. 192). In the process, of course, he goes over old ground, but he sprinkles it with interesting tidbits of new material like Agnes's reflection about the youthful lovers: "I think Hemingway and I were very innocent at that time—very innocent—both of us" (p. 202). But the big news comes in his conclusion that "Agnes von Kurowsky contributes little to Catherine Barkley other than her presence and her physical beauty" (p. 219).

There is other valuable information in Reynolds's book as well, including a careful study of the compositional process of

Farewell. Though Sheldon Grebstein reached some of the same conclusions earlier, Reynolds examines the holograph manuscript again to show both how Hemingway worked and how the novel developed.[6] Hemingway apparently moved from episode to episode, for example, unsure of exactly where he was going. And, as Reynolds points out, since the book divisions did not appear in the *Scribner's Magazine* serialization of the novel, it seems clear that Hemingway did not initially think of *Farewell* in terms of a five-act structure. In discussing the exceptional geographical and historical accuracy of the book in a later section, Reynolds is also able to show why Hemingway chose to write about an experience that required him to go scurrying to secondary sources: "He wanted to use the retreat from Caporetto as the crisis of his story" (p. 104) — and this because, as Reynolds makes clear in his conclusion, Hemingway came to realize that, "ultimately, Caporetto stood for the entire war experience, and that experience was defeat" (p. 282). There are various other insights along the way that Reynolds's careful examination of the novel's background makes possible. The retreat from Caporetto, for example, was not based on Hemingway's own war experience in Greece, as many have maintained, but rather on "a total knowledge of the military situation in northern Italy" (p. 105). And the rain that falls at such appropriate places during the retreat does not represent Hemingway's use of the pathetic fallacy: "Not once during Book Three of *A Farewell to Arms* does fictional rain fall when actual rain did not" (p. 116). At least this is Reynolds's apparently naive conclusion about the way an author makes use of fact in creating believable fiction; in attempting to show that earlier symbolic interpretations of Hemingway's use of rain are oversimplified — that, in other words, Baker, Young, and others see Hemingway turning the rain "off and on like some stage-prop spigot" (p. 116) — Reynolds unfortunately commits the very error he condemns.

Reviewers have had mixed reactions to the book. Almost all, however, praise Reynolds for his diligent research and for the corrective it provides. Richard Lehan, for example, sees *Hemingway's First War,* despite its flaws, some of which he

Hemingway: The Writer as Researcher

enumerates, as "an excellent book—one that calls for a more balanced look at Hemingway as an autobiographical novelist, and one that nicely defines qualities of Hemingway's imagination near the outset of his career." Scott Donaldson speaks of it as "valuable and exhaustively researched": "The author's digging has led him to important discoveries in three separate areas: the depiction of World War I in *A Farewell to Arms*, the role of Agnes von Kurowsky and the American Red Cross, and the way the novel was composed." Michael Howard thinks that Reynolds "has written a superb literary detective story, tracing Hemingway's sources in newspapers and historical works, digging out the originals of his characters and showing the lengths to which Hemingway went to ensure the accuracy of every incident he described." In a nicely balanced discussion, Jeffrey Meyers notes that the book is "original and valuable" and that "Reynolds' discussion of the historical and biographical background is by far the strongest part of the book." An apparently less-impressed Francis E. Skipp still feels that the work's value "arises mainly from the corrective its author . . . gives to those who read *A Farewell to Arms* as cunningly shaped autobiography." And even Walter Sullivan, whose comments about the book are essentially negative, observes that "Reynolds is a careful scholar."[7]

Yet though the various reviewers find the book impressively researched, they also point to a number of difficulties. Least damaging, perhaps, given the fact that the work argues for a new way of seeing Hemingway as writer, is Lehan's charge that the book is "overwritten and repetitious" (p. 472). Reynolds himself seems to recognize the problem; at one point in his presentation of evidence, he begins with the apologetic "To belabor what must now be obvious" (p. 132). Such plodding, of course, is inevitably tedious. As Skipp notes, Reynolds "achieves what would seem impossible in a book about Ernest Hemingway, a certain level of dullness" (p. 385).

Skipp also raises a much more serious, some say the central, issue—that Reynolds fails to show how Hemingway transformed his material into art. Despite the book's corrective value, Skipp notes, "the emphasis on Hemingway's purely inventive powers does not take sufficiently into account the ways in which the artist connects the stuff of his own experience to events beyond it, actual or imagined, and thereby gives them the felt pulse of life" (p. 386). Sullivan echoes the charge in discussing Reynolds's attempt to find the model for Catherine: "Reynolds knows that Catherine Barkley was a combination of Agnes von Kurowsky and Hadley Hemingway, who was older than Ernest, and Pauline, whose long and painful ordeal with the birth of Gregory I have already mentioned. But what Reynolds does not quite seem to comprehend is that all these women combined with God knows what other elements in the fertile imagination of Ernest Hemingway to produce a character who was different from them all" (p. 678). This and other problems lead Sullivan to conclude that Reynolds "has not found the meaning in his material" (p. 679).

Another major complaint involves Meyers's comment that "Reynolds' scholarship is superior to his criticism" (p. 272). Here, in fact, is the essential problem with the book. Reynolds argues, for example, that though Frederic Henry is the central character, he is not the hero (p. 271). Apparently following Delbert Wylder, Reynolds sees Catherine in that role (p. 255).[8] Nor does he read *Farewell* as a bildungsroman: "Neither Frederic nor Catherine is portrayed as an innocent in Europe at the beginning of the book. Neither expresses any ideals that have become besmirched by the war. If either Frederic or Catherine has any ideals, in the sense of American prewar ideals, they do not show them. Frederic is a cognoscente before he enlists with the Italians; he does not start innocent, and he does not end up more knowledgeable" (p. 271).

Both views suggest a serious misreading of the novel. Surely Frederic is Hemingway's tragic protagonist who, caught in an absurd and hostile universe, achieves heroic stature through his stoical endurance of a terrible war, a painful wounding, and the nonsensical loss of his beloved. Catherine, on the other hand, plays a decidedly secondary role, idyllic in large part because she is the ultimate male fantasy. And the book is obviously an initiation story. Traditional innocents, both Frederic and Catherine have romantic attitudes toward the war at the beginning. Frederic, after all, volunteers to help make the world safe for democracy long before America enters the conflict; his gradual withdrawl from it results from a progressive disillusionment with an event in which "finally only the names of places [have] dignity."[9] And Catherine joins the cause as a V.A.D. with the "silly idea [that her fiancé] might come to the hospital where [she] was. With a sabre cut . . . and a bandage around his head. Or shot through the shoulder. Something picturesque" (*Farewell*, p. 20). But she learns a frightful lesson: "People can't realize what France is like. If they did, it couldn't all go on. He didn't have a sabre cut. They blew him all to bits" (*Farewell*, p. 20).

Other problems occur as well when Reynolds's critical judgment fails him, as it does in the chapters on technique and structure. Reynolds surely stretches the text, for example, when he sees in the events of Frederic and Catherine's last night in Milan a foreshadowing of what will happen on a larger scale during the Caporetto retreat or again when he believes that the visits of Rinaldi and the priest to Frederic in the hospital represent the struggle between the flesh and the spirit: "Rinaldi offers a kiss, the touch of the flesh, which Frederic refuses. The priest merely pats Frederic on the shoulder, the laying on of hands" (p. 253). This kind of straining, all too plentiful in Chapters 9 and 10, is silly—an example of the very kind of error Reynolds later condemns. Such exertions, he remarks of various attempts to read *Farewell* as an Elizabethan tragedy, "sound very fine in the classroom, [but] tell us little about the novel" (p. 263). There are also Reynolds's wrongheaded belief that Frederic "bears little or no resemblance to Nick Adams" (p. 280), an extraneous and dull chapter on *Farewell* as travel literature, and an annoying adulation of Carlos Baker that runs throughout. In addition, Reynolds's surprising conclusion in the awkwardly constructed chapter on Miss von Kurowsky—that she contributed little to the portrait of Catherine except her presence and beauty—is misleading.[10] As Meyers remarks in his review, "It could certainly be argued, on the contrary, that apart from his mother, the most influential woman in Hemingway's life was Agnes von Kurowsky, who first taught him, when he was defenceless and vulnerable, to accept the care and protection of a woman" (p. 271). And Reynolds's speculation on Hemingway's early manuscript that Hadley lost in 1922—what the author calls the "*Ur-Farewell*"—is admittedly questionable.

Nonetheless, *Hemingway's First War* is a significant work. In showing that Hemingway took from books as much as he took from life, it acts as a needed corrective to the commonly held view of him as an autobiographical novelist. It also suggests the importance of making use once again of approaches that the New Critics were so quick to discard. As Reynolds himself observes in his conclusion: "Now that the first half of the twentieth century is no longer the 'modern age,' but an historical period of its own, it is time for critics to relearn the use of old tools. . . . Letters, manuscripts, source reading, social milieu, and literary biography must all be brought to bear on the published text. . . . We must begin the difficult and frequently tedious search for the hard data that will support, modify, or disprove our inheritance" (p. 283).

Notes

1. See Robert O. Stephens, ed., *Ernest Hemingway: The Critical Reception* (New York: Burt Franklin, 1977), pp. 69-104, for a collection of early reviews.

2. Young, *Ernest Hemingway: A Reconsideration* (University Park: Pennsylvania State Univ. Press, 1966); Baker, *Ernest Hemingway: A Life Story* (New York: Scribners, 1969); idem, *Hemingway: The Writer as Artist*, 4th ed. (Princeton: Princeton Univ. Press, 1972); Hanneman, *Ernest Hemingway: A Comprehensive Bibliography* (Princeton: Princeton Univ. Press, 1967); idem, *Supplement to* Ernest Hemingway: A Comprehensive Bibliography (Princeton: Princeton Univ. Press, 1975).

3. Price, "The Italians at Bay," *Century*, 73 (1917), 635-52; Douglas W. Johnson, *Battle Fields of the World War* (New York: Oxford Univ. Press, 1921); C. F. Horne and W. F. Austin, eds., *The Great Events of the Great War*, 5 vols. (New York: The National Alumni, 1920); Page, *Italy and the Great War* (New York: Scribners, 1920); Baedeker, *Guide to Italy* (New York: Scribners, 1928).

4. Charles Bakewell, *The Story of the American Red Cross in Italy* (New York: Macmillan, 1920).

5. Dalton, *With British Guns in Italy* (London: Methuen, 1919); *Reports by the Joint War Committee of the British Red Cross Society . . . 1914-1919* (London: n.p., 1921); Ernest Hemingway, "A Veteran Visits Old Front, Wishes He Had Stayed Home," *Toronto Daily Star*, 22 July 1922, p. 7; Stendhal, *The Charterhouse of Parma*, trans C. K. Scott-Moncrieff (Garden City, N.Y.: Doubleday, 1956). Robert O. Stephens, in *Hemingway's Nonfiction* (Chapel Hill: Univ. of North Carolina Press, 1968), pp. 254-68, first demonstrated Hemingway's use of his own newspaper articles in *Farewell*.

6. Sheldon N. Grebstein, *Hemingway's Craft* (Carbondale: Southern Illinois Univ. Press, 1973).

7. Lehan, rev. of *Hemingway's First War, American Literature*, 49 (1977), 473; Donaldson, rev. of *Hemingway's First War, Modern Fiction Studies*, 23 (1977), 269; Howard, "The Ordeal of Fire," *Times Literary Supplement*, 7 Oct. 1977, p. 1132, col. 3; Meyers, rev. of *Hemingway's First War, Criticism*, 19 (1977), 269, 272; Skipp, rev. of *Hemingway's First War, South Atlantic Quarterly*, 76 (1977), 385; Sullivan, "The Rose in the Fist: Hemingway Once Again," *Sewanee Review*, 85 (1977), 679.

8. Delbert E. Wylder, *Hemingway's Heroes* (Albuquerque: Univ. of New Mexico Press, 1969).

9. Ernest Hemingway, *A Farewell to Arms* (New York: Scribners, 1957), p. 185, hereafter cited in text as *Farewell*.

10. Scott Donaldson, however, believes that in Chapter 7 "Reynolds cleverly intersperses question-and-answer sections with fragments of Red Cross records and other biographical data on Agnes" and that "the result makes the most readable section of [the] book" (p. 269).

Dante, Shakespeare, and the Common Heritage

Calvin S. Brown

Francis Fergusson. *Trope and Allegory: Themes Common to Dante and Shakespeare.* Athens: University of Georgia Press, 1977. 164 pp.

The purpose of Fergusson's comparative study of Dante and Shakespeare is to show that, in spite of differences in time, place, and culture, they are in basic agreement on most aspects of human life. It is unfortunate that the title of this study might lead readers to expect merely a technical discussion of Dante's and Shakespeare's use of some rhetorical devices.

The subtitle is much more informative, and the chapter headings indicate the common themes which are considered and the general scope and plan of the investigation: "The Common Heritage of Dante and Shakespeare"; "Romantic Love as Lost: Paolo and Francesca and Romeo and Juliet"; "'Killing the Bond of Love': Ugolino and MacBeth"; "Human Government: *Purgatorio* 16 and *Measure for Measure*"; "Redeeming the Time: The Monarch as 'Figura' "; "The Faith in Romantic Love: Dante's Beatrice and Shakespeare's Comedies and *The Winter's Tale*"; and, finally, "Belief and Make-Believe: Poetry as Evidence of Things not Seen." Brief notes and a good index (good because it is not limited to a perfunctory listing of proper names) conclude the volume.

There is no attempt to prove, or even to suggest, that Dante influenced Shakespeare in any way, and Fergusson wisely makes this fact explicit in the first words of the book: "There is no reason to think that Shakespeare ever read Dante." What did influence both Dante and Shakespeare—indeed, it created them intellectually—is that "they share the classical-Christian vision of human nature and destiny which was composed of Aristotelian philosophy, Christian theology, and the heritage of pagan and biblical literature made relevant to their time by allegorical interpretation" (p. 1). They differ from other poets of their extended period not because they held this common "world picture," but because only they "were able to use it in all its harmonious complexity to mirror earthly life" (p. 2).

A study of this sort straddles the ill-defined boundary between comparative literature and the history of ideas. In the comparative field it falls into the category of comparison without influence, except for the influence of a shared tradition — a type of study approved by all but the most churlish comparatists. As a study in the history of ideas, it is necessarily concerned with a series of broad philosophical and theological problems, concretely presented as they affect the lives of historical or imaginary characters, but seen in the context of a long tradition and a body of generally accepted assumptions and beliefs. There is no reason, of course, why a study should be classifiable into some organized discipline, but we need not hesitate to say that this book is primarily a study in comparative literature simply because the approach and the significant values are themselves literary. As Fergusson points out, the tradition and ideas were generally available, and the thing that distinguishes Dante and Shakespeare from any number of their contemporaries is the ability to incorporate — really to incarnate — these concepts into credible and moving human beings and their experiences. This is essentially the task of literature, not of philosophy or theology, and it is the basic focus of Fergusson's approach.

He never formally defines *trope* and *allegory*, and there is really no need for such definitions, since they are implied in many passages and quotations. The fundamental one is Aquinas's "In Holy Writ no confusion results, for all interpretations are founded on one, the literal." (Would that some of our fancier critics who habitually misread or ignore an author's literal meaning in order to support the exhibitionism of their personal interpretations would take this text to heart!) The essential point, familiar enough to Dante and Shakespeare but now frequently missed, is that moral, philosophical, or religious significance is not something which a writer drags in from somewhere outside and dumps into his work; it is implicit in all human life and action and hence in all imitations of them in literature. If ideas have consequences, then consequences reflect ideas.

One of the most interesting points that emerges from this study is the intense practicality of both Dante and Shakespeare, which will probably come as a surprise to many readers. It is most clearly demonstrated in their treatment of human government. Fergusson conclusively shows us that neither Dante nor Shakespeare had much interest or faith in abstract principles of government or theories of the state. Both men considered that these matters could be profitably discussed only in connection with an actual, individual ruler, which to them meant a specific king or emperor. The personality, virtues, and flaws of the ruler are what make an actual government out of a set of abstract principles and conventional routines.

Fergusson writes for the intelligent reader as well as for the specialist. This approach is essential, since the author himself is probably the only specialist in both Dante and Shakespeare, and the function of a work of this sort is precisely to bring together things that are usually kept apart by specialization. Except when it is very obvious, he supplies the reader with whatever summary of plot or situation may be necessary. For Dante, he does exactly what is called for: he quotes him in the original, but follows the quotation with a translation. This prose version is an excellent one for the purpose, but, strangely enough, Fergusson does not identify it. (It appears to be a slightly revised form of the Carlyle-Okey-Wicksteed translation.)

There are other imperfections, including a few misprints, like Shakespeare's "twenty-eight years of playwrighting" (p. 2) and *though* for *thou* (p. 87). One can have only amused sympathy for a writer (or typesetter?) who, having had to refer repeatedly to Dante's *Commedia,* finally comes up with "Shakespeare's commedies" (p. 132). There is even one grammatical lapse: "the knowledge of good and evil which comes to whomsoever tastes" the fruit (p. 89).

There are other, more serious questions to be raised, however. In a study of this sort it is hard to keep from overstating one's case on occasion or making assertions that are not, and cannot be, supported. Fergusson has little of this sort of thing, but he cannot wholly escape it. He tells us, for example, that "for Shakespeare as for Dante the act of treachery was the most lethal sin; they both place it at the bottom of the scale of human actions" (p. 24). Dante arranged and ranked human actions, and the statement is clearly true for him. Shakespeare did not so rank them. As Fergusson points out, Macbeth agrees with Dante in making breach of trust a particularly bad form of fraud, but it is neither necessary nor possible to show that Shakespeare placed it at the bottom of the scale.

There are also questions of opinion and interpretation, and differences on matters of this sort are a sign of health. If a book says nothing that is not obviously true, it can say nothing that is not obvious, and it will be pointless either to write or to read it. Still, there are questions on which one feels impelled to dissent. The account of the love of Romeo and Juliet concludes with a paragraph beginning, "It would be gratifying to know exactly what Shakespeare read to enable him to transform his source (Bandello's story), lift it to poetry, and see its action in the light of the romance tradition as understood by classical Christianity" (p. 22). Surely this remark overrates the power of books. In the serious sense of the word, Dante was a scholar and Shakespeare was not. And it is Fergusson's thesis that both men shared their tradition with their contemporaries—i.e., read much the same things. If you could read something that would enable you to raise Bandello to the level of Shakespeare, we would have a plethora of Shakespeares. Shakespeare was not able to perform this feat by what he read, but by what he was.

A more serious objection involves the interpretation of Romeo's relationship to Rosaline. Fergusson quotes Romeo's elaborate speech about "brawling love" and "loving hate" and aptly compares it to the first sonnet in the *Vita Nuova*. But he does not point out the fact that what was genuine feeling in Dante is mere literary affectation in Romeo. If any proof were needed, surely Romeo's "Where shall we dine?" in the midst of his alleged transports and agonies provides it. With Rosaline, Romeo is merely admiring himself in the conventional role of the hopeless lover, and her function in the play is to make the sudden, genuine, overwhelming love for Juliet credible by contrasting it with the affected posturing of the relationship with Rosaline. Friar Laurence says that Rosaline knew this posing for what it was: "O, she knew well / Thy love did read by rote that could not spell." Fergusson explains this remark by saying, "He means that Romeo's love sees only literally, like a child who pronounces words without getting their meaning" (p. 7). But *by rote* means "by heart, from memory." Surely the friar's comparison is to a child who can't read (can't spell out the words) but who imitates the adults who have repeatedly read a story to him by holding up the open book and reciting the story. Thus he means that Romeo was not reacting to anything in Rosaline but was merely aping the postures and parroting the words of innumerable pseudo-Petrarchan lovers. A child who pronounces words from a book without getting their meanings must be able to spell.

But such objections are negligible in the light of Fergusson's achievement. He knows his two writers thoroughly and makes good use of recent scholarship without feeling any compulsion toward a breathless pursuit of the latest thing. He complements his scholarship with both common sense and wisdom, two qualities which are essential for any real grasp of Dante and Shakespeare. He writes well and convincingly. Finally, he achieves the goal of all true criticism: he sends his reader back to the literary works themselves with deepened understanding and renewed enthusiasm.

A New Edition of the Poems of the *Gawain*-Poet

Alexandra F. Johnston

Charles Moorman, ed. *The Works of the* Gawain-*Poet*. Jackson: University Press of Mississippi, 1977. xii, 452 pp.

The appearance of this edition of the four poems in Cotton Nero A x should have been a major event in the study of the *Gawain*-Poet. Unfortunately, it is not. Professor Moorman's project (which, he admits in his preface, ranged "somewhat unsteadily over ten years") seems to have been dogged both by delays and by strangely inconsistent assumptions about the nature of its audience.

The length of gestation has had two major effects on the value of the work. First, because it did not appear until 1977, it is not "the first 'collected edition' of Cotton Nero A x since the MS itself" (p. 3). This distinction must go to the normalized Everyman paperback edition brought out by A. C. Cawley and J. J. Anderson in 1976.[1] Secondly, the critical issues discussed and the works listed in the bibliography were, at best, five years out of date at the time of publication. No work published after 1972 is cited, and of the 208 items listed (a full and useful collection as far as it goes) only twelve were published after 1970.

The more important flaw in the work, however, is its assumptions about audience. In the first paragraph of the introduction, Professor Moorman states, "The book should prove useful both as a reading and a reference edition and as a graduate text" (p. 3), but on page 6 he writes, "I have attempted everywhere, moreover—in text, notes and glossary—to provide an edition that will be of use to the general student of literature as well as to the specialist." It is here that the problem lies. This edition is neither accessible enough for an undergraduate nor complete enough for a graduate student.

Paradoxically, its faults as an undergraduate or generalist text are its strengths as a graduate or specialist one. The text of poetry itself, for example, is excellent. Professor Moorman states clearly and well his principles, which are conservative in all but the order of the poems. Indeed, he has given us the only collected edition that retains the old letter forms and provides variant readings from other standard editions. The text, it seems to me, is at a high scholarly level with sensible notes discussing well not only variant readings but variant interpretations. This is the aspect of the edition that makes it useful for scholarly study. Such thoroughness, however, can do nothing but intimidate an undergraduate or a general reader. For them, the approach taken by Cawley and Anderson, where "the marginal gloss and footnote paraphrases are intended as a prosaic aid to the reader, not as a substitute for the poet's own language," is infinitely preferable.[2]

The most glaring example of the opposite problem in the Moorman edition is the absence of an etymological glossary. He meets this problem in the introduction: "There already exist detailed etymological glossaries for each of the four poems listing each meaning, if not each instance, of every word used, and a concordance which is thorough, even if occasionally confusing—in short, ample aid for the philologist-specialist engaged in a study of the *Gawain*-poet" (p. 8). Indeed, this is true. Besides the concordance, and language studies such as Marie Boroff's, there are glossaries that aim at completeness in each of the standard scholarly editions.[3] But full etymological glossaries that supply variant meanings for words are useful to readers other than the "philologist-specialist." Frequently, critical judgments rest on disputed meanings. Moorman supplies a marginal gloss and, at the end, a word list containing only "the most common meanings in their simplest forms of those words used eight or more times" (p. 445). In spite of the full notes in this text, unless the reader has the standard edition of each poem beside him, the wealth of subtle variations in meaning (surely one of the outstanding features of the work of this poet) is lost. Professor Moorman himself expresses the view that his approach "unfortunately tends to solidify a single

A New Edition of the *Gawain*-Poet

reading by neglecting ambiguities" (p. 8). It is regrettable that this failing is as apparent in this edition as it is in the Cawley-Anderson text. On the one hand, the detailed textual scholarship is intimidating for the generalist; on the other, the lack of a detailed glossary both flattens the meaning of the poems for the generalist and forces the specialist seeking to make his own judgment about the meaning of the poems to use other aids.

The problem of audience is compounded in the introduction by a curious method of citation. The critical discussion (pp. 11-46) is entirely without footnotes. After I had worked with it for some time, it became clear that each critic named in the discussion appears somewhere in the bibliography. This was not immediately apparent because the critics are listed alphabetically within separate subheadings (such as "Sources and Analogues") that bear some relationship to the subheadings in the introduction—but not a complete one. If only one work by a single author appears in the bibliography, nothing appears in the text. If more than one work appears, normally the date of the work being referred to and the page number appear after the name and in parentheses, e.g., "Norman Davis (1967: 132-52)" on page 47 of Moorman. Such a system has its own logic and economy, but it presents real problems. First of all, not to supply page references for single works of an author renders the citation almost useless. Secondly, when an opinion is being expressed that is not directly related to a critic's name, it is impossible to know whose opinion it is. For example, on page 14 there is no indication of the sources of the various suggestions concerning the possible identification of the poet. Such an indication may not be necessary for those as familiar with the scholarship as Professor Moorman, nor may it be necessary for the complete generalist. However, I was completely frustrated by the sentence "On the basis of his library he has been identified as one John of Erghome" (p. 14). I know something of John Erghome and his library (left to the Augustinian Friary in York),[4] and would like to pursue the reference. Here assumptions about audience have led to an unfortunate technical decision. It would have been far better to use the standard form advocated by the

Modern Language Association or some modification of it that would help rather than frustrate the reader.

There are technical problems in the physical layout of this book. For example, two lines were reversed in the setting on page 18. Perhaps the most important problem, however, is the way the text and the discursive notes are set up. These are the strength of the work, and yet it seems to me that their usability is hampered by having them at the bottom of the page in double columns. The page is already full enough with text, marginal gloss, line numbers and textual notes. Adding the discursive notes as well produces a page of almost eighteenth-century complexity. Real problems arise when a full and valuable discussion of variant interpretations spills over beyond the page containing the line or lines in question. Every effort seems to have been made to avoid this problem by varying the number of lines of text as the notes vary in length, but occasionally (as in the beginning where a discussion of lines 1-4 appears under lines 9-16) misplacements occur. Both the text and the notes would have been easier to read had the University Press of Mississippi followed the standard modern practice of putting the discursive notes together after the text.

A good feature of this edition is the inclusion of all the illustrations from the manuscript. No one else, except Gollancz in the facsimile edition, prints them all.[5] It is only unfortunate that they could not have been reproduced as color plates. Every effort seems to have been made in the printing process to capture the detail; in fact, one or two of the plates (such as the one depicting Gawain at the Green Chapel) are actually better than the facsimile reproduction. Even with all the care that has been taken, however, they are not particularly clear. Some explanation should have been given. Those of us who know about the illustrations can acknowledge the difficulties, but a generalist needs more explanation of the crude and faded drawings than the single sentence on page 10.

The Works of the Gawain-*Poet* was a laudable undertaking that has provided us with a good conservative edition of all four poems in the manuscript. The text itself is of scholarly value. But the lack of an etymological glossary and the idio-

A New Edition of the *Gawain*-Poet 371

syncratic method of citation limit the value of the volume as a whole for the specialist. I am afraid that generalist and specialist alike will prefer the Cawley-Anderson text for quick reading and cross reference while the specialist will continue to use the standard single editions for detailed study.

Notes

1. Cawley and Anderson, eds., *Pearl, Cleanness, Patience, Sir Gawain and the Green Knight* (London: J. M. Dent & Sons, 1976).

2. *Pearl*, p. vi.

3. Barnet Kottler and Alan M. Markman, *A Concordance to Five Middle English Poems: Cleanness, St. Erkenwald, Sir Gawain and the Green Knight, Patience, and Pearl* (Pittsburgh: Univ. of Pittsburgh Press, 1966); Borroff, *Sir Gawain and the Green Knight: A Stylistic and Metrical Study* (New Haven: Yale Univ. Press, 1962); E. V. Gordon, ed., *Pearl* (Oxford: Oxford Univ. Press, 1953); Robert J. Menner, ed., *Purity* (New Haven: Yale Univ. Press, 1920); J. J. Anderson, ed., *Patience* (Manchester: Manchester Univ. Press, 1969); J. R. R. Tolkien and E. V. Gordon, eds., *Sir Gawain and the Green Knight*, 2d ed. (Norman David, ed.) (Oxford: Oxford Univ. Press, 1967).

4. M. R. James, ed., "The Catalogue of the Library of the Augustinian Friars at York," in *Fasciculus Ioannie Willis Clark Dicatus* (Cambridge: Cambridge Univ. Press, 1909), pp. 2-96.

5. Sir Israel Gollancz, *Pearl, Cleanness, Patience and Sir Gawain* EETS, OS 162 (1923).

Basic Books

T. H. Howard-Hill

Robert C. Schweik and Dieter Riesner. *Reference Sources in English and American Literature, an Annotated Bibliography*. New York: W. W. Norton & Company, [1977]. xxiv, 13-258 pp. [sic].

The latest addition to the crowded field of students' bibliographical handbooks is the reissue of a work published in Germany with another title in 1976.[1] The preface is shorter, and the compilers have added a rather superficial introduction of seven pages, "Using Reference Sources," in which they attempt to prepare the reader for the inadequacies of their own work, and also a risible glossary of six pages to which, alas, attention must be paid later. The substance of the book, printed apparently without alteration from the German edition, consists of twenty-four classifications of material, most of them subdivided, starting from "I. English Literature" and "II. American Literature" and finishing with "XXIV. Catalogues of and Guides to Libraries, Archives, and other Repositories." Perfunctory indexes of subjects and names complete the listing of 1,217 entries, most of which are annotated.

Since the annotations provide the most patent claim of *Reference Sources* to the attention of potential users, they should be considered and commended at once. But to supply annotations — as I believe every work of this kind should — exposes compilers to two contrary charges, and Professors Schweik and Riesner are not exempt. Annotation is always subject to the pressures of concision: too long and the user will not read or the publisher be willing to print them, too short and they will serve no useful purpose. The present compilers have not resisted the temptation to an expansiveness which often merely summarizes what the user can derive readily enough for himself from the phrasing of the title-entry. For Item 14 ("The American Bibliographic Service. *Quarterly Check-List of Literary History.* Darien, Conn., 1958-1975."), we do not gain much from being told that it is "a quarterly check-list . . . on . . . literary history"; the compiler could convey that the publication is restricted to monographs on English, American, French, and German literary history without redundancy.[2] Or for *The Oxford History of English Literature* (Item 183), where ten volumes are listed by title under the names of their respective authors, it is irritating to be told it is "a multi-volume comprehensive history of English literature, with each volume prepared by a single specialist," and no less so to be informed that the fourteen-volume *Cambridge History* (Item 184) is "a very comprehensive multi-volume history of English literature." There is much similar redundancy in the notes, the excision of which might have made space for necessary information.

In a bibliographical handbook as selective as *Reference Sources*, the inclusion of each item must be justified by comparison with other items in the same category. If Item 1 is my *Index to British Literary Bibliography* and if the first volume (*Bibliography of British Literary Bibliographies*, 1969) is annotated[3] — without mention that it has about 5,000 entries — then the presence of C. S. Northup's *Register of Bibliographies of the English Language and Literature*, "a comprehensive bibliography of some 12,000 bibliographies on English language and literature," needs to be explained. Apart from the fact that Northup and Van Patten cover American as well as English authors and hence belong in an introductory section of books useful for both English and American literature, it needs pointing out that Northup, unlike *BBLB*, extends beyond 1890 and, also unlike *BBLB*, includes bibliographies of manuscripts. However, Northup is grossly inflated by references to the bibliographies printed in the *Cambridge History*, which provided the genesis of the *CBEL*; its continued usefulness is very much restricted. In other instances, a user may expect precise details where too often the annota-

Basic Books

tions yield only vexing generalities. If *CBEL* (Item 4) "remains useful for some classes of materials not included in [*NCBEL*] at all," while in *NCBEL* (Item 6) "other classes have been added or greatly enlarged," why are these not specified? For Greg's *Bibliography of the English Printed Drama to the Restoration* (Item 61) the would-be user is informed that there are "various author, title, and subject indexes," but he is not told what they are or in which of the four volumes they may be found. The annotation to this item fails completely to indicate the importance of a monumental bibliography which I heard described by a distinguished bibliographer friend as "the greatest single-handed achievement of English scholarship of this century." Sometimes the notes positively mislead the user. In section "XXI. History. B. British History," for example, the headnote to the bibliographies published by the Clarendon Press, Oxford (Items 1037a-40), subordinates them to the highly selective Conference on British Studies Bibliographical Handbooks issued by the Cambridge University Press (Items 1034-37), whereas the annotation should show that they are the most thorough and authoritative bibliographies of British history to which a student can have recourse. Again, reflection on the purpose of the annotations, and close editing, would greatly have enhanced their value. Nevertheless, the user will quickly find that the annotations provide him with substantial benefits he fails to receive from such handbooks as Altick and Wright's, where annotation is uncommon.[4]

The reader will find, however, the arrangement of items rather more vexatious. It is fallacious to assert that students first resort to the indexes of reference works, but if they did, they would get little help from the indexes to the present work. A more significant point is that the classification of entries should be comprehensible: the rationality of the classification should enable the user to "learn" the book. Apparently the arrangement of *Reference Sources* passes from the immediate literary concerns of its readers (English and American Literature), through more general literary classifications (literary forms; general and comparative literature) to "Interdisciplinary Literary Materials," whence follows a short connecting sequence of "The Literary Text: Printing [to] Editing" and "Guides to Scholarship and General Literary Reference Materials" before the second major sequence begins with "Guides to General Reference Materials": here not Literature but literature (i.e., books) is the main concern. Books and nonbooks: microforms and reprints; media; dissertations; serials (periodicals and newspapers—if serial fiction is included the subject index does not show it); review indexes; and indexes to books, collections of essays, etc. Then follows the "Rare and Used Book Trade" and a general grab-bag of biography, folklore, history, dictionaries, encyclopedias, and catalogues. All this is in what seems to be an arbitrary order, an impression not diminished when one surveys the items listed in the different sections. The main collateral effect of the separation of "Literature" from "Books" is to suggest to the student that what scholars say about books (secondary literature) is more important than the works themselves, but the immediate effect is to disperse widely throughout the work books that any user approaching the handbook in a rational manner would expect to find together. I am asserting here that all but the most sophisticated users of a bibliographical handbook approach it for enlightenment with a particular research topic in mind, not with a predisposition toward a certain kind of reference tool which might supply the information they require; that is, if a student needs information about a subject, it is by and large immaterial whether he finds it in a literary history, a biographical dictionary, a handbook, an analytical index, or an annotated bibliography, so long as he finds it. Put all those tools together and he can choose the one most likely to satisfy his search; scatter them throughout a closely classified work and provide a grossly inadequate index and he will give up—direct shelf search is easier. The compilers have been so infatuated with classification they have neglected to make suitable allowances for the potential user.

Consider the index entry for English drama. The first index number is 39: Stratman's *Bibliography of Medieval Drama*, which is listed under "I. English Literature. A. Bibliographical Materials. 2. Period. a. Medieval." The next sequence is items 61–65, "Renaissance," headed by Greg's *Bibliography*; items 67–73, which relate to Shakespeare, are not accounted to be relevant to Renaissance drama, apparently. The next sequence, "Restoration and Eighteenth Century," items 86–92, unlike the preceding, does not start with a primary bibliography. That should be the Woodward and McManaway *Checklist*, with the Bowers *Supplement* (Item 88), which is followed by MacMillan's *Drury Lane Calendar* (Item 90), Van Lennep's *The London Stage, 1600–1800: A Calendar* (Item 91) and Highfill's *A Biographical Dictionary* (Item 92), none of which, least of all the last, belongs with "Bibliographical Materials."[5] Next follow two items for the "Victorian Period," the first (Item 120a) not included in the index: apparently there is no primary bibliography of Victorian plays, Allardyce Nicoll notwithstanding. The next sequence (Items 141–44a) comes from "I. English Literature. A. Bibliographical Materials. 3. Form. b. Drama." It is headed by the Harbage-Schoenbaum *Annals*, which might just as appropriately have accompanied Greg's *Bibliography* in an earlier section: the two important items are pretty effectively separated. Then follow three items (152, 153, 168) from "I. English Literature. A. Bibliographical Materials. 4. Special topics" (Regional literature, Ethnic literature, etc.) which, so far as I can determine, could just as well have been placed in the previous section (with specific indexing: "Jew in Drama" rather than the "Jew in Literature" entry that 168 is given). The next entry (Item 178) is under "I. English Literature. B. Bio-Bibliographies": it is Vinson's *Contemporary Dramatists*, 1973, which belongs under "III. Literary Forms. B. Drama" since it supplies bio-bibliographies of American and Canadian dramatists as well as English. The next section, "I. English Literature. C. Histories. 2. Period and Genre Histories," introduces (at last amongst items 195–202) the fundamental works of Sir E. K. Chambers, *The Mediaeval Stage*, 1908, (not "*Medieval*"), *The Elizabethan Stage*, 1923, and *William Shakespeare*, 1930, and of Gerald E. Bentley, *The Jacobean and Caroline Stage*, 1941–68, all without indication of their paramount importance.[6] The final sequence I shall mention here is listed under "III. Literary Forms: Bibliographies, Indexes, and Handbooks. B. Drama": items 361-96, which are divided between "1. Primary Materials" and "2. Secondary Materials." These materials, which ostensibly pertain to drama in general rather than British and American drama, include the catalogue of the British Drama League (Item 361a),[7] Bergquist's *Three Centuries of English and American Plays* (Item 362), Firkins's *Index to Plays* (Item 363), which covers plays published in English (i.e., not American) anthologies and collections, and Dubois's *English and American Stage Productions* (Item 372). Later on *Nineteenth Century Theatre Research* (Item 386a) appears. It is devoted to English and American drama, and is included again as item 1206, one suspects inadvertently.[8]

The items mentioned thus far are recorded in the main under specific headings which clearly indicate to the user where he is in the book and what he should expect to find there. Very often, however, the sections have secondary, tertiary, even quaternary subarrangements, of which the user is given no other notice than the following statement in the preface: "We have tried in every case to adopt arrangements particularly suitable to the material at hand. Thus in some cases we have followed an historical arrangement; in others, an inverted chronology; and in still others, arrangements by level of generality or other organizational patterns according to the logic of the case" (p. x). As a consequence, items appear in apparently arbitrary orders which the user must discover for himself and which change from section to section. Under "4. Special Topics," for instance, items relating to literature in Ireland, Scotland, and Wales, subdivided by genre, are listed first, followed by regional novelists, picaresque literature — but not specifically English so the item is apparently misplaced — children's literature, and three items on Jews in literature, in generic order: these are apparently the only "special topics" a student needs help with. There are no subheadings. The confusing effect of the classifications is not mitigated, as the compilers hope, by "the analytic table of contents, the extensive system of cross-references, and the detailed

Basic Books

index" (p. x): they are simply not analytic, extensive, and detailed enough.

So much may be, perhaps, controversial: classifications are not subjects on which there is usually unanimity. All users, however, must deplore the exiguous bibliographical details of the entries themselves. Although the compilers can cite precedents for their practice of omitting collations and the names of publishers and series (Altick and Wright, and Kennedy and Sands, for instance), there is really no excuse not to provide information valuable for the identification of a work and assessment of its likely usefulness.[9] The entry for Philip Hepworth's *Archives and Manuscripts in Libraries* (Item 1186), for example, omits to notice that it was published by the Library Association and that it consists of only thirty pages, useful information for a potential purchaser or borrower. Entries in the style of item 1192 ("British Museum. *The Catalogues of the Manuscript Collection*. Rev. ed. by Theodore C. Skeat. London, 1962") are too sparse to be properly helpful. This pamphlet of forty-five pages was revised by Skeat from his article in the *Journal of Documentation*, 7 (1951), 18-60, an important fact for anyone who does not have the pamphlet but has access to the journal.[10] Periodical entries are rudimentary to the point of triviality, the information provided usually being limited to the title and the date of the first issue.[11]

The omission of issuing bodies and publishers is perhaps not of so great consequence since, for some unstated reason, corporate authors such as the Modern Humanities Research Association (Item 10) and the Modern Language Association (Item 11) are not indexed. The index is deficient in other respects. Titles are not indexed at all, and names are given in varying fullnesses which do not correspond to the style used on the title pages of the works listed in *Reference Sources* or in *NUC*, and of course are not internally consistent. The compilers do not appear to have appreciated the function of the subject index to compensate for the many unavoidable (and avoidable) difficulties of classification. The main subject headings generally repeat the headings of the classification but ignore the silent subclassifications of those comprehensive headings. The subject index entry for drama, for example, shows "English" after "American" as a subheading, followed by the string of item numbers (which I have previously analyzed: there are two indexing errors in 11 citations here). A user who resorts to the index to find "Drama: English: Eighteenth Century" or a bibliography of British dramatic periodicals (Item 144) will be disappointed: there are no appropriate subject headings. A reader who seeks to check the publication date of the first volume of the MHRA's *Annual Bibliography of English Language and Literature* will not find it under Bibliographies: Literature: Secondary" or "Literature: Bibliographies" because there are no such headings. At "English Literature, Bibliographies, Reviews of Research, and Indexes: general" the user is referred to twenty-one items, the tenth of which is *ABELL*.

The glossary lists "the chief terms and abbreviations used to describe the arrangement and contents of . . . works included in this book" (p. xviii). It is patently not a glossary of literary terms although students will be tempted to use it as such. It is incomplete: "enlgd." and other conventional abbreviations used in collations are omitted, and some contractions for periodical titles, e.g., *RQ*, are not included. Many of the "definitions" are unilluminating (e.g. Addenda, Catalogue, Checklist, Descriptive Catalogue, Dictionary List) or wrong (e.g., National Bibliography, Proctor Order, Reprint, STC Number, Textual Bibliography) and expose either the compilers' lack of familiarity with bibliographical matters or, more likely, the haste and lack of care with which the definitions were written.

No two readers will agree completely on the items which should be included in a compilation as highly selective as *Reference Sources* was obliged to be. One could have dispensed with the record of bibliograhies announced by Gale Research Company, many of which still await publication. The record of projected publications can only be partial and, as a matter of course, nothing useful can be said about publications the compilers could not examine or students use. Many readers will deplore the omission of works intended to guide the student in his study of a field or subject: I notice that helpful aids to manuscript studies by J. M. Osborn and G. N. Ray were absent—but then, so is Paleography. And concordances (despite Items 1003-5), and Computational Linguistics. There is no subject index entry for Language, and under "Linguistics" the user is referred to Kennedy and Sands's *Concise Bibliography for Students of English* (Item 647) and to "*style and stylistics*." The notion that students of literature need know nothing more of language than how to use Dictionaries (Items 1075-1128) is one which I hope will be widely rejected. However, materials on cinema are included, under the rubric of "topics of increasing interest to students of literature" (p. ix). The compilers have not attempted to supply even perfunctory access to the kinds of linguistic materials students of literature often require, and that is a serious omission. Nor does their preface or introduction explain the basis of the selection of topics to be treated.

It is an occasion for regret that the compilers did not seize their opportunity to publish a guide to supplant Kennedy and Sands and Altick and Wright, each of which shows signs of increasing age and debility, not repaired by intermittent updatings. *Reference Sources* shares many of the faults noticed here with those works and others. Yet it contains a plenitude of material which the user must learn of with gratitude, and the provision of annotations is almost sufficient to offset—for careless readers—the deficiencies I have mentioned. If only on account of its date, *Reference Sources* is the best available handbook in its price range. Severe editing would have made it very much better. As it stands, it is a counterproductive example of the craft of the enumerative bibliographer.

Notes

1. *English and American Literature, a Guide to Reference Materials* (Berlin: E. Schmidt, 1976), 258 pp. Grundlagen der Anglistik und Amerikanistik 8. I have not made a mechanical collation of the German and English editions.

2. The note continues: "The American Bibliographic Service pub-

lishes quarterly check-lists on a variety of subjects." The reader is not informed that these checklists include medievalia (Item 34) and Renaissance studies; and he cannot find whether the checklists are included, because there is no entry for American Bibliographic Service in the index of names.

3. The titles are as I give them. *Reference Sources* is also in error when it asserts that *BBLB* includes bibliographies of manuscripts. That will, however, be correct when the second enlarged edition is published this year. The annotation to the *Index* might also have mentioned—in accordance with the compilers' practice elsewhere—that the third part consists of a bibliography of British literary bibliography and textual criticism. (The third part consists of three volumes, published in 1979).

4. Richard D. Altick and Andrew Wright, *Selective Bibliography for the Study of English and American Literature*, 5th ed. (New York: Macmillan, 1975). However, most of the material (like special contents) to which the annotations draw attention is not indexed.

5. The fiction sequence follows: Item 93 is McBurney and Taylor's checklist *English Prose Fiction, 1700-1800, in the University of Illinois Library* (1965); Item 94 is McBurney's *Checklist . . . 1700-1739* (1960), an order which is inexplicable by any criterion I can conceive of.

6. Sir Edmund appears without the courtesy of his title but he could not complain; so does Lord Rothschild (Item 1184) and he is a baron: Chambers was only a knight. However, Sir Paul Harvey (Item 205) is suitably dignified. There are some peculiarities as well as inconsistencies in the treatment of names throughout.

7. Neither the corporate author nor the title (*The Player's Library*) appears in the "Index of Names."

8. One way of dealing with joint English and American items like Bergquist would be to insert references in the English and American drama sections at the exact point at which the user should find the material, not as a blind reference with other similar items at the end of the section.

9. Ion Trewin deplores the omission of publishers' names from bibliographies, to the detriment of would-be purchasers, asking that "all authors add the name of the publishing house. . . . And would all publishers' editors insist that authors do just this?" (*TLS*, 21 Apr. 1978, p. 445).

10. The Library Association, because it is not mentioned in item 1186, is not indexed; the British Museum, which is mentioned in item 1192, is also not indexed. The title has an error; and why there should be a typographical distinction between personal and corporate authors is hard

to fathom. An instance similar to the Skeat item is Coleman's *The Jew in English Drama* (Item 168) which was reprinted from the *Bulletin of the New York Public Library*, where it may often be more readily consulted.

11. *Reference Sources* does not go as far as it should in providing analyticals of collections of articles like Items 575 and 616, doubtless in the cause of economy. This principle is pressed beyond reasonable limits when Greg's "The Rationale of Copy-text," one of the most influential essays in modern literary history, reprinted five times in various collections in twenty years, is noted merely in connection with Tanselle's article (Item 620), which discusses it. (The section "Editing" is deplorable.)

Experiencing the Nineteenth Century: Two New Collections

Stephen W. Canham

U. C. Knoepflmacher and G. B. Tennyson, eds. *Nature and the Victorian Imagination*. Berkeley: University of California Press, 1977. xxiii, 519 pp.

Richard E. Levine, ed. *The Victorian Experience: The Novelists*. Athens: Ohio University Press, 1976. 273 pp.

A collection of essays sometimes succeeds or fails as much on the strength of its editorial premises as on the merits of its individual essays. This is the case with *Nature and the Victorian Imagination* and *The Victorian Experience*, both of which consist of new articles by major critics, but which, as volumes, reflect highly dissimilar editorial attitudes. *Nature and the Victorian Imagination* studies the pervasive influence of Nature on the period as a whole, not solely on its literature; it attempts to deal thoroughly, if not comprehensively, with the role of Nature in Victorian culture. Editors Knoepflmacher and Tennyson attempt to achieve unity in diversity by imposing a tight intellectual and organizational framework on their broad subject. *The Victorian Experience*, although fairly wide-ranging (from Dickens to Gissing), is more conventionally limited to literature as it studies the impact of nineteenth-century fiction on the modern consciousness. Editor Levine has rejected a thematic approach; his goal has been to achieve continuity by suggesting a particular point of view to his contributors, although he then apparently assumed a laissez-faire attitude toward the results. Despite their differences, both volumes offer new ways to approach Victorian studies and thus are important editorial experiments as well as noteworthy contributions to scholarship. They provide alternatives to the restriction of collections based on one author or work and to the amorphous nature of some festschriften (*Nature and the Victorian Imagination* is a festschrift dedicated to E. D. H. Johnson). Both collections, then, wisely respond to the need for some kind of unifying principle. Their success in attaining that unity, however, is markedly different.

In his introductory remarks to *The Victorian Experience*, Levine suggests that from the reflections of a refined and mature critical sensibility can come something of a comprehensive, unifying "experience" of Victorian fiction. This experience, he feels, represents the "relevance" of the fiction for contemporary audiences. He has therefore assembled eight new essays by prominent critics of the nineteenth century who bring to bear on the fiction their long personal and critical associations with the novels (William F. Axton on Dickens, Juliet McMaster on Thackeray, Ruth apRoberts on Trollope, Frederick R. Karl on the Brontës, Jerome Beaty on George Eliot, Lionel Stevenson on Meredith, Bernard J. Paris on Hardy, and Jacob Korg on Gissing). Levine states further that he "foresaw the essays as something more than personal testaments and qualitatively very different from critical introductions to major authors. . . . [He] saw the book offering to student and general reader alike a fresh, accessible, and new vantage point" (p. 5). Levine's provocative experiment seeks fresh ways of seeing, not simply individual authors, but all literary experience as well. The editor argues for a wholeness of approach, an intellectual and personal integration in reading which in turn prompts the rather numinous "Victorian experience." There is an anomaly here, one which underlies all literary criticism but which applies particularly to an approach so firmly based in the individual's response to the work. In reading *The Victorian Experience*, we become vicarious participants in someone else's experience of the fiction. All literature (and good criticism as well) demands the reader's imaginative participation, but will knowledge of another person's response allow us to appreciate the work in the same way that increased information about the work itself will enhance our reading? It is a question of primacy: which comes first, the critic or the work? Levine, for instance, is "sure that the reader will find enormously interesting the discussions of popular culture" (p. 7) in Axton's survey of Dickens. It may be charming to picture Axton "joyfully" seated before his "cat's-eye Philco" listening to "A Christmas Carol" (p. 30), but here the editorial thesis breaks down as the critic lapses into anecdote and nostalgia.

This is not to debunk Axton, for I would much rather perceive an individual, a vital human voice, in any writing, than have to endure voiceless, antiseptic prose. As George Eliot said, in the best style "one hears the very accent of living men."[1] One reads too much academic prose that, trying to be definitive, succeeds only in effacing the human being who at some time must have *felt* something about the work. Oscar Wilde notwithstanding, a set of values which raises analytical comment above human response to art seems disordered; ideally, the two are reciprocal. The problem in *The Victorian Experience* is uncertain editorial direction, for Levine also says that "certainly if we've learned something in the last quarter-century of academic criticism, it is precisely that explication of the text enriches the reader's experience of the work" (p. 4). Few would quarrel with him here. But where is the emphasis to lie in the volume, on textual explication or on subjective response? Can the two be cleanly separated or does the best criticism take both into account? Levine seems to believe that they should fuse, but several of his contributors have apparently reached a different conclusion.

The editor's introductory remarks describe his intentions, but they do not explore the issues raised by his hypothesis. Has he commissioned the volume out of dissatisfaction with previous critical attempts to express the "relevance" (a word he carefully considers) of nineteenth-century fiction? Is this to be a seminal work in a new critical direction? Will other volumes dealing with poetry, drama, or nonfiction prose follow? One would like more explanation of the issues and ideas that led Levine to his approach; he does seem, after all, to be trying to temper a mild form of New Criticism with Pateresque Romanticism. The bulk of the introductory remarks is devoted to unnecessary summation of the essays to come; the space would have been better used to discuss in detail the critical methodology employed in the book.

The essays are not to be "personal testaments" or literary memoirs; however, Levine does want the various authors to express, where possible, their individual relationships with the novels. This task has been construed by most of the writers as necessitating a certain amount of retrospection and recapitulation of their past work in order to assess the impact of Victorian fiction on their current attitudes and to propose some of the possibilities for the future inherent in the great novels of the last century. At its worst such an approach results in repetition of ideas and data already well recorded in prior critical works; that is perhaps the most frustrating aspect of the book. Stevenson's article on Meredith and Korg's on Gissing repeat a great deal of information from their critical biographies of those writers. The same is true for all the contributors: to discuss their experience of the fiction, they have to return to the best of what they have thought and said. If one is unfamiliar with the original critical works, the present essays are useful introductions and major assessments. If one *does* know the more thorough prior studies, the value of the essays is diminished, for the balance between textual explication and personal response then becomes tipped in favor of the response, creating the danger of reading the essays more as reminiscence than as critical inquiry.

Levine's suggestions have resulted in a pronounced emphasis on the relation of nineteenth-century literature to our own time. All of the essays seem to be implicitly informed by an understanding that the devotion of a career to the study of nineteenth-century fiction is "relevant." There is not, however, any hint of apology, for the authors are too firmly convinced of the importance of their subjects ever to lapse into special pleading. Most of the essays link Victorian and modern conceptions: Karl connects the Brontës to Franz Kafka and Doris Lessing in terms of the existentially modern themes of enclosure and self-identity. As apRoberts shows, Trollope's depiction of women and his sensitivity to their subjugation (marital, social, and political) remain important in the study of the history of women's consciousness. And in Korg's discussion of Gissing, Levine finds "the experience of modern history" (p. 17), a darkening vision that is in itself a defense against despair.[2] What emerges is an intentional examination of the nineteenth century in terms of the twentieth, an attempt to make the Victorian experience a modern experience. In one sense, this smacks of critical justification, a self-vindicating attitude which fears rebuke for looking to the past rather than to the present or future. But most of the essays demonstrate that the literature *can* be made to look toward the present and future by insightful, sensitive reading. If we cannot learn from the novels, why read them at all?

Levine states that he "gave the critics only the most broad and general guidelines and let them carry their essays as their imaginations and interests dictated" (p. 5). Such freedom attests to his trust in the contributors, but it has resulted in his premises being interpreted in widely divergent ways. McMaster stays painstakingly close to the texts of Thackeray's novels as she examines central images and symbols; her essay considers many issues, but its methodology is thoroughly conventional. Axton, on the other hand, does not hesitate to range freely in time, applying his findings on Dickens to our own media-saturated age. Beaty stays close to George Eliot's texts, while Karl is more comparative, bringing the writings of the Brontës to bear on modern literature. Some readers may applaud this diversity, but I think it reveals the weakness of the free rein granted the essayists. Levine's thesis has been *so* broadly interpreted that one must wonder if the contributors themselves had a clear idea of what was being asked for. Levine seems to have hoped for a centripetal impulse, a shared experience of fiction that would methodologically but not thematically unite the essays. What he received, however, is decidedly centrifugal. Individual essays succeed despite, more than because of, the vague editorial guidelines.

Paris's "Experience of Thomas Hardy" probably comes nearest to fulfilling Levine's ideas. Paris traces his relationship with Hardy, and especially *Tess of the D'Urbervilles*, through twenty years—from undergraduate infatuation to his current

Horneyean psychological esteem. His essay is a fine exposition of the maturation of a critical sensitivity, but it is also a solid revaluation of Hardy. To achieve this, Paris must repeat some of his former (now somewhat recanted) work, but the essay never falters into palinode, for he deliberately shows how and why he moved from one position to another. Paris combines the person underlying the writing—the experiencing human being—and critical commentary on the literary work; by refusing to extract himself from his ideas, Paris makes them humanly accessible without sacrificing either intellectual acuity or personal dignity. It is in this kind of balance between old and new, between textual exposition and the experiencing self, that the strength of Levine's thesis lies. Such balance is not easily achieved, but its power is formidable: by combining the ultimate relevance of the aesthetic response to art with close textual analysis, the method reconciles impressionistic criticism with the legacy of rigorous textual scrutiny we have inherited from New Criticism. It seeks the best of two modes, looking for a fusion of self and object which has interestingly Romantic overtones (which Levine does not discuss).

On page 3 Levine tells us that *The Victorian Experience* grew out of the "sometimes confused, often precarious state of literary studies in our own time." Unfortunately, by failing to address the implications of his hypothesis and, more importantly, by failing to provide a clearly defined sense of common purpose for the essays, the volume does little to clarify the critical situation. By commissioning new articles, Levine had a fine opportunity to test his theory. Unlike Ian Watt's eclectic *The Victorian Novel: Modern Essays in Criticism* (New York: Oxford Univ. Press, 1971), which reprints previously published work, Levine might have orchestrated the essays, without violating their integrity, into a cohesive, unified critical statement. But the essays are instead simply discrete discussions of individual authors, arranged chronologically from Dickens to Gissing. There is no thematic unity to them, nor do they stand in a developmental or contrapuntal relation to each other. Three of the eight are footnoted; from a sample of ten notes checked, only one proved inaccurate.[3] Most of the typographical errors involve punctuation and spelling rather than more substantive matters. The 273-page volume does not contain index, bibliography, or illustrations.

The Knoepflmacher-Tennyson book is more ambitious in scope and more academic in point of view than *The Victorian Experience*. What is unusual about *Nature and the Victorian Imagination* are not the types of essays it includes, which are conventionally academic, but rather its use of a theme that is at once limited to Nature but also wide ranging. The effort points toward synthesis, even holism; equal value is given all cultural manifestations of Nature. Scientific discoveries, for instance, are not ignored for more subjective observations in literature; instead, they are explored as major intellectual developments that often stimulated literary analysis. The goal of the book is to make the reader see the issue as a whole by assimilating information in diverse fields reported from various critical viewpoints.[4] But despite this breadth, there are important areas that do not receive attention, and a number of the essays are more suggestive than substantial.

Nature and the Victorian Imagination includes twenty-five new essays, supported by 131 illustrations, all designed to probe nineteenth-century attitudes toward Nature. In addition to an essay by each editor, there are pieces by George Ford, George Levine, R. H. Super, J. Hillis Miller, A. Walton Litz, and other luminaries in Victorian and early twentieth-century studies of literature and art. Some of the essays break new ground, others explore familiar territory from new perspectives, and still others argue that we need to reassess and redefine our critical and aesthetic stances toward the period. As a whole, they support the editors' contention that "the Victorian response to Nature . . . endures . . . as a source and origin to which we can reascend and which we can continue to reexplore" (p. 499).[5] This sounds remarkably similar to Levine's claim for the relevance of Victorian fiction, although few of the essays in *Nature and the Victorian Imagination* make explicit connections to contemporary attitudes or thought. The book definitely continues to explore its subject, from the domestication of Nature in interior design to developments in chemistry to T. S. Eliot and nineteenth-century poetry. The quality of "reascension," however, depends on the individual essayist's ability. When successful, to reascend is to recover, and a large number of the essays do reestablish the force of Victorian ideas.

The book is divided into six sections: "The Mind's Eye" (a photo essay on nature photography), "The Taming of Space" (the relation of human habitation to Nature), "Explorations" (geographic and intellectual), "Systems of Knowledge" (the sciences and Darwin), "Redefinitions" (the balance between tradition and innovation in nineteenth-century art and literature), and "Toward the Twentieth Century" (Victorian influences on modern conceptions). This arrangement serves the reader well, moving logically from images of landscapes and the *ways* they were seen through the camera, to man *in* Nature, ideas and discoveries *about* Nature, representations of Nature in the arts, and finally to the ramifications of these elements for the early twentieth century. The editors claim that the essays stand in an "interlocking relation" (p. xv); some do and some do not. David Robertson's discussion of early English mountain climbers and their motives leads directly to George Levine's "High and Low: Ruskin and the Novelists," a more "literary" inquiry into the role of mountains and the absence of sublimity in nineteenth-century fiction. The essays on Victorian painting in "Redefinitions" dovetail smoothly. But some of the connections seem rather pat, if not forced; Levine concludes his discussion with Dickens; this seems to be the only connection to Robert Patten's subsequent piece on Dickens and the hearth. The internal coherence that does develop in many of the sections will not prevent casual reading of individual essays and may well prompt readers to read more than they intended.

Most major Victorian authors receive attention; discussions of Wordsworth and Coleridge at one end of the century and Eliot and Lawrence at the other frame the Victorians nicely. Discussions of less well known figures, both in literature and art, substantiate the ideas expressed by their more famous contemporaries. Coverage of the major artists, however, is less satisfactory. Burne-Jones does not even merit an index entry, and the important use of motifs and themes from Nature in book design and illustration by such artists as William Morris and Charles Ricketts goes unmentioned. Although the impulse of the volume is clearly interdisciplinary, it goes beyond the usual art and literature yoke, looking at architecture, landscape design, the natural and physical sciences, and even Arctic exploration. The book is by no means comprehensive, but its breadth does suggest the degree to which the Victorian imagination was permeated with concerns for Nature in its many guises.

The desire to do so much in one volume is both courageous and stimulating. Even Joseph Warren Beach's landmark study *The Concept of Nature in Nineteenth-Century English Poetry* (New York: Macmillan, 1936), although discussing American authors, does not venture beyond poetry. More recent studies, such as Karl Krober's *Romantic Landscape Vision: Wordsworth and Constable* (Madison: University of Wisconsin Press, 1975) and major articles by Roger Shattuck and Carl Woodring, have restricted ranges.[6] *Nature and the Victorian Imagination* considers poetry, prose and prose fiction in a study of literature in its widest social, intellectual, scientific, historical, and psychological contexts. The wide scope is clearly a strength, but it necessarily invites questions about specific omissions. There is no discussion of the function of Nature in the great children's literature of the period (Ruskin's would have been particularly appropriate); even editor Tennyson's survey of childhood as a theme in literature gives virtually no space to the books written for children themselves. Little is done with the century's penchant for view-hunting, that almost programmatic response to Nature, and no effort is made to connect literature and music in terms of their shared reflections of Nature. Does the volume imply that what is excluded is of lesser importance? Perhaps any attempt to do so much is bound to tantalize as much as satisfy individual interests. Other readers will find other exclusions; one volume cannot do everything. Still, its breadth is impressive and permits an understanding of the subject which, if not complete, is certainly better rounded than a more restricted study of only literature and Nature would have allowed.

The physical design of *Nature and the Victorian Imagination* deserves attention; it is a handsome volume with an appropriately green cloth binding and dust wrapper. Page and type size are large enough to allow comfortable reading, and care has been given to page layout. An unobtrusive but revealing indication of this concern is the use of a small floral printer's device instead of numerals to identify the essays on their initial pages (two for the second, three for the third, etc.). The device is repeated for internal divisions in the essays and on the spine—William Morris might applaud this combination of the decorative and the functional. The numerous illustrations complement the text itself, and many of the essays rely heavily on their visual examples. There is a decided weakness here, however. All but five of the plates are halftones, appropriate for the reproduction of drawings and early photographs but obviously inadequate for the color and richness of nineteenth-century painting. It is not merely the black-and-white format that detracts from their impact; the poor quality of a significant number of the plates prevents proper appreciation of the artists' precision and delicacy (e.g., pls. 92, 93, 100). Quality is again inconsistent in the five tipped-in color plates. The best are only adequate, and in the worst (pls. 62, 117) the color-dot pattern is obtrusive at normal reading distance. And why a painting that receives only one line of textual comment (pl. 116) is reproduced in color while so many discussed at length by Martin Meisel and W. F. Axton appear in drab black and white remains a mystery.

There are other problems with the book. I counted nineteen typographical errors (some substantive), a surprisingly high number in a volume produced under what should have been rigorous editorial scrutiny. Even more disconcerting, and potentially damaging for the reputation of the volume, is inaccuracy in the textual apparatus, notably in footnote references. From a sample of twenty notes, five proved to be in error by volume and/or page citation.[7] The book is extensively footnoted, and full documentation is of course an asset in a study

Experiencing the Nineteenth Century

of this kind. But should the unreliability discovered in the sample hold true for the entire book, the utility of this documentation will be seriously undermined. The errors are not merely transpositions or obvious typographical mistakes; they thus afford the user great difficulty in locating the correct source. On the other hand, the index is thorough and accurate and provides quick entry to the broad subject. Individual contributors have occasionally included subject bibliographies, but a volume-wide selected bibliography would have been a useful addition.

Both *The Victorian Experience* and *Nature and the Victorian Imagination* attempt to make the nineteenth century more accessible to the twentieth, more comprehensible to us as we move farther away from it in time. Both go beyond introduction to more thorough analysis of their subjects, seeking depth as well as breadth. The greater success of the larger volume is not so much a matter of size as of more definite editorial direction. This control does not appear in the substance of the essays themselves, in their approach or point of view, but rather in the intellectual design and physical organization of the volume. Although the section divisions of *Nature and the Victorian Imagination* may strike some readers as arbitrary or even after-the-fact impositions, still they provide clear and helpful separation of the larger subject into its components. Like *The Victorian Experience*, *Nature and the Victorian Imagination* moves chronologically toward the end of the century, but here the movement seems (pardon the expression) natural. By the time we reach Lawrence and Eliot, we have a much better understanding of the ideas they inherited and incorporated (or modified) in their own work. The chronological arrangement, then, is more than the most obvious organizational scheme, for it is made to carry the period's developing, changing attitudes toward Nature. The welcome integration of feeling and textual exposition in Levine's book is seriously weakened by the absence of such editorial control. Had he been able to pull the essays together in an extended commentary (a prologue or epilogue, perhaps) on the shared Victorian experience implicit in the articles, his experiment in experiential criticism might have been more effective. As it is, the volume simply ends with the last line of the final essay, and the reader is left vaguely wondering what the book was all about. *Nature and the Victorian Imagination,* by contrast, generally fulfills its promises. Despite its problems, many of which could be resolved in a subsequent edition, *Nature and the Victorian Imagination* is both a useful reference work and a significant collection of critical essays. The *Victorian Experience: The Novelists* must remain a literary curiosity, a disappointing effort in a new critical direction.

Notes

1. Quoted in Miriam Allott, *Novelists on the Novel* (New York: Columbia Univ. Press, 1959), p. 314.

2. Korg's idea about Gissing as "one of the great prophets of the modern city" (p. 255) can be compared readily with A. Walton Litz's discussion of Baudelaire in the same capacity in *Nature and the Victorian Imagination,* pp. 470-88.

3. On p. 100 Ruth apRoberts misquotes from J. Hillis Miller's *The Form of Victorian Fiction* (South Bend, Indiana: Univ. of Notre Dame Press, 1968), p. 123. She says, "Characters come into existence in relation to other people"; Miller wrote, "A man comes into existence in his relations to other people," which changes the meaning of her sentence significantly.

4. In this impulse, *Nature and the Victorian Imagination* resembles Jerome Hamilton Buckley's *The Victorian Temper: A Study in Literary Culture* (Cambridge: Harvard Univ. Press, 1961) or Walter Houghton's *The Victorian Frame of Mind* (New Haven: Yale Univ. Press, 1957). But neither Buckley nor Houghton considers Nature in any detail, and therefore the new volume meets a longstanding need.

5. The editors' conclusion, from which the quotation comes, is titled "Afterglow and Aftermath." Interestingly enough, Chapter 20 of Joseph Warren Beach's *The Concept of Nature in Nineteenth-Century English Poetry* (New York: Macmillan, 1936) is titled "Victorian Afterglow" — are the editors tacitly acknowledging their forerunners here?

6. See Roger Shattuck, "Vibratory Organism: Seeing Nature Whole," *Georgia Review,* 31 (1977), 454-75, on Baudelaire and Western art; see also Carl Woodring, "Nature and Art in the Nineteenth Century," *PMLA* 92 (1977), 193-202. New York Univ. Press has recently published a collection of sixteen essays which provide significant comparisons to the two books reviewed here. Edited by Donald H. Reiman, Michael C.

Jaye, and Betty T. Bennett, the collection is titled *The Evidence of the Imagination: Studies of Interactions between Life and Art in English Romantic Literature.*

7. Four errors occur in the footnotes to Ellen E. Frank's "The Domestication of Nature: Five Houses in the Lake District" (pp. 68-92). I presume that Frank used the standard Library Edition of E. T. Cook and Alexander Wedderburn's *The Works of John Ruskin*, 39 vols. (London: George Allen, 1903), and not one of the reprints. Whichever edition she used, four of her six references to the *Works* are inaccurate by the Library Edition. Her initial citation to Ruskin (note 14), which she locates in X, 326, is actually found in IX, 411. Notes 17, 18, and 19 are likewise erroneous, and there are less serious inaccuracies throughout her notes. The other mistake was discovered in Chauncey Loomis's "The Arctic Sublime," in which note 5 refers to the wrong page in Marjorie Hope Nicholson's *Mountain Gloom and Mountain Glory: The Development of the Aesthetics of the Infinite* (Ithaca: Cornell Univ. Press, 1959). The quotation is located on p. 15, not p. 32, as cited by Loomis.

Professor Davis's Colonial South

Bruce Granger

Richard Beale Davis. *Intellectual Life in the Colonial South, 1585-1763.* 3 vols. Knoxville: University of Tennessee Press, 1978. xxxi, 1810 pp.

In a scholarly career that spans thirty years Richard Beale Davis, researching manuscript and printed material in American and British repositories, has published extensively on early southern life and culture. Two earlier books, *Francis Walker Gilmer: Life and Learning in Jefferson's Virginia* (1939) and *Intellectual Life in Jefferson's Virginia, 1790-1830* (1964), served as trial balloons for the present study, which he began contemplating more than twenty-five years ago. Although he says *Intellectual Life in the Colonial South* makes no claim to be a definitive account of its subject, it is difficult for even the informed student to think of an important aspect of the mind of the colonial South he has overlooked in a work that covers promotion literature and history, the Indian, education, books, libraries, reading and printing, religion and the sermon, science and technology, the fine arts, belles lettres, politics and economics, law and oratory. Incorporated into it is material from his earlier books *George Sandy: Poet-Adventurer* (1955) and *Literature and Society in Early Virginia, 1608-1840* (1973), and from his editions and anthologies *William Fitzhugh and His Chesapeake World, 1676-1701* (1963), *The Colonial Virginia Satirist* (1967), *Collected Poems of Samuel Davies* (1968), and with C. Hugh Holman and Louis Rubin, Jr., *Southern Writing, 1585-1920* (1970).

In this capstone to a career devoted to giving the early South its place in the sun, Davis undertakes to offset the view that New England dominated the colonial mind. The emphasis in Moses Coit Tyler's *History of American Literature, 1607–*

1765, first published just a century ago, is weighted heavily toward New England writers; many of the southern writers included are mentioned only in passing, and Tyler is as unaware of the existence of the southern poets Robert Bolling and Richard Lewis as he is of the New Englander Edward Taylor. It is unfortunate that Vernon Louis Parrington (who says in the foreword to *The Colonial Mind* [1927], "Perhaps I should add that the seeming neglect, in the present volume, of southern backgrounds, has resulted from the desire to postpone the detailed consideration of the mind of the South to a later volume") did not live to write such a book, since the only southern writer considered in the period covered by Davis's study is William Byrd and then for only two pages. "Explicit and implicit in the writing of the New England general or intellectual historian," writes Davis, "is the assumption that except in politics and law and perhaps agriculture the southerner before and after 1800 had no scientific inventive genius, no moral ethic, no appreciation of or creativity in the arts, and above all no sustained cerebration or rationally speculative mind" (p. xxiv). Of the massive evidence advanced in the course of this 1,800-page study to set the record straight, three examples will have to suffice here. Davis says that even though "education per se was an incidental result, not a major purpose, of English colonization" (p. 273), "for the first full century at least there was as great a proportion of literacy in the Chesapeake Bay colonies [Maryland and Virginia] as in the Dominion of New England" (p. 268). In an article which bears upon the question of literacy, Edwin Wolf refers mainly to libraries that have survived and names only Byrd and Jefferson among the dozen great American book collectors before 1800 in a list which includes the New England Mathers and Winthrops and middle-colony James Logan and Benjamin Franklin.[1] Davis, thinking of collectors like the Virginians John Mercer and Robert Carter, conjectures that "if southern records were intact or the actual contents survived, perhaps a dozen great libraries from below the Susquehannah might stand beside these northern ones, and every one of them was collected before the Revolution" (p. 518). Questioning

Richard H. Shryock's assessment of Americans elected to the Royal Society of London before 1763,[2] Davis believes that "at least half a dozen southern colonists on their merits deserved election ahead of Cotton Mather, and certainly ahead of William Brattle and Harvard President Leverett of Massachusetts" (p. 821), meaning men like the botanist John Clayton II, the silk and tobacco cultivator Edward Digges, and the historian John Lawson.

Davis tries to set the record straight in other ways as well. Contrary to Bridenbaugh and others who picture those southern Anglicans favoring an American bishopric as villains,[3] he suggests that "a church which wished for the authority inherent in its laws was hardly insidious, treacherous, or even anti-libertarian in so wishing" (p. 664). In answer to scholars like Perry Miller who see Anglican and Puritan sermon styles as standing in opposition to each other,[4] he remarks that the early Anglican sermon in the South "was *not* the opposite in form of the Puritan, but very much like it" (p. 705); the plain style "was by no means confined to New England or to nonconformists in general" (p. 709). Hugh F. Rankin, a historian of the colonial theater, believes that southern audiences were better mannered that those in the North because the artisan class was not present;[5] "there is no proof," says Davis, "that the representatives of skilled labor were not present in just as great a proportion in the South" (p. 1282). For a final example, Davis challenges Kenneth Silverman's assertion that the colonial South "developed no elegiac tradition" in poetry, demonstrating that "a strong funeral elegiac tradition persists in the colonial South" (p. 1400).[6]

Of the writers who contributed to the intellectual life of the colonial South, Davis places William Byrd II in the first position. As is well known, at Westover he had "one of the greatest of all American colonial libraries" (p. 555). Raymond P. Stearns calls Byrd the scientist "the most constant link between the Royal Society and Virginia during the first half of the eighteenth century."[7] Davis thinks him probably "the greatest collector of oil paintings, especially portraits, of the colonial period" (p. 1251). He is convinced, as others may not be, that

Byrd the writer is "first and last a satirist" (p. 1367) and approaches his correspondence, diaries, essays, histories, poems, even *A Discourse Concerning the Plague,* from this perspective. Among less well known writers the one Davis seems most anxious to upgrade—and in my opinion he succeeds—is the New-Light Presbyterian Samuel Davies, calling him "the glory of the Great Awakening [who] became a major international figure as preacher, hymn writer, and champion of religious toleration" (p. 691) and "perhaps the greatest colonial pulpit orator" (p. 767). He contends that it was Davies, not New England religious poets, whose *Miscellaneous Poems, Chiefly on Divine Subjects* (1752) "brought the muse of sacred poetry before the American public" (p. 1484).

The belletristic writings examined in the present study range through forms of nonfiction prose (public and private history, treatises, sermons, letters personal and public, essays) and religious and secular poetry. Davis finds no evidence that any novels were written before 1763 and notes that the earliest play was Robert Munford's *The Candidates,* not written until 1770. Faced with the impossibility of evaluating Davis's long, wide-ranging chapter on southern belles lettres, let me touch on his treatment of one genre popular in the eighteenth century, the essay serial. All the important published serials appeared in the Maryland, Virginia, and South Carolina gazettes. It was disappointing to see three lively literary serials, *The Monitor, The Meddlers Club,* and *The Humourist,* passed over lightly in favor of *The Centinel,* a serial of immediate purpose; but I realize that saying this only reflects my personal literary bias.[8]

My reservations about this steadily informative and comprehensive study are few and minor. In view of the frequently high literary quality to be found in such northern papers as the *New-England Courant* and its successor, the *New-England Weekly Journal,* I question Davis's observation, carefully worded though it is, that "with the possible exception of Franklin's *Pennsylvania Gazette,* the newspapers of the two Chesapeake Bay colonies and of South Carolina seem as generally informative, with as high a quality and variety of literary materials, as the newspapers in the north" (p. 623). Davis offers no evidence, if indeed any exists, to support his assertion that New York, unlike Philadelphia and Boston, "enjoyed plays much as did the southerners" (p. 1280); Rankin, for one, indicates that the theater history of New York and Philadelphia in the late colonial period was roughly comparable.[9] It is only because this book is so logically organized and clearly written throughout that I was aware of a few lapses. On two occasions, once at the end of a chapter (pp. 371-84), the other at the end of a section (pp. 593-95), the organization seems contrived and not altogether logical. And the following sentence is confusing: "The South no more than New England produced its best prose in the purely belletristic essay" (p. 1420); since the author has just said that "the most distinguished and abundant form of literary expression of the region and period is in prose, including a variety of essays," does he perhaps mean "no less" rather than "no more"?

John Crowe Ransom, addressing the American Literature Group of the Modern Language Association in Detroit on 28 December 1951, suggested that a definition of the southern "character" must take into account the importance the southerner attaches to history, form or ceremony, the earth or nature, religion, leisure, and family, as these have been affected by social inequality, social intimacy, and a sense of imminent breakdown. He was of course surveying 350 years of southern history. It is not surprising that Davis, calling attention from time to time in his study to "continuity in certain features of southern intellectual character from the colonial era to at least the mid-twentieth century" (p. 1636), should be so nearly in agreement with Ransom's definition even though he is surveying only the first 150 years of that history. At the end he suggests that the mental character of the colonial South was formed from such ingredients as the southerner's "strong belief in his own region," his religion, "love of the earth itself, or greed to possess it," the need for education, persistent reading, classicism (as opposed to neoclassicism), love of play and recreation, familial relationship, a code of honor, and a sense of humor. From John Smith to William

Faulkner, it would seem, there has been continuity of tradition in the southern character. Dramatizing this continuity is the epic theme Davis finds central to southern promotion literature and history like the collections of Hakluyt and Purchas and John Smith's *True Relation*—namely, "European man developing through a series of heroic actions in a strange new world" (p. 5). "Disillusioned as the modern southern writer may appear," remarks Davis, "he often seems still to be asking why there cannot be, for one brief shining moment or for ages, a Camelot located in his own land. And he often supplies his own answer" (p. 66).

As deeply researched and comprehensive as *Intellectual Life in the Colonial South* is, its author has to admit, "there is here no attempt at a complete picture: only the outlines of a portrait" (p. 1635). Having recently retired after a distinguished thirty-year career at the University of Tennessee where many of his students wrote dissertations on aspects of early southern literature and culture, the fruits of which are incorporated in the present study, Richard Beale Davis expresses the hope that other scholars will act on his suggested areas for further investigation and flesh out the portrait here so painstakingly outlined. These suggestions in the text together with the general bibliographies and notes to the chapters should encourage others to carry this task forward so that future historians, and especially literary historians, can present a more nearly balanced picture of the colonial mind.

Notes

1. Edwin Wolf, 2nd, "Great American Book Collectors to 1800," *Gazette of the Grolier Club*, NS, No. 16 (June 1971), 3-71.

2. Shyrock, *Medicine and Society in America, 1660–1860* (New York: New York Univ. Press, 1960).

3. Carl Bridenbaugh, *Mitre and Sceptre: Transatlantic Faiths, Ideas, Personalities and Politics, 1689–1775* (New York: Oxford Univ. Press, 1962).

4. Miller, *The New England Mind: The Seventeenth Century* (New York: Macmillan, 1939), Chapters 11 and 12 on rhetoric and the plain style.

5. Rankin, *The Theater in Colonial America* (Chapel Hill: Univ. of North Carolina Press, 1965), p. 190.

6. Silverman, ed., *Colonial American Poetry* (New York: Hafner, 1968), pp. 122, 259. See Jack D. Wages, "Elegy and Mock Elegy in Colonial Virginia," *Studies in the Literary Imagination*, 9 (Fall 1976), 77-93.

7. Stearns, *Science in the British Colonies of America* (Urbana: Univ. of Illinois Press, 1970), pp. 280ff.

8. See Bruce Granger, *American Essay Serials from Franklin to Irving* (Knoxville: Univ. of Tennessee Press, 1978), pp. 73-96, for information about *The Monitor, The Meddlers Club,* and *The Humourist.*

9. Rankin, *Theater,* pp. 77, 78, 80, 83, 116.

"Shadows and the shows of men":
The London Exhibition World
G. Blakemore Evans

Richard D. Altick. *The Shows of London.* Cambridge, Mass.: The Belknap Press of Harvard University Press, 1978. v, 553 pp. 181 illustrations.

Richard D. Altick's *The Shows of London* is a learned, packed (at times perhaps a little overpacked), and thoroughly documented study of English popular taste in entertainment—theater and reading aside—over a period of nearly three hundred years, from 1600 to 1862.[1] In undertaking this large and daunting enterprise, Altick again proves himself one of his own Scholar Adventurers. Behind his study lies massive reading in hundreds of related books and dedicated digging in the many collections of ephemera in all the major research libraries of England and America. A glance at the documentation for the first three chapters, for example, quickly reveals how wide (and deep) a net Altick has cast—works on manners, customs, and sports, personal memoirs and diaries, travel books, historical and antiquarian studies, literary works from Nashe to Wordsworth, collections of newspaper clippings, handbills, and illustrations, periodicals, public records, etc., etc. In a time so much given to the spinning of critical cobwebs, it is reassuring to encounter a work of such significant and definitive scholarship. "Panoramic" in "narrative landscape" and sheer length, it is a rewardingly good book and covers its large canvas, London, that "great and notid Sittey" (as it was elegantly described by Samuel Hadlock, a Yankee sea captain, who exhibited a troupe of Eskimos there in 1824) with a sure eye for the most telling detail and a generally well controlled sense of proportion, lightened by an occasional dry wit.

As used by Altick, the terms *show* or *exhibition* embrace

"displays of pictures, objects, or living creatures, including human beings, that people as a rule paid to see," the live humans limited, apart from madmen, generally to freaks or visitors from exotic climes. The study's main theme is the condition of, or changes in, popular taste from Tudor times to the great Crystal Palace exhibition of 1851. Two other themes are stressed: the democratic, leveling aspect of "show-going," where the social elite rubbed shoulders (not always very comfortably) with the laboring classes, united for the moment by a "common" curiosity, an element in "lowering, however briefly, the conventional barriers that kept class and class at a distance"; and the emerging insistence on "rational amusement," "education sugarcoated with entertainment," for the illiterate masses. This attitude grew out of the Enlightenment and was constantly voiced by reform-minded Victorians, becoming, unfortunately, too often a tag used to advertise shows with little or no claim to the *dulce* let alone the *utile*. Professor Altick also brings out sharply the intense competitiveness which both stimulated and ultimately destroyed new venture after new venture in the show-world. Since outré, exotic, or spectacular novelty was the very life breath of the entertainment industry, no sooner did a successful "new" show or exhibition open its doors than an enterprising rival would appear, determined to outdo it. But any novelty soon becomes old hat, and the race to capture and retain a fickle public's wandering tastes was a never-ending one; hence the words *open* and *close* run like a theme song throughout the volume.

Some measure of the wide-spread interest in the world of shows by all levels of society appears in the comments, not always approving, of well-known literary figures and other writers, and it is one of the strengths of Altick's study that he draws liberally on their views, critical or supportive, as evidence of how, at any given time, such shows and exhibitions were received by the more thoughtful and influential members of the society. A partial list reads like a small roll call of English literature: Nashe, Henry Peacham, Donne, Walton, Evelyn, Pepys, Tom Brown, Ned Ward, Steele, Swift, Johnson, Goldsmith, Smollett, Horace Walpole, Wordsworth, Byron,

The London Exhibition World 409

Leigh Hunt, Lamb, Hood, Dickens, Thackeray, Ruskin. Apart from these obvious literary connections, however, Altick's study has abiding relevance for the student of literature. Popular taste, good or (more frequently) bad, inevitably leaves its mark on the writings of any age, and no one can read this book without gaining a keenly increased awareness of the special "climates of opinion" and the shifting social mores revealed, consciously or unconsciously, in the works of, particularly, eighteenth- and nineteenth-century writers.

It is impossible here in a short review to give more than the merest suggestion of the range and variety of materials in a study of these generous proportions. The opening two chapters, for example, trace in considerable detail the growth of a large number of private and public collections and museums from 1600 to 1800, a subject picked up later for the nineteenth century in Chapter 31. Apart from the many small, miscellaneous "cabinets" of the virtuosi or "Nicknackitorians," a few collections stand out as historically noteworthy: "Tradescant's Ark," founded about 1628 and soon "regarded as the finest and largest natural history museum anywhere" (it was in part, I believe, the inspiration for the "House of Astragon" in Davenant's *Gondibert*, Bk. II); Don Saltero's Coffeehouse (1708), London's "first public museum," where gentlemen enjoyed coffee under the eye of some 293 "rarities"; Horace Walpole's neo-Gothic Strawberry Hill complex, "the first purpose-built exhibition structure in the London area"; and the British Museum (1759), housing Sir Hans Sloane's collection, the first "national museum" and "the first museum in Europe to be explicitly open to the public"—or so the by-laws declared, though it was not until the 1830s that the proletariat was allowed free entry, especially on holidays.

A survey of "Monster-mongers and Other Retailers of Strange Sights" (the phrase is Swift's) follows. Any freak, animal or human (or in between), seems to have attracted, then as now, the seamier side of man's insatiable curiosity.[2] "All out-o'-the-way, far-fetched, perverted things,/All freaks of nature . . . This Parliament of Monsters" as Wordsworth was to describe Bartholomew Fair in 1802, a fair that had changed little since the sixteenth century. The most revolting of the freak shows was Bedlam, where the antics of madness might be enjoyed for a small fee. But humanitarian feelings were stirring, and in 1770 Bedlam was closed to the public, though admission could still be obtained by special ticket. Even in the so-called "Age of Improvement" (Chapter 19), "Deformito-mania," as *Punch* dubbed it in 1847, was still a popular disease, witness such attractions as General Tom Thumb, Seurat, the Living Skeleton, the Sicilian Fairy, Daniel Lambert, who weighed 700 pounds, and Signora Girardelli, "the celebrated fireproof female." But not all were freaks. Aborigines from exotic lands were entertained and feted in the eighteenth century (Iroquois and Cherokee sachems, and Omai, the Tahitian youth) and celebrated as examples of the Noble Savage, unspoiled by the corruptions of civilization, so dear to eighteenth-century philosophical theory. But the tune changed in the nineteenth century, and the troupes of Laplanders, American Indians, Bushmen, Kaffirs, and "Aztec Lilliputians," not to forget the "Hottentot Venus," admired particularly for her extraordinary posteriors, were gawked at as reassuring reminders of the superiority of the white man, particularly of the Anglo-Saxon variety. This smug racism, an outgrowth of the Industrial Revolution and greatly increased material prosperity, is unpleasantly revealed, as Altick notes, by Dickens in an article on "The Noble Savage" in *Household Words*:

Think of the Bushmen. Think of the two men and the two women who have been exhibited about England for some years. Are the majority of persons—who remember the horrid little leader of that party in his festering bundle of hides, with his filth and his antipathy to water, and his straddled legs, and his odious eyes shaded by his brutal hand . . . —conscious of an affectionate yearning towards that noble savage, or is it idiosyncratic in me to abhor, detest, abominate, and abjure him? . . . I have never seen that group sleeping, smoking, and expectorating [shades of *American Notes!*] round their brazier, but I have sincerely desired that something might happen to the charcoal smouldering therein, which would cause the immediate suffocation of the noble strangers.[3]

If he tired of living (or bottled) exhibits, the Londoner

could from early times amuse himself with a plethora of waxworks (Chapters 7 and 24), from the funeral effigies of royalty in Westminster Abbey—the "Ragged Regiment" as they were called, a much visited "show" by the beginning of the seventeenth century—to the still flourishing Madame Tussaud's Baker Street establishment (1832), the proprietress of which, in an 1802 London debut, had caught the special taste of the moment by exhibiting victims of the French Revolution modeled from "the heads which were brought to her for the purpose, fresh from the guillotine." Considered as an exhibition offering "rational amusement" for the masses, Madame Tussaud's is a fair example of the delicate line such presumably "educational" ventures were forced to tread between the two poles of that term. It was indeed edifying to see the famous and the newsworthy personages of the past and the immediate present, skillfully realized in startlingly realistic wax forms, but it was the "Chamber of Horrors," filled with the figures of notorious murderers and other criminals captured as it were in the very commission of their crimes, that caught and held (as it still does) the morbid fancy of the public. As Altick again and again points out, too much emphasis on the rational, educational, or scientific intention of an exhibition proved fatal to continued financial success. More than education, which officially by the late eighteenth and nineteenth centuries the lower classes were supposed to desire above all else, the great mass of people still happily craved amusement and tended to go where they could get it.

From waxworks it was not a great step to automata operated by clockwork, air pressure, or hydraulics (Chapter 6). Mechanical wonders, such as Winstanley's "Water Theatre" (1703), Jaquet-Droz's writer, harpsichord player, and draftsman (1776), or Kempelen's celebrated chessplayer (1783), a presumed piece of ingenious fakery (an element that people continued to enjoy even in the new age of science), were later matched (Chapter 25) by Professor Faber's Euphonia or "Speaking Automaton" (1846), "capable of halting speech in French, Latin, Greek, and English in addition to his creator's native German," or by John Clark's Eureka (1845), "purported to realize a long-standing English ambition: the production of a limitless number of Latin hexameter verses unassisted by any muse." Another early development was the "moving picture," originally a sort of mechanized puppet show, that was adapted to display scenes of country life or topical events such as the Siege of Lille (1708) (in this respect and others a forerunner of the moving panorama). More seriously "philosophical" was the introduction to England of the orrery in 1713, a "moving picture" of the solar system and an ancestor of the modern planetarium. Here science mingled with wonder and instruction, an appeal also tapped by Vaucanson's gilded-copper duck (1742) that not only ate but literally digested its food and "discharge[d] it at the other End."

Apart from the annual fairs, the London sightseer intent on outdoor amusement and refreshment could disport himself in the various "Gardens" that became especially popular in the eighteenth and nineteenth centuries (Chapters 7 and 23) — Vauxhall, "Elysium-by-night" as it was called, and Ranelagh, or the much later Cremorne Gardens, the Surrey Zoological Gardens, and the Royal Park Zoo (1828). Originally such "Gardens" were instituted for "promenading, flirting, dining, drinking, listening to music, admiring vistas, pictures, and statuary," but in order to survive they later added shows of a spectacular nature: firework displays, naumachias, the Battle of Waterloo, Vesuvius by day and night (including an eruption), the Temples of Ellora, the Siege of Gibraltar, the Great Fire of London, etc., etc. But all this was not enough, and Vauxhall closed down in 1859 (Ranelagh had disappeared in 1803), and the Cremorne Gardens endured an increasingly disreputable existence until 1878.

But all was not "cakes and ale"! Serious educational exhibitions, archaeological, scientific, and industrial-technological, were also the order of the day in the nineteenth century. In 1812, for example, William Bullock opened his Egyptian Hall (officially known as the London Museum), offering the public a collection of "upwards of Fifteen Thousand Natural and Foreign Curiosities, Antiquities, and Productions of the Fine Arts" (Chapter 18). This curious architectural monstrosity quickly became a London institution and continued a long and varied career, under different owners and with an extraordinary variety of all sorts of exhibitions, until it finally disappeared in 1904, only to be replaced, nostalgically, by an "Egyptian House" devoted to shops and offices. Even more determinedly educational and scientific, complete with lectures, was the Polytechnic Institution (1838), a rival of the slightly earlier Adelaide Gallery (1832) and the abortive National Repository (1828; Chapter 27). While the Adelaide Gallery had its oxyhydrogen microscope (magnifying, it was claimed, 16,000 to 3,000,000 times) and its popular daily demonstrations of Jacob Perkins's steam gun (so devastating that it was advertised as putting an end to war) as well as a miniature canal in which model steam-driven paddlewheels could be observed as they "sailed," the Polytechnic boasted a *gas* microscope "projecting on a 425-square-foot screen the animal life present in the rich broth that was the metropolitan water supply," a diver who worked under water in an airtight diving dress, and a three-ton cast-iron diving bell (the Adelaide's was "a tiny glass diving bell occupied by a frantic mouse"), in which adventure-prone sightseers could actually be submerged in the Polytechnic's much larger artificial canal. The story illustrates once again the exciting but ruinous commercial rivalry, already referred to, that infested the exhibition trade, and the Adelaide Gallery was reduced by 1847 to an amusement hall. Despite its eventual surrender, however, the Adelaide Gallery was, as Altick observes, "the first direct English progenitor of the modern science and technology museums with its working machines and models and its visual dramatization of elementary scientific principles."

The culminating technological, scientific, and ethnological exhibition of the nineteenth century (a forerunner of Wembley and the various world fairs of the twentieth) was, of course, that held in the specially constructed Crystal Palace in 1851, originally located in Hyde Park (Chapter 32). Under royal auspices, though privately financed, it was planned and executed on a scale hitherto undreamed of and was a resounding and overwhelming success, attracting over four million visitors between the beginning of April and the end of September and turning London into one huge exhibition dormitory. After the exhibition was over, the extraordinary glass structure was carefully taken down and reassembled at Sydenham, where, sadly, this "last Victorian attempt to mix culture and amusement" became "more and more a gigantic variety entertainment." *Sic transit.* . . .

One more significant phenomenon of the exhibition world remains to be noticed. The panorama, and its various derivatives, from the moment of its debut in 1791, became what might be called the backbone of show business for the next sixty some years, and Altick devotes a number of somewhat repetitiously detailed chapters and part chapters to its development and eventual demise.[4] Pictorial art had received ever increasing attention in the eighteenth century, partly through Hogarth's realistic views of London life, prints produced cheaply enough to be available to a new middle- or lower middle-class buyer, and partly through the founding of the Royal Academy in 1768 with its annual exhibitions by the academicians and its growing interest in the painting of large canvases on historical subjects. (The National Gallery was not established until 1824, London being "the last major European capital to acquire a governmentally sponsored art collection.") This combination of a taste for realism and history, particularly current history, was abetted by the earlier advances in lighting and moving scenery engineered by Loutherbourg for Drury Lane in the 1770s (Chapter 9) and in 1781 was brought to its culmination in his famous Eidophusikon, or "Various Imitations of Natural Phenomena, represented by Moving Pictures" ("1. Aurora; or, the Effects of the Dawn, with a view of London from Greenwich Park. 2. Noon; the Port of Tangier in Africa, with the distant View of the Rock of Gibraltar and Europa Point. 3. Sunset, a view near Naples. 4. Moonlight, a View in the Mediterranean, the Rising of the Moon contrasted with the Effect of Fire. 5. The Conclusive Scene, a Storm at Sea, and Shipwreck").

The inventor of the panorama (from the Greek, meaning "an all-embracing view") was Robert Barker, who, evolving the novel idea of displaying a view as seen from some special height in its complete sweep of 360 degrees, perfected a technique for painting it on a cylindrical surface without distortion or loss of realism. The earliest such panorama (1794), a view of London from the Albion Sugar Mills, "the highest landmark between St. Paul's and Westminster Abbey," was an acknowledged success with its sense of immediacy and meticulously detailed realism (Chapter 10). Nearly forty years later (1829, Chapter 11), an indication of how firmly rooted the panorama craze had become, Thomas Hornor constructed The Colosseum to house his 134-foot panorama of London as viewed from his "observatory" atop the cross of St. Paul's, from which, with magnificent intrepidity, he had made his 2,000 initial sketches.

The panorama vogue soon spread all over Europe and America. As Altick says, "Panoramas became the newsreels of the Napoleonic era," a function they continued to serve for decades to come, bringing to a public avid for news pictorial views of the latest significant events or major battles. This same public was also becoming less parochial and had developed a taste for foreign travel, a taste that most could satisfy only vicariously through the medium of the panorama and its various offshoots, the Diorama (1822), the Cyclorama (1848), and the moving or rolling panorama, the last of which reached staggering lengths. One such was John Banvard's thirty-six scene panorama of the Mississippi (Chapter 13), reportedly three miles long, that unwound its way to London in 1848, only to find itself challenged by another "ORIGINAL GIGANTIC AMERICAN PANORAMA" that claimed to be four miles long, "one third larger than any other moving panorama in the world." Despite the competition posed by the invention of photography and the appearance of quickly produced illustrated journals like the *Illustrated London News* in the 1840s, so-called panoramas (the word was very quickly adapted to refer to almost any kind of large picture exhibition, cylindrical or not) survived down into the 1860s.

The volume is handsomely produced, with 181 carefully selected illustrations, though none, alas, of James Graham's fabulous "Celestial Bed" (1780), where "at a fee of £50 for a night's occupancy, sterility was purportedly cured in sybaritic luxury," assisted by romantic pictures, music, mirrors, perfumes, and (in Graham's words) "About 15 cwt. of compound magnets. . . continually pouring forth an ever flowing circle": But we may be sure none exists or Professor Altick would have found it for us.

Notes

1. The present book forms in many ways a companion study to Altick's *The English Common Reader: A Social History of the Mass Reading Public, 1800#1900* (Chicago: Univ. of Chicago Press, 1957).

2. Altick (p. 91) quotes an unpleasantly revealing anecdote from Samuel Pepys's *Diary* which comments on this aspect of human nature. Visiting Westminster Abbey, Pepys was "by perticular favour" allowed to touch the remains of Katherine of Valois, wife of Henry V: "I had her upper part of her body in my hands. And I did kiss her mouth, reflecting upon it that I did kiss a Queen, and that this was my birthday, 36 year old, that I did first kiss a Queen."

3. *Household Words,*7 No. 168 (1853), 337–38; quoted by Altick, p. 281. The reference to *American Notes* is the reviewer's.

4. The index entry for "panoramas" is, for example, some eight times longer than any other.

The *Review* Association

Major funding for *Review* is provided by a grant from the Research Division and the College of Arts and Sciences at Virginia Polytechnic Institute and State University. Additional support is provided by The *Review* Association, a group of major universities which support the aims and purposes of the series. Member universities are as follows:

Columbia University
Duke University
University of Minnesota
Pennsylvania State University
Princeton University
University of Virginia

Contributors

KENT BALES is Associate Professor of English and American Studies at the University of Minnesota.

LOUISE K. BARNETT is Assistant Professor of English at Douglass College, Rutgers University.

W. F. BOLTON is Professor of English at Douglass College, Rutgers University.

CALVIN S. BROWN is Alumni Foundation Distinguished Professor Emeritus of Comparative Literature at the University of Georgia.

E. C. BUFKIN is Associate Professor of English at the University of Georgia.

STEPHEN W. CANHAM is Assistant Professor of English at the University of Hawaii at Manoa.

RICHARD II. DAMMERS is Associate Professor of English at Illinois State University.

RICHARD A. DWYER is Professor of English at Florida International University.

A. S. G. EDWARDS is Associate Professor of English at the University of Victoria.

G. BLAKEMORE EVANS is Cabot Professor of English Literature at Harvard University.

CARL FICKEN is Assistant Professor of Theology and Culture at the Lutheran Theological Southern Seminary.

DAVID C. FOWLER is Professor of English at the University of Washington.

BRUCE GRANGER is Professor of English at the University of Oklahoma.

DONALD J. GRAY is Professor of English at Indiana University and Editor of *College English.*

MICHAEL GRODEN is Associate Professor of English at the University of Western Ontario.

CAROLYN G. HEILBRUN is Professor of English at Columbia University.

T. H. HOWARD-HILL is Professor of English at the University of South Carolina.

ALEXANDRA F. JOHNSTON is Executive Editor of Records of Early English Drama.

JOHN BUSH JONES is Professor of English at the University of Kansas.

ROBERT M. JORDAN is Professor of English at the University of British Columbia.

A. WALTON LITZ is Professor of English at Princeton University.

THOMAS L. MCHANEY is Professor of English at Georgia State University.

STEPHEN E. MEATS is Professor of English at Pittsburg State University.

CHARLES J. NOLAN, JR., is Assistant Professor of English at the United States Naval Academy.

DEREK PEARSALL is Professor of English at the University of York.

RONALD SHARP is Associate Professor of English at Kenyon College and Coeditor of the *Kenyon Review.*

PETER L. SHILLINGSBURG is Associate Professor of English at Mississippi State University.

DIANE TOLOMEO is Assistant Professor of English at the University of Victoria.